MOTIVATION, CONSCIOUSNESS AND SELF-REGULATION

PSYCHOLOGY OF EMOTIONS, MOTIVATIONS AND ACTIONS

Additional books in this series can be found on Nova's website
under the Series tab.

Additional E-books in this series can be found on Nova's website
under the E-book tab.

PSYCHOLOGY OF EMOTIONS, MOTIVATIONS AND ACTIONS

MOTIVATION, CONSCIOUSNESS AND SELF-REGULATION

DMITRY A. LEONTIEV
EDITOR

Nova Science Publishers, Inc.
New York

For permission to use material from this book please contact us:
Telephone 631-231-7269; Fax 631-231-8175
Web Site: http://www.novapublishers.com

NOTICE TO THE READER

The Publisher has taken reasonable care in the preparation of this book, but makes no expressed or implied warranty of any kind and assumes no responsibility for any errors or omissions. No liability is assumed for incidental or consequential damages in connection with or arising out of information contained in this book. The Publisher shall not be liable for any special, consequential, or exemplary damages resulting, in whole or in part, from the readers' use of, or reliance upon, this material. Any parts of this book based on government reports are so indicated and copyright is claimed for those parts to the extent applicable to compilations of such works.

Independent verification should be sought for any data, advice or recommendations contained in this book. In addition, no responsibility is assumed by the publisher for any injury and/or damage to persons or property arising from any methods, products, instructions, ideas or otherwise contained in this publication.

This publication is designed to provide accurate and authoritative information with regard to the subject matter covered herein. It is sold with the clear understanding that the Publisher is not engaged in rendering legal or any other professional services. If legal or any other expert assistance is required, the services of a competent person should be sought. FROM A DECLARATION OF PARTICIPANTS JOINTLY ADOPTED BY A COMMITTEE OF THE AMERICAN BAR ASSOCIATION AND A COMMITTEE OF PUBLISHERS.

Additional color graphics may be available in the e-book version of this book.

LIBRARY OF CONGRESS CATALOGING-IN-PUBLICATION DATA

Motivation, consciousness and self-regulation / editor, Dmitry A. Leontiev.
    p. cm.
 Includes index.
 ISBN 978-1-61324-795-2 (hbk.)
 1. Motivation (Psychology) 2. Consciousness. 3. Self-control. I. Leontiev, Dmitry A.
 BF503.M668 2011
 153.8--dc22
            2011017311

Published by Nova Science Publishers, Inc. ✠ *New York*

CONTENTS

PREFACE

The first part of this book is devoted to the old problem of fundamental motivations that can hardly be approached in another way, other than theoretically. The second part of the book is devoted to new or rather marginal concepts that seem capable to enrich general models of motivational processes. Part three of the book deals with the issues of self-regulation and self-determination; in the last two decades the problems of motivation can be hardly dealt with without touching these issues. The focus of the last part of the book is cultural context and cultural mediation of motivation. This book was planned not as a collection of discoveries to be considered, but rather as a collection of nontrivial views that may turn helpful for making a better sense of the discoveries actually made.

Chapter 1 - This chapter gives an overview of the evolution of explanatory models of the fundamentals of human motivation throughout the last century: from the concepts of instinct and drive to basic needs, and from the lists of biologically rooted needs to the discovery of non-biological, social, and existential imperatives to human behavior. The integrative model, proposed by the author, distinguishes three qualitatively different levels of individual-world relationships: the biological existence, the social existence, and the personal existence. Objective meta-necessities inherent in each level (including the actualization of potentialities and relating to the environment; social belongingness and integration; self-determination and autonomous choice) underlie special needs relevant to this particular level.

Chapter 2 - Motivation is a process of continuous exchange between the subject—individual—and the environment. From an existential perspective, we see this exchange as having a dialogical structure, connecting the given reality of both subject and object with the intentions of the individual. Motivation, being of existential relevance, has a causal link to the fundamental themes of existence. Further, the spiritual (i.e., noetic) power embedded in personhood functions as a tool for processing information in motivation. Thus, both existential structure and being a free person play the decisive role in the motivational process. This process is characterized by the repetitive and continuous decisions individuals make. The fundamental themes of existence bring shape to our understanding of motivation, while the spiritual (noetic) power within individuals is operative in all motivation. The paper illustrates the relation between the fundamental themes of existence and the motivational process. This process includes a coming to terms with the reality of one's existence, or "being in the world," with the reality of one's life and finally with an awareness of one's identity. Empirical phenomenological research over the past 30 years has confirmed that accepting these realities enables an individual to participate and be open to relationships and wider contexts from which personal meanings are discovered. These four fundamental themes of existence form a matrix for the psychopathological understanding of psychic disorders and provide a context for clinical interventions. Further, they represent the structural model of Existential Analytic Psychotherapy.

Chapter 3 - This chapter discusses the concept of future time perspective (FTP) as a cognitive-motivational concept. FTP results from formulating motivational goals in the rather near or more distant future. People do not only differ from each other for the content of their motivational goals or aspirations, but also for the extension or length of the time perspective that is involved in those goals. Individual differences in the length of FTP also have motivational consequences because they affect the anticipated incentive value of future goals and the perceived instrumentality of present actions for achieving those goals. In the second part of this chapter, we summarize empirical studies validating this motivational conceptualization of FTP. The third part illustrates the usefulness of taking into account individual differences in FTP in the realm of vocational and career planning behavior. Finally, we discuss empirical studies assessing the behavioral impact of the subjective organization of the personal FTP on the construction and evaluation of vocational projects in three stages of the career development and in critical decision moments within the Portuguese educational system. Extension and content of FTP were taken into consideration.

Chapter 4 - The chapter presents a theoretical analysis of applications of the concept of meaning in the psychology of motivation. The history of this concept in psychology and especially psychology of motivation is traced with special emphasis on the two most elaborated general theories of motivation where the concept of meaning is central: J. Nuttin's relational theory of human conduct and A.N. Leontiev's activity theory approach. In the present-day context, the relevance of the meaning concept for attributional theories of motivation and action regulation is discussed. Personal meaning may fulfill the role of common denominator for many special models of motivation linking them together as well as with more general theoretical contexts and other problem fields.

Chapter 5 - The following chapter is based theoretically on motivational psychology. It links the concepts of (1) implicit vs. explicit motives sensu David McClelland (1985), (2) Mihaly Csikszentmihalyi's (1975, 1997) concept of Flow Experience, and (3) Heinz Heckhausen's concept of volition and action (Heckhausen, 1977, Rheinberg, 2008). The core concept that links these three constructs is *Motivational Competence*, which is defined as "a person's competence to set goals in such a way that they can pursue the goals efficiently without being forced into permanent volitional control of his or her own actions" (Rheinberg, 2008; Rheinberg & Engeser, 2010). Empirical data how motivational competence could be measured and data supporting our assumption are presented.

Chapter 6 - The chapter presents an attempt to answer the basic question of the motivational roots of human activity in terms of varied principles and systems of activity regulation. Regulation is treated as the general principle explaining the capacity of living systems to move from less desirable outcomes to more desirable ones, based on feedback evaluated against the criteria of the desirable and causing corrections of the current activity. Forms of regulation may be of different complexity and subordinated to different kinds of criteria. The author offers a theoretical classification of possible logics of human regulation, each of them being an elementary mechanism; the proposed multiregulation personality model suggests that the whole system of individual autoregulation is made by the combination of the described elementary mechanisms in individually varied proportions that accounts for the qualitative interindividual differences.

Chapter 7 - This chapter consists of two parts. The first one presents a summary of the self-determination theory account of people's good living and optimal functioning. It highlights three motivational components identified by this theory: psychological needs (needs for autonomy competence and relatedness), aspirations and life strivings, and the continuum of motivational regulation. All these components are considered in relation to people's eudaimonic happiness and optimal, healthy functioning. The main conclusion of this section is that in order to be happy, people need to regularly and in a balanced way gratify their needs, have strong intrinsic strivings relative to extrinsic aspirations, and be relatively self-determined in their main domains of living and functioning. The second part addresses in more detail the controversial question of the nature of human autonomy as a fundamental condition for people's thriving and flourishing. It provides a conceptual analysis of this construct, uncovers the mechanisms of its beneficial performance, and addresses a highly discussed question of relationships of autonomy and culture. This section ends with a conclusion on the fundamental importance of human autonomy for people, communities and societies to survive and thrive.

Chapter 8 - The chapter conceptualizes hardiness as the existential courage that facilitates being able to turn stresses from potential disasters into growth opportunities. In this explanation, life is assumed to be an inherently stressful phenomenon, involving ongoing developmental requirements, which get added to imposed megatrends. In all of this, the hardy attitudes and skills involve not only surviving, but thriving. This leads to enhanced performance, health, and subjective fulfillment. Furthermore, this chapter summarizes relevant research, which supports the position, and has led to validated procedures for hardiness assessment and training.

Chapter 9 - Theories of aging consider subjective well-being (SWB) as a global indicator of sane psychological adjustment to life tasks and for successful aging. The present study is concerned with (a) SWB, (b) various personality variables, and (c) the influence these personality determinants have on SWB in old age. Participants were 259 females and 134 males ranging from 63 to 84 years of age at the first measurement wave. The sample was subdivided into three age cohorts: 63 to 68 (n=139), 69 to 72 (n=133), and 73 to 84 years (n=121). Three hundred and twenty-five participants were re-interviewed almost five years later. SWB is usually conceived of having a cognitive as well as an affective component, both of which were assessed. Personality variables included personal agency (self-efficacy, externality, hopelessness), motive dispositions (achievement, power, affiliation), coping strategies (accommodative flexibility, assimilative persistence), goal variables (goal commitment, goal attainability, goal probability), and subjective health perception. Results confirmed findings of SWB research, according to which SWB is at a rather high level, even in old age. Males indicated greater life-satisfaction and more positive affective well-being than females. The predictor variables formed a coherent pattern of four factors: (1) Assertiveness (persistence, achievement and power motives), (2) goals (commitment, attainability, probability, (3) flexibility, subjective health, (low) hopelessness, (low) externality, and (4) affiliation motive. Self-efficacy had equal substantial loadings on both the assertiveness and flexibility factors. This means that individuals with a strong sense of efficacy have both assimilative and accommodative coping strategies at their disposal. The association of subjective health with flexibility shows that individuals who are capable of adjusting their aspirations to age-related constraints feel less impaired by health restrictions. Gender differences relate to higher personal agency (self-efficacy, low hopelessness, low externality) and higher assertiveness (persistence, achievement, power) of males. However, there were no gender differences concerning accommodative flexibility and subjective health, and males and females were equally highly committed to their goals. There were distinct age-related changes: Personal agency, assertiveness and goal probability decreased, but the decline only began in the middle-age cohort and was mostly pronounced in the oldest cohort (age 78 upwards). The phase after entry into retirement was characterized by a rather high stability of personality, whereas a terminal decline occurred only in the oldest age. These results support the differentiation between a "third" and "fourth" age. Generally, goal commitment increased and subjective health decreased during the interval between the two measurement points. Regression analyses on the impact of the predictor variables on SWB revealed (low) hopelessness as being the main predictor of both life satisfaction and affect. Beyond that, cognitive and affective well-being were influenced by *different* predictors. Self-efficacy and flexibility had the highest impact on life satisfaction, especially in the youngest age cohort. However, in the oldest cohort, the most influential predictor of life satisfaction was the success probability of attaining personal goals. Affective well-being, in contrast, was mainly influenced by subjective health perception in all cohorts. Longitudinal analyses revealed that during the five-year interval, our participants' life satisfaction *increased*, whereas affective well-being *decreased*. These differing developmental trends could be explained by different predictor variables. Again, feelings of hopelessness had a detrimental effect on both changes in cognitive as well as in affective well-being. Beyond that, the increase in life satisfaction was mainly due to the ability to flexibly adjust one's own aspirations to reduced resources and, therefore, strive for achievable goals. The decrease in affect, in contrast, was primarily caused by poor subjective health.

Chapter 10 - Nuttin's critique of Thorndike's *Law of Effect* made a substantial contribution to the experimental study of motivation and its influence on learning and performance. The studies stimulated by this critique contributed much to Nuttin's formulation of his Relational Theory of human motivation and personality, a conceptual framework that can be used to analyze the main shortcomings of the traditional educational practice, both at macrosystem and at microsystem levels. This traditional educational system reproduces high rates of school dropouts and underachievement, as well as persistent emotional problems. The authors propose an alternative view on educational practice based on the ideas of task tension and of instrumental dynamic functioning proposed by J. Nuttin.

Chapter 11 - The aim of this chapter is to propose a model of the self-determination process, based on the cultural-historical view on human motivation. Before describing the model itself, the author elaborates the main ideas about human motivation, originated in the framework of cultural-historic approach in the broad sense of the term. Higher forms of motivation (such as self-determination and will) are understood as specific 'motivational abilities' which can be acquired in some social and educational environments but not in others. Relying on the concepts of P. Janet, L.S. Vygotsky, M. M. Bakhtin and B. F. Porshnev, the author considers the motivating speech influence to be the universal 'building block' of the complex social motivating systems, shaping our motivations in a very high degree. An act of speech influence can lead either to simple obedience/disobedience or it can start a real motivational dialogue. The latter is seen as a process in which new motives, desires and decisions emerge. Motivational dialogue can be internalized; in such a case, it is considered to be the real core of the self-determination process. So, creating a 'dialogical environment' is regarded as the main path for developing the self-determination ability in children.

Chapter 12 - A theory is presented that highlights the narrative role of language in moral development. Two stages in moral development are distinguished: the stage when children can speak and memorize events but are not yet capable of cheating and the stage when they are capable of creating deceptive stories in order to protect themselves from punishment for non-compliance with moral rules. When children reach the second stage, they may encounter situations of free moral choice – the situations in which they can transgress on a moral rule and yet get away with this by presenting adults with a deceptive story. From the view of the presented theory, these kinds of situations are key for the emergence of the intrinsic moral motivation – motivation based on respect for moral rules rather than on the fear of negative consequences for non-compliance. Various scenarios of the development of this kind of moral motivation are considered, and experimental studies that aimed to test the theory are reviewed.

Chapter 13 - This chapter presents a review of the current literature on theoretical and empirical studies of flow experience (or optimal experience) within Internet-mediated environments. The concept of flow as introduced by Csikszentmihalyi is described, the parameters characterizing optimal forms of experience are discussed, as well as data collection methods which are most often used to measure flow. The particular Internet-mediated environments connected with the studies of optimal experience and thoroughly reviewed in the chapter include online (1) shopping, (2) learning, (3) game playing, and (4) interaction. A brief overview of the projects in the field, initiated and performed by the author and his colleagues, is also presented.

In: Motivation, Consciousness and Self-Regulation
Editor: Dmitry A. Leontiev, pp. 1-6

ISBN 978-1-61324-795-2
© 2012 Nova Science Publishers, Inc.

Chapter 1

REEMERGING PERSPECTIVE FOR THE PSYCHOLOGY OF MOTIVATION

Dmitry A. Leontiev
Moscow State University, Russia

Psychology of motivation is a very special field of psychological inquiry – highly, and even intimately important for everyone and still very fragmented and obscure, despite its centennial history. It was not always made a separate field during this history. A period of much theoretical interest in motivation directly connected with the fascination of the riddle of human nature through the first half of the 20th century was followed after the Second World War by decades of disappointment in general theory, narrow specialization of research and straightforward methodological rigorism. The field of motivation was occupied by cognitive revolutionaries, split into pieces and largely dissolved in other problems, such as learning, personnel management, psychotherapy, etc.

In the last couple of decades this field seems to "reemerge" (Ryan, 2007). Among the factors of this reemergence R. Ryan mentioned a renewed interest to human nature, the rapid growth of cross-cultural psychology, new positive emphasis in research agenda, attention to profound existential issues, the discovery of sophisticated brain mechanisms of higher regulations, etc. Due to all these developments the psychology of motivation is now less than totally bound with old Manichean dichotomies like cognition vs. affect, conscious vs. unconscious, internal vs. external, etc. that now seem strongly delimiting if not misleading. It is less concerned with distinguishing easily measurable stable (that is, static) dispositional variables and attempts to get a better idea of the involved processes, relationships and complex systems.

New millennium requires new paradigms. The mainstream theoretical psychology of the last century seems to work out the resources of the development of Aristotelian-Cartesian approach to the human mind, at least what refers to its further development, though its special applications keep working effectively in many fields. These new paradigms should be comprehensive ones, giving due respect to the variability and complexity of human motivation, rather than narrow ones, providing a universally valid explanation. What the theory of motivation and of the entire human conduct needs now most of all is discovering the meaning of human action. Meaning of something is determined by its conceived or construed context: to get a meaning of something we are to put it into the appropriate context (see Leontiev, 2011, this volume). Does the psychology of motivation have such a context for the objects of its research and is this context comprehensive enough? If the context is narrow, the meaning will be also narrow. After decades of zoom-in research, a more zoom-out view would be helpful.

Alexander Asmolov, one of the leading Russian psychologists, in his historical evolutionary approach to personality development within multiple systems proposed an explanation of meaning of individual differences and even deviations from the mainstream trends. According to this approach, all individual variations present a store of potentialities, of eventual directions of further development of the whole, be it a species, a social group, a society or humanity at large. The larger this store, the more effective and flexible are the selection of the ways of further evolution. Some potentialities are selected, some rejected, but they may become contemporary and urgently demanded at another time when the objective situation and external challenges will change (see Asmolov, 1998).

Many hidden potentialities that may enrich the present-day psychology of motivation can be found in the history of the field, in theories and models that by some reason failed to receive the appreciation they deserve due to some biases in favor of the mainstream paradigms; in particular, overemphasis on rational mechanisms at the expense of irrational ones, overemphasis on quantitative methods at the expense of qualitative ones, overemphasis of analysis at the expense of synthesis, etc. Let's have a brief look at this history.

Historically (as well as logically) the first motivational paradigm was explaining behavior as determined by internal causes, rooted in the individual -- "Aristotelian way of thinking", in terms of K. Lewin (1935), or "explanation from the first sight", in terms of H. Heckhausen (1980). This paradigm persisted until the 1930's, when behaviorists, on the one hand, and Lewin, on the other hand, shifted the emphasis to the external causes ("explanation from the second sight") and, then, to the interaction between external and internal causes ("the third sight", in terms of Heckhausen, 1980). However, this was not the only paradigmatic shift in the psychology of motivation. No less important were, first, the introduction of the teleological perspective by A. Adler, as opposed to Freudian causal model (the innovation that V. Frankl later compared to Copernican revolution); second, the extension of the sources of human behavior from the individual mind to the collective mentality by C. G. Jung; third, the conceptualization of motivational units in terms of individual-world relations or connections, rather than mere interactions, by H. Murray; and fourth (but not least) the introduction of the idea of deliberate control over motivational processes through their mediation by L. Vygotsky. All these views developed through 1930es stayed marginal.

In the post-war period all these ideas have been developed further, though still outside the mainstream. The teleological perspective found the most convincing elaboration in Frankl's theory of will to meaning, the sociocultural perspective — in a number of academic theories, e.g. in the treatment of motives as cultural schematisms by R. d'Andrade, the relational perspective had been very elegantly construed by J. Nuttin, and the ideas of control over motivation (though without direct links and references to Vygotsky) became one of the central points of German psychology of motivation in the 1980s, not to mention much less known but very important theoretical and experimental works on volitional regulation by V. Ivannikov in Moscow. In addition, a very important explanatory concept of personal meaning has been introduced to the psychology of motivation by A.N. Leontiev, J. Nuttin, G. Kelly and some other scholars independently of each other.

I claim that it's time to better explore the resources of some approaches diverging from the mainstream of the last century to discover their fruitfulness for the treatment of present-day problems.

The idea of this book was born at the 7th International Conference of Motivation (Leuven, 2000) and took shape at the next, 8th Conference (Moscow, 2002) that I chaired. It was the insight of a common ground of some European approaches to motivation that seemed to be broader in scope of their vision of the psychology of motivation due to their basing on some non-classical concepts, underappreciated by the mainstream paradigm of the last century. These approaches are the cultural-historical activity theory approach by L. Vygotsky, A. N. Leontiev and A. R. Luria (originated in Russia), existential approach by L. Binswanger, M. Boss, V. Frankl, et al. (originated in Switzerland and Austria), and J. Nuttin's relational theory (originated in Belgium). Though these theories developed rather independent of each other, the key explanatory concepts are sometimes strikingly similar and they are capable of substantially enriching the mainstream psychology of motivation. The concept of meaning may bring meaning into it, the concept of future time perspective may open a perspective, the concepts of culture and psychological tools may enhance its culture and arm it with tools, and the concept of courage may support its courage.

It took however years to make this idea come true. The book includes a few keynote and selected papers given at the 8th International Conference on Motivation (Moscow, 2002), but most chapters have been written specially for it. Its authors represent eight countries. Besides the three approaches mentioned in the previous paragraph, each having a long history, more recent approaches in terms of autonomy, self-regulation and autotelic activity entered the common dialogue. This latter view is represented in this volume by chapters authored by Valery Chirkov, Falko Rheinberg & Stephan Engeser, Frank Halish & Ulrich Geppert, and Alexander Voiskounsky. Cultural-historical view is represented by Eugene Subbotsky and Catherine Patyaeva, existential approach by Alfried Längle and Salvatore Maddi, and relational theory by Manuel Viegas Abreu, Maria Paula Paixão, & Willy Lens. As for me, I was educated within the cultural-historical framework but try not to restrict my scholarly identity to a single tradition; in my chapters I try to create a dialogical space, bridging schools and helping them to reveal in this space their commonality and underappreciated potentialities.

The first part of the book is devoted to the old problem of fundamental motivations that can hardly be approached in a way other than theoretically. The chapter by D. Leontiev presents an overview of this field, tracing the development and change of the basic constructs used to make sense of the sources of human motivation – instinct, drive, need, etc. - and, parallel to this, the extension of the contexts and imperatives of human existence from biological adaptation to social integration and then, to personal self-determination. The summarizing model is based on the distinction of objective "metanecessities" inherent in each of the three levels and embraces the needs of biological, social, and personal existence as equally important for a non-reduced human being.

The chapter by Alfried Längle, one of the leaders of present-day existential psychology, specially concerns one group of fundamental motivations, namely existential ones. He highlights the role and the relevance of existential motivations largely neglected by the mainstream motivation theories. Thanks to Victor Frankl, his teacher, the idea of the will to meaning as a profound human striving is no more novel; Längle proposes a more comprehensive theory describing a system of four fundamental existential motivations. What is needed at this level is (to simplify his argument): (1) a place in the world, (2) a value of living, (3) a shared existence and (4) a meaning – last, but certainly not least.

The second part of the book is devoted to new or rather marginal (for the field of motivation) concepts that seem capable of enriching general models of motivational processes. It openss with the chapter by Maria Paula Paixão, Manuel Viegas Abreu and Willy Lens, who explicate the concept of future time perspective (FTP). This concept was introduced by their teacher Joseph Nuttin, who stressed that future is the space where all motivation is located. Though this concept is now an acknowledged one, its potential is rather poorly exploited in the psychology of motivation. The authors give a detailed theoretical analysis of the concept and a review of empirical studies; they also highlight its applied potential in the example of vocational guidance practice.

The next chapter by D. Leontiev highlights the relevance of the concept of personal meaning for the psychology of motivation. Though many authors, beginning with Freud, tried to put meaning and motivation together, few attempts generated coherent theories, and these did not win much recognition outside their countries of origin. Nevertheless, the concept of meaning seems now still more relevant for making a common ground for many phenomena like valence, instrumentality, control beliefs, etc., that are analyzed in this context.

The third nontrivial concept is that of motivational competence, proposed by Falko Rheinberg and Stefan Engeser. By motivational competence the authors understand the capacity to set goals in the way that would not create tensions and effortful control of their implementation. In their model they combine the approaches of D. McClelland, H. Heckhausen and M. Csikszentmihalyi, among others. They also provide empirical evidences in favor of their model that clearly show the covariation of self-regulation, goal attainment, flow and the congruence between one's implicit and explicit motives.

Part 3 of the book deals with the issues of self-regulation and self-determination; in the last two decades the problems of motivation can be hardly dealt with without touching these issues. As it is argued in one more chapter by D. Leontiev, the concept of self-regulation (autoregulation) refers to a general principle of human activity rather than to special processes. The author introduces the general explanatory framework based on this principle and proposes his Multiregulation personality model that describes a finite variety of basic forms and mechanisms of human regulations. Implications from this model provide theoretical answers to some controversial issues of developmental, clinical, and evolutionary psychology.

The next chapter by Valery Chirkov is devoted to the concept of human autonomy. The chapter gives a detailed account of this concept developed within the Self-Determination Theory. Its second part provides theoretical and empirical arguments in favor of the importance of personal autonomy for eudaimonic happiness and reveals psychological mechanisms of the impact of autonomy on good living. A special analysis of autonomy in different cultures shows that autonomy is beneficial in various cultures, and not only in the ones that foster it.

The chapter by Salvatore Maddi, a renowned representative of the existentialist tradition, is centered on existential courage operationalized in his concept of hardiness. The concept of hardiness is very important within the autoregulation context, though the chapter provides no direct references to this context. In fact, this learned capacity, as it is shown in manifold studies reviewed by the author, accounts for the meaningful and reasonable reactions in stressful or frustrating situations, in contrast to self-regulation breakdown occurring in similar situations with non-hardy individuals lacking existential courage.

The chapter by Abreu and Paixiao deals with some aspects of Nuttin's relational theory of motivation and their implications for education. The authors come back to Nuttin's critique of Tolman's theoretical explanation of the law of effect. New experiments allow them advancing further Nuttin's position that explains learning efficiency by the regulatory context of task tension. As it follows from the experimental data with different kinds of tasks, it is not the reward per se that is critical for learning efficacy; learning occurs more efficiently when its results are associated with the perspective of future improvement. The authors draw from these data important implications for educational practice, providing the general model of educational process based on the relational theory.

The last chapter in this part is authored by Frank Halisch and Ulrich Geppert. Unlike most other chapters, this one is mainly empirical; it is based on a large longitudinal study of predictors of well-being in the old age. The authors trace sophisticated interrelations between different groups of variables like personal agency, motive dispositions, regulatory coping strategies, goal variables, as well as measures of subjective health perception, different aspects of well-being, gender and age scale. Rich data contain many insightful findings; for me, the most intriguing seems to be the compensation of the declining with age positive affect and subjective health with flexible and rational autoregulation based on careful goal selection; this strategy helps to maintain well-being at a rather high level despite the objectively reduced agency.

The focus of the last part of the book is cultural context and cultural mediation of motivation. This part opens with a theoretical chapter authored by Catherine Patyayeva. She proposes a nontrivial approach to the issue of cultural historical determination of human motivations, treating sociocultural systems as a source of specific motivational influences; to denote these special kinds of urges, she uses the term *dispositif* coined by French philosopher Michel Foucault. The second part of the chapter is devoted to making sense of the way speech communication contributes to motivational processes. Patyaeva construes an original theoretical explanation that escapes reducing speech communication to suggesting stimuli or sign tools; she introduces the concept of motivational dialogue, proposing the model of joint determination of an action that grows into the cultural model of self-determination.

The role of speech in self-regulation processes is also the focus of Eugene Subbotsky's chapter focused on the development of moral regulation of action. His original Tape—Double Tape theory explains the emergence of intrinsic moral motivation out of an extrinsic one in the course of early personality development. Sophisticated experiments provide new insights of the social mechanisms of development of both capacity and motivation to evaluate one's own actions from another perspective than one's own immediate interests.

Finally, Alexander Voiskounsky in his chapter gives a detailed overview of a relatively new research field dealing with the conditions of optimal experiences (flow state) in internet-communications, including online shopping, learning, playing, chatting, hacking and other forms of online activity. World wide web appears as a modern form of cultural environment and tool at the same time, penetrating into most domains of human activity; its place and role in our lives is growing fast. Voiskounsky shows the relevance of flow theory for understanding the many important phenomena we meet on the online side of human living.

This book was planned not as a collection of discoveries to be considered, but rather as a collection of nontrivial views that may turn helpful for making a better sense of the discoveries actually made. Now the situation in psychology seems to be somewhat more favorable for "vigorous theorizing" (Maddi, 1980) than a decade or two ago.

To put it most vigorously, the ideas explicated in this book help to foresee the outline of a (the?) new psychology of motivation for the XXI century.

1. It is RELATIONAL in the sense that the sources of human motivation are sought not in inherent dispositions or in environmental factors, or in the combination of both, but rather in idiosyncratic, flexible, vital and imperative relations that bridge an individual to the world.
2. It is TELEOLOGICAL in the sense that human behavior always has meaning, or reasons, even if effective causes are evident. The answer in causal terms to the question "Why?" is a half–answer; the ultimate answer can be given only in final terms.
3. It is CULTURE-BOUND in the sense that much of the content and structure of motivation is acquired from the collective mind of the given social community and the treasury of artifacts and "significats", materially embodied and semantically embodied human creations.
4. It is PERSONAL in the sense that motivation is always motivation of a person that gives shape to it and controls it; even if a person is unable to personalize and control his/her own motivation, it is due to some personality features that are responsible for this.
5. It is just around the corner.

REFERENCES

Asmolov, A. G. (1998). *Vygotsky Today: on the Verge of Non-Classical Psychology*. New York: Nova Science Publishers.

Heckhausen, H. (1980). *Motivation und Handeln*. Berlin: Springer.

Leontiev, D. (2011b) Personal meaning as the basis of motivational processes. In D. Leontiev (Ed.) *Motivation, consciousness, and self-regulation* (pp. 000-000). New York: Nova Science Publishers.

Lewin, K. (1935). *A dynamic theory of personality: selected papers*. New York: McGraw-Hill.

Maddi, S. R. (1980). The uses of theorizing in personology. In E. Straub (Ed.), *Personality: Basic issues and current research*. Englewood Cliffs, NJ: Prentice-Hall.

Ryan, R. (2007). Motivation and emotion: A new look and approach for two reemerging fields. *Motivation and Emotion*, 31, 1-3.

PART 1. NEW LOOK AT FUNDAMENTAL MOTIVATIONS

In: Motivation, Consciousness and Self-Regulation
Editor: D. A. Leontiev, pp. 9-25

ISBN: 978-1-61324-795-2
© 2012 Nova Science Publishers, Inc.

Chapter 2

FROM DRIVE TO NEED AND FURTHER: WHAT IS HUMAN MOTIVATION ABOUT?

Dmitry A. Leontiev
Moscow State University, Russia

ABSTRACT

This chapter gives an overview of the evolution of explanatory models of the fundamentals of human motivation throughout the last century: from the concepts of instinct and drive to basic needs, and from the lists of biologically rooted needs to the discovery of non-biological, social, and existential imperatives to human behavior. The integrative model, proposed by the author, distinguishes three qualitatively different levels of individual-world relationships: the biological existence, the social existence, and the personal existence. Objective meta-necessities inherent in each level (including the actualization of potentialities and relating to the environment; social belongingness and integration; self-determination and autonomous choice) underlie special needs relevant to this particular level.

Keywords: Instinct, drive, need, value, social motivation, existential needs

INTRODUCTION

Motivation refers to the system of processes and mechanisms that bring a living creature into motion. It is inherent in the entire animal world, because characteristic of animal life, unlike vegetable life, is locomotion in search of safety and nutrition. Although this locomotion is usually treated as a causally determined process, it is triggered and regulated by a complicated interplay of external (environmental) and internal (organismic) states and processes and cannot be explained by the former or the latter alone; motivation may be thus defined in terms of this interplay.

When we approach the distinction between the human being and the subhuman species, the question arises whether human motivation can be treated in the same way as animal motivation. After many centuries of overestimating the difference between humans and other animals, Charles Darwin, and a few decades later Edward Thorndike and John Watson, changed this paradigm in favor of underestimating the difference between them. This underestimation prevailed throughout most of the 20th century.

This period in history coincided with the period of the most intensive development of the views regarding fundamental human motivations. Quite a number of theories of personality, created throughout the 1920s-1950s, were based on some assumptions about human motivation. In the postwar period, however, the interest in theoretical speculations about human nature in academic psychology has radically decreased. Psychologists shifted the emphasis to the situational mechanisms of motivation for special kinds of activity that could be investigated experimentally. The explosive development of studies of situational factors of behavior and motivation (see Heckhausen & Heckhausen, 2006), as well as the "cognitive revolution" of the 1960s, introduced many new intermediate variables into the model of transition from need to action._It has become evident that these intermediate variables (including personality variables such as the locus of control), and processes of cognitive elaboration (such as the subjective probability of success) account for the direction and energy of action to a much more substantial degree than do measurable need dispositions as the original energetic sources of activity. The focus of researchers' interest has shifted from needs to *ad hoc* motivation and its situational, cognitive, and personality determinants. This trend has proved to be stable and still pertains.

Indeed, the problem of definition of "need", connected with a meta-psychological context, as well as the problem of need classification and the problem of need measurement, make this concept hardly compatible with the dominating empirical tradition in psychology. Single motivational dispositions (needs) can be made measurable (with much limitations), but not the whole motivational system. Nevertheless, there is hardly any other hypothetical construct in psychological theory, whose relevance would be so evident phenomenologically. Since the 1970's new publications on specifically human fundamental motivations began to appear. Despite some inspiring theoretical advances, there are no recent publications that would summarize the present day state of the issue of fundamental human motivations.

Throughout the 20th century we observe the change from the concept of instinct elaborated in the natural sciences to the philosophically founded idea of existential needs specifically expressing a human way of being-in-the-world, a change that corresponds to the evolution of human sciences at large. The aims of this paper are (1) tracing the history of general views on fundamental human motivations, especially the history of the construct of "need", and (2) summarizing recent views regarding qualitatively different levels of human motivation as distinct from that of animals, and proposing an integrated theoretical model.

PREHISTORY OF PSYCHOLOGICAL THEORIES OF MOTIVATION

Viewing the first psychological theories of human motivation by William McDougall and Sigmund Freud, all of which remained without much competition throughout the 1900's-1930's, the question of the forces that energize human behavior and give it direction, has been answered in terms of drives. Both theories conceived drives as essentially the same as instincts in the animal world, that is, inherited impersonal forces of biological origin that make one to perform definite acts of behavior according to an inbuilt biological program. The idea of instinct, as an innate motivational force, has been elaborated by Charles Darwin, who made this word an explanatory scientific concept. Instincts in subhuman living species not only produce motivational effects, biological programs also account for the shape of special forms of behavior. Due to the lack of alternatives to these theories, by the early 1900's the word "instinct" was accepted as a rather common term for the motivational explanation of human behavior both by psychologists and by the lay audience; however, McDougall (1908) found a lack of conceptual clarity in the use of this concept by his contemporaries.

The concept of human instinct, as defined by McDougall, also stressed that human behavior is driven and directed by inborn forces. Instincts, however, have a complicated structure that include cognitive, affective, and conative components; and, only the affective component is inborn, while the other two components can be transformed through life experiences. Strong criticism against the application of the word "instinct" to human behavior forced McDougall to change this term for the term "propensity" in the later version of his theory (1932). Although McDougall tried to distinguish motivational propensities from actual behavioral tendencies, or wishes, his classification of propensities is totally based on the classification of observable forms of behavior. In the first version of his theory, McDougall distinguished 12 instincts, and in the later one 18 propensities that coincide with regular forms of human behavior or emotional responses; for example, food-seeking, disgust, sex, fear, curiosity, protection and parenting, gregariousness, self-assertion, submission, anger, appeal, construction, acquisition, laughter, comfort, rest or sleep, migration, bodily functions, and others.

The alternative concept of drive (*Trieb*, usually translated as *instinct*) proposed by Freud (1916) was similar to McDougall's instinct in that it was conceived as an inborn force of biological origins, which is the energy source and basis of all behavior. However, the difference was that Freud's *Trieb* concept appeared as nonspecific regarding forms of behavior. In McDougall's theory there was a special instinct or propensity that accounted for every distinguishable form of behavior, or, at least, for some class of behaviors. In Freud's theory all behavior stems from essentially the same motivational source. Though Freud used to speak of drives in the plural, he never tried to classify human drives by their content, except for his well-known, very general dichotomies like life drives versus death drives, ego drives versus id drives, Eros versus Tanatos; he considered this distinction just a working construction and asked not to take it as a real explanation (Freud, 1916). In general, it is the sophisticated psychodynamic processes that channel the energy stemming from the same source — the all-driving id — and that finally define which forms of behavior or symptoms will unfold in a given situation, fed by this non-specified energy.

Similar to Freud's concept was that of the non-specific drive proposed by Clark Hull (1943) that has become the basis of many experimental studies, mostly with animals. Despite the differences in explanation, Hull also assumed that drive, as the single energy source, might underlie various forms of behavior by virtue of associations established in learning processes throughout one's lifetime.

FROM DRIVE TO NEED

The concepts of drive and instinct dominated until the end of the 1930's. The necessity of changing the central explanatory principle came with the development of the Psychology of Personality, or Personology, as a special field of psychology (Allport, 1937; Murray, 1938). The emphasis in the psychology of motivation was shifted from impersonal mechanical forces, operating upon and within us, to more individual and controllable motivational forces. Etymologically, the German word "*Trieb*," or English "drive," contains the root that refers to the effect, stating what this force does with the subject, while the German word "*Bedürfnis*", or in English "need," refers to the experience of some demand. The latter term thus implies intentionality and potentiality, unlike the former term that implies an inescapable causal effect. In terms of human nature, as a driven being, one is a victim of uncontrollable forces; however, as a being with needs, one is an agent relating to the surrounding world.

The reasons against using the concept of drive or instinct as "a motivational unit in which the drive, motivated behavior and the goal object or the goal effect are all appreciably determined by heredity" (Maslow, 1970, p. 27), have been following: First, this concept implied a homeostatic view of motivation, and the reduction of any tension was treated as the final goal of all activity. In has been argued, however, that this is true for a sick, rather than a healthy organism, and such a model is only applicable to just a few human motivations (Allport, 1937; Goldstein, 1939; Maslow, 1970). Second, this view treated human motivation as essentially unchanging throughout the life circle, like in animals. On the contrary, the principle of functional autonomy of motives, introduced by Allport (1937), gave due respect to the development of human motivations. Third, the mixture of drive and behavior in the explanatory concept of instinct urged to explain every form of behavior by assuming a corresponding instinct; however, psychological data make it evident that a given form of behavior may be an expression of different motivations, and a given need may be channeled through different forms of behavior (Maslow, 1970, p. 23). Fourth, the concept of drive emphasized the energetic, "activational" aspects of behavior, while more importantly for human motivation there are more delicate processes of choice of goal objects and appropriate actions, such as the human urge for food, which is better conceived as appetite, rather than hunger (Maslow, 1970).

Already during the 1920s (e.g., Lewin, 1926) the term "need" was sometimes used instead of "drive"; however, its conceptual elaboration followed somewhat later, in the works of Henry Murray (1938) and Abraham Maslow (1943; 1970).

Beginning his book with the phrasing of "need or drive", Murray, however, preferred the word "need" in subsequent pages. He stressed that "need" is an unobservable, hypothetical construct. Each need has a directional, or qualitative aspect that differentiates it from other needs, and an energetic, or quantitative aspect. A need is dynamic: it comes into being, endures for a moment and perishes; one need succeeds another. It is convenient to group similar needs as different manifestations of one need (Murray, 1938, p. 60). Needs are inner dynamic forces inherent in the organism. Murray, however, discarded the term "instinct" for two reasons: first, motivational effect blended with behavior itself; and, second, it limits one to "needs" that can be proven innate; for many needs it is hardly possible to prove this (ibid., p. 74).

Murray classified needs into viscerogenic (or primary) ones, engendered by characteristic bodily events, and psychogenic (or secondary) ones, having no detectable bodily origins. The complete list of needs, composed by Murray, had, as he confesses, no sufficient basis except for its proven practical utility (ibid., p. 76). However, Murray's list stays to date, and is considered the most widely accepted and practically used list for research purposes of the classification of needs; and, some of the categories he introduced in the classification (e.g., achievement or affiliation) generated new fields of research. Different needs may be related to each other in various ways: some may fuse, counteract, or conflict with each other; some may be subsidiary to others (ibid., pp. 86-88). A need may be manifest (if it is objectified in real action) or latent (if it is not), relatively conscious or relatively unconscious.

A very important concept of *press* designated a positive or negative effect that an object or a situation is exerting or may exert upon the subject; it is a directional tendency on the side of the world that matches a need as a directional tendency on the side of the subject. Press may be positive (to the subject's benefit) or negative (to the subject's harm), mobile (active) or immobile (passive) (ibid., pp. 118-121). Summarizing, Murray defined need as a force within an organism, provoked sometimes by sequences of internal organic processes, but more often by the occurrence of some press (or its anticipation).

Maslow's concept of basic needs also referred to inner motivational forces. Maslow argued that basic needs could hardly be completely innate or completely free of the influence of heredity; he preferred to speak of them as "instinctoid", assuming that they are to some degree inherited (Maslow, 1970, pp. 80-81). However, human urges are not the same as those of other species; moreover, along with the ascendance up the evolutionary ladder, the role of hereditary components of motivation seems to have diminished (ibid., pp. 27, 91). The typical human desire is not tied to a local somatic base; it is the desire of the whole person, and it is the whole person, rather than a single organ, that can be gratified or frustrated (ibid., pp. 19-20).

Unlike Murray, Maslow refused to compose a list of drives or needs. Needs are not isolated from each other; they overlap, vary and are tied with each other in various ways (ibid., pp. 25-26). Maslow's own famous classification of needs is in fact the classification of five groups of needs without delineations within the groups. These five groups form a hierarchy; the lower needs are at the same time more urgent; they should be satisfied first, and only when they are mostly satisfied, the needs of the next level can direct behavior, etc. The needs of the lowest level are physiological, with the needs for safety representing the next level; next follow the needs of belonging and love, esteem; at the top level, there is the need for self-actualization (ibid., pp. 35-47). The criteria for labeling needs "low" or "high" are, in particular, the following: The higher needs appear later on, both in evolutionary and ontogenetic development, and they are less imperative for human survival and less urgent. Their pursuit and gratification account for better health and quality of life and produce more gratifying subjective experiences. They have more preconditions and more complicated requirements; they are more valued (ibid., pp. 98-100). Maslow recognized exceptions in this theoretical order (ibid., pp. 51-53) and, somewhat later, in his theory of deficiency motivation and growth motivation (Maslow, 1955), he refuted his own idea of a fixed order of the satisfaction of needs. Instead, he postulated a parallel existence of two forms of motivation, or needs. Deficiency needs can be defined through something lacking; to reach gratification, one has to find and consume it. Growth needs are defined through the processes of unfolding, development and realization of one's potentialities, not focused on special objects.

QUALITATIVE DISTINCTION OF HUMAN NEEDS: FROM CULTURAL ANTHROPOLOGY TO CULTURAL HISTORICAL ACTIVITY THEORY

The comprehensive theories of human motivation proposed by Maslow and Murray are still the most current ones today. Maslow's theory is most often taken as the reference point for criticism, development, and revision attempts (e.g. Yang, 2003; Kenrick et al., 2010), and Murray's theory is still used as the basis of motive measurement methodology. They are based on different explanatory principles: Maslow's theory is based on the principle of actualization, deducing motivation for some activity from potentialities to fulfill this activity; and, Murray's theory is based on the principle of interaction with the world, deducing motivation from the model of complementarity and interaction between the individual and the world. However, both principles equally apply to animal and human motivation, and both theories put little emphasis on the distinction between animals and humans.

Many thinkers and researchers have written on the special social nature of the human being, strongly differentiating between species, though interpretations of this social nature widely diverged. Beyond any doubt these differences must have strong implications for the theory of human motivation.

No wonder that specialists in the study of cultures were the first scholars who put into question the assumption of the primacy of basic needs. It was probably Bronislaw Malinowski, one of the most prominent leaders of cultural anthropology during the first half of the 20th century and the founder of functional sociology, who stressed in his posthumously published "Scientific Theory of Culture" that the social way of living produced the duplication of environment in humans (Malinowski, 1944). Acknowledging that a human being is a type of animal species and is thus to fulfill some basic requirements in order to survive and to procreate, he made some important additions. First, culture makes a special "second environment" that provides new ways and means of satisfaction of basic needs (the list of them includes nutrition, procreation, bodily comfort, safety, movement, development, and health). Second, individuals in society interact with the world through their social organization. Third, most cultural products serve the gratification of biological needs and culture provides new responses to needs rather than creates new needs. However, the culture also creates some new imperatives stemming from the social way of life inherent in humans. These imperatives are: permanent use and evolution of production equipment (response: economics), regulating individual behaviors by coded prescriptions (response: social control), intergenerational transmission of collective experiences and competences (response: education), and legally empowered authority privileged to enforce its decisions (response: politics) (Malinowski, 1944).

It is evident that these secondary imperatives are produced by the social way of living, one could say, by the meta-necessity of being in harmony with the social groups and organizations one belongs to. I shall elaborate on this point further; here I'd like to pay attention to one proof of the existence of such meta-necessity, namely its being the rationale for distinguishing between the norm and pathology. Indeed, throughout the 1960s several prominent scholars belonging to different branches of human sciences, — philosophy, sociology, and psychiatry, — independently of one another presented historical and sociological analyses of the development of the idea of norm and pathology, coming to the conclusion that these are sociological, rather than medical concepts, defined by "following" vs. "violating social rules and standards of behavior" (Foucault, 1965; Goffman, 1967; Szasz, 1961). It follows that being in harmony with society, or at least adjusting to it is a vital imperative, rather than just a convention.

Another renowned cultural anthropologist, Dorothy Lee, has come to still more radical conclusions about the lacking explanatory potential of the concept of basic needs, especially the ones derived from the biological imperatives. "I am not saying that there are no needs; rather, that if there are needs, they are derivative not basic. If, for example, physical survival was held as the ultimate goal in some society, it would probably be found to give rise to those needs which have been stated to be basic to human survival; but I know of no culture where human physical survival has been shown, rather than unquestioningly assumed by social scientists, to be the ultimate goal" (Lee, 1959, p. 72). Lee argued that culturally shared values, rather than needs, account for the most vital part of human motivation. Indeed, whether we agree with Lee or not in her denying the importance of needs in favor of values, it is evident that the concept of value in this context embodies different kinds of imperatives and a different motivational mechanism than that of the need—action sequence. It may be treated either (as Lee suggested) as alternative to the latter, or at least as complementary to it.

In the second half of the 20th century the idea of special forms of social motivation rooted in the "second nature" of human beings found detailed elaboration in the framework of the cultural-historical activity theory approach (CHAT), especially in the theoretical works of A.N. Leontiev, Lev Vygotsky's follower (Leont'ev, 1978). This approach departs from the individual's relating to the world, rather than from an isolated organism situated in some environment. A person's interaction with the world mediated by culturally transmitted tools, rather than inborn potentialities or environmental pressures, is considered the source of mental and personality development, the source of human motivation.

The simplest biological forms of needs are demands for some lacking substance or for a functional activity in the environment necessary for the preservation and development of both the individual and the species. These needs are always homeostatic; the activity they launch is aimed at reaching an optimal level of functioning of vital processes and stops as soon as this level is reached. Animal needs are all about self-preservation and procreation, metabolism, and the development of vital "orienting" and performing skills.

Human needs radically differ from animal needs. As, in particular, the studies with blind-deaf babies show, an (specially organized) interaction with the world is absolutely necessary to turn some vital deficiency into a need that would drive a special activity. Despite eventual inborn prerequisites, all human needs, in their elaborate forms, are determined by one's life experience, and thus are culturally shaped — both their goal objects, the forms of activities to fulfill, and the instrumental tools are culturally determined. Higher forms of human needs express human connections with the social and cultural aspects of the human condition, like lower forms, with its natural aspects.

The most precise distinction between the two different levels of human needs has been proposed by the Russian philosopher and historian, Herman Diligensky (1976; 1996). He distinguished the *needs for physical existence* and the *needs for social existence*. The former bridge an individual to the physical environment and implement the realization of vital relationships, causing a person to effectuate interaction with the world in order to survive and procreate. The latter emerge from interpersonal relationships (including relationships between a person and a group and intergroup relationships) and cause a person to effectuate interaction with one's fellows in order to provide a social balance. Social motivation cannot be deduced from biological motivation, because it refers to the level of functioning that is organized along with non-biological regularities.

BEYOND BIOLOGICAL AND CULTURAL MOTIVATION: DISCOVERING EXISTENTIAL NEEDS

In the first half of the 20th century the concept of need served as a transitory link between animal and human behavior, reminding us of our biological nature. The second half of the century brought forth the idea of existential needs, expressing the special human nature and way of being, different from the nature and way of being we find in animals.

The humanistic revolution of the 1950's-1960's, against the reduction of human psychology to blind drives, white rats, and computing machines, has returned the philosophical issue of human nature to the agenda of psychology and has given a new impulse to the development of the theories of needs based on the views of the specifically human motivation as distinct from the animal one. Without denying the importance of basic physiological needs, conceived as essentially the same as in other mammals, humanistic authors, belonging to different traditions, have proposed theories of human existential needs emerging from uniquely human ways of existence. By existential needs, I understand the imperatives stemming from the awareness of one's unique position in the world. Their relative gratification produces the feeling of humanness, and their frustration effectuates either the feeling of humiliation or the loss of conscious self-reflection. Some relevant ideas have been proposed in the first half of the 20th century, for example, in Victor Frankl's theory "the will to meaning" is considered to be the most fundamental human motivation (see Frankl, 1969). The most recent model of fundamental existential motivations has been proposed by Alfried Längle (2011). I shall dwell here on three elaborated theories of existential needs that should be mentioned in this context: First, the theory of Erich Fromm (1956), which he labeled as humanistic psychoanalysis; Second, the theory of Salvatore Maddi (1971), which can be classified as existential personology; Third, the most recent self-determination theory of Edward Deci and Richard Ryan, which is now a part of the positive psychology movement. Deci labeled his views as "empirical humanism" (Deci, Flaste, 1995, p.79).

Fromm's view of needs emerged from his analysis of the human situation. The uniqueness of this situation consists in the broken harmony between the biological nature and the transcendent existence of humans. A human being "has fallen out of nature, as it were, and is still in it; he is partly divine, partly animal; partly infinite, partly finite. *The necessity to find ever-new solutions for the contradictions in his existence, to find ever-higher forms of unity with nature, his fellowmen and himself, is the source of all the psychic forces that motivate man, of all his passions, affects, and anxieties.* The animal is content if all its physiological needs — its hunger, its thirst and its sexual needs — are satisfied. Inasmuch as man is *also* animal, these needs are likewise imperative and must be satisfied. *But inasmuch as man is human, the satisfaction of these instinctual needs is not sufficient to make him happy; they are not even sufficient to make him sane. The archimedic point of the specifically human dynamism lies in this uniqueness of the human situation; the understanding of man's psyche must be based on the analysis of man's needs stemming from the conditions of his existence*" (Fromm, 1956, p. 25).

The core of these conditions is the inescapable split between the two aspects of human nature – the inherited one, common for all the nature that drives us back to the mindless harmony with natural laws and ties, and the newly found one, based on self-awareness, transcendence and having been thrown away from the Garden of Eden. "All passions and strivings of man are attempts to find an answer to his existence" (ibid., p. 29). Fromm described five existential needs responding to different aspects of the human situation. Each of these needs has two forms, the one driving a person along the human way of self-awareness and transcendence of nature, and the other proposing an easier solution of moving back to the mindless dissolution in the laws or ties of nature or of its substitute, society.

1. The need of relatedness: "some form of relatedness is the condition for any kind of sane living. But among the various forms of relatedness, only the productive one, love, fulfills the condition of allowing one to retain one's freedom and integrity while being, at the same time, united with one's fellow man" (ibid., p. 36). Other forms of relatedness are based on narcissistic blindness to the reality of fellow humans.
2. The need of transcendence: a human being "is driven to transcend the role of the creature, the accidentalness and passivity of his existence, by becoming a "creator"" (ibid., p. 36). Creativeness is the human response to this need; however, it is a serious challenge. "*There is another answer to this need of transcendence: if I cannot create life, I can destroy it. To destroy life makes me also transcend it.* Indeed, that man can destroy life is just as miraculous a feat as that he can create it" (ibid., p. 37).
3. The need of rootedness: a human being "can dispense with the *natural* roots only insofar as he finds new *human* roots and only after he has found them can he feel at home again in this world" (ibid., p. 38). The key dichotomy here is brotherliness vs. incest. Brotherliness refers to the form of ties established voluntarily, free from the natural fixations. Incest refers to the incapacity of getting rid of the primary rootedness within the nuclear family and of seeking out new roots outside the family.
4. The need of a sense of identity: A human being "needs to form a concept of himself, needs to say and to feel 'I am I'" (ibid., p. 60). Full-range personal identity, that is full experience of individuality, the capacity "to feel 'I' in the sense that he was the center and active subject of his powers and experienced himself as such" (ibid., p. 62), is not so easily achieved. The majority is satisfied with its substitute, herd identity "in which the sense of identity rests on the sense of an unquestionable belonging to the crowd" (ibid.)
5. The need of a frame of orientation and devotion. It "exists on two levels; the first and the more fundamental need is to have some frame of orientation, regardless of whether it is true or false.... On the second level the need is to be in touch with reality by reason, to grasp the world objectively" (ibid., p. 65).

Unlike Fromm, Maddi has built his theory of needs on the basis of clinical psychology, rather than on philosophical anthropology. His basic assumption is that there are three groups of needs inherent in human nature: *biological*, *social*, and *psychological* needs. "The biological needs require metabolic requirements, and their continual frustration leads to intense suffering and even physical death. Included here are such well-known needs as that for food, water, air, and elimination" (Maddi, 1971, p. 149). Social needs refer to "at least those for communication and for contact" (ibid.). What is meant by psychological needs is "capabilities, even requirements, of mind as opposed to body or groups. Those needs have been described in various ways, but they seem well summarized by referring to the push to symbolize, to imagine, and to judge" (ibid., p. 151). Symbolization refers to "the mental act of generalizing from specific experiences so that you establish categories of things or events" (ibid.), imagination to "the process of developing ideas and sequences of ideas that resemble possible experiences in the world, but have no actuality outside the mind" (ibid.), and judgment to "any sort of evaluation, be it moral or preferential" (ibid., p. 152).

All the three groups of needs are considered equally necessary for human functioning. "Only by expressing them all will a person be able to avoid the accumulation of frustration and other dire consequences attendant upon need deprivation. But when one or more of the three sets of needs are stifled, or defended against, the result is a lopsided personality – too biological or too social or too psychological – undermined and limited by the fact that it insufficiently expresses all that is in man's nature" (ibid., p. 155). However, psychological needs are the most crucial for human nature. Maddi called the type of personality "in which psychological needs are a source of anxiety and have been defended against" the conformist type; a conformist person "defines himself as *nothing more than a player of social roles and an embodiment of creature needs*" (ibid.). Such a person feels powerless in the face of both kinds of pressures. "Soon he will become his social roles and biological needs – there being no longer any act of consciousness worth speaking of to mark the fact that his identity is not the only one possible" (ibid., p. 157). This type of personality is vulnerable to existential sickness – the profound feeling of meaninglessness and alienation; Maddi describes conformism as a premorbid state. On the contrary, when psychological needs are expressed along with the other ones, we are facing the personality type Maddi called individualistic. This is "someone with a mental life through which he can understand and influence his social and biological experiences and urges" (ibid., p. 163). Psychological needs – symbolization, imagination and judgment – are powerful resources an individualistic person uses to find meaning in life and to pursue meaningful possibilities rather than to follow the pressures of facticity (Maddi, 1998).

The short list of three basic needs proposed in the self-determination theory (SDT) of Edward Deci and Richard Ryan (Deci & Flaste, 1995; Deci & Ryan, 2000; Deci & Vansteenkiste, 2004) is probably the most recent of relatively well-known approaches to fundamental human needs. Though the authors work in the empirical tradition, they stress the necessity of meta-theory; however, the basic needs are conceived not as a part of SDT meta-theory, but rather as "a theoretical postulate that was formulated because it provided an interpretation of various empirical results" (Deci & Vansteenkiste, 2004, 26).

The basic needs proposed by SDT theory are: *the need for competence* that concerns people's inherent desire to be competent in dealing with the environment; *the need for relatedness* that concerns the universal propensity to interact with, be connected to, and experience caring for other people; and *the need for autonomy*, that concerns the human universal urge to be causal agents, to experience volition, to act in accord with one's integrated sense of self and to endorse one's actions at the highest level of reflective capacity. Without any specifications, these three needs refer to the uniquely human aspects of being, and they amazingly overlap with Fromm and Maddi's views.

However, unlike both Fromm and Maddi, Deci and Ryan speak of universal basic needs rather than special existential needs and find the roots of these needs in the general biological nature of human organisms, rather than in a human being's transcendence of this biological nature. "Innate psychological needs for competence, relatedness, and autonomy concern the deep structure of the human psyche, for they refer to innate and life-span tendencies toward achieving effectiveness, connectedness, and coherence" (Deci & Ryan, 2000, p. 229). In this sense their view of the highest human motivations is similar to Maslow's (1976) latest theory of meta-motivation at the level of Being. Maslow, however, stressed that Being-values that motivate those who have reached the level of Being, though rooted in human biology, are not the same as basic needs that motivate us at the lower level of Becoming, on the way toward growing into a human person. For Deci and Ryan, needs for competence, relatedness and autonomy are of vital necessity for every human individual, rather that a luxury that the most successfully advanced individuals can afford. Nevertheless, they draw a crucial difference between these psychological needs and traditional views of basic physiological needs; while for the latter the set point of the human organism is passivity, "in SDT, the set point is growth-oriented activity" (Deci & Ryan, 2000, p. 230). Another difference is that the dynamic of a need in course of active interaction with the environment is more important that its strength. This makes the basic needs in SDT similar to existential needs in Fromm and Maddi's theories.

The criterion to identify a need is purely empirical: its satisfaction should have positive psychological consequences, and its frustration negative ones. The needs are defined as universal necessities; they are an inherent aspect of human nature and "constitute the nutriments that are required for proactivity, optimal development, and psychological health of all people.... To the extent that the needs are thwarted, one would expect to find passivity, ill-being, fragmentation, and alienated functioning" (Deci & Vansteenkiste, 2004, p. 25). The concept of basic needs "...implies that some desires are linked to or catalyzed by our psychological design, as it were, while others are not" (Deci & Ryan, 2000, p. 232). Deci and his co-authors refer to numerous experimental studies that provide tangible support to the assumption that psychological well-being and positive development are being promoted by satisfaction and support of the needs for competence, relatedness and autonomy.

Let's summarize the output of the three approaches presented in the last two sections. First, in contrast to classical pre-war theories, the origins of fundamental human motivations are found in person-world relationships, rather than in human biology. This is true even for biological motivations, or "needs for physical existence" (Diligensky); at approximately the same time (1950's-1960's) animal psychologists collected numerous data, finally discarding the concept of instinct as an inborn motivational force (e.g., Lehrman, 1956). Second, on one level of these relationships, human needs are homological to needs of other mammals, while on other levels they are unique for the human species; the shift of the emphasis from the former to the latter in current publications is quite visible. Third, the uniqueness of human nature is seen not so much in the social way of being, but rather in the mature autonomous personhood based on self-determination, construing one's own life trajectory in line with one's goals rather than adjusting to biological and social pressures. Quite a number of scholars mentioned in the recent decades two opposite motivational tendencies or needs: a tendency toward integration with a social group and a tendency toward standing out, individual autonomy and self-affirmation (e.g. Diligenski, 1996, p. 117).

BACK TO CLASSIFICATION: NEEDS AT DIFFERENT LEVELS OF PERSON-WORLD RELATIONSHIPS

The most integral and well-structured view on human needs, as ties between an individual and the world embracing biological, social and existential levels can be found in Joseph Nuttin's relational theory of motivation, based upon the ideas of Lewin, Murray and Woodworth, among others (Nuttin, 1984).

Nuttin defined needs as "behavioral relationships in as far as they are 'required' to insure the individual's optimal functioning" (ibid., p. 60), and the reference point for his analysis was the system I—E (individual—environment). "Rather than beginning with these two entities which, once in existence, come into contact, the starting point is within the relational network itself in which the personality and the environment are the two poles. Independent of this relational network, neither the person, nor the environment are relevant to the analysis of behavior" (Nuttin, 1984, 58).

The ultimate basis of behavioral dynamics in Nuttin's theory is a person's interaction to the physical and social environment rather than the biochemical state of tissues or the electrical stimulation of the central nervous system (ibid., 57). It is the inherently dynamic nature of the "individual—environment" relationship that gives needs their dynamic power; "specific motivations are the *regulators* — not the initiators — of an ongoing stream of behavioral functioning" (ibid., p. 60). Needs "are related to different modalities of functioning that make up the functional structure of a given species of living beings" (ibid., p. 77). A state of deficit has no dynamic power in itself; it becomes a source of activity only due to inherent dynamism to overcome the deficiencies (ibid., p. 63). What we find "within" a living organism is an inherent need for relational functioning. "Each person is motivated for specific objects as well as for specific types of relationships" (ibid., p. 61); hence, need objects are crucial for the definition of the nature of a need. However, before a need has found adequate objects and relevant behavioral patterns have been elaborated, it exists in a pre-behavioral, diffuse form, with a very limited range of selectivity and directionality, to be further concretized or canalized (ibid., p. 65-67). The fundamental orientation of needs is innate, but develops and concretizes itself into countless motives and goal objects depending on learning, situational cues, and cognitive processing of needs (ibid., p. 78).

Needs are integral; they relate to the personality functioning in its entirety, which can hardly be subdivided into distinguishable and classifiable units. His view of "the basic behavioral dynamism as an inherent need for relational functioning in the living organism," (ibid., p. 62) destroys the popular distinction of the "primary," biological vs. "secondary," psychological or social motives.

Nuttin argued that drawing up a list of needs would be neither helpful nor possible; the results would depend on the level of abstraction chosen by the researcher. The multitude of dynamic orientations we find in adult human beings stems from the differentiation of the basic need for relational functioning along with actually occurring behavioral relationships; the goal objects demanded and met in the world serve as the basis of this differentiation and a possible classification of needs. "Their proposed number and label are of minor importance…. Of major importance, however, are the processes through which the basic dynamics differentiate and are elaborated into concrete behavioral motives, goals, and plans of action" (ibid., p. 214).

Nevertheless Nuttin in his earlier works did propose a classificatory structure, and his structure seems to be very precise, though rough. Following Maslow's example, rather than composing a list of motives he distinguished three levels of relational functioning and two directions of human motivational tendencies. One direction is that of self-actualization, achievement, growth, and security, that refers to purely individual existence; another direction is associated with the giving of oneself, contact, affiliation, participation, union and love, that is, with transcendence of individual existence. The levels he described are the psychophysiological, the social, and the spiritual (Nuttin, 1962, 244-246) or the biological, the psychosocial, and the ideational (Nuttin, 1984, 132). The first refers to the processes rooted in the physiological structures of the organism; the second refers to the processes that link us to the surrounding world in ways that make sense for us; the third refers to our relationship to the transcendent (not necessarily supernatural) reality that raise our living above adjustment. Correspondingly, on the first level we find the basic needs for vital development and biological contact; on the second one the basic needs for personality development and psychosocial contact; on the third level the basic needs for existential support and universal integration.

OUTLINES OF THE INTEGRATIVE MODEL

What seems to be the most important aspect in Nuttin's theory of needs is, first, a conceptualization of the three distinct and mutually independent levels of a human relating to the world, each of which produces a dynamic of its own; and, secondly, the idea of "the inherent need for relational functioning" as the only need we find inherent in the organism. His structural model is a helpful prototype for a renewed multilevel model of human needs presented below. This model presents an attempt to integrate the ideas of Fromm, Nuttin, Maddi, Diligenski, and Deci and Ryan in a present-day context.

1. Need refers to a basic form of connectedness of living organisms to the outside world, the motivational source of one's activity.
2. Subhuman animal species, as living organisms, are connected to the environment by vital biological ties; all the necessities of their lives (survival, metabolisms, and procreation) are deducible from these ties.
3. A human being is connected to the world at multiple levels, largely independent of one another. On the biological level, common for all species, one is connected to the world as a biological unit, one individual organism. However, humans relate to the world not only on this level, as biological units. On the second level, that of social existence common for all humans, our relations to the world are no longer direct. Rather, they are mediated by our belongingness to social units. We are connected to these social units that interact with the world as a whole; our individual well-being is thus dependent on our social belongingness. We relate to the world on this level as parts of social units, rather than as individuals. The second class of human imperatives emerges from this aspect of the human condition; needing social integration, we accept the imperatives proposed by social units as our own. Such socially transmitted non-individual imperatives have been conceptualized in terms of

values (e.g. Kluckhohn, 1951; Lee, 1959) or extrinsic motivation (Deci & Ryan, 1985).

4. Many humans, belonging to the conformist type, in S. Maddi's terms (Maddi, 1971), have no fundamental motivations besides the ones emerging from the *biological existence* and the *social existence*. One may distinguish, however, the third optional level of *personal existence*; relating to the world at this level is not obligatory for survival and adjustment. Each individual is to discover personally the possibility to relate to the world on this transcendent level (though many of them never come to such an insight). This level is a challenge and relating to the world on this level radically increases the quality of life, the fullness of the realization of the human potential, and the control over one's life process and outcomes. In fact, a person meets *the world* at large only on the personal level of existence; on the two other levels we are dealing just with the physical and social *environment* (cf. Frankl, 1982). The separate needs we may distinguish on this level include the need for personal identity, the will to meaning, the need of transcendence in Fromm's terms, and others.

5. It has been stated more than once that distinguishing separate single needs is a deliberate construction, a matter of convention and convenience. However, it would make sense to speak of *metanecessities*, inherent in each level of human existence. Metanecessity is not a motivational construct; it refers to the objective peculiarities of the basic structure of relationships with the world, a prerequisite for all the specific motivation emerging at the given level. The metanecessities of the biological level of existence have been precisely characterized by Kurt Goldstein and Joseph Nuttin: the former spoke of the actualization as the universal tendency of all the inherent potentialities to unfold (Goldstein, 1939, p. 204); the latter spoke of the need for relational functioning as the only one we find "within" a living organism (Nuttin, 1984, p. 62). *Actualizing potentialities and relating to the environment thus seem to be the two metanecessities of the level of biological existence*, necessary and sufficient for one's functioning as a biological unit. The basic *metanecessity of the level of social functioning is one's establishing harmonious or, at least, satisfactory, or adjusted relationships to the social groups and communities one belongs to*; all special forms of social motivations are implied by this metanecessity. The basic *metanecessity at the level of personal existence seems to be personal autonomy and self-determination*. Indeed, without them no existence at the personal level seems possible. Autonomy thus appears as much more than just a basic need. The role of autonomy for successful functioning at all the levels is highlighted by recent findings, suggesting that the freedom of choice is the variable mediating the impact of nearly all the economic and social indicators on the well-being of nations (Inglehart et al., 2008).

It is difficult to overestimate the contribution of the self-determination theory (Deci & Ryan, 2000): all the three basic needs postulated by SDT refer to the metanecessities described above. Indeed, competence is a very important aspect of any relating to the environment, the capacity to produce desired outcomes; relatedness is a different name for social belongingness; and autonomy is the metanecessity of the level of personal existence. A somewhat similar hierarchical motivational model has been proposed by Skinner & Edge

(2002) who linked the three basic needs postulated by SDT to special social contexts and coping processes.

CONCLUSION

The aim of this chapter was to present a general theoretical overview of the problem of fundamental human motivations. This problem is now far from the center of academic discussions and the field develops slowly; nevertheless it will never be out of date. The historical trend in the field of basic motivations goes toward the growing edge of this field, namely a shift of emphasis to the differences between human beings and subhuman species in their way of being, as well as differentiating between "obligatory" motivations and "facultative" ones; the latter develop in course of an individual life at the level of personalized relations with the world, and may not develop at all in some individuals. I distinguished three levels of human functioning, or, one may say, of being-in-the-world: the level of biological existence where we function as biological units, the level of social existence where we function as elements of social units, and the level of personal existence where we function as autonomous self-conscious agents. Each of these levels is characterized by objective metanecessities underlying all the varieties of motivational structures and mechanisms developing on this level: the actualization of potentialities and relating to the environment on the level of biological existence, integration with social systems on the level of social existence, and self-determination on the level of personal existence. This model is an attempt to summarize the recent development in the field of fundamental human motivations.

REFERENCES

Allport, G. W. (1937). *Personality: a psychological interpretation*. New York: Holt.

Deci, E. L., & Flaste, R. (1995). *Why we do what we do*. London: Penguin.

Deci, E., & Ryan, R. (1985). *Intrinsic motivation and self-determination in human behavior*. New York: Plenum.

Deci, E. L., & Ryan, R. M. (2000). The "what" and "why" of goal pursuits: Human needs and the self-determination of behavior. *Psychological Inquiry, 11*(4), 227-268.

Deci, E. L., & Vansteenkiste M. (2004). Self-Determination Theory and basic need satisfaction: understanding human development in positive psychology. In A. Delle Fave (Ed.), *Positive Psychology: Special issue of Ricerche di Psicologia, anno XXVII*, N 1, 23-40.

Diligenski, H. H. (1976). Problemy teorii chelovecheskikh potrebnostei (Problems of theory of human needs). *Voprosy Filosofii*, Nr. 9, 30-43.

Diligenski, H. H. (1996). *Sotsialno-politicheskaya psikhologiya (Social Political Psychology)*. Moscow: Novaya Shkola.

Foucault, M. (1965). Madness and civilization, ed. by R. D. Laing, D. G. Cooper. New York: Pantheon Books.

Frankl, V. E. (1969). *The will to meaning: foundations and applications of logotherapy*. New York: Plume.

Frankl, V. (1982). *Der Wille zum Sinn. 3., erw. Auflage*. Bern: Huber.

Freud, S. (1916). Introductory Lectures on Psycho-Analysis. The Standard Edition of the *Complete Psychological Works of Sigmund Freud, Volume XV (1915-1916): Introductory* Lectures on Psycho-analysis (Parts I and II), 1-240.

Fromm, E. (1956). *The sane society*. London: Routledge and Kegan Paul.

Goffman, E. (1967). Interaction ritual: essays on face-to-face behavior. New York: Pantheon Books.

Goldstein, K. (1939). *The organism*. New York: American book company.

Heckhausen, J., & Heckhausen, H. (Hrsg.) (2006). *Motivation und Handeln. 3 Aufl.* Heidelberg: Springer Medizin Verlag.

Hull, C. L. (1943). *Principles of behavior*. New York: Appleton-Century-Crofts.

Inglehart, R., Foa, R., Peterson, C., & Welzel, C. (2008). Development, freedom, and rising happiness: A global perspective (1981—2007). *Perspectives on Psychological Science*, *3*(4), 264-285.

Kenrick, D. T., Griskevicus, V., Neuberg, S. L., & Schaller, M. (2010). Renovating the pyramid of needs: Contemporary extensions built upon ancient foundations. *Perspectives on Psychological Science*, *5*(3), 292-314.

Kluckhohn, C. (1951). Values and Value Orientations in the Theory of Action. In T. Parsons (Ed.). *Toward a General Theory of Action* (pp. 388-433). Cambridge: Harvard University Press.

Längle, A. (2011). The Existential Fundamental Motivations Structuring the Motivational Process. In D. Leontiev (Ed.) *Motivation, consciousness, and self-regulation* (pp. 00-00). New York: Nova Science Publishers.

Lee, D. (1959). *Freedom and Culture*. Englewood Cliffs, NJ: Prentice-Hall.

Lehrman, D. S. (1956). On the organization of maternal behavior and the problem of instinct. In P. P. Grasse (Ed.) *L'instinct dans le comportement des animaux at de l'homme* (pp. 475-514). Paris: Masson.

Leont'ev, A. N. (1978). *Activity, Consciousness, and Personality.* Englewood Cliffs, NJ: Prentice-Hall.

Lewin, K. (1926). *Vorsatz, Wille, und Bedürfnis*. Berlin: Verlag von Julius Springer.

McDougall, W. (1908). *An Introduction to Social Psychology*. London: Methuen.

McDougall, W. (1932). *The Energies of Men*. London: Methuen.

Maddi, S. (1971). The search for meaning. In W. J. Arnold & M. M. Page (Eds.), *Nebraska symposium on motivation 1970* (pp. 137-186). Lincoln, NB: University of Nebraska Press.

Maddi, S. (1998). Creating Meaning Through Making Decisions. In P. T. P. Wong & P.S. Fry (Eds.). *The Human Quest for Meaning* (pp. 1-25). Mahwah, NJ: Lawrence Erlbaum.

Malinowski, B. (1944). *A Scientific Theory of Culture.* Chapel Hill, NC: University of North Carolina Press.

Maslow, A.H. (1943). A Theory of Human Motivation. *Psychological Review*, *50*, 370-396.

Maslow, A. H. (1955). Deficiency motivation and growth motivation. In M. R. Jones (Ed.), *Nebraska Symposium on Motivation* (Vol. 3, pp. 1-30). Lincoln, NB: University of Nebraska Press.

Maslow, A. H. (1970). *Motivation and Personality. 2nd ed.* New York: Harper & Row.

Maslow, A. H. (1976). *The Farther reaches of human nature*. Harmondsworth: Penguin.

Murray, H. A. (1938). *Explorations in personality*. New York: Cambridge University Press.

Nuttin, J. (1962). *Psychanalyse et conception spiritualiste de l'homme*. Paris: P.U.F.

Nuttin, J. (1984). *Motivation, Planning, and Action: a Relational Theory of Behavior Dynamics*. Leuven: Leuven University Press; Hillsdale, NJ: Lawrence Erlbaum Associates.

Skinner, E., & Edge, K. (2002). Self-determination, coping, and development. In E. Deci, & R. Ryan (eds.). *Handbook of Self-determination Research* (pp. 297-337). Rochester, NY: The University of Rochester Press.

Szasz, T. S. (1961). *The Myth of Mental Illness: Foundations of a Theory of Personal Conduct*. New York: Harper & Row.

Yang, K.-Sh. (2003). Beyond Maslow's Culture-Bound Linear Theory: A Preliminary Statement of the Double-Y Model of Basic Human Needs. In V. Murphy-Berman & J. J. Berman (Eds.). *Nebraska Symposium on Motivation. Vol. 49. Cross-Cultural Differences in Perspectives on the Self* (pp. 175-255)*.* Lincoln, NB: University of Nebraska Press.

In: Motivation, Consciousness and Self-Regulation   ISBN: 978-1-61324-795-2
Editor: D. A. Leontiev, pp. 27-38   © 2011 Nova Science Publishers, Inc.

Chapter 3

THE EXISTENTIAL FUNDAMENTAL MOTIVATIONS STRUCTURING THE MOTIVATIONAL PROCESS

Längle Alfried[*]
International Society for Logotherapy and Existential Analysis, Vienna

ABSTRACT

Motivation is a process of continuous exchange between the subject—individual—and the environment. From an existential perspective, we see this exchange as having a dialogical structure, connecting the given reality of both subject and object with the intentions of the individual. Motivation, being of existential relevance, has a causal link to the fundamental themes of existence. Further, the spiritual (i.e., noetic) power embedded in personhood functions as a tool for processing information in motivation. Thus, both existential structure and being a free person play the decisive role in the motivational process.

This process is characterized by the repetitive and continuous decisions individuals make. The fundamental themes of existence bring shape to our understanding of motivation, while the spiritual (noetic) power within individuals is operative in all motivation.

The paper illustrates the relation between the fundamental themes of existence and the motivational process. This process includes a coming to terms with the reality of one's existence, or "being in the world," with the reality of one's life and finally with an awareness of one's identity. Empirical phenomenological research over the past 30 years has confirmed that accepting these realities enables an individual to participate and be open to relationships and wider contexts from which personal meanings are discovered.

These four fundamental themes of existence form a matrix for the psychopathological understanding of psychic disorders and provide a context for clinical interventions. Further, they represent the structural model of Existential Analytic Psychotherapy.

[*] Alfried LÄNGLE, M.D., Ph.D. (psychology), *1951, is Founder (1983) and actual President of the International Society for Logotherapy and Existential Analysis (Vienna), scholar and former collaborator of Viktor E. Frankl. He is Professor of Psychotherapy at the State University Higher School of Economics (Moscow, Russia), the Sigmund Freud University, Vienna, and the University of Klagenfurt, Faculty of Psychology. For his over 200 publications, he got two honorary doctorates and three honorary professor degrees.

Keywords: Existential motivation, existential analysis, existential psychology, Person

INTRODUCTION: WHAT MAKES FOR MOTIVATION?

Talking about motivation is ubiquitous in social sciences such as psychology, psychotherapy, pedagogiy, sociology, and politics as well as in marketing and economics. It seems obvious that we need good motivation for the achievement of our life tasks, for creativity, growth, social functioning and personal fulfillment.

But a substantial question arises from the very beginning about the nature of motivation: do we really need to *become motivated from outside,* or are we already and *originally motivated* due to our nature? Is the essence of what we call "motivational process" an act of *receiving* something? Or does the motivational process merely consist in shaping the process of being primordially, constantly and generally moved? In this latter case, motivating someone would simply mean to provide a theme for that pre-established energy. This would mean that we do not help people to be motivated, but help them to find *what for* they can best implement the existent motivational force in their lives. The motivational process would provide a theme, a direction for the intentional power, a reason for the decision, and show the value of the particular action for one's life. In other words, motivating someone means helping him/her to find possibilities, values, authenticity and meaning for what one is doing.

Alfred Adler and George Kelly (cf. Brunner et al. 1985, p. 290) took the position that humans are originally motivated by their nature and need not be moved from outside. So did Viktor Frankl, an adherent of Adler's circle. This position was also taken by the "potentialists" of the humanistic psychology movement, like Carl Rogers ([1961] 1988, 49): if the circumstances are favorable for activity, humans develop all their activities and potentials of their own.

Existential Analysis has an integrative view of motivation. Motivation arises from a correspondence between an external stimulus and subjective, inner potential. Motivation also arises from the continuous internal needs of the individual. This includes a spiritual, and, therefore, essentially human, striving to become oneself by seeking engagement and communication with others. This concept of motivation is rooted in the fact that existence can be characterized as "*being* in the world." This means being—and becoming—an integral part of the world, and living "*in between*" both internal and external worlds (in the sense of existing being at once both subject and object). Conceptualizing existence as an inseparable connection with *otherness* and with a "world," in a similar way as Heidegger (1979), in the concept of *Dasein*, forms the basis for motivation.

FRANKL'S "WILL TO MEANING"

For Frankl, humans are indeed motivated by *biological* and *social* drives, but primarily and most profoundly, they are motivated by their personal "will to meaning." This means that any person is fundamentally moved by a *spiritual* striving for a deeper *understanding* of what one experiences or does. This motivational force is regarded to be a direct result of the essence of human "nature." It is seen in the spiritual (i.e., noetic or personal) dimension of (wo)man, and the will to meaning is rooted in this dimension.

In Frankl's theory (1973, p. XVIII ff.; 1959, p. 672), this spiritual dimension is marked by the three basic human potentials[1], which consist of "psychological" spirituality, freedom and responsibility. The quest for meaning, and with it the primary motivational process, can, therefore, be understood as a concomitant necessity inherent in this dimension. It basically consists in the challenge created by our freedom[2].

Freedom paradoxically brings along a compulsion of choice—being free means that we are forced to choose. A prerequisite of any real choice is the notion of the content and the understanding of the context in which the decision has to be made. The intentional goal of the will arises from this horizon, and if adopted by the subject, it turns out to be a value, probably the highest value one can see in the given situation. These are the elements of *existential meaning*: the greatest (or highest or deepest) value in the given situation, which can be seen and understood by the individual to be within the reach of his abilities. Frankl's primary motivation thus turns out to be an immediate consequence of the realization of the person's will, the human expression of freedom.

Frankl developed this logotherapeutic concept of motivational theory in an era that was dominated by determinism, reductionism, subjectivism and monadology, all of which he fervently combated. His education took place in that period, and hence his thinking was exposed to some of these ideas. Frankl's personal and scientific accomplishment was certainly the overcoming of these tendencies in his overall concept of logotherapy. He especially achieved this with his concepts of meaning and of self-transcendence, both cornerstones of his anthropology. But it seems that in the motivational angle of his theory, he may have adopted some individualistic thinking by tracing back the concept of existential motivation to the concept of will. He even reinforced the pertaining concept by naming it "will" to meaning. Frankl himself explained the decision of calling his motivational concept "will" to meaning by his intention to formulate a counterweight to Nietzsche's "will to power." At the same time, he wanted to define the "true" content by replacing the instrumental value of "power" by the more spiritual value of "meaning."— Below this critical remark will be brought to its conclusion by describing a concept, which is formulated on an existential ground.

THE MODERN QUEST FOR MEANING

In our times, it is not the theme of freedom that dominates the discussion of social problems, psychopathologies, and the scientific discourse. No longer pertinent is the neo-Darwinian discussion that arose as a consequence of the genetic discoveries in the 1960ies and 1970ies and that led to the polarity of "freedom and necessity" and to the outburst of free will against repression in 1968.

---

[1] Frankl calls them also "existentials"—referring to Heidegger's term "Existentialien."

[2] "Psychological spirituality" explains what is meant. It captures the meaning of the situation and activates the person's potential of being free. Responsibility, on the other hand, is also related to freedom—it imposes itself only there where humans are free. Seen from these practical aspects, freedom reveals itself as the decisive factor of the spiritual dimension. The importance of freedom explains why it is more often treated in philosophical and psychological theories than meaning and responsibility.

Nowadays, different problems are predominant: marital and family life have widely evolved into broadly accepted forms of single life; the communities, social experiments and sexual promiscuity of the 1970s have turned to fantasy games in virtual worlds, TV-channel-hopping or internet surfing. For sexuality, the open acceptance of homosexuality is broadly achieved. The social cohesion in politics and economy has been loosened in favor of a high degree of individualism, of liberal economic concepts with competition and rivalry, of a new feeling of freedom by utilizing and challenging the resources of the individual to the utmost degree. This new feeling of freedom brings along more isolation not only for the elderly people, but also for entire cultures.

The *schizophrenic aspect of our times* is that we have the best structures of communication mankind has ever had, that we travel more internationally than any generation before us, but that finally we feel lonelier and that there is probably less real exchange among the cultures than before. The increase in contact between people of different cultures has led to a consumption of the pleasant aspects of cultures but not to a true dialogue. This lack of profound dialogue, and consequently understanding, provokes anxiety of alienation and of loss of identity. This phenomenon can be observed in tourism and immigration. The increase of speed has brought along a decrease of contact; the increase of information has led to a decrease of communication; and the increase of traffic has destroyed much of personal encounter. September 11 has to be seen on this background. It shows the huge and frightening failure in communication and encounter between different cultures.

EXISTENTIAL PARADIGM

As children of our time, faced with its specific problems, we have to adapt our theories to the needs and sufferings of today. We have, therefore, further elaborated the motivational concept in Existential Analysis into an approach that is by no means less humanistic or less personal, though it follows a different paradigm. As a complement to the individualistic concept of freedom and personal will, which laid ground to the development of this post-modern era, we now need as a counterweight to the shadow of freedom an *interpersonal paradigm.*

This is the line we have adopted in modern Existential Analysis. We have enlarged our motivational concept by basing it on the probably most original activity of personhood: on our being essentially dialogical, prone to and directed towards exchange with others. Being oneself, finding oneself, needs the field of tension of the "inter-," the "between," the "aida" as the Japanese say (Kimura 1982; 1995, 103ff.). This spiritual need of communication and dialogue is also underlined by the numerous personality disorders related to the loss of self!—There is no "me" without a "you," as Buber and also Frankl were saying. Being oneself as a person means being in communication, being in a continuous inner and outer exchange of contents, means fine-tuning the outer with the inner reality and, vice versa, oneself with the objective meaning of the situation. Motivation is understood as engaging in that continuous flow that is established by nature between the person and his/her world. They are inseparably connected and interrelated, in uninterrupted reciprocal action. Or as Heidegger has defined it: being a person, "Dasein," means "being-in-the-world," means dealing with "otherness."

EXISTENTIAL CONCEPT OF MOTIVATION

From an existential point of view, *dialogue* (or "communication" as Jaspers says) is an essential constituent in human psychology and in the understanding of the essence of human existence. If we take the capacity for dialogue as a *characteristic* of being a person (i.e., a being with mind and spirit and a potential for decision-making), then humans are always waiting for their completion by a "partner" in the broadest sense. As dialogical beings, humans expect and look for something or someone "speaking" to them, calling them, needing them, talking to them, looking for them, challenging them. One gets the necessary pro*vocation* through everything one is confronted with, one has in front of oneself, one is dealing with. At exactly that moment, the object before us starts "speaking" to us. Being provoked means being called. This provocation is the *starting point of any motivation.*

In other words: seen from an existential point of view, *motivation means involvement of the person*, initiating the personal processes by provocation in some kind of vis-à-vis. Of course the best vis-à-vis is a partner interacting with us. This processual capacity of the person is described in the theory of "Personal Existential Analysis (PEA)" (Längle 1994c) and made applicable by its methodological formulation. This method is an application of this dialogical concept of the human being with the goal of engaging personal potentials in a process of dealing with information, thus giving rise to encounter.

The PEA-model is fundamental for any kind of involvement of the person. As such it helps to distinguish *three steps* within the motivational process:

1. *Recognizing* something in its worth or value, insofar as it speaks to us. This is often a challenge demanding action on our part. To see what a situation provokes in us means to recognize the situational meaning involved.
2. *Harmonizing.* Bringing the perceived value, challenge or meaning into accordance with one's inner reality, i.e., examining the consistency with the rest of our values, with attitudes, abilities and capabilities and with our conscience.
3. The final step in the development of motivation is the *inner consent* to one's own *active* involvement. This consent and the act of harmonizing the new value with inner (already existing personal) reality leads to the presence of the inner person in one's actions. It brings up the integration of the new value and the person himself into a *wider context* (meaning).

Without this involvement of the person in the motivational process, human beings would not be dealing with a question of motivation. Instead, there would be a sort of reflex or reaction, but no "action." Any act, any deed, is defined as a *decided* act and is therefore *voluntary* and free—which is to say "personal."

If we take motivation as a *free* decision to act, then we must also take into consideration the concept of *will*. Frankl (1970, pp. 37-44; 1987, pp. 101-104) saw meaning as the moving part in free will. An existential view of will takes it as the anthropological axis of existence. A *processual description* of will, however, relies on the fundamentals of existence and therefore shows more than just meaning as being basic for constituting will. Free and realistic will is based on three more elements:

1.   on the real ability and *capacity* of the subject;
2.   on the *emotional* perception of the situational *value*;
3.   on the inner *permission* for that act, emerging from an agreement with one's concepts of life and morality.

Before we go into this, let us conclude this part of the exposition dealing with the structure of motivation by adding a reflection on the initial problem of the two basic concepts of motivation. Do people need to be motivated from *outside*, or can the motivation only be shaped, canalized, because people are *intrinsically* motivated? Our theory is that this existential concept results in forming a *bridge between two opposite positions*:

a)   It is the *interrelation* with the vis-à-vis from which motivation emerges. Being touched and provoked, as well as understanding the situation, is like *being called* on by something or someone. This appeal activates the constitutional "being-in-the-world" because of a recognition or understanding of what this particular situation is about. This equals the recognition of the situational or existential meaning. Furthermore, this means that we *receive an impulse* from the recognition of the essential message from our vis-à-vis (outer world, but also body, feeling, thoughts).
b)   By our *understanding* of the context and by our inner agreement, the motivation gets its shape and receives its content.

Seen in that light, the notion of "being-in-the-world" provides the grounds on which the personal forces are activated. This happens by a perceptive encounter with some form of otherness or with oneself.

Let us now have a closer look at the four fundamental motivations for a fulfilled existence.

THE FOUR FUNDAMENTAL CONDITIONS FOR A FULFILLING EXISTENCE

In the first part, we have elaborated the crucial point for motivation, which lies in attaining the *dialogical potential* of the subject. Its "pro*vocation*" can be taken as the starting point for any motivation, because the need and the ability for dialogue are seen as the dynamic essence of the person (with subsequent potentials like freedom and will). This dialogue (with the world and with oneself) is a prerequisite for building up a motivation. We have pointed out that for this reason, there is *no motivation without cognition, accordance, bringing into harmony, inner consent and meaning*. For the aspect of freedom in motivation—seeing it as moving a person towards a *free* act within the world—the structure of will has to be taken into account. Will is fundamentally related to the structure of existence, which in turn is shaping the motivation substantially. This—the provocation into dialogue and the relation to the fundamental structure of existence—is the *central hypothesis* of this paper.

If we look more closely, we see that this concept of motivation implies a dialogical *confrontation* with the given facts of our existence. All preconditions of existence can be summarized in four fundamental structures, the "cornerstones of existence":

- the *world* in its factuality and potentiality
- *life* with its network of relationships and its feelings
- *being oneself* as a unique, autonomous *person*
- the *wider context* where to place oneself = *development* through one's activities, opening one's *future*

Existence in our understanding needs a continuous *confrontation* and a dialogical *exchange* with each of these four dimensions. It is on this basis that the subject forms his specific notions about reality. These four realities challenge the person to give his response, they ask for his inner consent, activate his inner freedom. But they are not only challenging dimensions—they are also structures that, at the same time, allow to entrust oneself to each of these given realities. Their facticity is the fundament of what we call existence. As such, they fundamentally move our existence and can be called "fundamental existential motivations" (Längle 1992a,b; 1994a; 1997a,b; 1998c).

1. The World—Dealing with Conditions and Possibilities

The first condition arises from the simple fact that I am here at all, that I am in the world. But where to go from here? Can I cope with my being there? Do I understand it? I am there, and as an old German saying from the 15th century goes in free translation: "I don't know where I am from, I don't know where to go—I wonder why I am so glad." I am there, there is me—how is that even possible? Questioning this seemingly self-evident fact can go to great depth, once I go into it. And if I really think about it, I realize that I cannot truly comprehend this. My existence appears like an island in an ocean of ignorance and of connections that surpass me. The most adequate and traditional attitude towards the incomprehensible is one of astonishment. Basically, I can only be astonished that I am there at all.

But I am there, which puts *the fundamental question of existence* before me: *I am—can I be?* For making this question practical, I may apply it to my own situation. Then I may ask myself: Can I claim my place in this world under the conditions and with the possibilities I have? This demands three things: *protection, space and support.*—Do I enjoy *protection*, acceptance, do I feel at home somewhere?—Do I have enough *space* for being there?—Where do I find *support* in my life?—If this is not the case, the result will be restlessness, insecurity and fear (cf. Längle 1996). But if I *do* have these three things, I will be able to feel trust in the world and confidence in myself, maybe even faith in God. The sum of these experiences of trust is the fundamental trust, the trust in whatever I feel as being the last support in my life.

But, in order to be there, it is not enough to find protection, space and support—I also have to *seize* these conditions, to make a *decision* in their favor, to *accept* them. My *active* part in this fundamental condition of being there is to accept the positive sides and to endure the negative sides. To *accept* means to be ready to occupy the space, to rely on the support and to trust the protection; in short "to be there" and not to flee. To *endure* means the force to let be whatever is difficult, menacing or unalterable and to "support" what cannot be changed. Life imposes certain conditions on me, and the world has its laws, to which I must bend myself. This idea is expressed in the word "subject" in the sense of "not independent." On the other hand, these conditions are reliable, solid and steady. To let them be, to accept them as given is only possible, if I can be at the same time. Therefore, to accept means to let each other be, because there is still *enough space* for me, and the circumstances do not menace me anymore. Man procures himself the space he needs with his ability to tolerate and to accept conditions.—If this is not the case, psychodynamics takes over the guidance in the form of coping *reactions,* which are to secure life (Längle 1998a).

2. Life—Dealing with Relationships and Emotions

Once someone has his/her space in the world, he/she can fill it with life. Simply being there is not enough. We want our existence to be *good*, since it is more than a mere fact. It has a "pathic dimension," which means that it does not simply happen, but that we experience and suffer or enjoy it. Being alive means to cry and to laugh, to experience joy and suffering, to go through pleasant and unpleasant things, to be lucky or unlucky and to experience worth and worthlessness. As much as we can be happy, so, too, can we suffer. The amplitude of emotionality is equal in both directions, whether this suits us or not.

Therefore, I am confronted with the *fundamental question of life*: I am alive—do I *like* this fact? Is it good to be there? It is not only strain and suffering that can take away the joy of life. It may also be the shallowness of daily life and the negligence in one's lifestyle that make life stale. In order to seize my life, to love it, I need three things: *relationship, time and closeness.*—In verifying the presence of life in one's own situation we may ask ourselves questions like this: Do I have *relationships*, in which I feel closeness, for which I spend time and in which I experience community?—What do I take *time* for? Do I take time for valuable things, worthy to spend my time for? To take time for something means to give away a part of one's life while spending it with someone or something.—Can I feel close and maintain *closeness* to things, plants, animals and people? Can I admit the closeness of someone else?— If relationships, closeness and time are lacking, *longing* will arise, then *coldness* and finally depression. But if these three conditions are fulfilled, I experience myself as being in *harmony with the world and with myself,* and I can sense the depth of life. These experiences form the fundamental value, the most profound *feeling for the value* of life. In each experience of a value this fundamental value is touched upon; it colors the emotions and affects and represents our yardstick for anything we might feel to be of worth.—This is what our theory of emotion as well as the theory of values relates to.

Still, it is not enough to have relationships, time and closeness. My own consent, my active participation is asked for. I *seize* life, engage in it, when I *turn to* other people, to things, animals, intellectual work or to myself, when I go towards it, get close, get into touch or pull it towards me. If I turn to a loss, *grief* arises. This "to turn to" will make life vibrate within me. If life is to make me move freely, my consent to being touched (to feeling) is necessary.

3. Being a Person—Dealing with Uniqueness and Conscience

As pleasant as this emotional swinging may be, it is still not sufficient for a fulfilling existence. In spite of my being related to life and to people, I am aware of my being separate, different. There is a singularity that makes me an *"I"* and distinguishes me from everybody else. I realize that I am on my own, that I have to master my existence myself and that, basically, I am alone and maybe even solitary. But, besides, there is *so much more* that is equally singular. The *diversity, beauty and uniqueness* in all of this make me feel respect.

In the midst of this world, I discover myself unmistakably; I am *with* myself and I am given *to* myself. This puts before me the *fundamental question of being a person*: I am myself—*may* I be like this? Do I feel free to be *like that*? Do I have the *right* to be what I am and to behave as I do?—This is the plane of identity, of knowing oneself and of ethics. In order to succeed here, it is necessary to have experienced three things: *attention, justice and appreciation*.—Again, one can verify this third cornerstone of existence in one's own existence by asking: by whom am I *seen*? Who considers my uniqueness and respects my *boundaries*?—Do people do me *justice*?—For what am I *appreciated*—for what can I appreciate myself?—If these experiences are missing, *solitude* will be the result, *hysteria* as well as a need to hide behind the *shame*. If, on the contrary, these experiences have been made, I will find myself; find my authenticity, my relief and my self-respect. The sum of these experiences builds *one's own worth*, the profoundest worth of what identifies my own self at its core: the self-esteem.

In order to be able to be oneself, it is not enough to simply experience attention, justice and appreciation. I also have to say "yes to myself." This requires my *active* participation: to *look* at other people, to encounter them and, at the same time, to demarcate myself and to stand by my own, but to refuse whatever does not correspond to me. *Encounter* and *regret* are the two means by which we can live our authenticity without ending up in solitude. Encounter represents the necessary bridge to the other, makes me find his essence as well as my own "I" in the "you." Thus, I create for myself the appreciation requisite for feeling entitled to be what I am.

4. Meaning—Dealing with Becoming, Future and Commitment

If I can be there, love life and find myself therein, the conditions are fulfilled for the fourth fundamental condition of existence: the recognition of what my life is all about. It does not suffice to simply be there and to have found oneself. In a sense, we have to transcend ourselves, if we want to find fulfillment and to be fruitful. Otherwise, we would live as if in a house where nobody ever visits.

Thus, the transience of life puts before us *the question of meaning of our existence*: I am there—*for what* is it good? For this, three things are necessary: *a field of activity, a structural context and a value to be realized in the future*.—For a practical application, we can ask ourselves questions of the following type: is there a *place* where I feel *needed*, where I can be productive?—Do I see and experience myself in a *larger context* that provides structure and orientation to my life? Where I want to be integrated?—Is there anything that *should still be realized* in my life?

If this is not the case, the result will be a feeling of *emptiness, frustration, even despair* and frequently *addiction*. If, on the contrary, these conditions are met, I will be capable of *dedication* and *action* and, finally, of my own form of *religious belief*. The sum of these experiences adds up to the meaning of life and leads to a sense of fulfillment.

But it does not suffice to have a field of activity, to have one's place within a context and to know of values to be realized in the future. Instead, the *phenomenological attitude* is needed, which we spoke about at the beginning. This attitude of openness represents the *existential access* to meaning in life: i.e., dealing with the questions put before me in each situation (Frankl 1973, XV, 62). "What does this hour want from me, how shall I respond?" The meaningful thing is not only what *I* can expect from life, but, in accordance with the dialogical structure of existence, it is equally important what *life wants from me* and what the moment expects *from me* and what *I* could and should do *now* for others as well as for myself. My *active* part in this attitude of openness is to bring myself into *agreement* with the situation, to examine whether what I am doing is really a good thing: for others, for myself, for the future, for my environment. If I act accordingly, my existence will be fulfilling.

Viktor Frankl (1987, p. 315) once defined meaning as "a possibility against the background of reality." In another context, Frankl (1985, p. 57) referred to the potentialities underlying the meaning: "The potentialities of life are not indifferent possibilities; they must be seen in the light of meaning and values. At any given time, only one of the possible choices of the individual fulfills the necessity of his life task."

This notion of valuable possibilities endorsed with the theory of the fundamental existential motivations, defines meaning even more concretely as "the *most valuable, realistic* possibility of the given situation, for which I feel I should decide myself." *Existential meaning* is therefore what is possible *here and now*, on the basis of facts and reality, what is possible *for me,* may it be what I need now, or what is the most pressing, valuable or interesting alternative now. To define and redefine this continually is an extremely complex task for which we possess an inner organ of perception capable of reducing this complexity to livable proportions: our sensitivity as well as our moral conscience.

Besides this existential meaning, there is an *ontological meaning*. This is the overall meaning in which I find myself and which does not depend on me. It is the philosophical and religious meaning, the meaning the creator of the world must have had in mind. I can perceive it in divination and in faith (cf. Längle 1994b) for the differentiation between the two forms of meaning.

There is a *story* that Frankl used to tell and that illustrates in a simple way the importance of the ontological meaning for understanding life (cf. Längle 2002, p. 60ff).

It was at the time when the cathedral at Chartres was being built. A traveler came along the way and saw a man sitting at the roadside, cutting a stone. The traveler asked him, astonished, what he was doing there. "Don't you see? I am cutting stones!" Nonplussed, the traveler continued on his way. Around the next bend, he saw another man, also cutting stones. Again, he stopped and asked the same question. "I am cutting corner-stones," was the reply. Shaking his head, our man traveled on. After a while, he met a third man who was sitting in the dust and cutting stones, just as the others had been. Resolutely he walked up to him and asked: "Are you also cutting corner-stones?"—The man looked up at him, wiped the sweat from his brow and said: "I am working at a cathedral."

CONCLUSION

Since motivation is a "movement of the will" of a person, it is basic to consider the structure of the will. Will as expression of the human freedom is seen in existential analysis as the core of being a person. Personhood itself is considered as dialogical in its essence— what brings up a dialogical concept of freedom or will and motivation. The lines of such dialogues can be found in motivation and build a fundamental structure of any motivation: the connection with the world, with one's life, with one's being a person, with meaning. These dimensions of existence hence provide a conceptual basis for motivation.

REFERENCES

Brunner R., Kausen R., Titze M. (Eds.) (1985) *Wörterbuch der Individualpsychologie.* München: Reinhardt.

Frankl V. E. (1959) Grundriß der Existenzanalyse und Logotherapie. In: Frankl V., v. Gebsattel V., Schultz J. H- (Eds-) *Handbuch der Neurosenlehre und Psychotherapie.* Vol III, pp. 663-736. Munich: Urban & Schwarzenberg.

Frankl V. E. (1970) *The Will to Meaning. Foundations and Applications of Logotherapy.* New York: New American Library.

Frankl V. E. (1973) *The Doctor and the Soul. From Psychotherapy to Logotherapy.* New York: Random House.

Frankl V. E. (1985) *Psychotherapy and Existentialism. Selected papers on Logotherapy.* New York: Washington Square Press.

Frankl V. E. (1987) *Ärztliche Seelsorge. Grundlagen der Logotherapie und Existenzanalyse.* Frankfurt: Fischer.

Heidegger M. (1979) *Sein und Zeit.* Tübingen: Niemeyer.

Kimura B. (1982) The phenomenology of the between: on the problem of the basic disturbance in schizophrenia. In: de Koning et al. (Eds.) *Phenomenology and Psychiatry.* pp. 173-185 London: Academic Press.

Kimura B. (1995) *Zwischen Mensch und Mensch. Strukturen japanischer Subjektiv*ität. Darmstadt: Wissenschaftliche Buchgemeinschaft.

Längle A. (1992a) Was bewegt den Menschen? Die existentielle Motivation der Person. Vortrag bei Jahrestagung der GLE in Zug/Schweiz. Published (1999) Die existentielle Motivation der Person. In: *Existenzanalyse* 16, 3, 18-29.

Längle A. (1992b) Ist Kultur machbar? Die Bedürfnisse des heutigen Menschen und die Erwachsenenbildung. In: *Kongreßband „Kulturträger im Dorf."* pp. 65-73. Bozen: Auton. Provinz, Assessorat für Unterricht und Kultur.

Längle A. (1994a) Lebenskultur-Kulturerleben. Die Kunst, Bewegendem zu begegnen. *Bulletin der GLE* 11, 1, 3-8.

Längle A. (1994b) Sinn-Glaube oder Sinn-Gespür? Zur Differenzierung von ontologischem und existentiellem Sinn in der Logotherapie. In: *Bulletin der GLE* 11, 2, 15-20.

Längle A. (1994c) Personal Existential Analysis. In: *Psychotherapy East and West. Integration of Psychotherapies.* pp. 348-364. Seoul: Korean Acadamy of Psychotherapists 1995.

Längle A. (1996) Der Mensch auf der Suche nach Halt. Existenzanalyse der Angst. In: *Existenzanalyse* 13, 2, 4-12.

Längle A. (1997a) Das Ja zum Leben finden. Existenzanalyse und Logotherapie in der Suchtkrankenhilfe. In: Längle A., Probst Ch. (Hrsg.) *Süchtig sein. Entstehung, Formen und Behandlung von Abhängigkeiten.* pp. 13-33 Wien: Facultas.

Längle A. (1997b) Modell einer existenzanalytischen Gruppentherapie für die Suchtbehandlung. In: Längle A., Probst Ch. (Hrsg.) *Süchtig sein. Entstehung, Formen und Behandlung von Abhängigkeiten.* pp. 149-169 Wien: Facultas.

Längle A. (1998a) Verständnis und Therapie der Psychodynamik in der Existenzanalyse. In: *Existenzanalyse* 15, 1, 16-27.

Längle A. (2002) *Sinnvoll leben. Logotherapie als Lebenshilfe.* Freiburg: Herder; 5. Aufl.

Rogers C. R. ([1961] 1988) On Becoming a Person. A Therapist's View of Psychotherapy. Houghton Mifflin Co. – German: *Entwicklung der Persönlichkeit.* Stuttgart: Klett-Cotta.

PART 2. ENRICHING EXPLANATORY MODELS OF MOTIVATION

In: Motivation, Consciousness and Self-Regulation   ISBN: 978-1-61324-795-2
Editor: D. A. Leontiev, pp. 41-63   © 2012 Nova Science Publishers, Inc.

Chapter 4

MOTIVATION, FUTURE TIME PERSPECTIVE, AND VOCATIONAL PLANNING BEHAVIOR

M. P. Paixao and M. V. Abreu
University of Coimbra, Portugal
W. Lens
University of Leuven, Belgium

ABSTRACT

This chapter discusses the concept of future time perspective (FTP) as a cognitive-motivational concept. FTP results from formulating motivational goals in the rather near or more distant future. People do not only differ from each other for the content of their motivational goals or aspirations, but also for the extension or length of the time perspective that is involved in those goals. Individual differences in the length of FTP also have motivational consequences because they affect the anticipated incentive value of future goals and the perceived instrumentality of present actions for achieving those goals. In the second part of this chapter, we summarize empirical studies validating this motivational conceptualization of FTP. The third part illustrates the usefulness of taking into account individual differences in FTP in the realm of vocational and career planning behavior. Finally, we discuss empirical studies assessing the behavioral impact of the subjective organization of the personal FTP on the construction and evaluation of vocational projects in three stages of the career development and in critical decision moments within the Portuguese educational system. Extension and content of FTP were taken into consideration.

Keywords: Future time perspective, motivation, career planning, decision-making

INTRODUCTION

In this chapter, we want to show how future time perspective as an individual personality characteristic has a double motivational significance. In the first part, we discuss Nuttin's motivational conceptualization of FTP (Nuttin, 1964, 1984; Nuttin & Lens, 1985). For him, FTP results from motivational goal-setting processes. In the second part of this chapter, we will discuss our more recent theoretical and empirical research that grew out of Nuttin's work and that shows that individual differences in FTP also have motivational consequences.

THE MOTIVATIONAL MEANING OF FUTURE TIME PERSPECTIVE

It is evident from Nuttin's Relational Theory of Human Behavior (Nuttin, 1984; Abreu, 2001; Abreu & Paixão, 2011) that for Nuttin, motivational processes in humans and lower animals are very different. Higher cognitive functioning is the main reason for this difference. We humans are able to develop complex thinking. Covert cognitive functioning is much more developed and functionally important in human than in animal behavior. Due to long-term episodic memory, we can bring parts of our very distant, or rather near past alive in the present and benefit from it (or not). Our present life space (Lewin, 1943) is not limited to the *here and now*, it extends also into the past. Higher human cognitions also make it possible to anticipate the future. We can imagine what will come, what we would like to happen or not, tomorrow, next week, month, and even years from now. The anticipated future becomes also a part of the psychological present. We live of course in the present but the (remembered) past and the (anticipated) future are integrated in the individual psychological present or life space.

There are, however, important individual differences in the temporal life space of human beings (De Volder, 1979). Some people are mostly past-oriented. Their past is the most important part of their temporal world. They live in the past that was very traumatic or very rewarding for them. Others are present-oriented and completely absorbed by the present. They do not take their past nor their future into consideration when they act. A third category includes predominantly future-oriented people. The anticipated future is the largest part of their temporal life space. Most of their actions are future oriented, what they are doing in the present is in the service of their future. For Nuttin (1980), it is psychologically adaptive to live in the present, but a present that integrates the past, present, and future, that is experienced as evolving from the past and as being directed towards the future, than to live in the past, or the future, or the present without any reference to the past and future.

"Time perspective" refers to the integration of the past, present, and future in the psychological life space of an individual. Future Time Perspective (FTP) is then the degree to which and the way in which the anticipated chronological future is part of the present life space (Lewin, 1943; Nuttin, 1980). As we will explain later, there are large individual differences in the extension or length of FTP. The future dimension of the psychological present can be short or very long. It may even go beyond an individual lifetime.

NUTTIN'S COGNITIVE-MOTIVATIONAL THEORY OF FUTURE TIME PERSPECTIVE

Nuttin (1964, 1980; Nuttin & Lens, 1985) conceptualizes future time perspective as an acquired personality characteristic that results from motivational goal setting. People cognitively elaborate or translate their more general and vague needs, motives, and cravings into more specific motivational goals, means-end structures (sub-goals and end-goals), behavioral plans, and projects. Students, for example, specify their need for achievement and/or their need for self-realization by planning to succeed in their exams, to go to college, to become a teacher, a farmer, etc. The need for achievement becomes the need for success in a particular achievement task (e.g., being selected for the Olympics; winning a gold medal; scoring more winning games than last season). It is only after such specifications that needs and motives will affect overt behavior. Nuttin (1984) stresses the importance of this motivational process for need gratification and psychological well-being. Needs that are not cognitively elaborated into a more or less specific goal or plan are doomed to be frustrated. That explains, for example, why adolescence is such a frustrating period for many youngsters. They want to do something important with their life (e.g., need for self-realization), but many of them do not know yet what specifically they want to do or become. In numerous experimental and correlation studies, validating their Goal Setting Theory, Locke and Latham (1990, 2002) and their collaborators showed that goals must be specific and difficult (but not too difficult) in order to motivate action.

Such motivational goals and behavioral plans can be analyzed for their content or the motivational domain to which they belong (e.g., hunger, thirst, sex, affiliation, curiosity, achievement, power) and by their spatio-temporal localization (where and when will they be achieved). By definition, motivational goals are situated in the future. But the temporal distance to sub-goals and final goals may vary from very short (e.g., to go for a swim this afternoon) to very long (e.g., the student who prepares an entrance examination for college because (s)he intends to become a successful surgeon). They can even extend beyond the individual's lifetime (e.g., saving money for one's funeral). Setting motivational goals in the rather distant future and developing long range behavioral projects to achieve those goals creates a long or extended future time perspective. FTP can be defined as the present anticipation of future goals. People with a rather short FTP set most of their goals in the near future. People with a much longer or deeper FTP have set for themselves relatively more goals that can only be achieved in the distant future. In comparison with people with a short FTP, people with a long FTP have relatively more long-term than short-term goals. Thus "future time perspective evolves from motivational goal setting. It is formed by the more or less distant goal objects that are processed by an individual," (Nuttin & Lens, 1985, p. 22). However, a long FTP is for Nuttin also a prerequisite to be able to elaborate long-term motivational projects. These two assumptions are not contradictory if one accepts – as Nuttin did – reciprocal influences within developmental processes. He assumed reciprocal influences between the development of a long FTP and long term motivational planning. The anticipation of a rather long chronological future is indeed necessary, but not sufficient, to develop a long motivational future time perspective by formulating goals in the distant future. One must also psychologically be able to bridge the temporal distance between the present and the future moment where the goal is expected or hoped to be reached or achieved.

Nuttin's conceptualization of FTP is strongly related to Mischel's (1981) concept of delay of gratification. In one of Mischel's research paradigms, children had to make a number of choices between an immediate smaller reward and a delayed but larger reward (e.g., one pencil now or two pencils tomorrow). Some children have a more or less systematic preference for the delayed larger reward, while other children have a clear preference for the immediate but smaller reward. A number of experimental and correlational studies tried to identify the variables that are correlated with the preference of the children. In a second series of studies, children had to choose between two rewards (e.g., an apple or an orange). Then they were told to sit down and wait for the experimenter to return spontaneously in order to receive the preferred reward. But the children were also told that they could stop waiting at any moment and call back the experimenter by ringing a bell. The children also knew that in the second case they would not receive the preferred reward but the other non-preferred one. Mischel and his collaborators studied individual and situational determinants of how long children could wait.

As explained before, people with a long FTP have set, and are striving towards, relatively more goals in the distant future than in the near future. Since they have fewer goals in the near future, they will experience less immediate goal satisfaction. They postpone the satisfaction that results from goal attainment.

Nuttin's conceptualization of FTP as resulting from goal setting and motivational planning has a long history in psychology, especially in Europe (Lens, 1986). Lewin (1931) discussed the effect of the past and especially the future on present behavior and explained how the past and the future are progressively integrated by the child in its life space:

> The child no longer strives solely for present things, not only has wishes that must be realized at once, but his purposes grasp toward a tomorrow. The goals which determine the child's behavior are thrown continually further into the future. A decisive extension of the psychological present life-space of the child is based upon this temporal displacement of goals (Lewin, 1931; English translation, 1935, p. 173).

Lewin (1942) defined future time perspective as the present anticipation of future goals:

> The setting of goals is closely related to time perspective. The goal of the individual includes his expectations for the future ... (Lewin, 1948, p. 113).

Also, Lersch (1938; 10th edition in 1966) stressed the fact that, at each moment in time, the past and the future are part of an individual's psychological situation and that the orientation toward the future is due to motivational aspirations.

Bergius (1957) distinguished a conative and a cognitive component in future orientation. The conative component represents a motivational, dynamic orientation towards future goals. The cognitive component has to do with the subjective expectation that the anticipated goals will be realized.

Fraisse (1957, 1963) understood future time perspective in the same sense as Lewin:

> ... the future only unfolds in so far as we imagine a future which seems to be realizable ... There is no future without at the same time a desire for something else and awareness of the possibility of realizing it ... (Fraisse, 1963, p. 172 & 174).

Fraisse (1963, p. 173) quoted Guyau (1902, p.33) to stress that the psychological future originates in motivational strivings:

We must desire, we must want, we must stretch out our hands and walk to create the future. The future is not what is coming to us but what we are going to.

Future time perspective became the object of predominantly correlational studies relating individual differences in length (depth, extension) of FTP to other personality characteristics or situational circumstances such as age, gender, intelligence, socio-economic status, need for achievement, student motivation, psychopathology, delinquency, imprisonment, hospitalization, etc. (Nuttin, Lens, Van Calster & De Volder, 1979).

MOTIVATIONAL EFFECTS OF INDIVIDUAL DIFFERENCES IN FTP

FTP is a cognitive-motivational concept not only because it results from motivational goal setting (Nuttin, 1980), but also because it has motivational effects. More recent theoretical and empirical work in the Leuven Research Center for Motivation and Time Perspective (founded by Professor J.R. Nuttin) was aimed at explaining the motivational consequences of individual differences in the extension of FTP. We will now discuss this research. We will first formulate a theoretical model that explains why people with a longer FTP are (in general) more motivated than people with a short FTP. We will then describe a series of empirical studies validating the model. The underlying process is formulated in terms of the psychological distance to future moments (Gjesme, 1982) and the expectancy x instrumentality x value models (VIE-models) of human motivation (Eccles, 1984; Feather, 1982).

In the previous section we explained how motives, needs, or cravings are cognitively processed into more specific motivational goals and into behavioral plans and projects assumed to be instrumental in achieving those goals. Nuttin (1980; Nuttin & Lens, 1985) developed a coding system to identify the motivational content of the goals and he also developed a technique to situate the expressed goals on an individual temporal scale. This allows a measure of the extension, length, or depth of the individual time perspective (see above).

In this section, we describe the psychological variables and processes that can explain the motivational effects or consequences of individual differences in the extension of FTP. These effects are mediated by the psychological distance to future moments. The extension of FTP and the psychological distance to future moments are negatively correlated (Gjesme, 1982; Lens & Moreas, 1994; Moreas & Lens, 1991). For individuals with a long FTP, the psychological distance to a given moment in the future, for example 2 or 5 years from now, is psychologically much shorter than for individuals with a short FTP. The latter group does not take the future into account as much; they live more in the present. Five years from now is much too far away for them, and it is not part of their life space. For very short and very long time intervals into the future, the length of FTP does not seem to affect the psychological distance to a substantial degree. Tomorrow or next weekend is very near for everybody, independent of her or his FTP and 20 or 30 years from now is for most adolescents, for example, chronologically too far away to matter, whatever the extension of their FTP is. For example, two high school graduates, one with a long FTP and the other with a short FTP, start medical school to become a medical doctor in seven years. Graduating from medical school in 7 years will look much closer in time for the student with a long FTP than for the student with a short FTP. This difference has important motivational consequences.

To explain these effects, De Volder and Lens (1982) distinguished a cognitive and a dynamic aspect in FTP. The cognitive aspect of FTP makes it possible to anticipate the more distant future, to bridge chronologically longer time intervals into the future. Individuals with a longer FTP dispose of longer time intervals in which they can situate motivational goals, plans, and projects. Their present actions can also be directed toward goals, not only in the rather near future, but also in the more distant future. As a consequence, those actions acquire a higher utility value, as they are more instrumental. For example, doing your best in high school is not only a means to succeed in the exams and receive a reward, it is also seen as important to pass a difficult entrance examination for university studies, and to become a very good professional and to develop an exciting professional career later on. People with a short FTP cannot think that far into the future.

We understand the dynamic aspect as an ability to ascribe high valence to goals, even if these goals can only be reached in the (very) distant future. Normally, the anticipated incentive value of a reward decreases the more it is delayed in time (Ainslie, 1992; Logue, 1988; Mischel, 1981; Rachlin, 1995). For example, what would you prefer as a reward for helping me today, one dollar now or one dollar in a month from now? In his research on the determinants and correlates of delay of gratification, Mischel (1981) created approach-approach conflicts between a smaller immediate reward (e.g., 1 pencil now) and a larger but delayed reward (e.g., 2 pencils in a week from now). The psychological distance towards goals in the rather distant future is shorter for people with a longer FTP than for people with a shorter FTP. As a consequence, the decrease in anticipated value as function of temporal delay is less steep for them. Again, this effect of individual differences in FTP and experienced psychological distance is not very relevant for very short and very long time intervals. For most people, the incentive value of, for example, a free ski-vacation in 30 years will not be affected by their FTP. It is much too far into the future for everyone.

Summarizing, the longer the FTP, the shorter the psychological distance towards future moments. That explains why present actions can have a higher utility value or instrumentality for people with a longer FTP and why people with a long FTP are better able to attach higher incentive values to future goals.

Well-validated cognitive motivational theories such as the *Expectancy x Value* theories (Feather, 1982) and *Valence x Instrumentality x Expectancy* or VIE models in work motivation (Pinder, 1998) hold that the strength of motivation is a positive function of the product of expectancy that an action will lead to the desired outcome (instrumentality, utility of that action) and the anticipated value of that outcome or goal.

EMPIRICAL EVIDENCE

We will now summarize some of our empirical studies validating the cognitive-motivational theory of future time perspective explained above.

De Volder and Lens (1982) found that highly motivated 11th graders (17-18 years old) who were given a list of potential goals in the near and the distant future, attached significantly more value to goals in the distant future than less motivated students. They also found that highly motivated students attached a significantly higher instrumental value to their schoolwork for reaching goals in the near and the distant future. Lens and Decruyenaere (1991) found that high, moderate and low motivated subgroups of high school students significantly differed (in the predicted direction) in the instrumental value or utility of "doing your best in school" for success in life in general. The more the pupils were aware of the importance of schoolwork for later, the more motivated they were. It seems however, that perceiving the future importance does not always increase student motivation. Van Calster, Lens, and Nuttin (1987) found a significant main effect of perceived instrumentality on student motivation in grade 11 and 12 (age 17-19). Students who perceived their education as important for their future (high instrumentality) were significantly more motivated than their peers, scoring low for perceived instrumentality. They did however, also find an interaction effect of instrumentality and affective attitude towards the individual future. Perceived instrumentality does enhance student motivation, but only for those students who have a positive attitude towards their future. Attaching high instrumentality to present school grades had the opposite effect on motivation for students with a negative outlook on their future. The combination of a high instrumentality of doing your best in school for the personal future and a high positive affective attitude towards the personal future has a positive effect on motivation and school grades. A very bleak outlook on the future seems to be a de-motivating variable. Moreas and Lens (1991; Lens, 2001) asked ninth grade students to rate the value of ten motivational goals in the near future (within a two year period) and ten other goals in the more distant future (after at least a two year period). The near and the distant goals cover the same motivational content categories. They measured the instrumentality of "doing my best for my studies" for reaching those 20 goals. Student motivation was measured by questionnaire. Twelve items measured "Study Persistence" and seven items measured "Study efficiency". Future time perspective was measured by the proportion of the number of goals for the near future (within two years) to the number of goals to be situated in the more distant future (beyond a two year period). The smaller this proportion, the longer the individual FTP is. The goals were spontaneously expressed as sentence completions to the Motivational Induction Method (MIM; Nuttin & Lens, 1985).

An analysis of variance reveals the expected significant effect of FTP on student motivation. Pupils with a very long FTP (highest quartile) were significantly more motivated than pupils with a short or very short FTP. The length of FTP was expected to have a positive effect on the anticipated value of goals, on the perceived instrumentality of study behavior for reaching future goals, and on the product of value and instrumentality. For distant goals, this effect was stronger than for near goals. This expected interaction-effect of FTP and time period on the value of goals was indeed significant. There was no effect of FTP on the value of the near goals but the predicted effect of FTP on the value of distant goals was significant. The anticipated value of distant goals was significantly higher for people with a long or a very long FTP than for people with a very short FTP. As predicted, length of FTP also had a stronger effect on the perceived instrumentality for the distant goals than for the near goals.

The last study (Creten, Lens, & Simons, 2001) in this series started from a practical problem. Many pupils in lower level vocational schools have serious motivational problems, be it more so for theoretical than for practical courses. They are no more intrinsically motivated to study, certainly not for their more theoretical courses. If they are motivated at all, it is because of extrinsic reasons (Lens & Decruyenaere, 1991). Many vocational students also have a rather short future time perspective (Lens & Decruyenaere, 1991; Phalet & Lens,

1995). They do not look very far into the future, they rather live 'here and now'. They are not well aware of, or do not care much about, the instrumentality or utility of their present school career. Creten, Lens, and Simons (2001) were interested in whether the relationship between FTP and motivation would also apply to this group of students. Are students in vocational education who perceive the future relevance of, for example, a second language, more motivated for that course than students who are not aware of the future importance of the same course? Is it possible to motivate these students by pointing to the future contingencies of their present schoolwork? They found that the students were significantly more motivated for their practical courses than for each of the two theoretical courses. They also found that the perceived instrumentality differed from course to course, for both near and distant goals. For the near future goals, the instrumentality of French (second language) was as high as for practical courses. For long-term goals, practical courses were perceived as most useful. Students also found French important for the future, whereas for the other theoretical courses, many students had problems in seeing its utility both for the near and the distant future. For the whole sample of 733 students, a significant correlation between instrumentality and student motivation was found. In general, students who perceived their studies as having a low impact for their goals in the near or the more distant future were less motivated. Students who ascribed more utility to their practical courses were more motivated for these courses than they were for the theoretical courses. The students were not more motivated for French than for their general theoretical courses, although they attached a higher utility value to French. It seems that perceived instrumentality or utility was an important but not a sufficient condition for developing student motivation. Also, the specific content of the course and the way in which it is taught matters a lot.

Summarizing, we can indeed conclude that perceiving the instrumentality or utility of a present task for future goals enhances the motivation for that task, in comparison with a task that is a goal in itself, with no implications for the future.

It must be made very explicit here that we are not comparing the motivational effects of near versus distant goals, as Bandura (1986) did when he argued that proximal goals are more motivating than distal goals. We compare the motivational effect of having only immediate goals versus having proximal goals which are at the same time means towards more distant goals (Lens & Rand, 1997). Persistent striving towards long-term goals will be facilitated by formulating a series of such short-term subgoals, leading to the (provisional) final goal in the more distant future (Bandura & Schunk, 1981; Bandura & Simon, 1977). Long-term goals require more work and are achieved by first reaching subgoals. Zaleski (1987; 1994) found that "... if proximal goals are intermediate, instrumental subgoals necessary for attainment of the final end states, then those who have distal goals work harder on the proximal ones," (Zaleski, 1987, p. 34). In comparison with individuals with a short future time perspective, people with a long future time perspective are more persistent in working for a goal, and derive more satisfaction from such present goal-oriented actions. They are not only more motivated for distant goals, but also for near subgoals.

THE ORGANIZATION OF THE SUBJECTIVE FUTURE AND CAREER PLANNING BEHAVIOR

The theoretical context in which our psychological intervention in the career realm is rooted results from the combination of the Developmental and Ecological approaches to Vocational Guidance and Counseling (Super, 1996; Vondracek, Lerner, & Schulenberg, 1986; Vondracek & Porfelli, 2002) and the Relational Theory of Motivation and Personality (Nuttin,1984). Within this context, human behavior, in order to be understood in its whole, needs to be analyzed in its life space or psychological field and, in our view, the career psychologist working in an educational setting should act as a multidisciplinary intervention programs manager (Santos & Paixão, 1992), aiming at the activation of the psycho-social factors of identity construction. This activation will increase the systemic plasticity and the spreading of a "secure basis" (Blustein, 1988, 1994) for identity development. Thus, psychological interventions can be planned, either at the individual level or at the level of the systemic context (Bronfenbrenner, 1986).

According to the Relational Theory of Motivation proposed by Joseph Nuttin (Nuttin, 1984; Nuttin & Lens, 1985), motivational functioning is analyzed through several dimensions pertaining to the temporal axe of goal-setting processes: extension of the future time perspective (FTP), density of the main temporal and content categories, time attitudes, and time orientation. Motivational goal-setting analysis derives from an explanatory model of behavioral functioning, which is built upon the concept of intentionality. This model stresses the need to study motivation and the dynamics of goal functioning in order to understand individual behavior within significant interaction contexts. This is the reason why several authors working within the vocational psychology domain have recently stressed the need to harmonize the study of career behavior, integrating cognitive, affective, and motivational factors in the research efforts directed to the comprehension of vocational decision-making and development (Osipow, 1993, Lent & Brown, 2006).

Within this goal-setting model, vocational guidance and counseling can be conceived as a process of intervention that is able to activate personal agency and a set of behavioral self-determinating factors, thus promoting the "internal" means that facilitate positive changes in the social context, making it subjectively more controllable, predictable, or permeable to creative factors. As such, the main role of the psychologist or the career counselor is to activate individual "transformational" potential via the utilization of goal directed procedures (Nuttin, 1987; Ford, 1992). In general, these procedures endorse the study of work roles within all the other life roles and reinforce the importance of the development of positive characteristics of the subjective future time in the construction of the vocational and psychosocial identity.

The subjective organization of the future constitutes a motivational dimension influencing several developmental areas, functioning as the cognitive and affective support for the performance of a large number of instrumental and exploratory tasks and activities within the career realm: choice-making throughout the life-span, cognitive and behavioral performance in significant transitional moments within the educational system and between school and the world of work and the psychological integration of diverse personal and social phenomena affecting the decision-taking process (Markus & Nurius, 1986, Paixão, 1996, Savickas, 1990). According to Cantor and Fleeson (1994), future time perspective has an "anticipatory socialization" function, performing also an instrumental role in relation to the protection and maintenance of the intentions activated by the working self-concept. FTP can be conceived as a style of coping with the personal future in the most significant life contexts, constituting the main dimension in the motivational activation of career or vocational development, especially during the first stages of dominant career intervention strategies (Herr & Cramer, 1996).

The application of the fundamentals of the relational theory of motivation to the most significant human developmental domain bears relevant implications (Nuttin, 1985), not only to the study of career, but also to other educational and growth contexts and is largely connected to the study of the process of elaboration, construction, and implementation of personal projects (Pervin, 1989). This focus on personal projects is designed to answer this fundamental question: how do cognitive-motivational factors underlying, respectively, the setting of new goals, the development of self-regulation strategies, and the structuring and evaluation of the plans of action direct and organize behavioral functioning in domains that are important for the development of a well integrated identity? Plus, taking into account that motivational psychology over the years (Lens, 1993) has pointed out a very close connection between goal-setting and planning, on one side, and the organization of future orientation or FTP on the other, how do the structural, motivational, and attitudinal characteristics of FTP influence the self-regulation and developmental processes in career-related decisions?

The analysis of motivational and cognitive components underlying the general structure and evaluation of planning behavior can be carried out at three epistemological levels explaining the problem of the passage from representation to action (Kuhl & Beckmann, 1985):

a) The interaction of cognitive and motivational processes explaining the formation of goals and intentions, that is, explaining typical pre-decisional and decisional processes (choice motivation);

b) The interaction of cognitive and motivational processes explaining the maintenance and enactment of intentions, enabling the comprehension of how intentions are first translated into a sequence of actions, which we can integrate in typical post-decisional processes (control motivation);

c) The interaction of cognitive and motivational processes involved in the performance and evaluation of the actions (the problem of performance control motivation).

Kuhl considers that most motivational theories, namely Nuttin's Relational Theory, Lewin's motivational conceptions, and the dominant expectancy-instrumentality-value models mainly focus on the problem of goal or intention formation, developing explanatory concepts and processes that allow us to understand which action tendencies are dominant at each moment. It is assumed that the successive motivational constellations - that is, the underlying hierarchy of motives organizing the stream of behavior - automatically determine the passage from intention to action. Nuttin (1984) also contends that the same system of needs that activated the cognitive-motivational processes of goal formation continues to activate and direct the organism during the behavioral executive phase. The discrepancy between the final goals and the actual situation of the organism creates a state of tension that supports the executive processes until the goal or intention is completely reached. In sum, according to Kuhl (1992), dominant cognitive theories of motivation, namely Nuttin's theory, sustain that the interaction of motivational and cognitive processes that explain goal formation is responsible for their automatic translation into action. Kuhl and Beckmann (1985) consider this an incomplete view of the problem of explaining the passage from intention to action. In the research line of Ach, they developed an action control theory that tries to understand how decisions, choices, or goals are translated into actions; that is, how relevant volitional processes explain post-decisional behavioral patterns.

We have to agree that, in the vocational or career realm, most classical decisional and career choice theories imply that the motivational processes underlying goal formation will automatically be translated into goal execution and evaluation, which is a very fragmented view of the decisional reality, not accounting for the dynamics of post-decisional processes. Even when they account for the existence of a specific post-decisional reality, they try to deal with it in a purely didactic way (help building the sequence of a chain of instrumental acts or teaching the principals of contingent planning). Several authors in the motivation field considered this view as a very inadequate way to address ambiguous, complex, and difficult situations, as most vocational or career decisions are. Such a view, once again, does not deal with the existence and dynamic functioning of volitional processes in the maintenance and enactment of previously formed or activated intentions. Additionally, most counseling procedures do not deal with the fact that increasing self-knowledge, by using a multiplicity of methodologies, is not sufficient to guarantee that the counselees will engage in the implementation of alternatives or actions that they prefer or that they have previously chosen to be carried out. The consideration of important volitional processes and the level of effectiveness they promote in the use of self-regulatory mechanisms seems an essential condition to help counselees be involved in instrumental paths, allowing a more positive evaluation and a more firm personalization of important career developmental tasks.

Nevertheless, and contrary to Birch's view (1985), we think that Nuttin's theory contains relevant considerations regarding goal implementation, namely those involved in his general time perspective theory: the temporal structure characteristics of motivational projects and plans and the type of general organization of significant and/or routine life activities ("master plan") may inhibit or facilitate the translation of goals and intentions into action. In fact, a moderate or high extension of FTP, for instance, contributes to increasing the level of reality of the final goal, thus facilitating the involvement of the subject in instrumental chains leading to that goal. We cannot forget the extensive attention Nuttin gave to the regulatory function of instrumental motivation, a typical self-determined form of behavioral regulation, according to the self-determination theory (Ryan & Deci, 2000, 2001).

In the same line of thought, when we look at the state of the art in the study of careers, we are also forced to recognize that the role ascribed to motivational processes within the "post-modern" approaches to the study of vocational behavior and career development (Savickas, 1995, Chen, 2003) takes into account the dynamics of both pre-decisional, decisional, and post-decisional processes (Paixão, 2004). There are, basically, three "post-modern" approaches (the ecological and systemic paradigm, the narrative and hermeneutical paradigm, and the constructivist paradigm), whose main concern is the understanding of the process of construction of the subjective career or the ascription of meaning to work in people's lives (Richardson, 1993). The constructivist paradigm implies that the personal construction of vocational behavior reinforces temporal integration via the establishment of cognitive links between present decisions, past choices, and future possibilities. Vocational projects are perceived as cognitive schemata organizing social representations and guiding intervention. The narrative paradigm is interested in the process of articulation of actions within a narrative which is organized via temporal ordering, using a methodological framework that takes into account the future consequences, desired or not, of present vocational actions. Innovative and creative examples of these methodologies are the narrative elaboration of the decision cycle by Cochran (1997) and the analysis of narrative themes proposed by Savickas (1989), in the line of the early extrapolation method based on the analysis of career themes developed by Super (1954). Finally, the ecological and systemic paradigm, materialized in the concept of "embedded identity" (Blustein, 1994), contends that the temporal variables can be conceived as both cognitive and affective schemata that articulate the establishment of reciprocal relations at different levels of the behavioral ecosystem. Memories from the past and, mainly, anticipations of the future (Nuttin & Lens, 1985) are both the products and producers (Lerner, 1984) of affective and cognitive-symbolic attachments with spaces and time zones that are virtual or possible. Within this latter paradigm, the motivational, developmental, and systemic model of decision-making proposed by Vondracek and Kawasaki (1995), following the motivational systems theory of Ford (1992), occupies a central place. According to this model, the motivational activation of career development is a central and fundamental dimension in the organization of vocational interventions, mainly when these interventions aim to obtain long term behavioral changes.

Thus, within these "post-modern" approaches, all levels of motivational functioning — mobilization, direction, and instrumental behavior regulation and evaluation — imply the impact of the organization of important temporal variables working in a subjective future dimension. This fact led Savickas (1990), in the line of Nuttin's relational theory of motivation (Nuttin & Lens, 1985), to the elaboration of a temporal model of career intervention organized around three important temporal constructs: extension, differentiation, and integration of future orientation. This temporal career model underlines the fact that the research carried out on the motivational content, affective quality, and cognitive structuring of people's representations about the future, that is, the study of future time perspective (FTP) or future orientation, must be discussed and integrated in the study of career development.

THE TEMPORAL LOGIC OF VOCATIONAL PROJECTS IN SOME CRUCIAL MOMENTS OF THE LIFE-SPAN: SOME EMPIRICAL STUDIES

We have carried out three complementary exploratory studies in which the temporal variables are viewed as predictors of behavioral criteria pertaining to planning behavior, both as a goal-setting and as a project evaluation process in the larger context of career development (Paixão, 1996, 1997). In order to understand the behavioral impact of the subjective organization of the personal future or FTP on the construction and evaluation of vocational projects in three career developmental moments (Boutinet, 1992) – the vocational project of the beginning of adolescence, the pre-occupational project of late adolescence/beginning of autonomous adult life and the vocational project of the occupationally active adult – we used the Motivational Induction Method (MIM) to measure future time extension and density, and the Time Attitude Scale (TAS), to measure future time attitudes or the dimension of optimism towards the personal future (both questionnaires developed by Nuttin and Lens, 1985).

The MIM includes two small booklets with 20 and 10 pages respectively. On top of each page, a motivational inducer is printed. These sentence beginnings are formulated in the first person and the verb always expresses a tendency, an effort, desire, intention, etc. The sentence beginnings in the first booklet are formulated in order to induce positive motivational objects (e.g., I intensely desire....), while the second one asks for negative objects; objects that are avoided, feared, etc. (e.g., I would not like it if ...). Participants are invited to write a full sentence by expressing what they desire or fear. Each goal object expressed in the sentence completions is coded according to both a content code, which comprises eight main categories of content analysis (self, self-realization, realization, contact, cognitive exploration, possession, leisure, and transcendental) and some dozens of sub-categories, as well as a temporal code comprising calendar units (near future) and social/ biological units (intermediate and distant future, as well as the historical future and the open present).

The TAS was constructed to measure individual attitudes towards the personal past, present, and future (we only used it to measure future time attitudes), and it is based on Osgood's semantic-differential rating technique. It comprises (in its Portuguese adaptation) 22 bipolar pairs of adjectives, mainly expressing the subject's affective attitude towards each one of the temporal dimensions (but also their attitudes concerning the structure, internal control, degree of difficulty, instrumental value, and subjective temporal distance). Each pair of adjectives corresponds to a 7-point scale ranging from "very positive" to "very negative". Participants are asked to indicate on each scale how they spontaneously experience their personal past, present, and future.

In the first study, we focused on the impact of the organization of the subjective future on the construction of vocational projects in the beginning of adolescence, where the main developmental task is the consolidation of a sense of identity, requiring the construction and articulation of extended plans of action ("progressive narrative"). Taking into account an extended body of research, we expected the extension of FTP and the global attitudinal value towards the future, independently and/or in interaction, to predict several aspects of planning behavior in early adolescence (total quantity of developmental tasks anticipated for different future moments, quantity of specific tasks anticipated for the near and intermediate future, quantity of the content categories involved in the tasks anticipated for the global future, motivation to participate in systematic vocational guidance activities, and level of instrumentality assigned to these activities and level of certainty of current vocational project).

In a sample of 159 8th grade students (both male and female) attending basic schools in Coimbra, we found that the extension of FTP did not produce any main effect on the majority of the dependent variables (the exception being the level of decision and compromise of the subject's vocational project, which was higher in the group, showing a more extended FTP). On the other hand, the global attitudinal value towards the future showed main effects (in the expected direction) in several of the dependent variables considered (e.g., number of tasks for the near future, number of specific tasks for the near future, number of tasks for the intermediate future, number of specific tasks for the intermediate future, number of tasks for the very distant future, etc). There were no interaction effects between the two independent variables on any of the components of the vocational planning behavior.

In the second study, we focused on the impact of the organization of the subjective future on the construction of projects in late adolescence/beginnings of adulthood, a nuclear period of ecological transition between secondary and higher education. Several studies pertaining to the career and personality psychological literature (Abreu, 1986; Markus & Ruvolo, 1989; Pelletier, 1986) stated that both the temporal structure of future orientation and the degree of optimism towards the personal future have a strong influence on important vocational development criteria in periods of ecological transition, promoting planning and coping behaviors that facilitate the successful performance of relevant occupational insertion tasks and activities. Thus, using Little's "Personal Projects Analysis" (Little, 1983, 1989), we expected the extension of FTP and the global attitudinal value towards the future, independently and/or in interaction, to predict the temporal range of current personal projects, preferred types of personal project formulations (mainly oriented towards behaviors *versus* mainly oriented towards final results), and personal project evaluation in the dimensions of structure and efficacy. In a sample of 42 subjects (both male and female) who had completed secondary education in Coimbra and were applying to higher education institutions, the analysis of the impact of the temporal variables upon several indexes of personal project structures and evaluations were carried out via a 2 x 2 factorial plan of analysis of variance (2 levels of extension *versus* 2 levels of attitude), which revealed a significant interaction effect on the perceived level of control of significant personal projects. Post-hoc comparisons showed that the group containing subjects with a more extended and optimistic subjective future obtained significantly higher values in all the comparisons, whereas the group containing subjects with a more extended and pessimistic subjective future obtained significantly lower values than the short extension and pessimistic group. This result indicated that a longer extension of FTP only has a positive impact on the perceived level of control when associated with an optimistic attitude. The global attitudinal value towards the future showed main effects (in the expected direction) on several dependent variables: density of projects in some content categories, time adequacy, outcome and other's views. On the other side, the extension of FTP showed main effects (in the expected direction) on the following dependent variables: density of projects in some content categories, percentage of projects with a short and medium temporal span, percentage of projects with a high degree of specificity, percentage of projects formulated in behavioral terms, and time adequacy.

Finally, in the study that tried to analyze the impact of the organization of the subjective future on the construction of projects during the active occupational life period, we viewed adult career development as mainly dependent upon the functioning of the motivational structure of the working individual (Vondracek & Kawasaki, 1995). Within the transactional perspective of adult career development (Leitão & Paixão, 2001), the concept of "anticipatory coping" (Fassinger & Schlossberg, 1992; Gibson & Brown, 1992) is fundamental in describing the subject's efforts in trying to deal with the more important behavioral processes and changes that occur during the working adulthood. An extended body of research carried out in the areas of adult career behavior and adult project construction and evaluation (Vondracek & Kawasaki, 1995) has shown that the attitudinal dimension of future orientation has been pointed out as the one having a most enduring impact on the structure and efficacy of personal projects. On the other hand, several studies (Little, 1989; Palys & Little, 1983) established a positive link between different components of future orientation and life satisfaction. Accordingly, we expected the extension of FTP and the global attitudinal value towards the future, independently and/or in interaction, to predict personal project evaluations in the dimensions of structure and efficacy. We also expected the extension of FTP, the global attitudinal value towards the future and personal project evaluations in the dimensions of value, structure and stress (as factors respectively promoting the integration of relevant developmental tasks in the self-concept, personal project degree of reality, and expressing the type of coping with ambiguous and difficult tasks), to predict work satisfaction. In a sample of 101 subjects (both male and female) who worked as managers in several private and public organizations (in the Central Region of Portugal) belonging to the economic areas of education, occupational training, health, agriculture, industry, and tourism, the global attitudinal value towards the future showed main effects on several indexes of personal project evaluations: visibility, control, initiation, outcome, self-prototypicality, other's views, and progress. Complementarily, the extension of FTP showed main effects in two evaluation indexes, namely personal project importance and value congruency. There were no interaction effects between these two independent variables on any indexes of personal project evaluation. As to the impact of both temporal variables and personal project evaluations on work satisfaction, the extension of FTP and the global attitudinal value towards the future were the single predictors that contributed the most to the portion of variance explained by all the predictors.

Thus, based on these empirical studies, we can conclude that the global attitudinal value towards the personal future facilitates the process of translation of intentions into creative and effective action and influences personal project evaluation concerning their efficacy or subjective probability of success and their social impact. In fact, the global attitudinal value towards the personal future maintains close relationships with more intentional and productive planning behavior processes, independently of age or specific life contexts and situations. On the other hand, the extension of FTP seems to bear a more visible impact on the type of structure evidenced by personal projects (relevant expressions of people's subjective career) mainly in critical periods of ecological transition (in which people are encouraged to develop new goals in order to be able to experience a successful transition). It also shows some impact on the level of work satisfaction in occupationally active adults. In more stable phases or periods of the career development process, its motivational influence or impact is not clearly evident. The cognitive-motivational impact caused by each one of the temporal variables seems to be relatively independent and autonomous of each other.

Keeping this data in mind, we argue that, in the career domain, future research and intervention should focus on nuclear periods of ecological transition and follow individuals along their processes of personal project elaboration, implementation, and evaluation. Once the cognitive and behavioral impact of future orientation seems to be mainly attitudinal, career counselors should invest in comprehensive models of career intervention (Paixão, 2004, 2008; Savickas, 2002; Spokane, 1991).

FUTURE TIME PERSPECTIVE AND VOCATIONAL DECISION-MAKING: AN EXPLORATORY STUDY OF THE MOTIVATIONAL FUNCTIONING IN CRITICAL TRANSITIONAL MOMENTS WITHIN THE PORTUGUESE EDUCATIONAL SYSTEM

Traditionally, vocational decision-making has been viewed as a strictly cognitive and rational process (Gelatt, 1962; Jepsen & Dilley, 1979; Pitz & Harren, 1980). Only recently the role of motivational and affective factors in this process have been recognized, both as facilitators as well as inhibitors of the successive vocational choices the students are required to make along their career (Gelatt, 1989; Phillips, 1994). Vocational decision-making models have for a long time recognized the role of the future as a task characteristic, but they have not attributed any behavioral function to FTP as a personality characteristic. According to these models, the orientation towards the future is implicit in the cognitive concepts of estimation, expectancy, instrumentality, and subjective probability, which explain the decision processes via the strategic organization of the information within the cognitive evaluative systems of the decider (Paixão, 1988; Silva, 1997; Paixão & Silva, 2001). More recently, however, the focus of attention has been directed to the role motivational factors play in the decision-making process (Lent, Paixão, Silva & Leitão, 2010): as a matter of fact, some authors suggest that the activation of FTP reduces anxiety towards the personal future, while at the same time it increases its degree of reality, thus reinforcing the subject's realistic attitudes in relation to the career planning behavior (Paixão, 1996; Peavy, 1992, 1997/8; Savickas, 1990).

This is the reason why Paixão & Silva (2001) carried out a research study where they tried to understand the relations between the main components of FTP as conceived by Nuttin (Nuttin & Lens, 1985) and the degree of anxiety towards significant vocational choices in critical transitional moments within the Portuguese educational system. Paixão & Silva (2001) collected the data in two samples of students attending basic and secondary schools (9th and 12th grades, 127 and 189 students, respectively) in the Central Region of Portugal and focused on the relationship between FTP and the degree of anxiety towards main vocational choices. They also checked if the student's typical time extension and time content profiles differed in the two transitional and vocational decision making moments. Keeping in mind an innovative body of research carried out in the areas of the subjective organization of the future and vocational indecision and anxiety (Savickas, 2002), they expected to find a negative correlation between the extension of FTP and, respectively, the degree of anxiety associated with the choice process, the difficulty in decision-taking, the need to collect further educational and occupational information, and the need to improve self-knowledge. In order to assess FTP, they used the LMT, a Portuguese adaptation and self-rating version (Santos, Paixão, Silva & Castro, 1995) of the MIM (Nuttin & Lens, 1985), which consists of a list of 97 items corresponding to goal objects representing different time and content categories. Subjects are free to choose whatever item corresponds to a desired or feared personal goal object. They also used the Career Factors Inventory (CFI; Chartrand et. al., 1990) to assess career indecision components. The CFI is a multidimensional self-rating decision scale comprising 21 items organized around two informational factors and two personal-emotional factors.

The main results of this study were somewhat disappointing: we only found a significant negative correlation (in the expected direction) between the extension of FTP and the need to collect further educational and occupational information among 12th grade students. These students also selected a significantly lower number of goal objects than their 9th grade colleagues, a fact that certainly has to do with the type of specific career development tasks which are characteristic of each group: vocational exploration tasks (predominant among the 9th graders) presuppose a higher number of cognitive and affective connections with significant interaction contexts than the vocational specification tasks that are characteristic of a group of subjects who are about to complete their secondary education. As to the motivational profiles, both time content and time extension were very similar in both groups of students and revealed a predominance of goal objects located in the distant future, thus translating the students' constructive behavioral organization in critical moments of decision-making. The data also indicated a good balance between the relative number of goal objects located in the near future and in the open present, a fact that is illustrative of the necessary flexibility of the behavioral means-ends structure in nuclear transitional life periods. However, the low consistency of the results with the initial research hypothesis demands further studies where the connections between the motivational variables (both time extension and content) and the main components of the decision-making process are more clearly traced and understood.

CONCLUSION

All the empirical studies we discussed in this chapter are in total agreement with Nuttin's saying that "the future is our motivational space." To be motivated, it is important to translate needs and cravings into specific motivational goals in the near and distant future. By doing so, one develops a long FTP perspective. This has positive motivational consequences because the psychological distance to such future goals decreases and the instrumental value of present actions increases. The delay in gratification that is associated with striving for distant goals is not frustrating because achieving more near subgoals as means towards those future goals creates intermediated satisfaction. One can at the same time strive for goals in the distant future and enjoy the present. For individuals with a longer FTP, it is easier to take future consequences of present actions into account. This is very adaptive in many domains of human endeavors (e.g., health behavior, delinquency, education, professional life). As shown above, developing a long, realistic, and well-structured motivational FTP is an important process in the vocational and career realm. It helps adolescents and emerging adults when planning and making important decisions regarding their educational and/or vocational career.

REFERENCES

Abreu, M.V. (1986). Para uma nova teoria dos interesses [About a new theory of interests]. *Biblos, LXVII*, 217-229.

Abreu, M. V. (2001). Desenvolvimento vocacional e estratégia de motivação para aprendizagens persistentes [Vocational development and motivational strategies among life long learners], *Psychologica, 26*, 9-26.

Ainslie, G. (1992). *Picoeconomics: The strategic interaction of successive motivational states within the person.* Cambridge, UK: Cambridge University Press.

Bandura, A. (1986). *Social foundations of thought and actions. A social-cognitive theory.* EnglewoodCliffs NJ: Prentice Hall.

Bandura, A., & Schunk, D.H. (1981). Cultivating competence, self-efficacy, and intrinsic interest through proximal self-motivation. *Journal of Personality and Social Psychology, 41*, 586-598.

Bandura, A., & Simon, K.M. (1977). The role of proximal intentions in self-regulation of refractory behavior. *Cognitive Therapy and Research, 1,* 177-193.

Bergius, R. (1957). *Formen des Zukunftserlebens* [Types of experiencing the future]. München: Johann Ambrosius Barth.

Birch, D. (1985). From needs to action – almost. *Contemporary Psychology, 30,* 395.

Blustein, D. (1988). Applying current theory and research in career exploration to practice. *The Career Development Quarterly, 41,* 174-184.

Blustein, D. (1994). The question of who am I: A cross-theoretical analysis. In M. Savickas & R. Lent (Eds.), *Convergence in theories of career choice and development.* Palo Alto, CA: Counseling Psychologists Press.

Boutinet, J. P. (1992). *Anthropologie du projet* [Anthropology of projects]. Paris: Presses Universitaires de France.

Bronfenbrenner, U. (1986). Recent advances on the ecology of human development. *In* R. Silbereisen, K. Eyferth & G. Rudinger (Eds.), *Development as action in context: Problem behavior and normal youth development.* Berlin: Springer-Verlag.

Cantor, N. & Fleeson, W. (1994). Social intelligence and intelligent goal pursuit: A cognitive slice of motivation. *The Nebraska Symposium on Motivation, 41,* 125-179.

Chartrand, J., Robbins, S., Morrill, W. & Boggs, K. (1990). Development and validation of the Career Factors Inventory. *Journal of Counseling Psychology,* 37, 491-501.

Chen, C. (2003). Integrating perspectives in career development theory and practice. *The Career Development Quarterly, 51,* 203-216.

Cochran, L. (1997). *Career counseling. A narrative approach.* Thousand Oaks: Sage Publications.

Creten, H., Lens, W., & Simons, J. (2001). The role of perceived instrumentality in student motivation. In A. Efklides, J. Kuhl, & R.M. Sorrentino (Eds.). *Trends and prospects in motivation research (pp. 37-45).* Dordrecht: Kluwer Academic Publishers.

De Volder, M. (1979). Time orientation: A review. *Psychologica Belgica, 19,* 61-79.

De Volder, M., & Lens, W. (1982). Academic achievement and future time perspective as a cognitive-motivational concept. *Journal of Personality and Social Psychology, 42,* 566-571.

Eccles, J. (1984). Sex differences in achievement patterns. *Nebraska Symposium on Motivation, 32,* 97-132.

Fassinger, R. & Schlossberg, N. (1992). Understanding the adult years: Perspectives and implications. In S. Brown & R. Lent (Eds.), *Handbook of counseling psychology (2ª ed.).* New York: Wiley.

Feather, N.T. (1982). *Expectations and actions: expectancy-value models in psychology.* Hillsdale, NJ: Erlbaum.

Ford, M. (1992). *Motivating humans:. Goals, emotions and personal agency beliefs.* Newbury Park: Sage Publications.

Fraisse, P. (1957). *Psychologie du temps* [The psychology of time]. Paris: Presses Universitaires de France.

Fraisse, P. (1963). *The psychology of time.* Westport: Greenwood.

Gelatt, H. B. (1962). Decision-making. A conceptual frame of reference for counseling. *Journal of Counseling Psychology, 9,* 240-245.

Gelatt, H. B. (1989). Positive uncertainty: A new decision-making framework for counseling. *Journal of Counseling Psychology, 36*(2), 252-256.

Gibson, J. & Brown, S. (1992). Counseling adults for life transitions. In S. Brown & R. Lent (Eds.), *Handbook of counseling psychology (2nd edition)*. New York: Wiley.

Gjesme, T. (1982). Psychological goal distance: The lost dimension in achievement motivation research. In W. Hacker, W. Volpert, & M. von Cranach (Eds.), *Cognitive and motivational aspects of action* (pp. 86-98). Amsterdam: North Holland.

Guyau, J.M. (1902) La genèse de l' idée de temps The development of the concept of time]. Paris: Alcan.

Herr, E.L. & Cramer, S.H. (1996). *Career guidance and counseling through the life span. Systematic approaches* (5th ed.) New York: Harper Collins.

Jepsen, D. & Dilley, J. (1979). Vocational decision-making models: a review and comparative analysis. In S. Weinreich (Ed.), *Career counseling. theoretical and practical perspectives*. New York: McGraw-Hill.

Kuhl, J. (1992). Motivation and volition. In G. d'Ydewalle, P. Eelen & P. Bertelson (Eds.), *International perspectives on psychological science. Vol. 2: The state of the art*. State of the Art lectures presented at the XXVth. International Congress of Psychology, Brussels. Hillsdale: Lawrence Erlbaum Associates.

Kuhl, J. & Beckmann, J. (1985). *Action control: From cognition to behavior*. Berlin: Springer-Verlag.

Leitão, L. & Paixão, M. P. (2001). Consulta Psicológica Vocacional para Jovens Adultos e Adultos. In M. C. Taveira (Coordenadora), *Educação e Desenvolvimento Vocacional*. Coimbra: Quarteto Editora.

Lens, W. (1986). Future time perspective: A cognitive-motivational concept. In D.R. Brown & J. Veroff (Eds.), *Frontiers of motivational psychology* (pp. 173-190). New York: Springer-Verlag.

Lens, W. (1993). *Future time perspective, motivation and behavioral regulation in educational and professional counselling*. Leuven, Belgium: Department of Psychology, Catholic University of Leuven.

Lens, W. (2001). How to combine intrinsic task-motivation with the motivational effects of the instrumentality of present tasks for future goals. In A. Efklides, J. Kuhl, & R.M. Sorrentino (Eds.). *Trends and prospects in motivation research* (pp. 23-36) Dordrecht, The Netherlands: Kluwer Academic Publishers.

Lens, W., & Decruyenaere, M. (1991). Motivation and demotivation in secondary education: Student characteristics. *Learning and Instruction, 1,* 145-159.

Lens, W., & Moreas, M.-A. (1994). Future time perspective: An individual and a societal approach. In Z. Zaleski (Ed.), *Psychology of future orientation* (pp. 23-38). Lublin: Towarzystwo Naukowe KUL.

Lens, W., & Rand, P. (1997). Combining intrinsic goal orientations with professional instrumentality/utility in student motivation. *Polish Psychological Bulletin, 28,* 103-123.

Lent, R. W., Brown, S. D. (2006). Integrating person and situation perspectives on work satisfaction: A social-cognitive view. *Journal of Vocational Behavior, 69,* 236-247.

Lent, R., Paixão, M.P., Silva, J.T. & Leitão, L.M. (2009). Predicting occupational interests and choice aspirations in Portuguese high school students: A test of social cognitive career theory. *Journal of Vocational Behavior*, 76, 244-251.

Leontiev, D. (Ed.) *Motivation, consciousness, and self-regulation* (pp. 000-000). N.Y.: Nova Science Publishers

Lerner, R. (1984). *On the nature of human plasticity*. Cambridge: Cambridge University Press.

Lersch, Ph. (1966)). *Aufbau der Person* [Construction of the person]. München: Johann Ambrosius Barth.

Lewin, K. (1931). An address given in February 1931 at a convention on problems of the Montessori Method. *Die Neue Erziehung, 2,* 99-103.

Lewin, K. (1935). *A dynamic theory of personality: Selected papers*. New York: McGraw-Hill.

Lewin, K. (1942). Time perspective and morale. In G. Watson (Ed.), *Civilian morale*. Boston: Houghton Mifflin.

Lewin, K. (1943). Defining the "field at a given time". *Psychological Review, 50,* 292-310.

Lewin, K. (1948). *Resolving social conflicts. Selected papers on group dynamics.* (edited by G.W. Lewin). New York: Harper & Brothers.

Little, B. (1983). Personal projects: A rationale and method for investigation. *Environment and Behavior, 15,* 273-309.

Little, B. (1989). Personal projects analysis: Trivial pursuits, magnificent obsessions and the search for coherence. In D. Buss & N. Cantor (Eds.), *Personality psychology. Recent trends and emerging directions*. New York: Springer-Verlag.

Locke, E.A., & Latham, G.P. (1990). *A theory of goal setting and task motivation*. Englewood Cliffs, NJ: Prentice Hall.

Locke, E.A., & Latham, G.P. (2002). Building a practically useful theory of goal setting and task motivation: A 35-year odyssey. *American Psychologist, 57,* 705-717.

Logue, A.W. (1988). Research on self-control. An integrating framework. *Behavioral and Brain Sciences, 11,* 665-709.

Markus, H. & Nurius, P. (1986). Possible selves. *American Psychologist, 41,* 954-969.

Markus, H. & Ruvolo, A. (1989). Possible selves: Personalized representation of goals. In L.A. Pervin (Ed.), *Goal concepts in personality and social psychology*. Hillsdale, NJ: Erlbaum.

Mischel, W. (1981). Objective and subjective rules for delay of gratification. In G. d'Ydewalle & Lens, W. (Eds.), *Cognition in human motivation and learning*. Leuven & Hillsdale, NJ: Leuven University Press & Erlbaum.

Moreas, M.-A. & Lens, W. (1991). *De motivationele betekenis van het individueel toekomstperspectief - project OT/88/6* (3 vols) [The motivational significance of the individual future time perspective: An unpublished research report]. K.U.Leuven: Departementement of Psychology.

Nuttin, J. (1964). The future time perspective in human motivation and learning. In *Proceedings of the 17th International Congress of Psychology* (pp. 60-82). Amsterdam: North-Holland

Nuttin, J. (1980). *Motivation et perspectives d'avenir* [Motivation and future time perspective]. Leuven: Presses Universitaires de Louvain.

Nuttin, J. (1984). *Motivation, planning, and action: A relational theory of behavior dynamics*. Leuven & Hillsdale, NJ: Leuven University Press & Erlbaum.

Nuttin , J. (1985). Le fonctionnement de la motivation humaine [The functioning of human motivation]. *L'Orientation Scolaire et Professionnelle, 14* (2), 91-103.

Nuttin J. (1987). Développement de la formation et motivation [The development of education and motivation]. *Éducation Permanente, 88/89,* 97-110.

Nuttin, J., & Lens, W. (1985). *Future time perspective and motivation: Theory and research method*. Leuven & Hillsdale, NJ: Leuven University Press & Erlbaum.

Osipow, S. (1993). Toward mainstreaming the study of career psychology. Paper presented at the *Third International Symposium on Career Development*, University of Toronto, Canada, August.

Paixão, M.P. (1988). A perspectiva temporal de futuro em algumas teorias do comportamento vocacional [Future time perspective in a few theories of vocational behavior]. *Psychologica, 1*, 47-56.

Paixão, M.P. (1996). *Organização da Vivência do Futuro e Comportamento de Planificação. Compreensão dos Processos Motivacionais e Cognitivos na Elaboração e Avaliação de Projectos Pessoais* [The organition of the subjective future and planning behavior: Understanding the motivational and cognitive processes involved in the elaboration and evaluation of personal projects]. Unpublished doctoral dissertation, Faculty of Psychology and Eductional Sciences, University of Coimbra, Portugal.

Paixão, M.P. (1997). A organização do futuro subjectivo e a construção de projectos no início da idade adulta [Subjective future organization and projects' elaboration in early adulthood]. In Actas da Conferência Internacional *A Informação e a Orientação Escolar e Profissional no Ensino Superior: Um Desafio da Europa.* Coimbra: Universidade de Coimbra.

Paixão, M.P. (2004). A avaliação dos factores e processos motivacionais na orientação vocacional [The consideration of motivational processes and factors in vocational guidance]. In L.M. Leitão (Ed.), *Avaliação Psicológica em Orientação Escolar e Profissional (*pp. 387-425). Coimbra: Quarteto Editora.

Paixão, M.P. (2008). Auto-determinação em contextos de formação e de trabalho: Promoção do desenvolvimento pessoal e da qualidade de vida. *Revista Psicologia e Educação, 7*(1).

Paixão, M.P. & Silva, J.T. (2001). Estudo do funcionamento motivacional em momentos críticos de tomada de decisão vocacional: estudo exploratório [Motivational functioning in critical decision taking]. *Psychologica, 26*, 175-185.

Palys, T. & Little, B. (1983). Perceived life satisfaction and the organization of personal project systems. *Journal of Personality and Social Psychology*, 44, 1221-1230.

Peavy, V. (1992). A constructivist model of training for career counselors. *Journal of Career Development, 18*, 215-229.

Peavy, R.V. (1997/98). Postmodern vocational development and counselling: Constructing possible futures. *Cadernos de Consulta Psicológica, 13-14*, 28-37.

Pelletier, D. (1986). Le projet ou l'élaboration cognitive du besoin [The project or the cognitive elaboration of needs]. *Éducation Permanente* (Projet, formation-action, 1ère partie), *86*, 29-40.

Pervin, L. (1989). *Goal concepts in personality and social psychology.* Hillsdale, NJ: Lawrence Erlbaum Associates.

Phalet; K., & Lens, W. (1995). Achievement motivation and group loyalty among Turkish and Belgian youngsters. In M.L. Maehr & P.R. Pintrich (Eds.), *Advances in motivation and achievement. Volume 9. Culture, motivation and achievement (pp. 32-72)*.Greenwich, Conn.: Jai Press Inc.

Phillips, S. (1994). Choice and change: convergence from the decision-making perspective. In M. Savickas & R. Lent (Eds.), *Convergence in theories of career choice and development.* Palo Alto, CA: Consulting Psychologists Press.

Pinder, C.C. (1998). *Work motivation in organizational behavior.* Upper Saddle River, NJ: Prentice Hall.

Pitz, G. & Harren, V. (1980). An analysis of career decision-making from the point of view of information-processing and decision theory. *Journal of Vocational Behavior, 16,* 320-346.

Rachlin, H. (1995). Self-control: Beyond commitment. *Behavioral and Brain Sciences, 18,* 109-159.

Richardson, M.S. (1993). Work in people's lives: A location for counseling psychologists. *Journal of Counseling Psychology, 40,* 425-433.

Ryan, R. & Deci, E. (2000). Self-determination theory and the facilitation of intrinsic motivation, social development and well-being. *American Psychologist, 55,* 68-78.

Ryan, R. & Deci, E. (2001). On happiness and human potentials: a review of research on hedonic and eudaimonic well-being. *Annual Review of Psychology, 52,* 141-166.

Santos, E. & Paixão, M.P. (1992). *Algumas linhas programáticas sobre o desenvolvimento de carreira de mulheres jovens.* Coimbra: Núcleo de Orientação Escolar e Profissional da Faculdade de Psicologia e de Ciências da Educação da Universidade de Coimbra.

Santos, E., Paixão, M.P., Silva, J.T. & Castro, I. (1995). Apresentação de um estudo empírico sobre a "Localização dos Motivos no Tempo (L.M.T.)": relação com o rendimento escolar. *Avaliação Psicológica: Formas e Contextos,* 3, 541-548. APPORT, L. S. Almeida & I. S. Ribeiro (Eds.).

Savickas, M. (1989). Career-style assessment and counseling. In T.J. Sweeney (Ed.), *Adlerian counseling: A practical approach for a new decade.* Muncie, IN: Accelerated Development Inc.

Savickas, M. (1990). Improving career time perspective. In D. Brown & L. Brooks (Eds.), *Career counseling techniques.* Boston: Allyn & Bacon.

Savickas, M. (1995). Uma nova epistemologia para a Psicologia Vocacional. *Cadernos de Psicologia Educacional.* Lisboa: Edições Universitárias Lusófonas.

Savickas, M. (2002). Career construction. A developmental theory of vocational behavior. In D. Brown & Associates (Eds.), *Career choice and development (4th Edition).* San Francisco: Jossey-Bass.

Silva, J.T. (1997). *Dimensões da Indecisão de Carreira. Investigação com Adolescentes.* Coimbra: Faculdade de Psicologia e de Ciências da Educação da Universidade de Coimbra (Doctoral Dissertation).

Spokane, A. (1991). *Career intervention*: Englewood Cliffs, NJ: Prentice Hall.

Super, D. (1954). Career patterns as a basis for vocational counseling. *Journal of Counseling Psychology, 1,* 12-19.

Super, D. (1996). A life-span, life-space approach to career development. In D. Brown, L. Brooks and Associates, *Career choice and development (3rd ed.).* San Francisco, CA: Jossey-Bass.

Van Calster, K., Lens, W., & Nuttin, J. (1987). Affective attitude toward the personal future: Impact on motivation in high school boys. *American Journal of Psychology, 100,* 1-13.

Vondracek, F. & Kawasaki, I. (1995). Toward a comprehensive framework for adult career development theory and intervention. In W. B. Walsh & S. Osipow (Eds.), *Handbook of vocational psychology. Theory, research and practice (2nd Ed.).* Hillsdale, NJ: Erlbaum.

Vondracek, F., Lerner, R. & Schulenberg, J. (1986). *Career development: A life-span developmental approach.* Hillsdale, NJ: Lawrence Erlbaum Associates.

Vondracek, F. & Porfelli, E. (2002). Counseling psychologists and schools: Toward a sharper conceptual focus. *The Counseling Psychologist, 5* (30), 749-756.

Zaleski, Z. (1987). Behavioral effects of self-set goals for different time ranges. *International Journal of Psychology, 22*, 17-38.

Zaleski, Z. (1994). (Ed.). *Psychology of future orientation*. Lublin: Towarzystwo Naukowe KUL.

In: Motivation, Consciousness and Self-Regulation   ISBN: 978-1-61324-795-2
Editor: D. A. Leontiev, pp. 65-78   © 2012 Nova Science Publishers, Inc.

Chapter 5

PERSONAL MEANING AS THE BASIS OF MOTIVATIONAL PROCESSES

Dmitry A. Leontiev
Moscow State University, Russia

ABSTRACT

The chapter presents a theoretical analysis of applications of the concept of meaning in the psychology of motivation. The history of this concept in psychology and especially psychology of motivation is traced with special emphasis on the two most elaborated general theories of motivation where the concept of meaning is central: J. Nuttin's relational theory of human conduct and A.N. Leontiev's activity theory approach. In the present-day context, the relevance of the meaning concept for attributional theories of motivation and action regulation is discussed. Personal meaning may fulfill the role of common denominator for many special models of motivation linking them together as well as with more general theoretical contexts and other problem fields.

Keywords: personal meaning, motivation, life-world, context, attribution

INTRODUCTION

Like a hundred years ago, today psychology finds itself in a state of an "open crisis". The explanatory potential of the 20th century mainstream seems to be largely exhausted. Though the disposition-situation approach is still working well in many applied tasks, the "zone of proximal development" of the psychological explanation seems to be shifted to new paradigms just taking shape. In particular, the concept of personal meaning that came to psychology from the humanities gradually attracted more and more attention of psychologists throughout the last century. Though most of the psychology of motivation did without this concept, we believe that it can now breathe a new spirit into the old problem of motivation: "what [and in what way – D.L.] moves people to act, think and develop" (Deci& Ryan, 2008, p. 14).

The aim of this chapter is finding the place of meaning in the explanatory models of human motivation. I shall, first, briefly observe the field of motivation and the field of personal meaning research in their historical development, paying special attention to the already existing approaches using the concept of meaning for the analysis of motivation, and then propose a theoretical model of meaning as the common ground for a number of contemporary models of motivation, especially the ones based on the ideas of causal attribution and control.

MOTIVATION, MOTIVE, AND MEANING

Human motivation (I restrict myself here with humans only) refers to the field covering all the psychological structures and processes that make any human activity happen, i.e. that accounts for the determination of comprehensible units of human activity. This field is best structured by the distinction of three levels of motivational processes (Asmolov, 1987; Leontiev D., 2004). The highest level is comprised of stable transsituational structures that are supposed to explain why humans do something at all, or "motivational constants" (Patyaeva, 1983). Explanatory concepts used in this context include instincts, drives, needs, energy, self-actualization, ergs, a.o., and are usually discussed in the context of the idea of the "human nature": *what people are generally supposed to do*. The structures and processes we find at the second level explain, *"why people do what they do"* (Deci&Flaste, 1995), that is, how the actual direction of activity in a given situation is defined or chosen (choice being understood as overcoming the indeterminacy and variability of opportunities, be it conscious and voluntary, or unconscious and automated process). Motive and goal serve as the key explanatory concepts at this level. The third level is that of the secondary processes that account for influences providing regulation and completion of the activity along with its motive and/or goal, since it started, or goal disengagement in relevant cases (Carver &Scheier, 1998). These processes explain why we usually pertain in implementation and completion of the once motivated activity, or *why people keep doing what they are doing*.

The psychology of motivation started proposing its explanatory models in the 1910s (Freud, McDougall; see Leontiev, 2011). Early theories of human motivation put the emphasis on consructs of the 1st level and proposed linear models that deduced behavior more or less directly from a relevant drive or need, even though sometimes a sophisticated interpretation was needed to uncover the hidden unconscious drive finding its transformed output by a compromise with cultural taboos and restrictions. The most critical transformation of the field occurred in the post-war decades (late 1940s-1960s). It became clear that the predictive value of motivational constants (needs, etc.) is rather low compared to *ad hoc* situational determinants, and that other processes than purely motivational ones (wish or will) are deeply involved, in particular, beliefs or disbeliefs in existence of causal links between one's resources, the activity, and the outcome, cognitive appraisal of the probability to accomplish the desirable, etc. This transformation resulted in shifting the emphasis to the situational processes of the 2nd and the 3rd levels, to the profound integration of the psychology of motivation with cognitive psychology, and to the transition from linear models (need – motive — intention – activity) to the system's ones; in the latter the ways different components of the motivational system are connected with each other are more important than the components themselves. In our days speaking of psychology of motivation as a field or discipline is questionable, because there seem to be no purely motivational processes apart from cognitive, regulatory and other processes involved in the motivational functions.

MEANING IN THE STRUCTURE OF MOTIVATION

The concept of personal meaning (Sinn) has not to date received a clear enough conceptualization in psychology and human sciences, despite its evident importance. It is partly due to linguistic confusion: the German conceptual opposition *Sinn vs. Bedeutung* (personalized, spiritual meaning *vs.* cultural, common semantic meaning), that has been playing a crucial role in the humanities since the end of the 19th century, cannot be precisely translated into English or French; Russian translation is, however, possible. This is why the authors that contributed most to the elaboration of the concept of meaning, were initially German-speaking ones (Gottlieb Frege, Max Weber, Alfred Adler, Victor Frankla.o.); then Russian-speaking ones (Gustav Schpet, Mikhail Bakhtin, Nikolai Berdyaev, Lev Vygotsky, Alexey Leontiev), and only since the 1960s English- and French-speaking authors started assimilating this concept (George Kelly, Joseph Nuttin, Eugene Gendlina.o.) (see a historical review in Leontiev D., 1996; 1999).

The meaning of the concept of meaning was quite diverse in different views elaborated without much considering of each other. Some authors used the concept of meaning to explain consciousness and cognition, some to explain activity regulation, some to explain personality structure and dynamics; some treated meaning as referring to objective reality, some as referring to subjective, or intersubjective, conversational reality; some spoke of *the* meaning as the superordinate integrating instance of human conduct, and some of a network of elementary meanings functioning at all the levels of activity regulation (see D. Leontiev, 1996). What was invariant for all the conceptualizations of personal meaning (*Sinn*) as distinct from cultural meaning (*Bedeutung*) were two of its basic features (D. Leontiev,1999; 2007). The first one is context dependence: something has meaning for a person only within some meaningful context, and changing the context would change the meaning of the same action, image or utterance (this argument has been most consistently put forward by Bakhtin (1979) and Bateson (2002)). The second one is its intentional or transcendent quality: personal meaning points toward the world that makes its essential context; personal meaning bridges the person to the world, and the world to the person's subjective experience; personal meaning implies the potential for activity and is thus regulating this activity; it is "a possibility against the background of reality" (Frankl, 1985, p.260).

The concept of meaning can be found in many classical theories of motivation, though usually in a marginal place. Freud in his early writings explicitly pointed at motives and wishes as the source of the special meaning of dreams or their elements (Freud, 1916), without defining meaning as a special term. Still more important is his later concept of cathexis that refers to special objects in the world becoming firmly connected to the basic drives; in other words, definite objects become meaningfully related to the satisfaction of essential drives, and such idiosyncratic connections established individually in one's living process become the frame for the channeling of psychodynamic transformations of motivational energy up to its output in behavior or mental imagery, including dreams. An analogy can be found in ethological concept of imprinting (K. Lorenz): though the species specific behavior successions are largely inborn, connecting these successions to special environmental objects or conditions occurs in individual development through *ad hoc* establishing of the meaning relations.

The first author who made a serious attempt to revise the psychology of motivation on the basis of the idea of *Sinn* (personal meaning) was Alfred Adler, who was the first to put into question the causal explanation of human motivation in line with the traditions of natural sciences as "*causaefficiens*" of activity and proposed instead its teleological explanation as its "*causafinalis*". In his latest works in the 1930s, Adler introduced this concept as the central one (Adler, 1980).

The most elaborated version of such an approach was proposed by Victor Frankl, who was for a few years a member of Adler's circle, though always stressed the divergence between his and Adler's views. Frankl deduced the whole human activity from the basic striving to discover a meaning of one's life and to fulfill it. "Even a suicide believes in some meaning, the meaning of death, if not the meaning of life. If he did not believe in any meaning, he could not move a finger to commit the act" (Frankl, 1979, pp. 236-237). Following the basic ideas of Max Scheler's philosophical anthropology, Frankl distinguished three levels of a human person – the biological, or bodily one, the psychological, or mental one, and the spiritual, or noetic one. The last one is, according to Frankl, the level of meanings, governed by the special laws of noodynamics; thanks to these laws, a person is able to confront with the causal influences located on the two lower levels, to say "No" to external pressures and to one's own needs. Lower motivations can direct and regulate behavior only inasmuch as the person loses meaning or loses the sensitivity to its "voice" (cf. Jung, 1934/1954). As a rule, all human motivation is guided by meaning.

Parallel to this, the same principle of explanation has been introduced in somewhat different terms of valence and demand character, to oppose the associationist explanations of motivational phenomena. The concept of conditioning, put forward by Ivan Pavlov and American behaviorism, proposed the explanation of behavioral dynamics based on the laws of associations (Thorndike, 1913; 1932). There was however numerous experimental evidence that a mere association is not enough to explain goal-directed activity; what matters is not occasional associations but rather meaningful relations between the components of activity and behavioral field (Lewin, 1926; Nuttin, 1953; see also Abreu &Paixao, 2011).

In particular, Lewin has elaborated this idea in his concept of *Aufforderungscharakter*, or demand character (Lewin, 1926), a special regulatory potential acquired by the objects in the behavioral field due to their relations to the whole "tense system" of the action regulation. Demand character manifests itself in the object's "appeal" for doing something special with it (like "eat me" on a cake in Carroll's "Alice in Wonderland"). The subsequent development of this concept led, however, in the direction of its abstract formalization and quantification at the expense of qualitative peculiarities and rich phenomenology of corresponding processes. The concept of demand character degenerated into a simplified concept of the objects' valence, that is, their easily measurable approach-avoidance potential of varied intensity, a better manageable one, but lacking a big portion of original qualitative phenomenology (see Lewin, 1938). Parallel to this, Edward Tolman developed a close concept of demand (Tolman, 1932 a, b; 1951). The result was his *Expectancy x Value* model widely accepted and elaborated in the next decades; it generated a multitude of derivative models of the ways people set and pursue their goals and subgoals as means to distant goals and motives (e.g.

Atkinson, 1957; 1964; Vroom, 1964; Feather, 1982; Raynor, 1970; Raynor&Entin, 1983, to name only a few of them).

Summing up this section, by the middle of the 20th century there was a growing awareness that the concept of meaning, though still ill defined, is relevant and important for the psychology of motivation. Medard Boss, in his overview of the main trends in psychological theory, listed among others the shift from psychic cause and psychodynamics to an understanding of motivational contexts. "Psychic cause and psychodynamics cannot exist, because the psychic part of them is concerned exclusively with a person's way of relating — emotional, rational, hopeful, active, perceptive, and so forth — to what matters to him in his world, and in his dimension there are only comprehensible motivational contexts. Any psychological theory that translates a motive or motivational context into a psychic cause or a psychodynamic causal chain destroys the very foundation of human being" (Boss, 1979, p. 152).

RELATIONAL THEORY AND ACTIVITY THEORY APPROACHES TO MOTIVATION

After World War 2 the explanatory potential of the concept of meaning gradually got recognition in academic theories of motivation. In particular, Joseph Nuttin in his relational theory of human conduct treated behavior as related to a meaningful situation in the meaningful world (Nuttin, 1984, p. 23). Meaning is rooted in the relationships between situation and motivation. "The meaning of a behavior, as well as the meaning of an object is to be seen in the types of relationships existing between definite parts of the world with their special functional properties... and, on the other hand, the person needing this kind of relations to the world" (Nuttin, 1973, p. 183). "The meaningful object virtually contains the scheme of behavior" (Nuttin, 1973, p. 182). More than this, "behavior is not 'movement plus the cognitive element of meaning', but meaning that is incorporated in motor responses" (Nuttin, 1984, p. 171). The meaning of behavior is constituted by its final goal; separate behavioral "segments" acquire their meaning within the context of the whole, parts of which they are. Discussing the distinction of extrinsic vs. intrinsic motivation, Nuttin argued that the difference lies in the relations between motivation and behavior: "Generally speaking, the motivation that is extrinsic to one form of behavior is intrinsically related to another need and type of activity" (Nuttin, 1984, p. 71). Here's one of the examples he uses to illustrate this argument: "a student can engage in study behavior in order to gain his parent's affection, but he can also engage in affective behavior in order to be allowed to study. Thus, we have to deal with two types of means-end structures, and not with two basically different kinds of motivation" (ibid.)

The most elaborated view that linked human motivation to meaning has been proposed in the activity theory approach by Alexei N. Leontiev, developed through the 1940s-1970s. Leontiev's approach was based on G.W.F. Hegel's ideas of the structure of object-related activity, essentially reproduced in the writings of his disciple Karl Marx, Lev Vygotsky's theory of mediated structure of higher human mental functions, and Kurt Lewin's early theory of the action dynamics (in fact, due to pressing political and ideological contexts in the USSR, Leontiev quoted Marx rather than Hegel, and never directly referred to Lewin). In his writings the above mentioned binary opposition of personal meaning (Russian *smysl*, German *Sinn*) vs. cultural meaning (Russian *znachenie*, German *Bedeutung*) played a critical role; due to this the former term used to be translated into English as "sense", or "personal sense", and the latter as "meaning" (e.g. A.N. Leont'ev, 1978).

A.N. Leontiev defined motive as, "the object of a need – be it material or ideal, sensually perceived or existing only in imagination" (Leont'ev, 1998, p. 12). A need that is not yet objectified, that is, that has not yet found its object, cannot be called a true need. It "finds", or "meets" its object in the world; the object, after its being met and "recognized" as such, becomes the motive of an intentional activity. This process of need meeting its object, that A.N. Leontiev called "crucial", has been described by different authors in somewhat varying terms: a need meeting the situation of its gratification (Uznadze, 1940/2004), a person finding meaning (Frankl, 1979), etc.

Most human activity is multimotivational, or polimotivated, that is, determined by more than one need (A.N.Leont'ev, 1978, pp.122-123). In fact, many human activities and many objects motivating them correspond to more than one need, satisfying them or contributing to their satisfaction at the same time. The most spectacular example is money and multiple activities motivated by earning money. However, it is the relation of the object to a need or needs that makes it the motive of a goal-directed activity. Money satisfies no need, but it is meaningfully related to the satisfaction of a multitude of needs. It is, however, due to their meaning, due to the special relations between money and human needs, that it becomes a motive for human activity. For Robinson Crusoe a pack of gold founded on a crushed ship near his desert island had neither personal meaning, nor motivating power.

A.N. Leontiev distinguished three main functions of a motive: driving, directing and sense-forming (meaning-making) ones, sometimes merging the first two of them. The sense-forming function underlies the distinction of two classes of motives: sense-forming (meaning-making) motives and stimuli motives deprived of meaning-making function (A.N.Leont'ev, 1978; 1998). This distinction is similar to the distinction of extrinsic vs. intrinsic motivation (Deci, 1971; Deci, Flaste, 1995). A special analysis (D. Leontiev, 1999) revealed that meaning-making function, that is relating to superordinate meaning-making contexts, needs and values, underlies the motivating power of any motives; if this meaningful link is broken, no driving or directing can occur. What distinguishes between both types of motives is the following: "sense-forming motives" are tied with corresponding needs and values in a natural way; the satisfaction one gets from fulfilling the activity is intrinsically implied by the nature of the activity (having a dinner in a restaurant in order to satiate hunger or to enjoy the chef's art). "Stimuli motives" are tied with the corresponding needs in a conventional, conditioned, occasional or other alienated way not implied by the nature of activity itself (having a dinner in a restaurant in order to facilitate flirtation or to beat a food consumption record in the Guinness Book of Records). In the second cases the activity may be said to have an extrinsic meaning rather than no meaning; however, the motivating power is also meaning-dependent, for it pertains as long as the relation between the activity and underlying need or value (flirtation failure may cause the complete loss of appetite in the above example).

The concept of motive has been first introduced by A.N. Leontiev (1936/2009) for extrinsic, alienated motives only to explain the cases when children fulfill some activity for the sake of something that does not coincide with its goal, that is, its anticipated result. Amazingly, A.N. Leontiev showed that this type of motivation, when motive and goal are not the same, makes the child's activity more stable and engaged than the intrinsic interest to the content of activity. Indeed, doing something for the sake of something different is characteristic of humans only. All human labor activity, based on the division of labor and specialization, self-discipline and delay of gratification, social regulations and moral choice, etc. is structured this way: what the subject is doing does not immediately explain why he or she is doing this. The activity however has a definite meaning, that is, is related to the meaning-making contexts that provide such a motivational explanation. The meaning-based explanation of motivation underlying any human activity includes two necessary components: the reference to the superordinate need(s) and/ or value(s), that are the source of the motivating power, and the reference to the special psycho-logical structure of relations that tie the motive to this source and explain the channeling of this motivating power through the given activity and its motive. Recently some theories have been proposed construing the structure of such relations (e.g. Smedslund, 1988; D.Leontiev,1999); however, the first and still unbeaten version is Spinoza's "Ethics".

Explaining motivation in terms of activity related to meaning contexts finds additional support in the activity theory approach to volitional regulation (Ivannikov, 1991). Volition is explained in this theory as deliberate regulation of the driving force of a motive (its increase or decrease) by means of establishing or cutting the relations of the given activity to various motivational contexts, and thus changing the personal meaning of this motive. For instance, a promise or an oath to do something plugs the motivational energy of self-esteem to the action that otherwise could have littlemotivation of its own.

Summing up, within the activity theory approach (A.N.Leont'ev, 1978; D. Leontiev, 1999; 2007) motivation is explained in terms of meaning, and meaning, in its turn, in terms of relations to the world. It is a meaningful relationship rooted in the being-in-the-world that connects a person with a situation, rather than an oblique cross between them. Activity theory approach and Nuttin's relational theory are thus forerunners of more recent models based on the assumption than meaning is a relation (Baumeister&Vohs, 2002; Heine, Proulx, &Vohs, 2006). When we say that something is meaningful or meaningless, it is basically about structure. A word is meaningful inasmuch as it is understood and linked to the context; a life is meaningful inasmuch as it is coherent and linked to a larger whole. Coherence and connectedness account for meaningfulness; fragmentation (dissociation) and disconnectedness (alienation) decrease meaning. A motive of the current activity is its intentional object that becomes in the given situation the focus of the subject's significant relations to the world. It possesses the motivating power due to its meaning, its being related to what is ultimately significant for the subject, be it due to its inherent nature, as in the case of intrinsic motivation, or due to learned or forced links, as in the case of extrinsic motivation. In turn, the goal is the anticipated result that is meaningfully related to the motive; it is only due to this relation that a goal may direct an action.

Unlike Lewin's concept of valence, A.N. Leontiev's concept of personal meaning has maintained and even deepened the qualitative aspect of the idea of demand quality of things due to their correspondence to needs or intentions at the expense of poor quantification and prediction of these processes. In other words, activity theory approach to motivation and self-regulation in terms of personal meaning gave due respect to the dynamic, fluent, Protean qualities of motivational processes, presenting a model that is qualitative, rather than quantitative, continual, rather than discrete, irrational, rather than rational, processual, rather than structural. Personal meaning transcends the ancient dichotomy *cognitive vs affective*; its nature cannot be reduced to one or another; it is much closer to what S. Epstein (1990) called experiential conceptual system. Meaning relations is the common denominator for such explanatory concepts as psychodynamics, conditioning, imprinting, valence, instrumentality, and attribution, to list only the most important ones.

ATTRIBUTION SCHEMESAS MEANING RELATIONS

In the recent decades the psychology of motivation assimilated many findings and concepts of cognitive psychology, including the concept of beliefs or representations about varying structural relations (in fact, meaning relations) between the goals of one's actions, its means, the motives, actual outcomes and their determinants. Instrumentality (Vroom, 1964; Emmons, 1999) and self-efficacy (Bandura, 1997) refer to the contingency between means and goals; locus of control (Rotter, 1966) and attributional pattern (Weiner, 1974) to the contingency between result and its causes; learned helplessness (Seligman, 1975; 1990) to the contingency between efforts and the outcome; causality orientations (Deci& Ryan, 1985) to the contingency between action and its determinants, etc. E. Skinner (1995; 1996) has conveniently classified various types of such relations and corresponding attributional schemes into (1) *means-ends* relations and strategy beliefs about them; (2) *agent-means* relations and capacity beliefs about them; (3) *agent-ends* relations and control beliefs about them. I add to this list (4) post-action relations between the action's *outcomes* and their desirable *consequences* (see Heckhausen&Kuhl, 1985) and implication beliefs about them and (5) pre-action relations between one's *wish and the goal* one is committed to and determinism beliefs about them. All five kinds of above relationships mentioned above (there may be some others missed so far) may be conceptualized as special forms of *if-then* behavioral relationships and contingency beliefs about them. W. Mishel called such *if-then* patterns "behavioral signatures of personality" claiming that "such reliable patterns of behavior variability characterize individuals distinctively as a rule, rather than an exception" (Mischel, 2004, p.8).

By attributional schemes I understand all these kinds of contingencies, which an individual may consider existing or nonexisting, effective or ineffective. It would be misleading to call them cognitive representations, for cognition refers to the identification of environmental invariants (Royce & Powell, 1983, p.11), that is, of something existing independent of cognition itself. Attribution does not reflect anything existing there "in reality"; it cannot be right or wrong. The ideas that one's successes or failures are due to one's efforts or due to external controlling forces are self-fulfilling constructions. They are "right" in a practical sense, because behaving in line with some attributional idea produces outcomes concordant with the initial idea; at the same time they are "wrong" in a gnosiological sense, because they don't correspond to any objective fact. However, any attributional scheme creates a meaning-making context that defines the meaning of an action: viewed in the helplessness context, any action is meaningless, while viewed in the high self-efficacy context, it appears as a way toward the goal; in the context of external control it is experienced as coercive, and in the context of autonomous causality as authentic. This evidently makes a great difference for the key parameters of motivation and action regulation. Researchers of such a closely related field as coping also note"attributions play a wider role in meaning-related processes than previous researchers have acknowledged" (Park &Folkman, 1997, p. 127).

Quite explicit treatment of attributions in terms of meaning-making contexts was proposed by D.C. Molden and C.S. Dweck (Molden&Dweck, 2000; 2006; Dweck&Molden, 2005). They examine "how the meaning that people assign to an achievement situation affects their motivation — how it affects the goals they pursue, the effectiveness with which they pursue them, and the interest and enjoyment that accompanies their pursuit" (Molden&Dweck, 2000, p. 131). Without referring to above mentioned authors outside the achievement motivation tradition, they come to essentially the same conceptualization: "The fundamental question that goal-based theories ask — 'What is the purpose toward which a person's strivings are directed?' — must be amended by 'What meaning does this purpose have for the person who has undertaken it'" (Molden&Dweck, 2000, p. 137). Meaning is defined here in terms of Dweck's well-known conceptualization of implicit theories of intelligence, or self-theories. She distinguished two principal kinds of such lay theories: *entity theory*, suggesting that intelligence is something that is fixed and cannot substantially change over time, and *incremental theory,* suggesting that intelligence is malleable.

Dweck and Molden state that different theories create different systems of meaning. Experimental studies support the hypothesis that these different meaning-making contexts have diverging consequences for goal choice, intrinsic motivation and behavior. E.g., Mueller and Dweck (1998) in their studies compared different forms of praise for students' performance: praise for intelligence, praise for effort and unspecified praise. Six studies revealed manifold differences in performance predicted by the student's implicit theory and the type of praise; combination of both factors accounts for the special meaning a success or failure may acquire. "People for whom an achievement task is measuring something permanent behaved markedly different from people for whom an achievement task reveals information only about an immediate process, like effort, or a malleable skill" (Molden&Dweck, 2000, p. 152). More recent studies overviewed by Dweck&Molden (2005) and Molden&Dweck (2006) confirm substantial effects of these two underlying meaning systems on coping with failure, resisting stereotype threat, responding to social challenges, coping with dysphoria, and many other domains. Besides, entity self-theory has proved to covariate with a broader concept of lay dispositionism, phrased by Ross and Nisbett (1991). "In summary, research on people's lay theories of personality has shown that, beyond any culturally shared assumptions about social behavior or universal principles for the processing of social information, the distinct meaning created by different beliefs about personality can have profound effects on social perception and social information processing" (Molden&Dweck, 2006, p. 199).

The authors conclude that meaning systems built around lay theories affect behavior and coping due to contrasting idea of competence. "An entity theory creates a meaning system focused on the goal of measuring and validating competence, and is thus associated with ability-oriented performance goals, ability attributions for setbacks, and the belief that effort indicates low ability... An incremental theory, in contrast, creates a meaning system built around the acquisition of competence and is thus linked to learning goals, effort and strategy attributions for setbacks, and the belief that effort increases ability" (Dweck&Molden, 2005, p. 137).

The theory developed by Dweck and Molden is the first experimentally founded attempt of introducing the idea of meaning into attribution-based motivation theory. To be sure, incremental vs. entity theories of intelligence or competence is just one of many meaning-making contexts that account for major differences in action regulation. Another meaning-making context of this kind is exemplified by the implicit belief in willpower as a limited resource in line with the self-control theory (Baumeister, Vohs, & Tice, 2007) as opposed to the belief in unlimited resource of control. In a recent study (Job, Dweck, & Walton, 2010) it was shown that implicit willpower theories predict whether the ego-depletion effect, described by the self-control theory, occurs. In particular, these implicit theories account for self-regulation in the real world. It is amazing that the degree of felt exhaustion after stressing tasks did not vary depending on the implicit theory; what indeed varied was the relation between the exhaustion and subsequent effort and performance! However, though this study has much in common with that of Dweck and Molden (the main difference is in the implicit theory taken as the independent variable), there was no direct mention of meaning in this publication.

One more relevant example presents R. Ryan's research on varied psychological meaning of rewards. In fact, the same reward may be interpreted by the person in a radically different way, either as a means of control, or as an acknowledgement of a job well done. Depending on which psychological meaning is attributed to the reward, the latter has different psychological consequences (see Ryan, 1982; Koestner at.al.,1984; Deci&Flaste, 1995).

What follows from this line of research is that the components of activity regulation (the agent, goal, means, motive), being meaningfully linked to a coherent system, make a necessary condition for the activity to be properly motivated and successful, or even to start and pertain. An open question is still whether these links are just cognitive representations, ideas, as most mentioned approaches assume, or are ontologically grounded beyond their mental representations, as it is implied by meaning regulation theory.

CONCLUSION

As I tried to show, there is growing evidence that the concept of meaning as intentional relation of activity components to broader contexts may serve as the integrative basis for the explanation of human motivational processes. This concept makes it possible to bring together the multitude of definitions of meaning, on the one hand, and psychological theories of motivation, on the other. Beginning with Freud and Adler, many motivation theorists felt the need of integrating the concept of meaning into their explanatory models. All these attempts could not be finally successful because of the lack of common terminology and of shared understanding over what is meaning. In the second half of the last century, elaborated motivation theories have appeared (J. Nuttin and A.N. Leontiev) that have explicitly built the concept of meaning into general models of human conduct; unfortunately, these theories did not win much recognition outside their countries of origin.

Present-day theories seem to be still more ready to assimilate the concept of meaning. The main benefits from this are the following. First, the meaning emphasis allows better considering the qualitative–phenomenological side of human motivation, largely neglected by both behaviorist and social-cognitive theories. Second, understanding motivation as an aspect of meaning dynamics may serve as the common denominator and the unifying theoretical frame for diverse processes and regularities, from the global meaning of life to minor "current concerns", thoroughly studied in special branches and problem contexts and described in special languages, including both academic and applied approaches, both "depth" and "height" psychology.

REFERENCES

Abreu, M. V. &Paixao, M. P. (2011). Motivational foundations of learning and motivational strategy for educational practice. In D. Leontiev (Ed.), *Motivation, consciousness, and self-regulation* (pp. 000-000). New York: Nova Science Publishers.

Adler, A. (1980). *Whatlife should mean to you*. London: Allen and Unwin.

[Asmolov, A. G.] (1987). Motivation. In A. V. Petrovsky, & M. G. Yaroshevsky (Eds.), *A Concise Psychological Dictionary* (p.193). Moscow: Progress Publishers.

Atkinson, J. W. (1957). Motivational determinants of risk-taking behavior.*Psychological Review, 64*, 359-372.

Atkinson, J. W. (1964). *An Introduction to Motivation*. Princeton, NJ: Van Nostrand.

Bakhtin, M. M. (1979).*Estetikaslovesnogotvorchestva.(Aesthetics of literary creativity)*. Moscow: Iskusstvo.

Bateson, G. (2002). *Mind and Nature: A Necessary Unity*. Cresskil, NJ: Hampton Press, Inc.

Bandura, A. (1997). *Self-efficacy: the exercise of control*. New York: W.H.Freeman& Co.

Baumeister, R. F., &Vohs, K. D. (2002). The pursuit of meaningfulness in life. In C. R. Snyder, & S. J. Lopez (Eds.), *Handbook of Positive Psychology* (pp. 608-617). New York: Oxford University Press.

Baumeister, R. F., Vohs, K. D., & Tice, D. M. (2007). The strength model of self-control.*Current Directions in Psychological Science, 16*, 351-355.

Boss, M. (1979). *Existential Foundations of Medicine and Psychology*. New York; London: Jason Aronson.

Carver, C., &Scheier, M.(1998). *On the Self-Regulation of Behavior*. New York: Cambridge University Press.

Deci, E. L. (1971). Effects of externally mediated rewards on intrinsic motivation.*Journal of personality and social psychology, 18,* 105-115.

Deci, E., &Flaste, R. (1995). *Why We Do What We Do: Understanding Self-motivation*. New York: Penguin.

Deci E., & Ryan R. (1985). *Intrinsic motivation and self-determination in human behavior.* New York: Plenum.

Deci, E. L., & Ryan, R.M. (2008). Facilitating optimal motivation and psychological well-being across life's domains. *Canadian Psychology, 49*, 14-23.

Dweck, C. S., &Molden, D. C. (2005). Self-theories: Their impact on competence motivation and acquisition. In A. J. Elliot, & C. S. Dweck (Eds), *Handbook of Competence and Motivation* (pp. 122-140). New York: Guilford.

Emmons, R. (1999). *The Psychology of Ultimate Concerns*.New York: Guilford.

Epstein, S. (1990). Cognitive-experiential self-theory. In L. A. Pervin (Ed.), *Handbook of Personality Theory and Research* (pp.165-192). New York: The Guilford Press.

Feather, N. (Ed.) (1982).*Expectations and actions: Expectancy-value model in psychology*. Hillsdale, NJ: Erlbaum.

Frankl, V. E. (1979). *Der Mensch vor der Fragenachdem Sinn*.München: Piper.

Frankl, V. E. (1985). Logos, Paradox, and the Search for Meaning. In M. Mahoney, & A. Freeman (Eds.), *Cognition and Psychotherapy* (p.259-275). New York: Plenum.

Freud, S. (1916). Introductory Lectures on Psycho-Analysis. *The Standard Edition of theComplete Psychological Works of Sigmund Freud, Volume XV (1915-1916): IntroductoryLectures on Psycho-analysis (Parts I and II)*, 1-240.

Heckhausen, H. ,&Kuhl, J. (1985). From wishes to action: the dead ends and short cuts on the long way to action. In M. Frese, & J. Sabini (Eds.), *Goal Directed Behavior: The Concept of Action in Psychology* (pp. 134-159). Hillsdale, NJ: Lawrence Erlbaum.

Heine, S. J., Proulx, T., &Vohs, K. D. (2006). The meaning maintenance model: On the coherence of social motivations. *Personality and Social Psychology Review, 10*, 88-110.

Ivannikov, V. A. (1991). *Psikhologicheskiyemekhanizmyvolevoiregulatsii (Psychological mechanisms of volitional regulation)*. Moscow: Moscow University Press.

Job, V., Dweck, C. S., & Walton, G. M. (2010). Ego depletion — is it all in your head? Implicit theories about willpower affect self-regulation. *Psychological Science, 21*, 1686-1693.

Jung, C. G. (1954).The development of personality (Originally published 1934).In *The collected works of C.G.Jung.Vol. 17* (pp. 167-186). London: Routledge and Kegan Paul.

Koestner, R., Ryan, R. M., Bernieri, F., & Holt, K (1984). Setting limits on children's behavior: The differential effects of controlling versus informational styles on children's intrinsic motivation and creativity. *Journal of Personality, 54*, 233-248.

Leont'ev, A. N. (1978). *Activity, Consciousness, and Personality*. Englewood Cliffs, NJ: Prentice-Hall.

Leont'ev, A. N. (1998) Bedürfnisse, Motive und Emotionen.*Mitteilungen der Luria-Gesellschaft*, Jg. 5, No 1, S. 4-32.

Leontiev, A. N. (1936/2009). Psikhologicheskoe issledovanie detskikh interesov vo Dvortse pionerov I oktyabryat (Psychological investigation of children's interests). In Leontiev, A. N. *Psikhologicheskie osnove razvitiya rebenkai obucheniya (Psychological Foundations of Child Development and Education)* (pp.46-100). Moscow: Smysl.

Leontiev, D. A. (1996).Dimensions of the meaning/sense concept in the psychological context. In C. Tolman, F. Cherry, R. van Hezewijk, & I. Lubek (Eds), *Problems of theoretical psychology,* (pp.130-142). New York: Captus University Publications.

Leontiev, D. A. (1999). *Psikhologiyasmysla (The psychology of personal meaning)*. Moscow: Smysl.

Leontiev, D. (2004). Obscheepredstavlenie o motivatsiicheloveka (General conception of human motivation). *Psikhologiya v vuze*, No 1, 51-65.

Leontiev, D. (2007). The phenomenon of meaning: How psychology can make sense of it. In P. T. P. Wong, L. Wong, M. J. McDonald, & D. K. Klaassen, (Eds.), *The Positive Psychology of Meaning and Spirituality* (pp. 33-44). Abbotsford, BC, Canada: INPM Press.

Leontiev, D. (2011). From Drive To Need and Further: What is human motivation about? In D. Leontiev (Ed.), *Motivation, consciousness, and self-regulation* (pp. 00-00). New York: Nova Science Publishers.

Lewin, K.(1926). *Vorsatz, Wille, und Bedürfnis*. Berlin: Verlag von Julius Springer.

Lewin, K. (1938). *The conceptual representation and the measurement of psychological forces*. Durham, NC: Duke University press.

Mischel, W. (2004). Toward an integrative science of the person.*Annual Review of Psychology, 55*, 1-22.

Molden, D. C., &Dweck, C. S. (2000).Meaning and motivation. In C. Sansone, & J. M. Harackiewicz (Eds.), *Intrinsic and Extrinsic Motivation: The Search for Optimal Motivation and Performance* (pp. 131-159). San Diego: Academic Press.

Molden, D. C., &Dweck, C. S. (2006). Finding "Meaning" in Psychology: A lay theories approach to self-regulation, social perception, and social development. *American Psychologist, 61,* 192-203.

Mueller, C. M., &Dweck, C. S. (1998). Intelligence praise can undermine motivation and performance. *Journal of Personality and Social Psychology, 75*, 33-52.

Nuttin, J.(1953).*Tâche, réussite et échec: Théorie de la conduite humaine.* Louvain, Publications Universitaires.

Nuttin, J. (1973). Das Verhalten des Menschen; der Mensch in seiner Erscheinungswelt. In H. G. Gadamer (Ed.), *PsychologischeAntropologie* (pp. 163-199). Stuttgart: Georg ThiemeVerlag.

Nuttin,J. (1984). *Motivation, Planning, and Action: a Relational Theory of Behavior Dynamics.* Leuven: Leuven University Press; Hillsdale, NJ: Lawrence Erlbaum Associates.

Park, C. L., &Folkman, S. (1997). Meaning in the context of stress and coping. *Review of General Psychology, 1*, 115-144.

Patyaeva, E. Yu. (1983). Situativnoyerazvitie I urovnimotivatsii (Situational development and levels of motivation).*VestnikMoskovskogoUniversiteta, Ser. 14 Psikhologiya*, No. 4, 23-33.

Rotter, J. B. (1966).Generalized expectancies of internal versus external control of reinforcements.*Psychological Monographs, 80* (whole no. 609).

Raynor, J. O. (1970). Relationship between achievement-related motives, future orientation, and academic performance.*J. of Personality and Social Psychology, 15*, 28-33.

Raynor, J. O., &Entin, E. E. (1983).The function of future orientation as a determinant of human behavior in step-path theory of action.*International J. of Psychology, 18*, 463-487.

Ross, L., &Nisbett, R. E. (1991). *The person and the situation: Perspectives of social psychology.* New York: McGraw-Hill.

Royce, J. R., & Powell, A. (1983). *Theory of personality and individual differences.* Englewood Cliffs, NJ: Prentice-Hall.

Ryan, R. M. (1982). Control and information in the intrapersonal sphere: An extension of cognitive evaluation theory. *Journal of Personality and Social Psychology*, 43, 450-461

Seligman, M. E. P. (1975).*Helplessness: On depression, development, and death.* San Francisco: Freeman.

Seligman, M. E. P. (1990).*Learned Optimism.* New York: Simon & Schuster.

Skinner, E. A. (1995). *Perceived Control, Motivation, and Coping.* Thousand Oaks, CA: Sage.

Skinner, E. A. (1996). A guide to constructs of control.*Journal of Personality and Social Psychology, 71,* 549 –570.

Smedslund, J. (1988). *Psycho-logic.* Heidelberg: Springer.

Thorndike, E. L. (1911). *Animal Intelligence.* New York: MacMillan.

Thorndike, E. L. (1932). *The Fundamentals of Learning.* New York: Teachers College.

Tolman, E. C. (1932 a).Lewin's concept of vectors.*J. of General Psychology, 7*, 3-15.

Tolman, E. C. (1932 b).*Purposive behavior in animals and men*. New York: The Century C*.

Tolman, E. C. (1951).A psychological model. In T. Parsons, & E. Shils (Eds.), *Toward a general theory of action* (pp. 277-361). Cambridge: Harvard University press.

Uznadze, D. N. (1940/2004).*ObschayaPsikhologiya (General Psychology)*. Moscow: Smysl; St.Petersburg: Piter-Press.

Vroom, V. H. (1964).*Work and motivation*. New York: Wiley.

Weiner, B. (1974). *Achievement motivation and attribution theory*. Morristown, NJ: General Learning Press.

In: Motivation, Consciousness and Self-Regulation
Editor: D. A. Leontiev, pp. 79-89

ISBN: 978-1-61324-795-2
© 2012 Nova Science Publishers, Inc.

Chapter 6

MOTIVATIONAL COMPETENCE: THE JOINT EFFECT OF IMPLICIT AND EXPLICIT MOTIVES ON SELF-REGULATION AND FLOW EXPERIENCE

Falko Rheinberg and Stefan Engeser

University of Potsdam and University of Trier, Germany

ABSTRACT

The following chapter is based theoretically on motivational psychology. It links the concepts of (1) implicit vs. explicit motives sensu David McClelland (1985), (2) Mihaly Csikszentmihalyi's (1975, 1997) concept of Flow Experience, and (3) Heinz Heckhausen's concept of volition and action (Heckhausen, 1977, Rheinberg, 2008). The core concept that links these three constructs is *Motivational Competence*, which is defined as "a person's competence to set goals in such a way that they can pursue the goals efficiently without being forced into permanent volitional control of his or her own actions" (Rheinberg, 2008; Rheinberg & Engeser, 2010). Empirical data how motivational competence could be measured and data supporting our assumption are presented.

Keywords: Motivational competence, implicit motive, explicit motive, volition, self-regulation, flow

INTRODUCTION

Of course, situations and/or other people sometimes dictate the goals for which we are to strive. However, there are broad areas in our everyday lives where we can set goals or select projects based on our own decisions. This is particularly the case for leisure time pursuits. If we focus on these areas of life, we see people engaged in activities which they obviously like very much. Even if their activities are challenging, risky or strenuous, they seem to function smoothly; they are totally absorbed by what they are doing and show further characteristics of Flow.

Nevertheless, in the same type of situation, we can also observe people who need all of their volitional and self-regulatory resources to force themselves to pursue the goals they have set themselves. The freely chosen activities seem to be hard, demand continuous self-control and cause negative feelings. Their self-chosen projects turn out to be unpleasant duties. How can this happen?

IMPLICIT VS. EXPLICIT MOTIVES

In the late 1980s and early 1990s, the distinction of two basically different kinds of motive systems that cause human striving were much regarded and influential in terms of our thinking on motivation (cf. Brunstein, 2008; Schultheiss & Brunstein, 2010). These are the *implicit* vs. the *self attributed motives*. Self attributed motives are also referred as explicit motives. The main characteristics of both motive systems are contrasted in Table 1.

Traditionally, motives such as need achievement, need power, or need affiliation have been assessed using projective measures, traditionally the Thematic Apperception Test (TAT; McClelland, 1985), which is today also referred to as the Picture Story Exercise (PSE; Pang & Schultheiss, 2005). In addition, the Grid Technique is often used as a semi-projective measure (Schmalt, Sokolowski, & Langens, 2000). These measures reflect individual differences in preferred incentives and types of activities. Most importantly, they operate below the level of person's self-perception and conscious self-description. They are *implicit* in person's perceptions and operations. Thus, McClelland called these motives "implicit".

Table 1. Some characteristics of implicit and self-attributed motives (McClelland, 1985; Weinberger & McClelland, 1990)

Implicit (basic) motives	Self-attributed motives (motivational self-concept; explicit motives)
Affective core	Cognitive core
Biologically based; particular hormone profile	Based on self-schemata
Non-conscious	Conscious self-representations
Triggered by situational cues that indicate rewarding types of activity	Activated by evaluations of expected outcomes, goals and consequences and by ego-involvement
Individual differences are due to genetic factors and early prelinguistic learning	Individual differences are due to linguistically based learning and communications/ attributions
Projective measures (TAT; Grid)	Self-report (questionnaire)

The main characteristics of these implicit motive systems are shown on the left-hand side of table 1: they have an affective core, are biologically based and non-conscious. Implicit motives are triggered by the chance to perform rewarding activities. Individual differences in implicit motives are due to genetic and pre-linguistic learning. As already mentioned, implicit motives can be captured using projective measurement.

If people are asked what is important and valuable in their lives and what things they usually prefer and strive for, then they do *not* generally give these implicit motives because humans are not usually aware of these basic and implicit systems. Instead, people will offer information about their self-attributed motives, as McClelland and others called these verbalized and consciously represented types of motives. We will refer to these as *motivational self-concepts* or *explicit motives*. If questionnaires are used to assess motivation, then these motivational self-concepts are being measured. The right-hand side of Table 1 shows the main characteristics of this self-system: it has a cognitive core and is based on conscious self-schemata. The self-system is formed, learned and coded linguistically and is measured via questionnaires.

The correlation between the two types of motive systems is surprisingly low, or even non-existent (cf. Spangler, 1992; Brunstein, 2008). One implication of this is that for many persons, the motivational self-concept is in line with their implicit motives. However, there are also a great number of people whose consciously represented schema of their own preferences and values differs substantially from their implicit motives.

Whether or not people's motivational self concept is in line with their implicit motives is quite important. Following McClelland (1985), implicit motives influence what type of situations and activities are stimulating and rewarding for a person. For instance, a woman with a strong implicit achievement motive feels good when she is engaged in challenging activities and has the sensation that she is operating effectively and perfectly – with the feeling of increasing her competence (cf. Brunstein & Heckhausen, 2008).

Figure 1 will illustrate the influence of the implicit motive and motivational self-concepts on action. The figure is based on the extended cognitive model of motivation by Heckhausen (1977) and the modification by Rheinberg (1989; cf. Rheinberg, 2008). In a given situation, we act to obtain outcomes which have attractive consequences for us. The link between the outcome and the consequences is also called instrumentality. This strictly rational representation of motivation based on the consequences was later extended with incentives that are inherent in the activity itself (task-related incentives; Rheinberg, 1989). Linking motives to this model, implicit motives have a strong impact on the incentives of the activity, as represented by a thick arrow directed from "implicit motives" to "action". Motivational self-concepts will impact the incentives of the expected consequences, with a thick arrow from the "motivational self-concept (explicit motives)" to the "expected consequences".

The motivational self-concept, however, has its main impact on the intended consequences. These are the goals of actions. In particular, if an individual thinks about the value of a goal in question and whether or not this goal fits with his or her values, she or he is operating with his or her motivational self-concept, because this is the basis of information which his or her conscious and deliberate evaluation process can use (cf. Schultheiss, 2008).

If you pursue a valuable goal where the goal leading action fits your implicit motives, you are in a comfortable situation; your implicit motives support your way to the goal. The type of activity you have to perform is attractive and rewarding for you. Thus, there is no need to force yourself on the path leading to the goal. And, after all, you have even produced outcomes that have desirable consequences.

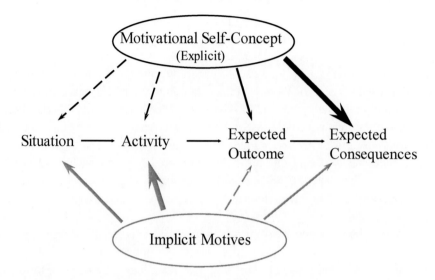

Figure 1. The structure of action (Heckhausen, 1977) and the hypothesized impact of implicit motives and motivational self-concepts (Rheinberg & Engeser, 2010).

Now imagine the following situation: You have decided or have been forced to reach a valuable goal, but the activities leading to the goal do not fit with your implicit motives. For example: You think it is important for your university to invest more money to foster excellent research projects and invest less money into tutoring programs for students – or *vice versa*. To reach this goal, you would have to influence the opinions of your colleagues; you would have to convince important leaders of your university and so on. All of these activities are most attractive for people with a strong implicit power motive. Such people love this type of activity anyway.

However, if you lack this implicit power motive, influencing other people has no incentive *per se*. Thus, you have to focus a lot of attention and place a lot of control on yourself to pursue the important goal. You have to make sure that you really get started with the activities leading to the goal and that you continue with the actions you don't really like. This structure demands a continuous volitionary self-control. Over and over again, you have to create a conscious representation of the goal state and its valuable consequences. You can't flow with your preferred action tendencies.

Table 2. The components of motivational competence

1.	Congruence between one's implicit motives and self-attributed motives
2.	The ability to evaluate the potential incentives of future situations
3.	The Ability to enrich situations with motive-congruent incentives
4.	Commitment to long-term projects not only based on benefits upon their completion, but also on the pleasure derived from the engagement in the activities themselves
5.	Metamotivational knowledge, that is the knowledge of thoughts / internal pictures that increase vs. decrease the current motivation
6.	In achievement-oriented societies: an additional component may be the knowledge of how to elicit a success-oriented motivational state (Rheinberg & Engeser, 2010).

STRIVING FOR MOTIVE-(IN)CONGRUENT GOALS

Brunstein and colleagues found out that pursuing motive-incongruent goals does not cause overwhelming happiness – even if you have succeeded in reaching your goal (Brunstein, Schultheiss, & Grässmann, 1998). In their study, students described the goals they were trying to reach in the following few weeks. Goals were coded for achievement, power, affiliation and intimacy. Subsequently, participants continuously rated (1) their emotional well-being, and (2) their progress in reaching these goals. At the beginning of the study, the students' implicit motives had been assessed using the TAT. Progress toward pursued goals increased emotional well-being only for those persons whose goals were congruent with their dominant implicit motive. High commitment to motive-incongruent goals decreased emotional well-being.

MOTIVATIONAL COMPETENCE

What makes a student pursue a motive-incongruent goal? As stated above, situational constraints, or other people, sometimes have the power to dictate our goals to us. However, in our leisure time, we are quite free to choose the activities we like to do. Why, then, not all people do engage in activities that fit with their implicit motives? We assume that this is partly due to a person's motivational competence, and refers to the capacity to make motive-congruent decisions. It is the person's ability to reconcile *current* and *future* situations with his or her activity preferences such that he or she can function effectively, without the need for permanent volitional control (Rheinberg, 2008). Table 2 shows the main components of this construct.

This represents the congruence between a person's implicit motives and his or her motivational self-concept. If a person is misinformed about his or her basic motives, he or she is frequently in danger of taking on goals that require activities that do not fit with his or her motive-determined action preferences. In contrast, people with high congruence between implicit motives and motivational self-concept have increased probabilities of engaging in projects that require activities that fit with their implicit motives. If our consciously selected goal and the activity leading to the goal both refer to the same preferred type of motivation, our whole capacity can flow into the action and we will be totally absorbed by it. We call this the *Flow hypothesis of motivational competence* (Rheinberg, 2004).

We measure Flow with the *Flow-Short-Scale* (FKS, Rheinberg, Vollmeyer, & Engeser 2003; Engeser & Rheinberg, 2008). This scale allows the assessment of all components of the Flow state within 40 seconds, with items such as "I am completely absorbed in what I am doing", "I know what I have to do each step of the way" and "I feel that I have everything under control". The scale is highly homogeneous (Cronbach's alpha .85> .94) and standardized with T-norms (for T-norms, see Rheinberg, 2004).

FIRST EMPIRICAL EVIDENCE:
MOTIVATIONAL COMPETENCE AND FLOW

Clavadetscher (2003) investigated $N = 60$ adults who devoted their leisure time to a non-profit club that supports concerts in the Swiss city of Bern. Club members can do quite different things for the club – from drafting beer in the bar to organizing and managing a concert. Using the *Flow Short Scale*, Clavadetscher assessed the Flow state which a club member experienced with the activity he or she had chosen.

Members' implicit motives for achievement, power and affiliation were measured with the Multi-Motive Grid from Schmalt et al. (2000). The motivational self-concept was measured with the Personal Research Form (PRF) from Jackson (1984). Each measure was z-standardized. Thus, it was possible to determine the difference between the implicit motive and the motivational self-concept for each of the three motives and sum it up. This sum was subtracted from an arbitrary constant in order to reach a positive score for the motive-congruence, which is our core variable for motivational competence.

The correlation between this estimation of motivational competence and Flow is $r = .34$ and is significant (p <. 01). This coefficient is not particularly high. However, two issues need to be taken into account here: (1) Motivational competence is only *one* out of *several* factors that influence Flow, and (2) Motive congruence is only *one* out of *several* components of motivational competence.

MOTIVATIONAL COMPETENCE, SELF-REGULATION, AND FLOW

A more complex study related motivational competence, self-regulation and Flow to one another. Engeser (2009) investigated $N = 246$ psychology students taking part in statistics courses (University of Potsdam and Technical University of Berlin). Among many other variables, he measured students' implicit achievement motive with the TAT according to Winter (1991). Students' self-concept of achievement motivation was measured with the PRF from Jackson (1984). One dependent variable was the *Self-regulation scale* (SSI) from Kuhl & Fuhrmann (2001). This scale measures different modes of attaining and sticking to the actions leading to a goal.

Persons high in self-regulation often have the feeling of self-determination and of being the origin of their own action. A typical item is: "I'm usually sure that the things I do depend on my own will and decisions". As expected, this mode of self-regulation is correlated significantly with motivational competence as measured in the aforementioned study by Clavadetscher ($r = .25; p < .01$).

However, Engeser analyzed not only the difference but also the interaction between the implicit motive and the motivational self-concept. Figure 2 shows the z-scores for self-regulation. The solid line represents participants with low scores for implicit achievement motives, while the dashed line stands for high scores. Now, if the implicit achievement motive is low (the solid line), it becomes quite irrelevant whether or not the student believes him or herself to be achievement-motivated. The solid line is rather flat. However, if the implicit achievement motive is strong (the dashed line), then it becomes important what the student thinks about his own achievement motivation.

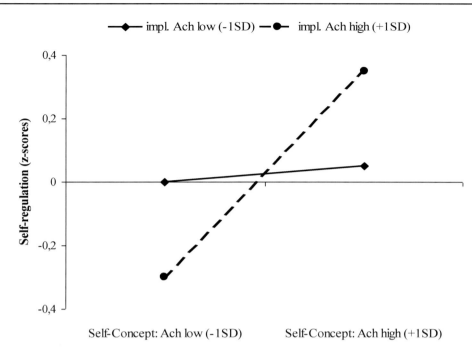

Figure 2. Self-regulation, implicit achievement motive and self-concept of achievement motivation (Engeser, 2009).

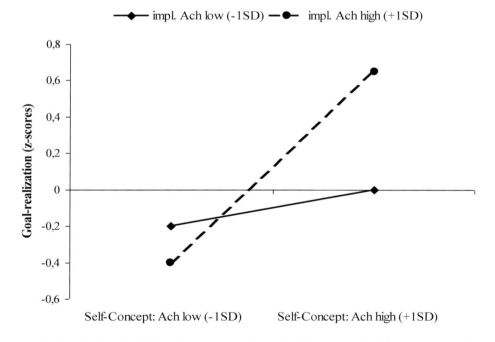

Figure 3. Goal-realization, implicit achievement motive and self-concept of achievement motivation (Engeser, 2009).

If the student has an appropriate self-concept of his or her own motivation, the self-regulation score is high: the student often feels that he or she is the origin of his or her own activities. The interaction between *implicit achievement motive* and *self-concept of one's own achievement motivation is also* significant; $t(236)$ = 2.22; p < .05. This is exactly what we should predict for persons with high motivational competence. Such persons set themselves goals that allow them to carry out activities that fit in with their implicit motives. Thus, they increase the chance of rewarding experiences and flow during goal-pursuing.

Most interesting are the students who are actually high in their implicit achievement motive but attribute themselves a low tendency for achievement-related striving. This combination is detrimental for self-regulation. We assume that the wrong concept of one's own preferences and values hinders these students from doing the things that would be supported by their implicit motive. Thus, they miss many chances to feel themselves to be the origin of their own actions and projects.

Data for *goal-realization* show a somewhat similar structure (see Figure 3). The dependent variable is goal-realization (SSI, Kuhl & Fuhrmann, 2001). This scale refers to persistence and strategies to optimize one's own goal-striving. A typical item is: "Once I have decided to go for a goal, I don't quit."

If the implicit achievement motive is actually low - i.e. the solid line in the illustration – it is not particularly important in terms of persistence what the student thinks about his or her achievement motivation (see Figure 3). However, if the implicit motive is high (the dashed line), then the self-concept of achievement motivation has clear effects. Students who have not only a strong implicit achievement motive but also a self-concept of high achievement motivation are most persistent in pursuing their goals. The interaction is significant: $t(236)$ = 2.75; p < .05.

This is understandable. If the goals you choose with respect to your motivational self-concept can be reached by activities you prefer because of your implicit motive, then it is not difficult to be persistent. You are doing the things you like to do anyway. However, if an inadequate self-concept of one's own preferences and values directs a person with a dominant implicit achievement motive to inadequate goal areas (for instance trying to become a powerful and important man or woman or having a lots of friends), then the path to the goal is not supported by the dominant implicit motive. Thus, pursuing the goal requires volition in order to hold on to it. The chance of persisting is clearly reduced.

But do students with high motivational competence really experience more Flow - even when learning about statistics? In Engeser's study, the students were given the Flow Short Scale (FKS) while they were working on a statistics task. Figure 4 shows the results: Again, there is a significant interaction between the implicit motive and motivational self-concept: $t(236)$ = 1.97; p =.05. Students with a strong implicit achievement motive (the dashed line) only have more flow experience when they know about their motivational preferences and, thus, have a self-concept of high achievement motivation.

Finally, the FKS score was a substantial predictor of the students' performance in the final statistics examination later on. In a hierarchical regression analysis, the FKS score predicted an additional 4 % of the variance of the final performance test when all other achievement-relevant predictors had already been taken into account (Engeser & Rheinberg, 2008).

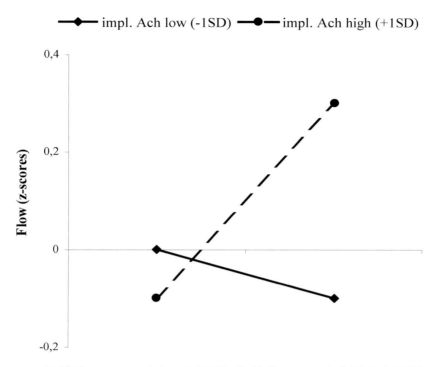

Figure 4. Flow experience (FKS), implicit achievement motive and self-concept of achievement motivation (Engeser, 2009).

CONCLUSION

The data of Clavadetscher (2003) and Engeser (2009) showed evidence for the importance of motivational competence. The studies were concerned with the relationship between motivational competence, self-regulation, flow, and performance. The results showed that for the first component of motivational competence, higher congruence between one's implicit motives and self-attributed motives is associated with better self-regulation, goal attainment and Flow.

The *concept of congruence* is not particularly new. For instance, we are already aware of it from Carl Rogers (1961) or Sheldon and Elliot (1999), and indeed from the concept of Freud (1938). We have merely specified this concept for motivational phenomena and linked it to McClelland's distinction between implicit and self-attributed motives. In so doing, we have gained a theoretically based measurement for the theoretical construct of Motivational Competence. Other studies of motive incongruence showed that it was related to negative affect (Langens, 2007; Schüler, Job, Fröhlich, & Brandstätter, 2008) and to unhealthy eating behavior. This indicates that fostering motivational competence would lead to higher well-being.

The relationship between motive incongruence and negative affect also fits in with the assumption that individuals with incongruence require more volitional control. Conversely, this would mean that actions with higher flow experience are more in accordance with the individual motive. The experience itself is therefore an indicator of the strength of the motive (Rheinberg, 2008). In line with this, research indicates that vividly imagining the actions toward goals helps a person to ascertain whether or not the action is in line with his or her personal motive (Schultheiss & Brunstein, 1999). Training to help people to better imagine the action should help to foster motivational competence. People will then be able to see the incentives of the action, and, if necessary, take steps to enrich the activities. Further research indicates that the ability to deal with stress helps to foster motive congruence and motivational competence (Baumann, Kaschel, & Kuhl, 2005).

We also related the construct of motivational competence to Heinz Heckhausen's general structure of action – that is situation, action, outcome, and consequences (see Figure 1). In this way, we were able to derive the *Flow hypothesis of motivational competence* (Rheinberg, 2004, a, b), which helps to provide an understanding of why implicit and self-attributed motives also have different impacts in the motivational sequence.

REFERENCES

Baumann, N., Kaschel, R., & Kuhl, J. (2005). Striving for unwanted goals: Stress-dependent discrepancies between explicit and implicit achievement motives reduce subjective well-being and increase psychosomatic symptoms. *Journal of Personality and Social Psychology, 89*, 781-799.

Brunstein, J. C. (2008). Implicit and explicit motives. In J. Heckhausen & H. Heckhausen (Eds.), *Motivation and action* (pp. 227-246). New York. Cambridge University Press.

Brunstein, J. C. & Heckhausen, H. (2008). Achievement motivation. In J. Heckhausen & H. Heckhausen (Eds.), *Motivation and action* (pp 137-183). New York: Cambridge University Press

Brunstein, J. C., Schultheiss, O. C. & Grässmann, R. (1998). Personal goals and emotional well-being: The moderating role of motive dispositions. *Journal of Personality and Social Psychology, 75*, 494-508.

Clavadetscher, Ch. (2003). *Motivation ehrenamtlicher Arbeit im Verein Mahogany Hall, Bern*. Abschlussarbeit NDS BWL/UF. Bern: Hochschule für Technik und Architektur.

Csikszentmihalyi, M. (1975). *Beyond boredom and anxiety*. San Francisco: Jossey-Bass.

Csikszentmihalyi, M. (1997). *Finding Flow. The psychology of engagement with everyday life*. New York: Basic Books.

Engeser, S. (2009). *Lernmotivation und volitionale Handlungssteuerung* [Learning motivation and self-regulation]. Saarbrücken: Südwestdeutscher Verlag.

Engeser, S., Rheinberg, F. (2008). Flow, moderators of challenge-skill-balance and performance. *Motivation and Emotion, 32*, 158 - 172.

Freud, S. (1938). *Abriss der Psychoanalyse*. Frankfurt: Fischer.

Heckhausen, H. (1977). Achievement motivation and its constructs: A cognitive model. *Motivation and Emotion, 1*, 283-329.

Jackson, D. N. (1984). *Personality Research Form* (3.ed.). Port Huron, MI: Assessment Systems, Inc.

Kuhl, J. & Fuhrmann, A. (1998). Decomposing self-regulation and self-control: The volitional component inventory. In H. Heckhausen & C. S. Dweck (Eds.), *Motivation and self-regulation across the life span* (pp. 15-49). Cambridge: Cambridge University Press.

Langens, T. (2007). Congruence between implicit and explicit motives and emotional well-being: The moderating role of activity inhibition. *Motivation and Emotion, 31*, 49-59.

McClelland, D. C. (1985). *Human motivation.* Glenview, Ill.: Scott, Foresman & Co.

Pang, J. S., & Schultheiss, O. C. (2005). Assessing implicit motives in U.S. college students: Effects of picture type and position, gender and ethnicity, and cross-cultural comparisons. Journal of Personality Assessment, 85, 280-294.

Rheinberg, F. (2008). Intrinsic motivation and flow-experience. In H. Heckhausen & J. Heckhausen (Eds.), *Motivation and action* (pp. 323-348). Cambridge, UK: Cambridge University Press.

Rheinberg, F. (2004). *Motivationsdiagnostik* [Measurement of motivation]. Göttingen: Hogrefe.

Rheinberg, F. & Engeser, S. (2010). Motive training and motivational competence. In O. C. Schultheiss & J. C. Brunstein (Eds.), *Implicit Motives* (pp. 501-548). Oxford: University Press.

Rheinberg, F., Vollmeyer, R. & Engeser, S. (2003). Die Erfassung des Flow-Erlebens [Measuring flow experience]. In J. Stiensmeier-Pelster & F. Rheinberg (Eds.), *Diagnostik von Motivation und Selbstkonzept (Tests und Trends N.F. Bd. 2)* (pp. 261-279). Göttingen: Hogrefe.

Rogers, C. R. (1961). *On becoming a person.* Boston: Mifflin.

Schüler, J., Job, V., Fröhlich, S., & Brandstätter, V. (2008). A high implicit affiliation motive does not always make you happy: A corresponding explicit motive and corresponding behavior are further needed. *Motivation and Emotion, 32*, 231-242.

Schultheiss O. C. & Brunstein J. C. (Eds.) (2010). *Implicit Motives.* Oxford: University Press.

Schmalt, H.-D., Sokolowski, K. & Langens, T. (2000). *Multi-Motiv-Gitter (MMG) [The Multi-Motive Grid (MMG)].* Lisse, Netherlands: Swets.

Schultheiss, O. C. (2008). Implicit motives. In O. P. John, R. W. Robins & L. A. Pervin (Eds.), *Handbook of Personality: Theory and Research* (3 ed., pp. 603-633). New York: Guilford.

Schultheiss, O. C. & Brunstein, J. D. (1999). Goal imagery: Bridging the gap between implicit motives and explicit goals. *Journal of Personality, 67,* 1-38.

Sheldon, K. M. & Elliot, A. J. (1999). Goal striving, need satisfaction, and longitudinal well-being: The self-concordance model. *Journal of Personality and Social Psychology, 76,* 482-497.

Sheldon, K. M. & Elliot, A. J. (1999). Goal striving, need-satisfaction, and longitudinal well-being: The self-concordance model. *Journal of Personality and Social Psychology, 76,* 482-497.

Spangler, W. D. (1992). Validity of questionnaire and TAT measures of need for achievement. *Psychological Bulletin, 112,* 140-154.

Weinberger, J. & McClelland, D. C. (1990). Cognitive versus traditional motivational models. In E. Higgins & R. M. Sorrentino (Eds.), *Handbook of motivation and cognition: Foundations of social behavior* (pp. 562-597). New York: Guilford Press.

Winter, D. G. (1991). *Manual for scoring motive imagery in running text* (3 ed.). Michigan: Unpublished manuscript, University of Michigan, Department of Psychology.

PART 3. REGULATION AND SELF-DETERMINED ACTION

In: Motivation, Consciousness and Self-Regulation
Editor: D. A. Leontiev, pp. 93-103
ISBN: 978-1-61324-795-2

Chapter 7

WHY WE DO WHAT WE DO:
THE VARIETY OF HUMAN REGULATIONS

Dmitry A. Leontiev
Moscow State University, Russia

ABSTRACT

The chapter presents an attempt to answer the basic question of the motivational roots of human activity in terms of varied principles and systems of activity regulation. Regulation is treated as the general principle explaining the capacity of living systems to move from less desirable outcomes to more desirable ones, based on feedback evaluated against the criteria of the desirable and causing corrections of the current activity. Forms of regulation may be of different complexity and subordinated to different kinds of criteria. The author offers a theoretical classification of possible logics of human regulation, each of them being an elementary mechanism; the proposed multiregulation personality model suggests that the whole system of individual autoregulation is made by the combination of the described elementary mechanisms in individually varied proportions that accounts for the qualitative interindividual differences.

Keywords: Motivation, regulation, autoregulation, evolution, activity, personality, individual differences

INTRODUCTION

The question quoted in the title of this chapter has been articulated some time ago as the key problem of human motivation (Deci & Flaste, 1995). It is typically assumed that the question has *the* answer; the point is to discover the universal motivating force, be it libido, the will to meaning, or terror management. Now it's getting more and more evident that the answer cannot be but multiple and the question is to be differentiated.

I do not mean proposing some new basic needs. First of all, the issue is to be split into at least three more detailed questions: (1) Why we do anything at all; (2) Why we do what we do rather than something else; (3) Why we keep doing what we are doing (see Leontiev, 2011 b for more details). The first question is usually answered in terms of a more or less founded postulation of some basic needs (see Leontiev, 2011 a for a review), the second one in terms of *ad hoc* cognitive and attributional mechanisms of action causation (Leontiev, 2011 b), and the third one in terms of action regulation, or autoregulation. I prefer the term autoregulation (see Valsiner, 2001), rather than self-regulation; the former means essentially the same as self-regulation, but without reference to "self" as some agent, and is thus usable in broader contexts.

I do not, however, treat regulation as a special kind of process inbuilt into a comprehensive structure of human motivation. On the contrary, both classic theories and recent research suggest that regulation is a superordinate concept embracing motivation as its special subsystem. The aim of this paper is thus, first, theoretical explication of the regulation concept as the principal framework for the analysis of motivation, and second, distinguishing a number of regulatory principles that are intertwined in human activity and can serve as variable explanations for different forms of human motivation.

REGULATION AS THE BASIC EXPLANATORY FRAMEWORK

The concept of regulation, born in life sciences and cybernetics, is steadily growing in its popularity among psychologists. Regulation refers to keeping some controlled process up to some preset criteria, and making necessary corrections when the process diverges from the criteria. The process may be autoregulated if monitoring of fitting the criteria and corrections are functions of the same system and the results of monitoring automatically cause necessary correcting actions.

The regulated process we are dealing with in psychology is activity that bridges an individual to the world. This embraces not only observable behavior but also mental activity without directly externalized products. Autoregulation is an inalienable property of all the living creatures striving to improve their living conditions and able at least to move in space, as well as of quasi-living artificial systems with programmed goal criteria and mechanisms of corrections toward better fitting them. In the most general formulation, life as the process developing between a living creature and the environment, or the world, should correspond to the way the creature exists and to the way the world exists. Vassily Davydov (1979) called this double imperative bilateral plasticity of human activity; in a sense, Freud's famous distinction of pleasure principle and reality principle refers to the same bilaterality. We are to fit to reality and to ourselves. If our activity fits to the world in line with the reality principle, we are realistic, if not, we are narcissists. If what we do corresponds to what we are, the activity is authentic, and if it doesn't, it is alienated.

Usually Norbert Wiener is referred to as the pioneer of the regulation paradigm (see Rosenbluth, Wiener, & Bigelow, 1943). The key idea was that of negative feedback – the recurrent incoming information about the divergence between the desired and the factual state of affairs that allows to correct/improve the performance. No adjustment or learning is possible without it. Still earlier, in 1929, the same idea has been pointedly articulated by prominent Russian physiologist Nikolai Bernstein. Arguing with Ivan Pavlov's reflex arc model, Bernstein introduced the idea of feedback reflecting the divergence between the actual and the desired, and proposed the model of reflex circle instead of reflex arc (see Bernstein, 1967). He kept elaborating these ideas for several decades, but his seminal works seem to be hardly known outside Russia, where they were and still are very influential.

The structure of an autoregulated process, as it is generally acknowledged, includes several necessary elements: 1. The process to be regulated. 2. The criterion or criteria of the desirable parameters of the process. 3. The monitoring subsystem, providing the feedback on the actual course of the process. 4. The matching subsystem that evaluates the process fitting the criteria and eventually calls for corrections. 5. The correcting subsystem, implementing corrections of the process for better fitting the criteria.

The explanatory principle of regulation provides an alternative to the principle of linear determinism. The latter presumes that human activity is determined by the multiplication of stable internal (dispositional) and external (environmental) forces. The former presumes that no stable forces or factors predict the activity of the living creature if we do not consider the dynamic system of activity regulation, its only stable element being the criteria of the desirable. Traditional mode of explanation, stemming from Aristotle (it might be called natural explanatory paradigm) says that all creatures behave along with their underlying inherent nature. Correspondingly, individuals are equal to themselves and strive to maintain their stability. Alternative framework that might be called functional explanatory paradigm says that all creatures are in a constant motion toward a better state of affairs and evolve in course of this motion, motivated by the challenge of adaptive change: improve or fail. We are not just what we are; we interact with the world and change (or fail to change). Autoregulation is the mechanism underlying the necessary, adaptive change; it can be defined as the functional capacity of moving from less desirable outcomes to more desirable ones through ongoing monitoring and correcting the current activity.

EVOLUTION OF REGULATORY PRINCIPLES AND HUMAN NATURE

It follows from what has been argued in the previous section that regulation in the broad meaning of the term refers to the universal principle of activity of all living and quasi-living systems directed by goals or other superordinate criteria of the desirable. Autoregulation is a flexible system including both stable and *ad hoc* components that links various determinants and factors of activity into an integrated whole.

More than this, regulatory systems and mechanisms tend to become more complex and multifaceted along with the evolution of life on Earth (see Csikszentmihalyi, 1993). Much of the evolution of living creatures can be explained in terms of evolution of regulatory principles and contours. The most intriguing aspect of this evolution is the development of criteria of the desirable. The most ancient and universal criterion of homeostasis was supplemented by the criteria of balanced adjustment to environmental challenges and successful procreation and natural selection. Later, with the evolution of Homo sapiens, the imperatives of the collective good and transcendent criteria emerged. This suggests that the activity of humans may be regulated along with different criteria and to a notable degree this is up to us (inasmuch as we are mature and self-conscious) to define, which criteria and underlying principles would guide our actions.

However, while in the case of subhuman species the architecture of their regulatory systems is species specific; in humans we meet a broad interindividual and sometimes intraindividual variability. It is possible both to let lower regressive principles direct our way and to follow the highest values that very few are able to accept as the ultimate goal. The XXth century more pointedly than ever posed the old question, what a human being is like — a godlike creature or a beast. The answer, however, is not simple. The variety of human manifestations ranges from unbelievable heights of human spirit to complete betrayal of humanity. This led some prominent thinkers of the post-war period to the argument that human nature is not fixed; rather, it is flexible and able to transcend any essence we might attribute to it (Fromm, 1964; Giorgi, 1992). In line with this, Rollo May (1967) noticed that our consciousness fluctuates within the continuum between the states of an active subject and a passive object; in some cases we let ourselves be driven by something, in some cases we take the initiative into our own hands, but we may voluntarily switch from one state to another. This means that we may function at different levels. There are human potentialities inherent in every person, but not in every person are they actualized at the given point of time.

I propose the image of *dotted human being* as a philosophical metaphor for catching this phenomenon. The idea of dotted human functioning means that the trajectories of our lives are not all the time at the same level. We sink to lower subhuman levels, and then we ascend to human levels again. Human level is the level of principles of behavior regulation that are inherent in human beings alone as distinct from the animal world. Subhuman levels are the levels of the mechanisms of regulation that are common for all animal species. There are not much experimental data that could directly support it, but it is enough to look at the world around us to see the evidence.

THE ISSUE OF ULTIMATE CRITERIA

The most consistent application of the idea of regulation to psychological explanation has been elaborated by Charles Carver and Michael Scheier (*Carver & Scheier*, 1981; 1998; 2000; *Carver*, 2004). These authors directly depart from the assumptions of cybernetics, information processing approach and control theory (*Carver & Scheier*, 1981, p. 108) and share the common model of regulation depicted above as the goal-directed process correcting itself on the feedback basis. They view their approach as associated with the cognitive paradigm but dealing with behavior rather than with cognition (*Carver & Scheier*, 2000) and substitute the metaphor of robot for that of computer (ibid.).

Carver and Scheier, like most other psychologists who make use of the regulation approach, treat a goal as the starting point and the ultimate criterion of any self-regulation process; goal disengagement equals to the cessation of self-regulation regarding this goal. This makes human behavior hyperrational, goals being "the measure of all things". In fact, this is often, but not always the case; Carver and Scheier are being criticized, in particular, for their failure to explain the emergence of goals they just assume (*Csikszentmihalyi & Nakamura*, 1999). Csikszentmihalyi and Nakamura (1999) proposed instead a more universal and basic, in their opinion, ultimate criterion, namely subjective experiences. Their primacy is especially evident in early ontogenesis; goals may pertain or change depending on the kind of experiences they produce. This criticism seems justified; it suggests, at least, that the criteria in regulatory systems can be of varied nature. Another implicit assumption of Carver and Scheier's theory that seems too simplifying of the real picture of human autoregulation is their equating feedback to information based on a widespread delusion that purely informational processes might generate dynamic phenomena by themselves. Two classic examples of this delusion is defining George Kelly's personal construct theory as a cognitive one and classifying Leon Festinger's theory of cognitive dissonance as a theory of motivation. In fact, Kelly in the classic version of his theory (*Kelly*, 1955) explained the dynamics of personal constructs in terms of experience rather than information. Experience refers to personally meaningful information in the context of one's life and does not include irrelevant information. In the last of Kelly's writings the concept of personal construct was being replaced by the concept of personal meaning (*Kelly*, 1970); quite a number of his followers classify his theory as an existentialist one. Festinger's theory (Festinger, 1957) is usually perceived as explaining motivation from the discordance between some cognitive elements. However, Festinger himself explicitly (however, without special emphasis) mentioned the necessary requirement of *significance* of both the discordant elements and the corresponding situation. If they are not significant, no motivation will emerge from discordant information.

We are approaching thus a broader view on dynamic autoregulation of individual-world interaction. This view implies the acknowledgement of multiple regulation criteria and mechanisms, both conscious and unconscious, voluntary and automated ones that may change or merge. Sometimes a person may even deliberately change the ultimate criteria of one's activity, as some researchers of human agency state (Harre, 1983; Rychlak, 1979). We do good if we put aside the assumption of a preset goal and investigate a variety of regulations available for humans, considering their importance for different forms and modes of individual-world relationships.

MULTIPLE LOGICS OF HUMAN BEHAVIOR

It follows from the idea of dotted human functioning that the question, why people do what they do, has no single universal answer. The model depicted below presents an attempt to consider the variety of possible explanations of human actions, each of them being valid in some cases, but not permanently valid even for one person. The finite variety of possible answers reflects different principles of behavior regulation, or different logics of human behavior.

A. The logic of drive gratification produces the answer: "Because I want (need, strive to) something". This is the simplest explanatory principle, common for human and animal behavior (with the reservation that an animal cannot say it); in many simple cases such an explanation seems rather evident, but in more complicated ones it is at least insufficient. It is psychodynamic psychology that deals mostly with this logic.

B. The logic of responding to stimuli produces the answer: "Because something or someone provoked or teased me". This is also an explanation valid both for human and animal behavior; it plays an important part in personal strategies of denying responsibility for one's actions. The main problem with humans, however, lies in interindividual variety of responses to many stimuli. The studies of conditioning, environmental psychology, and psychology of advertising deal mostly with this logic.

C. The logic of learned habits and dispositions produces the answer "Because I always behave this way". Quite a number of psychological problems are embraced by this logic, including skills acquisition, attitude formation and change, character and individual style, etc.

All the three above logics are common for humans and animals. The next step would be analyzing the difference between humans and animals in terms of logics of behavior that is, singling out distinctively human logics.

D. The logic of social norms and expectations. The relevant answer: "Because this is the way one should behave and most people behave in this situation". This logic is determined by the distinctively human phenomenon of society, mediated by the collective culture.

The manifestations of the social logic D, though distinctively human, characterize an impersonal hypersocialized individual, "social animal" or *das Man*, rather than personality. An individual in this case is a battlefield of macrosocial forces and regularities, rather than an autonomous agent. This logic is prevailing in the type of mass individual of mid-century as described by Ortega y Gasset (1930/1994), Fromm (1941), May (1953), etc. The most precise theoretical conceptualization of the distinction between "social individual" and personality has been proposed by S. Maddi (1971), who distinguished two paths of personality development: the conformist path of those who perceive themselves as nothing but the embodiment of biological drives and social roles and live up to their biological and social needs, and the individualist path of those who have "psychological needs" for symbolization, imagination and judgment; thanks to these needs they are able to build future time perspective, to investigate options and to deliberately construe their lives. The logic of behavior underlying the latter path is depicted below.

E. The logic of life-world or the logic of life necessity. The relevant answer: "Because this is necessary (important) for me". This logic is also inherent in humans alone due to another fundamental difference between humans and animals explicated by several thinkers in very close terms: while for animals there is nothing but an environment, for humans, there is the world (Vygotsky, 1934/82, p.280; Frankl, 1982, p.116). All animal behavior (logics A, B, and C) is tied to the immediate environment and to internal impulses, in other words, to the situation "here and now"; all the sources of its determination lie within the (external + internal) situation. We find no factors influencing animal behavior besides the actual external stimuli and the actual internal urges (drives and programs). Unlike animals, humans are able to measure their activity up to their entire *life-world* far beyond the actual situation; their activity is determined by the world at large, rather than by the environment. So by following this logic, reasons and incentives that are located far beyond the situation, including distant consequences and complicated connections, are then taken into account together with immediate incentives. It is not a purely rational logic, or a purely cognitive, abstract capacity, though cognitive schemes play an important role in the regulation processes based on this logic. It is the product of meaning-related regulation of human behavior (see Leontiev, 1999, 2007 for more details).

Explaining an action in terms of its meaning means linking it to the broader contexts of the individual's life world and its significant elements. We are speaking here of objective links inherent in the objective ontological structure of one's life, rather than of cognitive representations. As a rule these links are beyond awareness; however, a human being is the only creature capable of becoming aware of oneself, of one's life, and of one's relations to the world, rather than of the surrounding reality as it is. This kind of regulation serves to subsume individual activity to one's life-world at large, rather than to the demands of the current situation, to the logic of life necessity rather than to the logic of actual need satisfaction, or responding to external stimuli, or applying stereotyped operations, or conforming to social shoulds.

The dominance of E level or higher levels over subordinate ones makes the regulatory basis of personality as the distinctively human way of being (Leontiev, 1999). The function of personality can be depicted as orientation in the relations, which connect the individual to the world and the subordination of his/her activity to the structure of these relations. Personality is viewed as a system of self-regulation based on a structured subjective representation of one's relations to the world, and subjugation of one's life activity to the stable structure of such relations rather than to external stimuli, momentary urges, learned readiness or social pressures.

F. The logic of possibilities produces the answer in form of a new question: "Why not?" This logic transcends the logic of life necessity; it represents the next developmental stage of personal maturity. Not every human adult reaches this stage that roughly corresponds to the individualist way of personality development (Maddi, 1971); indeed, maturity is a developmental trajectory rather than a fixed level. It allows one to see the limitations of the logic of life necessity (E): making a person able to transcend any given situation and to adjust to his/her life-world at large; meaning-related regulation ties a person to the facticity of this life-world and its anticipated development and cannot account for the manifestations of human freedom from this facticity. The ability to transcend this facticity, that is to transcend the determination of behavior by the life-world, inherent in mature personality, is described in terms of human freedom (see May, 1981), or in terms of one's way of following the law of one's own (see Jung, 1934/1954).

In order to act at this level one has to switch on the capacity of self-reflexive awareness that only allows denying all kinds of pressures and external regulations acting upon us. Rollo May (1981) wrote that the pause between stimulus and response is the place where human freedom originates. We often tell a small child when we want her to behave herself: "Stop and count to ten!" This often helps because, in doing this, she stops swimming with the stream and becomes able to initiate a new action based on what *can* be done rather than what *presses us* to be done.

G. The logic of ultimate understanding. The relevant answer: because this corresponds to the way the things are. The person feels he or she has no choice because the world is arranged in such a way that there is the only way to do this and this. This is the type of regulation usually associated to enlightened, extremely wise persons like saints or sages. It is the level of mission, the level of understanding some kind of ultimate truth beyond the scope of everyday understanding. Very few ever reach it; nevertheless, it is a special logic that cannot be reduced to lower levels. Of course, subjective certainty cannot be a good criterion; the strength of self-confidence rarely covariates with the depth of understanding. There is, however, a good criterion to tell a spiritual leader from a self-confident maniac: two genuine sages will come to an agreement despite inevitable differences in their teachings but two maniacs will never. This level was depicted by the Strugatsky brothers, bestselling Russian writers, as the state when you are absolutely free because you have no choice – you just perfectly know what must be done. At this level one deeply penetrates into the essence of things that are imperative rather voluntary; if one is to act in line with the essence of things, one has no choice indeed.

MULTIREGULATION PERSONALITY MODEL

Now let us look at the interrelations between the described logics of human behavior. I suppose that there are special mechanisms and regulatory systems underlying each of them; however, in actual behavior they don't function separately, but rather are combined in multilevel systems. The seven above principles may be treated as seven dimensions of human behavior. Every action can be split into seven vectors, with each of the vectors representing a projection of the whole action to the dimension of this or that logic. These logics however are rarely present in pure forms; as a rule, they are combined and intertwined even in relatively simple behavioral acts and successions; taken together, they make human behavior multicontrolled and provide the basis for individual differences in regulation.

Keeping the proposed model in mind, we may, first, see *considerable individual differences* in the manifestations of all seven principles. There are people more or less acting out their actual urges; more or less easily responding to external stimuli; more or less automatically applying standard schemes and habits; more or less sensitive to social expectations and pressures; more or less considering (either consciously or intuitively) multidimensionality and distant consequences of their actions; more or less able or unable at all to transcend the given determinants of their action and to make a free choice.

Second, there are *developmental trends and successions* with respect to all of the logical principles mentioned. Logics A, B, and C start developing at birth (at least) in a parallel way; logics D and E are taught from a very early age but hardly ever function before the age of 1 year, and only after 3 they take a considerable place in the spectrum of human logics of behavior. The critical period for logic F is adolescence; the essence of adolescent crisis is the conflict between the striving to autonomy and development of psychological mechanisms of autonomous behavior regulation. Our studies (Kaliteyevskaya, Leontiev, 2004; Kaliteyevskaya, et al., 2006) show 4 possible constellations of personality mechanisms of freedom and responsibility in senior adolescents; only one of them corresponds to autonomous behavior regulation, and the others reflect different types of failures in reaching psychological maturity. One of the starting points for this model was the question where the personality starts; from what age we may state that personality (rather than just a constellation of individual traits) is already there? The model offers an explanation: all the seven logics develop in a parallel way, though not at the same time; the manifestations of the fifth logic characteristic of personality can be seen in a rather early age, but has a chance to become the defining one at a much later stage. The quantitative measure of personality is thus the ratio of the logic E related to A+B+C+D.

Third, clinical psychology provides enough evidences for separate types of *distortions* of these regulatory systems; in particular, *anorexia nervosa* gives an example of the disability of need satisfaction system, autism of the disability of responding to stimuli system, psychopathy presents the distortion of meaning-based regulation that results in behavior totally determined by momentary urges, etc. The task of psychotherapy may be articulated as restoring the balance of all the regulation systems.

The ability of self-management, characteristic of a psychologically sound person, presupposes the balanced development of, at least, the first five regulatory systems; the dominant role should belong to the highest, distinctively human ones. Daniel Elkonin, a prominent Russian developmental psychologist, put it the following way (personal communication, February 1984): "You say personality is regulation? Just the contrary, it is overcoming all sort of regulations". To be sure, to overcome some regulations one should introduce other ones that impose new, higher laws and regularities on the whole system of behavior regulation, which prevail over lower ones; the latter, however, are in no way totally disabled but just controlled. The relationship between these higher laws of the regulation of behavior, and the lower ones, has been brilliantly expressed by Hegel: "Circumstances or urges dominate a person only to the extent to which he allows them to do it" (1927, p.45). A person is thus able either to allow the lower principles of logic to guide the definite action, or not to allow this to happen. It is worth noting that manipulation as an effort to control another person's behavior always appeals to logics A (seduction), B (teasing), C (stereotyping), and D (imposing a duty); it is a success inasmuch as the manipulator succeeds in blocking self-determining logics E and F in the manipulated one.

The theoretical model proposed above may be called *multiregulation personality model* (Leontiev, 1999). I sketched only some of its implications and research perspectives and, surely, it is impossible to predict its possible explanatory potential. The model does justice to the only commonly shared belief about personality - its complexity (Pervin, 1990) and claims to account for "the person as a system, thereby involving the interplay between consistency and diversity, stability and change, and integration and conflict" (ibid., p.726).

CONCLUSION

As it has been mentioned above, the evolution of human beings can be best understood in terms of developmental progression of forms of autoregulation. And this refers both to individual ontogenetic development and to the evolution of social groups, human societies and humanity as a whole. Our ability to develop, to maintain and to reproduce the higher forms of autoregulation seems to be the most important condition for survival and development of the human civilization.

If you look around, you will see very different persons, as if they belonged to different species. Indeed, they regulate their lives and construe their relations to the world in very different ways, according to quite different criteria. These differences in autoregulation seem not to be a matter of genes, race, or normally distributed individual variations, linked to any kind of inborn differences. It is the matter of qualitative level differences, linked to one's own choices, one's own activity and one's wish to invest efforts to ascending the developmental stairs of regulatory mechanisms, individually evolving throughout one's personal history. A special field of research can be anticipated that would investigate and facilitate one's personal evolution; this field deserves the name of differential anthropology. However, this point transcends the scope of this chapter.

REFERENCES

Bernstein, N. A. (1967). *The co-ordination and regulation of movements.* Oxford: Pergamon Press.

Carver, C. (2004). Self-regulation of Action and Affect. In R. Baumeister, & K.D. Vohs (Eds.), *Handbook of Self-Regulation: Research, Theory, and Applications* (pp. 13-19). New York: Guilford.

Carver, C., & Scheier M. (1981). A Control-Systems Approach to Behavioral Self-Regulation. In L. Wheeler (Ed.), *Review of Personality and Social Psychology: 2* (pp. 107-140). Beverly Hills, CA: Sage.

Carver, C., & Scheier, M. (1998). *On the Self-Regulation of Behavior.* New York: Cambridge University Press.

Carver, C., & Scheier, M. (2000). *Perspectives on Personality. 4th ed.* Boston etc.: Allyn & Bacon.

Csikszentmihalyi, M. (1993). *The Evolving Self.* New York: HarperPerennial.

Csikszentmihalyi, M., & Nakamura, J. (1999). Emerging goals and the self-regulation of behavior. In R.S. Wyer (Ed.), *Advances in social cognition. Vol. 12. Perspectives on behavioral self-regulation* (pp. 107-118). Mahwah, NJ: Erlbaum.

Davydov, V. V. (1979). Kategoriya deyatelnosti i psikhicheskogo otrazheniya v teorii A.N.Leontieva (Categories of activity and mental reflection in A.N.Leontiev's theory). *Vestnik Moskovskogo universiteta. Ser. 14. Psikhologiya, No 4, 25-41.*

Deci, E. & Flaste, R. (1995). *Why We Do What We Do: Understanding Self-motivation.* New York: Penguin.

Festinger, L. (1957). *A Theory of Cognitive Dissonance.* Stanford, CA: Stanford University Press.

Frankl, V. E. (1982). *Der Wille zum Sinn. 3, erweit. Aufl.* Bern: Huber.

Fromm, E. (1941). *Escape from freedom.* New York: Rinehart.

Fromm. E. (1956). *The sane society.* London: Routledge and Kegan Paul.

Fromm, E. (1964). *The Heart of Man. Its Genius for Good and Evil.* New York: Harper & Row

Giorgi, A. (1992). Whither Humanistic Psychology? *The Humanistic Psychologist, 20* (2-3), 422-438.

Harré, R. (1983). *Personal Being: A Theory for Individual Psychology.* Oxford: Basil Blackwell.

Hegel, G.W.F. (1927). Philosophische Propadeutik (Philosophical Introduction). In *Samtliche Werke (Collected Works), Bd. 3.* Stuttgart: Frommann.

Jung, C.G. (1954). The development of personality (Originally published 1934). In *The collected works of C.G.Jung. Vol. 17* (pp. 167-186). London: Routledge and Kegan Paul.

Kaliteyevskaya, E., & Leontiev, D. (2004). When Freedom Meets Responsibility: Adolescence As The Critical Point Of Positive Personality Development. In A. Delle Fave (Ed.) *Positive Psychology. Special issue of Ricerche di Psicologia, 2004, anno XXVII,*(1), 103-115.

Kaliteyevskaya, E., Borodkina, I., Leontiev, D., & Osin, E. (2006). Meaning, Adjustment and Autodetermination in Adolescence. In A. Delle Fave (Ed.), *Dimensions of well-being. Research and intervention* (pp. 157-171). Milano: Franco Angeli.

Kelly, G. (1955). *The psychology of personal constructs*. New York: Norton.

Kelly, G. (1970). A brief introduction to personal construct theory. In D. Bannister (Ed.) *Perspectives in personal construct theory* (pp.1-29). London; New York: Academic press.

Leontiev, D. (1999). *Psikhologiya Smysla (The Psychology of Personal Meaning)*. Moscow: Smysl.

Leontiev, D. (2007). The Phenomenon of Meaning: How Psychology can Make Sense of It? In P. T. P. Wong, L. Wong, M. J. McDonald, & D. K. Klaassen (Eds.). *The Positive Psychology of Meaning and Spirituality* (pp. 33-44). Abbotsford, BC: INPM Press.

Leontiev, D. (2011a) From Drive To Need and Further: What Is Human Motivation About? In D. Leontiev (Ed.) *Motivation, consciousness, and self-regulation* (pp. 00-00). New York: Nova Science Publishers.

Leontiev, D. (2011b) Personal meaning as the basis of motivational processes. In D. Leontiev (Ed.) *Motivation, consciousness, and self-regulation* (pp. 000-000). New York: Nova Science Publishers.

Maddi, S. (1971). The search for meaning. In W. J. Arnold, & M. M. Page (Eds.), *Nebraska symposium on motivation 1970* (pp. 137-186). Lincoln, NB: University of Nebraska Press.

May, R. (1953) *Man's search for himself*. New York: Norton.

May, R. (1967) *Psychology and the human dilemma*. Princeton, NJ: Van Nostrand.

May, R. (1981). *Freedom and Destiny*. New York: Norton.

Ortega y Gasset, J. (1994). The Revolt of the Masses. New York: W. W. Norton & Company (Original work published in 1930).

Pervin, L. (1990). Personality theory and research: prospects for the future. In L. Pervin (Ed.). *Handbook of personality theory and research* (pp. 723-727). New York; London: The Guilford Press.

Rosenbluth, A., Wiener, N., & Bigelow, J. (1943). Behavior, Purpose and Teleology. *Philosophy of Science, 10,* 18-24.

Rychlak, J. (1979). *Discovering free will and personal responsibility*. New York: Oxford University Press.Valsiner, J. (2001). Process Structure of Semiotic Mediation in Human Development. *Human Development, 44,* 84-97.

Vygotsky, L. S. (1982). Problema razvitiya v strukturnoi psikhologii (The problem of development in the structural psychology, Originally published 1934). In L. S. Vygotsky. *Sobranie Sochineniy (Collected Works), Vol. 1.* (pp. 238-290). Moscow: Pedagogika.

In: Motivation, Consciousness and Self-Regulation
Editor: D. A. Leontiev, pp. 105-126

ISBN: 978-1-61324-795-2
© 2012 Nova Science Publishers, Inc.

Chapter 8

THE MOTIVATIONAL NATURE OF GOOD LIVING: HUMAN AUTONOMY AND WHY IT IS GOOD FOR PEOPLE AND SOCIETIES

Valery Chirkov
University of Saskatchewan, Canada[*]

ABSTRACT

This chapter consists of two parts. The first one presents a summary of the self-determination theory account of people's good living and optimal functioning. It highlights three motivational components identified by this theory: psychological needs (needs for autonomy competence and relatedness), aspirations and life strivings, and the continuum of motivational regulation. All these components are considered in relation to people's eudaimonic happiness and optimal, healthy functioning. The main conclusion of this section is that in order to be happy, people need to regularly and in a balanced way gratify their needs, have strong intrinsic strivings relative to extrinsic aspirations, and be relatively self-determined in their main domains of living and functioning. The second part addresses in more detail the controversial question of the nature of human autonomy as a fundamental condition for people's thriving and flourishing. It provides a conceptual analysis of this construct, uncovers the mechanisms of its beneficial performance, and addresses a highly discussed question of relationships of autonomy and culture. This section ends with a conclusion on the fundamental importance of human autonomy for people, communities and societies to survive and thrive.

Keywords: Motivation; psychological autonomy; eudaimonia; the good life

Across the globe, people strive to live healthy, long lives, to be happy, to be loved and accepted by others, and to be effective and productive in their daily endeavors. In light of this, philosophers, social scientists and policymakers have struggled to understand the best pathways to achieving these aims and to identifying the conditions and supports that facilitate

---

[*] The author wants to thank Richard M. Ryan for insightful and helpful suggestions during the preparation of this manuscript.

their attainment. This chapter is a continuation of this inquiry into the basis of optimal living and wellness using the theoretical propositions of *Self-Determination Theory* (SDT; Ryan & Deci, 2000). Specifically, it will outline the theoretical framework and some of the empirical research that supports SDT's motivational account of factors that facilitate or thwart people's attempts at attaining the good life.

CONCEPTUAL FRAMEWORK

To address the goal of living well, this chapter employs the Ancient Greece concept of *eudaimonia* (Ryan & Deci, 2001). Eudaimonic conceptions have been increasingly studied in recent years (Ryff & Singer, 2008; Waterman, Schwartz, & Conti, 2008). They address the issue of how people can live and act in accord with their best capabilities and characteristics (self-realization) and aim toward goals that have intrinsic value and worth, thereby building a meaningful life (May, 2010). That is, eudaimonic living entails pursuing excellence and virtues, and it emanates from a person's self and thus reflects a person's self-determination and autonomy (Ryan, Huta, & Deci, 2008).

To the extent that a person manifests a *eudaimonic way of living,* other indicators of *well-being* will be in evidence. Such well-being typically includes happiness or feelings of enjoyment, pleasure, and satisfaction but is not defined by them (Feldman, 2004; Ryan, et al., 2008). Indeed, eudaimonic living does not aim directly for pleasure or happiness, and at times it involves arduous effort and even suffering. Moreover, because hedonic happiness can also be obtained through superficial, selfish actions that do not result in meaning or harmonious living, it is not the central or defining element in wellness from the eudaimonic viewpoint. Indeed, this is where *hedonic conceptions of wellness* differ from eudaimonic conceptions (Ryan et al., 2008).

Among current motivational theories, SDT has specifically focused on a deeper understanding of eudaimonic living. In fact, according to SDT, eudaimonic living is rooted in human motivation: factors that energize people to develop their capabilities and strive for intrinsic goals that satisfy their basic psychological needs. SDT specifically proposes three groups of energizing and directing factors that constitute human motivation: *psychological needs*, *life goals,* and *motivational regulations* of specific activities. Together, these three groups of factors determine to a large degree whether an individual will experience optimal and harmonious living and wellness or not.

Within SDT, *psychological needs* are considered to lie at the heart of human nature—they are defined as innate organismic factors that are fundamental or essential for people's optimal functioning and personal growth. There are three basic psychological needs according to SDT: the *need for autonomy*—a necessity to be volitional, self-governing, and self-organizing in one's own actions and life choices; the *need for competence*—a need for feeling effective and capable in one's interactions with the environment; and the *need for relatedness*—a fundamental requirement to be connected to other people and to care for and be cared for by them (Ryan, 1995). The major thesis of SDT is that the nutrients and factors that support and facilitate the gratification of psychological needs comprise a fundamental condition for eudaimonic living. Empirical research indicates that when people experience satisfaction of their psychological needs, they report better well-being and health and higher levels of vitality and happiness (Patrick, Knee, Canevello, et al., 2007; Reis, Sheldon, Gable, et al., 2000; Sheldon, Ryan, & Reis, 1996; Vansteenkiste, Ryan, & Deci, 2008). In order for people to be happy, healthy, and successful, their psychological needs have to be gratified regularly and in a balanced way (Sheldon & Niemiec, 2006).

A second motivational constituent of eudaimonic living is comprised of the goals that people hold as their values and ultimate aims. SDT distinguishes between *intrinsic and extrinsic* goals (Kasser & Ryan, 1996). *Intrinsic goals and aspirations*, such as being a productive and efficient citizen, caring about people, creating peace and harmony in one's surrounding, and striving for self-improvement, self-development and self-understanding, are considered to be the goals that relate to and often directly satisfy basic psychological needs. This means that when people strive to achieve these goals, they will be much more likely to gratify their basic psychological needs (Ryan, Sheldon, Kasser, et al., 1996) because, in SDT, intrinsic goals are considered to reflect *first-order values*, which are not reducible to and not serving as means for other values (Ryan et al., 2008). These dialectical relations between psychological needs and intrinsic life goals create a favorable motivational background for eudaimonic, harmonious, and productive living and as a result for more a happy and satisfying life.

Extrinsic goals, such as strivings for wealth, fame, the desire to be attractive, popular, or powerful, and being able to control other people's thoughts, feelings and actions, are mainly considered substitutes or surrogate satisfiers of the basic psychological needs. Although the dynamics between extrinsic values and psychological needs can be very complex, when achieved, these goals do not bring satisfaction of psychological needs. If people are obsessed by this type of life goals and these goals prevail over their intrinsic aspirations, then people's harmonious living could be seriously shattered and their well-being will be deleteriously impacted (Kasser & Ryan, 1993; Niemiec, Lynch, Vansteenkiste, et al., 2006). This conclusion holds true across countries (Ryan, Chirkov, Little, et al., 1999; Schmuck, Kasser, & Ryan, 2000).

It is important to stress that people strive for both intrinsic and extrinsic goals, and there is nothing wrong, for example, with wishing to be wealthy and good looking. The problem arises when these extrinsic aspirations prevail over people's intrinsic strivings and start dominating their lives, overshadowing the intrinsic goals that are important for the eudaimonic living. Many studies within SDT established positive relations between the relative importance of intrinsic aspirations and peoples' well-being (Kasser, 2002; Kasser & Ryan, 1993; Kasser & Ryan, 1996; Niemiec, Ryan, & Deci, 2009).

The third constituent of motivation that, according to SDT, lies at the basis of eudaimonic well-being is a continuum of *motivational regulations* that govern people's ongoing activities. Motivational regulations in SDT are said to differ as a function of a person's *perceived locus of causality* (Heider, 1958/1982) of his or her actions, that is, whether these actions are experienced as determined by external (controlling) factors (*external and introjected regulations*), or as determined by internal (autonomous) personal factors based on valuing particular behaviors or on a deliberate reasoning and reflection (*identified* and *integrated regulations*) (Ryan & Connell, 1989; Ryan & Deci, 2000). Thus, there is a distinction between controlled and autonomous forms of motivation. A relatively separate form of motivational regulation is known as *intrinsic motivation* or the motivation that is based on enjoyment, pleasure, and interest in pursuing certain activities.

An important concept of SDT that ties together controlled and autonomous forms of motivational regulation is the concept of *internalization* (Wallis & Poulton, 2001). Internalization is understood as the psychological process of taking on or adopting external demands, norms, and social proscriptions and prescriptions and integrating them into one's identity and sense of value. Motivational internalization in SDT is considered to occur along the continuum of the types of motivational regulations mentioned above. The more internalized the behavior, the more volitional or autonomous it is experienced to be (Grolnick, Ryan, & Deci, 1997; Williams & Deci, 1996). Intrinsic motivation does not build on any forms of internalization, as it has a biological origin.

For the purpose of the current presentation, we will focus on three basic forms of regulations: *controlled motivation*, when either external rewards or punishments, or internalized expectations of other people or authority figures are perceived to be the causal factors of one's actions; *autonomous motivation*, when a person perceives that he or she volitionally chooses a certain action; and *intrinsic motivation*, when people act exclusively based on their interests, enjoyment, and pleasure that accompanied their behavior. Any behavior is determined by a combination of all three forms of motivational regulations, and again, as with previous constituents (needs and life aspirations), the relative prevalence of autonomous over controlled motivation is what is most important for promoting healthy, happy and eudaimonic living. At this point, hundreds of empirical studies guided by SDT have confirmed the beneficial role more autonomous forms of motivation play in people's learning, creativity, and well-being (Deci & Ryan, 2002; Ryan & Deci, 2000; Vansteenkiste, et al., 2008). The self-determined motivation is beneficial because it directly represents one of the most powerful psychological needs—the need for autonomy; that is, the need to be self-governed, to be oneself, to be genuine, and to live in accord with one's own will and capabilities.

Evidence suggests that the relations among life goals and the motivational regulation that underlies actions can be complex (Chirkov, Safdar, de Guzman, et al., 2008; Deci & Ryan, 2000; Sheldon, Ryan, Deci, et al., 2004). The goals reflect the *content* of people's aspirations and answer the question, "What are people striving for?" Conversely, governing motivational regulation answers the question, "Why are people striving for these goals?" In this case, the relations between goals, and especially extrinsic ones, and the motivation behind them could create complex dynamics, meaning that extrinsic goals (money, for example,) could be pursued either for controlled or autonomous reasons (Carver & Baird, 1998). For the intrinsic goals, there is a tendency (though not an invariant one) for people to be self-determined while pursuing them (Sheldon, 2002). In any case, both the "what" and "why" aspects of behaviors contribute independently to the prediction of productivity, energy, and wellness outcomes (Vansteenkiste, Lens, & Deci, 2006).

To briefly summarize: according to SDT, in order to live eudaimonic lives, people need to satisfy their basic psychological needs for autonomy, competence and relatedness. This satisfaction may be related to pursuing of intrinsic goals, which have to predominate over extrinsic ones, and to exercise self-determined forms of motivation in their everyday living, which should predominate over controlled motivation (Chirkov, Ryan, &Sheldon,2010). But what are the social conditions that promote and facilitate these goals and motivations? What relations should be established between parents and children, between partners, between teachers and students, bosses and subordinates, among citizens of a state and between them and representatives of different social and political institutions in order for people to be autonomous and agentic, and experience rich and fulfilling lives? The next sectionwill try to answer these questions.

SOCIAL CONDITIONS THAT PROMOTE AND FACILITATE OPTIMAL MOTIVATION

Self-determination theory provides answers to the questions about social conditions that promote motivation that is optimal for the good living. Specifically, SDT posits influences from both *proximal* and *distal* social conditions. *Proximal social relations* are those relations in a person's closest social environment that are based on face-to-face interactions in a family, between teachers and students, bosses and their subordinates at work and similar interactions in other domains of life. *Distal social relations* are the relationships among people and various social institutions that are based on the dominant cultural ideology, and the political and economic organization of a social life of societies. These relations are based on the shared cultural norms, practices, and meanings of what is good, right, and normal in this society. Distal relations create a background for more personal interactions, so these two layers of relations constantly interact with each other providing a social context for people's motivation.

Based on the SDT propositions, healthy proximal social relations are those that are supportive of basic psychological needs of people. For example, in order to demonstrate such support, teachers need to acknowledge and respect their students' needs, interests, and goals; they need to convey confidence that their students are capable of achieving these goals; teachers need to provide unconditional love and support to children if they fail or have problems. It is also important for teachers to consider children's points of view and provide them with different options of how to handle their lives in order for these students to be autonomously motivated (Assor & Kaplan, 2001; Assor, Kaplan, Kanat-Maymon, et al., 2005; Deci, Eghart, Patric, et al., 1994; Reeve & Jang, 2006). Similar requirements have been discovered to be important for creating basic needs supporting environment in a family (Grolnick, 2003), in a physician's office (Williams, 2002), or in a sport gym (Hagger & Chatzisarantis, 2007), and at work places (Gagne & Deci, 2005). The SDT researchers have also identified important relations between supportive environments and the goals that people try to achieve (Vansteenkiste, et al., 2006; Vansteenkiste, Simons, Lens, et al., 2004). The psychologically supportive relations facilitate achievement of intrinsic vs. extrinsic goals, and both intrinsic goals and autonomous motivation synergically enhance students' performance. The relations that support psychological needs are also beneficial because they facilitate internalization of the demands and norms of a social group. Through internalization, an individual incorporates rules and prescriptions for successful functioning in a society. A problem that may come out here is that the values and norms that are put forward for the internalization may be detrimental for a person's well-being, health and even life in a long run. Imagine autonomy supportive "brainwashing" of child soldiers in Africa or convincing a Muslim adept in fundamentalist ideas, leading him or her to a suicide bombing.

Chirkov et al. (in press) categorized the distal social conditions that relate to people's motivation as horizontal and vertical, and these relations, together with the meaning, values, and norms that regulate them, were labeled the *culture of horizontality* and *the culture of verticality. The culture of horizontality* is comprised of those relations that are based on and promote norms and values of trust, equality, respect, tolerance, sharing, an appreciation of human dignity and individuality among people in a society at large, within different social institutions, and between people and these institutions. The values and practices related to them were addressed by scientists at a political level as liberal democracies (Inglehart, 2000; Sen, 1999), and on a level of social infrastructure as social capital and social cohesion (Berger-Smith, 2000; Chirkov, et al., in press; Coleman, 1988; Grootaert & van Bastelaer, 2001). *The culture of verticality* is based on values, norms and practices of obedience, loyalty, and inclination to control people. This culture implicitly or explicitly is guided by the assumptions that some people are more worthy than the others, that the worthy people have a right to control and guide the unworthy ones, who have to be obedient and loyal. Because of these differences in unworthiness, people cannot be trusted and it is not necessary to treat unworthy people with respect and dignity. This type of relation is based on high valuing of power and status hierarchy, around which most of the social interactions in this culture are built (de Botton, 2004).

Ancient Greek philosophers, who were later followed by humanistic thinkers, were the first to recognize the culture of horizontality and its role in promoting human autonomy. Friendship, cooperation, trust, solidarity, respect, mutuality, dialog, and similar constructs were continuously mentioned by Epicurus (Bergsma, Poot, & Liefbroer, 2008), Spinoza (Uyl, 2003), Kant (Guyer, 2000, 2003), Habermas (1979, 1990), Kohlberg (1990), by humanistic psychologists and thinkers such as Erikson (1964), Rogers (1961)and Maslow (1968), Buber (1970) and Bakhtin (1984). The same scholars constantly mentioned the detrimental role the relations of autocratic control and dictatorship have on people's agency, optimal functioning, and flourishing. The principles of horizontality were suggested by Tremblay (2010) as a basis for the global ethics on our planet. Among ten ethical principles that he proposes for these universal ethics, six are based on the promotion of horizontal relations: dignity and equality; respect for life and property; tolerance and empathy; sharing; no domination and exploitation; and democracy. According to Habermas (1979, 2003), the strength of horizontality is based on an equal distribution of social power among the participating parties and their ability to express their needs, interests, and values through a dialog and be sure that their voices will be heard. This power and relational symmetry produces the fundamental symmetry of responsibility, which is required for healthy and ethical self-reflection and self-understanding. This self-reflection and self-understanding lie at the basis of people's mature autonomy and responsible and moral lives. In addition, in the egalitarian and horizontal relations a person can "trust in mutuality with the other" and, as a result, be able to "discursively form (his or her) will"; and to get "communicative access to (his or her) own inner nature" (Cote & Levine, 2002, p. 192-193). Also, according to Habermas, "human dignity," as one of the basic pillars of humanist ethics, "comes to have significance only in interpersonal relations of mutual respect, in the egalitarian dealings among persons" (2003, p.33). The vertical culture that is based on values of social dominance and social dependence "is foreign to the reciprocal and symmetrical relations of mutual recognition proper to a moral and legal community of free and equal persons" (p.65).

Both horizontal and vertical cultures are rooted in the historical, socio-economic, and religious heritage of a society and exist in the forms of institutionalized practices, laws, formal regulations and also shared informal norms and roles that prescribe people's appropriate behaviors. Each society has both of these dimensions but in different proportions.

Those societies where the culture of horizontality is a dominant one and the vertical relations and norms are under democratic control provide better conditions for people's optimal living and flourishing than those societies where the vertical culture is predominant, with little or no restrictions. The distal social relations provide a socio-cultural context for the proximal relations and, finally, for the satisfaction of basic psychological needs and promotion of self-determined motivation. It is important to note that in addition to psychological health and eudaimonic well-being, these conditions, both proximal and distal, promote people's creativity and innovativeness, which constitute a central feature of a fully human functioning (Amabile, 1983; Deci & Ryan, 1985).

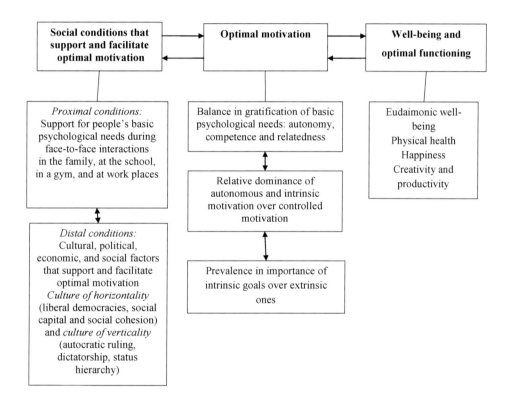

Figure 1. The motivational basis of the good living from the Self-Determination Theory perspective.

To summarize this presentation of the SDT account of social conditions, people's motivation, and optimal functioning, I provide a schema that reflects the basic components of this analysis (Figure 1). This schema emphasizes the interactive nature of relationships among social conditions, motivations and people's well-being. It is not only that social conditions provide support for healthy motivation, but that people with healthy motivation strive to be in and co-create more favorable social contexts for themselves, thus contributing to the maintenance of these conditions. In a similar way, it is not only positive motivation that promotes psychological well-being and eudaimonia, but also people, who optimally function, tend to elicit in themselves and others more positive motivation, more autonomy and stronger intrinsic goal orientation. But these predictions about the interactive nature of these components' functioning have to be studied empirically.

WHAT IS PSYCHOLOGICAL AUTONOMY?[1]

SDT is a well-structured and coherent psychological theory of human motivation and optimal functioning; it deals with complex ideas and constructs, such as autonomy, agency, authenticity, self, eudaimonia, internalization, and many others, which require close attention to their interpretation and understanding, as these constructs are also used by psychologists of other theoretical orientations and by scholars from other disciplines. This part of the chapter will focus on the central concept of the SDT's account of human motivation, which is the notion of *human psychological autonomy*. This concept, together with related notions of agency, free will, and freedom, is one of the most complex and challenging concepts within the social and human sciences, which have hundreds years of history in Ancient and modern philosophy, social, and human sciences (Archer, 2000; Baer, Kaufman, & Baumeister, 2008; Christman, 2009; Dennett, 1986; Dworkin, 1988; Frankfurt, 1971; Frie, 2008; Haworth, 1986; Martin, Sugerman, & Thompson, 2003; Mele, 2001; Paul, Miller, & Paul, 2003). Psychological autonomy is considered to be the fundamental aspect of not only mere human existence, but a happy, fulfilling, and satisfying one (Gruen, 2007). Despite the fundamental role autonomy plays in people's lives, this construct has been misunderstood, devalued, and sometimes discouraged at different historical times of its existence. In modern human sciences, it also holds a controversial position, where, on the one hand, there is a renaissance of an interest in it and related notions of agency, freedom and fee will (Frie, 2008; Haworth, 1986; Libet, Freeman, & Sutherland, 1999; Martin, Sugarman, & Hickinbottom, 2009; Martin, et al., 2003), but on the other hand, a strong inclination not only to diminish its importance for people's lives but also to question its right to exist as a real psychological phenomenon (Baer, et al., 2008; Bargh, 2008).

The goal of this section is to clarify the nature of psychological autonomy, to explain why it is so essential and beneficial for people's good living and eudaimonia, and to address some of the critiques raised against this concept.

CONCEPTUAL CLARIFICATION OF THE TERM

The emergence of the idea of human autonomy and the construction of the term for it is attributed to the philosophers of Ancient Greece. Socrates, Stoics, Aristotle and their contemporaries and followers are considered to be the major figures behind this new conceptual development (Bobzien, 1998; Cooper, 2003). Etymologically the words "autonomy" and "autonomous" mean "self" (*auto*) ruled by its own "laws" (*nomos*) (Soanes & Stevenson, 2008). Similar ideas related to the emergence and functioning of the human conscious self—which is the basis of the phenomenon of human autonomy—were contemplated by Ancient Chinese and Indian philosophers and thinkers, although the further destinies of the ideas in these countries are different from the ones in the Western world (Cheng, 2004; Elvin, 1985; Sanderson, 1985).

---

[1] This section of the chapter is based on the author's presentation at the Fourth International conference on Self-Determination Theory; Ghent, Belgium, May, 2010.

In modern times, human autonomy is a frequently misunderstood phenomenon both among scholars and the general public. It is often confused with individualism, independence, and even egotism and selfishness. Human autonomy is different from all these characteristics. Summarizing old and modern interpretations of this phenomenon (Bobzien, 1998; Cooper, 2003; Guyer, 2000, 2003; Oshana, 2003; Uyl, 2003), it is possible to identify the following most important aspects of it:

1. Autonomy is a state of affairs in a person's life when he or she is capable of and motivated to reflect on one's own desires, wants, and motivations; is driven to understand their origins, mechanisms, and consequences; and rationally decides either to follow or to ignore them. A crucial condition for this aspect of autonomy to function is the awareness of one's internal world and sensitivity to one's authentic needs and feelings.

2. An autonomous person sets in a self-determined fashion (without external coercion) his or her own life goals, criteria for a good and happy life, and moral standards of what are appropriate and right ways of achieving these goals. These goals, criteria, and standards lay at the basis of a person's rational decision to have a happy and fulfilling life. An important condition here is that these standards and criteria should not jeopardize other people's capacities to lead their own free and happy lives.

3. Finally, autonomy includes the capacity to reflect on various external demands, including but not limited to cultural traditions and prescriptions, social norms, and expectations of others. An autonomous person is aware of these influences and demands, understands their origins and consequences, and is able to rationally decide either to accept them as the guiding principles of his or her life or to reject them. For an autonomous person, the criteria to evaluate these socio-cultural demands are the reflected authentic needs and feelings (aspect 1) and rationally evaluated one's own life goals and values (aspect 2).

It is important to differentiate between the *personal* and *motivational* forms of autonomy (Chirkov, 2010; Oshana, 2003). *Personal autonomy* is a property of one's life when it is lived according to self-generated or freely internalized rules and norms, which become the laws that guide the ends and directions of this life. In its ideal form, these norms are built on the reflections on one's own needs and capacities, on the consideration of the needs, goals, and personal autonomy of other people, as well as of the needs and goals of communities and societies, and they are governed by reflective and rational reasoning. When these "personal laws" are fully developed, the autonomous person must care about them. People are considered to be personally autonomous if they not only use these "laws" to govern their lives, but if they also stay true to them, regardless of their social disapproval or life hardships. *Motivational autonomy* is a property of a person's specific actions and behaviors, which can be embedded into more or less autonomously governed lives. Examples of such behaviors are academic performances, interpersonal relations, work-related behaviors, physical exercises, health care practices, and many others. When autonomously executed, these actions and practices are experienced as self-governed and self-directed and are built on reflections and rational reasoning with regard to different pressures both internal—biological urges and psychological wants and desires—and external—the demands and expectations of other people regarding this particular behavior. It is this form of autonomy that is studied by self-determination theory.

Following this interpretation, autonomy emerges as a central and exclusively human capacity that lies at the centre of conscious, rational, authentic, and deeply satisfying living. Without autonomy, human beings are mere robots governed either by unreflected wants and desires or by the strings of ideological, political and religious manipulators.

Why is autonomy fundamentally essential for people's happy and healthy living? Starting with the Ancient Greek philosophers, several generations of scholars in one way or another reiterated the same thesis: that in order for people to be happy, they need to be free politically, socially, and psychologically (Engstrom & Whiting, 1996; Frey & Stutzer, 2000; Giri, 2000; Guyer, 2000; Inglehart & Oyserman, 2004; Veenhoven, 2000). According to these accounts, only a psychologically free (autonomous) person knows what he or she really wants, what his or her personal goals and criteria for good and happy living are, and what the best ways of reaching them are. Only a free person can choose. Autonomy, both personal and motivational, allows a person to be in contact with his or her authentic needs, motives, goals, and moral principles (Christman, 2009; Horney, 1950). Without this contact, a person develops self-alienation—a condition that lies at the core of various psychological and social pathologies (Fromm, 1941; Gruen, 2007). Kant provided even a more encompassing account of why autonomy is so important for happy fulfilling functioning (Guyer, 2000, 2003). His logic on this issue could be interpreted as follows: Human activity and the promotion of life in all its manifestations constitute the deepest pleasure in life. But only freely executed activity can promote a full life. Therefore, only an autonomous person, who has access to this freedom, may experience this fullness of life and, as a result, experience the deepest eudaimonic pleasure that comes with it.

SYMBOLIC MENTAL REPRESENTATIONS AS A BASIS OF PSYCHOLOGICAL AUTONOMY

The best way to introduce the idea of human autonomy as a psychological phenomenon is to consider its basic constituents and their development. According to the current philosophical and psychological understanding, human autonomy is based on the emergence of symbolic mental representations and the ability of human beings to use them to regulate their behavior as well as their thoughts and feelings (Deacon, 1997; Martin, 2008; Murphy & Brown, 2007). This exclusively human form of regulation is evolutionarily evolved and built upon less sophisticated forms of regulations, such as reflexes, learning through conditioning, and non-symbolic reflective regulation. The human brain has the ability not only to perceive information from the environment, to form images of the outside world, to memorize them, and to initiate behavioral responses based on these impressions, but also to create mental representations of these primary images, memories, and intentions. Because of this second capacity, people acquire the power to reflect on the situations they are in, on their thoughts and feelings about them, and to contemplate and plan their future actions. Human beings are capable of working off-line and manipulating all the available information without necessarily directly acting upon it. High animals can generate non-symbolic mental representations, but only humans can produce symbolic—based on language—forms of mental representations, which moves human beings away from a direct dependence on environmental contexts, from primary cognitive and emotional reactions to them, and from impulsive behavioral responses. We have the capacity to reflect upon, postpone, or revert these perceptual, cognitive, emotional, and motivational primary forces. This capacity lies at the core of human potentiality toward psychological autonomy.

These symbolic mental representations serve several important functions (Murphy & Brown, 2007). They free people from the immediacy of a situation and from dependence on immediate environmental stimuli. This freedom from immediate perceptual fields provides people with enormous flexibility in their behavior. The second feature of humans' symbolic representations is their ability to create scenarios of future actions and, as a result, to mentally entertain various behaviors before executing them. Another characteristic of these representations is their ability to signify the processes of a person's own mental activity and to make it the object of one's awareness, reflective understanding, and rational decision making. The fourth attribute allowes them to represent the minds of other individuals and, through constructing the mental representations of social relationships, to open unrestricted opportunities for social interactions and communication. And finaly symbolic representations allow a person to reflect on relations among other symbolic representations, within one's mind. This capacity to signify relations and the relational properties of the world allows human beings to construct abstract concepts and associations among them; this power of abstraction gives people not only the freedom from their immediate environments and biological states, but also the freedom of studying and comprehending the outside world.

Because of the presence of these off-line representations, humans have "gaps," as philosopher Searle (2010) worded it, in the chain of executing any intentional actions. These gaps mean that humans have the freedom to change, reverse, or stop the execution of any component in this chain of commands and executions. The ability to use these gaps effectively brings people their psychological autonomy: the autonomy to reflect, to postpone, to think, to imagine, and then to act or not to act. This autonomy gives us "psychological freedom," It is not autonomy per se that has evolved during evolution and has brought evolutionary advantages to human species but the symbolic mental representations that have made humans the best adapted creature on earth. Autonomy results from the successful implementation of all five functions of symbolic representations, executed intentionally under the guidance of rational reasoning. Based on these arguments, it is possible to say that autonomy is human natural potentiality that may evolve into a real and powerful source for actions if people are trained to use it.

SELF AND HUMAN AUTONOMY

Another important acquisition that accompanied the emergence and functioning of symbolic mental representation is a *sense of self*: a sense that a reflecting individual develops as a result of learning how to use symbolic representations. Based on this learning, a person acquires the capacity of seeing the external and internal worlds from "within" his or her own frame of reference, the feeling that it is he or she who is doing all these reflections, reasoning, planning, and acting. This sense of self is built on a person's body awareness, body-in-the-environment models and a historical memory of being the same person over time (Murphy &

Brown, 2007). Archer (2000) argued that "the self, that continuous sense of being one and the same subject ... is the source of reflexive self-consciousness which lasts throughout life—continually informing us that the things which happen to us ourselves and the things that we make happen, all pertain to the self-same being" (p.255). These arguments lie at the basis of the SDT's understanding of *self* as a center of experience and actions from the point of view of an experiencing and acting individual and only in this phenomenological sense do the SDT researchers use this concept in terms such as self-ruled, self-governed, and self-determined. This sense of self is a universal attribute of all human beings. As Mauss (1985) worded it "... there has never existed a human being who has not been aware, not only of his body, but also at the same time of his individuality, both spiritual and physical" (p.3). The symbolic mental representations, the sense of self, and psychological autonomy are dialectically related phenomena that constitute the essence of humanness in every human being.

This sense of self and the ability of one's self to manipulate various mental representations was labeled "homunculus" by medieval scholars—a metaphorical small person who sits in our heads and guides our body and mind though life. This metaphor has become a straw man for the representatives of various deterministic trends in psychology and philosophy who fight the whole idea of human autonomy and freedom as unscientific and indeterministic (Bargh & Chartrand, 1999; Skinner, 1971). "Homunculus" is a metaphor, but the sense of self and the power of self-determination built on it are real psychological phenomena.

CULTURE AND HUMAN AUTONOMY

The relationship between culture and autonomy is one of the most highly discussed and disputed topics in modern social and human sciences (Archer, 1996; Benson, 2001; Markus & Kitayama, 2003; Martin, 2008; Martin, et al., 2003; McCrone, 1999). Cultural determinists argue that autonomy is culturally relative because it can only emerge in social and symbolic environments and continuously stays dependent on these environments. Their opponents—cultural universalists—argue that autonomy is a universal attribute of human beings across countries and cultures, and that cultures only shape its manifestations. Following our above arguments, it can be stated that human autonomy exists in human beings as a universal potentiality and requires culture and a symbolic-linguistic context to be developed into actuality. Human society (as a system of interconnected social relations) and Culture (with a capital "C," as it refers to any intentional reality maintained through shared meanings and practices) are absolutely necessary for human autonomy as potential to be developed into real psychological power.

Culture is understood here as a community of people who, through sharing language and other symbolical features, negotiate the meanings and practices that govern their lives, regardless of time and space in these communities. We define "cultures" (small "c") as particular communities and systems of shared meanings and practices, which exist in time and space, such as Chinese culture, Islamic culture, culture of white, middle-class North Americans, etc. Culture is absolutely important for the emergence of symbolic representations as a necessary prerequisite for autonomous regulation (Kagan, 2004; Martin, 2008). Culture gives people tools in the form of language and other symbolic forms of regulation that they need to learn, to internalize and to transform into their own inter-subjective mental symbolic representations (Vygotsky, 1978, 1986). The emergence of symbolic representations, which are the basis of human autonomy and sense of self, depends on Culture. This is how Habermas (2003) worded this thesis: "Subjectivity, being what makes the human body a soul-possessing receptacle of the spirit, is itself constituted through intersubjective relations to others. The individual self will only emerge through the course of social externalization, and can only be *stabilized* within the network of undamaged relations of mutual recognition" (p.34). "Individuation, as a part of life history, is an outcome of socialization. For the organism to become, with birth, a person in the full sense of this term, an act of social individuation is required, that is, integration in the *public* context of interaction of an intersubjectively shared lifeworld." (p.34). "... It takes entrance in the public sphere of a linguistic community for a natural creature to develop into both an individual and a person endowed with reason" (p.35). This is where the thesis that autonomy depends on culture comes into play, and in this context this thesis is absolutely correct. Symbolic environments (any symbolic environment) enable emergence of mental representations through directed social interactions.

Because of the advantages that symbolic representations bring to people, all societies are interested in teaching and training their members to properly use them. Almost all societies show young individuals through education and training that they have this symbolic reflective capacity. Educators try to stress its importance and train students in the appropriate uses of it. This training could include, but is not limited to, learning the skills of delaying responses to immediate environmental and internal (bodily and psychological) demands, gaining competence in reflecting on one's own reactions to these demands, developing the habits of planning and contemplating further actions, and taking into consideration thoughts and feelings of other people in planning one's responses.

When this system of symbolic representations at different levels is in place and all the relevant skills of using these representations are learned, a person has all the prerequisites to exercise his or her autonomy. Then, more complex and dialectical relations between an autonomous individual and his or her cultural environment start unfolding. The dialectics here is that when a person acquires these representations and learns how to use them effectively, he or she becomes relatively independent of those cultural influences that have enabled these capacities in the first place. An autonomous individual can reflect on his or her society and culture, which made this autonomy possible, and becomes relatively independent from its norms, rules, expectations and traditions (Martin, et al., 2003). As a result of this, an autonomous individual can accept, resist, or deny societal and cultural demands and act on his or her own will and governance. The fact that Culture supplied him or her with the tools for these emancipated actions does not mean that a person is a slave of a culture.

And this is where the struggle between an autonomous person and Culture starts. Any culture has members with different levels of autonomy development, and each culture created its own politics to deal with these potentially creative, innovative, but also critical and rebellious individuals. For example, Ancient Greece, starting with Socrates, cherished this capability and believed that human autonomy enabled people to be the builders of their own happiness and good life. They created a social order—democracy—where human autonomy flourishes. The Greek civilization was the cradle of the modern ideology of individualism. Modern liberal democracies in general welcome autonomous, creative and self-reflecting individuals (Inglehart & Welzel, 2005).

In Ancient China, philosophers were also aware of humans' capability for conscious and self-conscious reflections and based on them the capacity to be autonomous and relatively independent from society. They refer to the concept *zhi* which means "the will of the self"(Chong, 2003). There were arguments in the history of Ancient China between philosophers who cherished this capacity and those who wanted to put it under a strict societal control (Elvin, 1985). The second trend has won. The arguments of the winning side were that people fail to exercise their autonomy and freedom efficiently, because pursuing personal moral values and goals created nothing but chaos in communities. The remedy for this problem was found in a centralized government and the development of the ideology of vertical collectivism. According to this ideology, it is not the development of individuals but the maintenance of harmony within hierarchically structured communities that are the central points of concern for rulers and ordinary people, and this maintenance leads to good and moral living. But the development of this ideology does not mean that Chinese people do not have autonomy as a psychological capacity. The ideology of vertical collectivism puts it under a very strict societal control, but the autonomy as a capacity for reflective thinking and self-government never disappeared.

Thus, Culture plays various roles in the functioning of autonomous individuals: it enables people's symbolic mental representation that make autonomy, sense of self, and self-determination possible. It facilitates the development of autonomy through systematic education and training of children on how to use these mental representations properly. But, when autonomy emerges, the personal life of any autonomous person becomes a battlefield between the striving for autonomy and the demands of the society to subordinate this autonomy to the collective norms, values, and ideologies and make autonomous people externally controlled. In societies where the culture of horizontality prevails over the culture of verticality, this struggle can be pretty subtle, whereas in vertical cultures, and especially in countries with extreme forms of totalitarianism and autocratic dictatorships, this battle can be very severe, meaning that autonomous people either conform to the dictators or die.

Another aspect of the thesis that human autonomy depends on society and Culture states that autonomy is not a natural propensity but a socially and linguistically constructed phenomenon. Being socially constructed means that certain things or phenomena and their meanings exist only if a community of people believes in their existence, shares these beliefs and enacts them in their everyday activities (Searle, 2010). Let's take as an example the ideology of individualism, which is culturally constructed. The socio-culturally constructed nature of individualism means that all the members of a community where this ideology is propagated believe that an individual should be at the center of attention and the starting point for evaluation of societal traditions, norms and practices. They also believe that it is a valuable ideology and should be facilitated and propagated by any means. They also know that other people believe in this ideology and act on this assumption of mutual understanding. Thus, the ideology of individualism emerges through the communal negotiations and is maintained as long as there is a community of people who believe in it, think about it positively, and enact it in their actions. In philosophy, this is called "collective intentionality" (Searle, 2010). As soon as the members of a community stop believing in individualism and stop acting based on this belief, this ideology as a phenomenon will disappear. Human autonomy, when it is developed and functions fully, exists independently of what other members of the community, including an autonomous person, think about it or believe about it. It is a part of our make-up, and it exists as a natural and not a socially constructed condition. What is constructed in this case is the meaning of autonomy and being autonomous: Is it good or bad? Should autonomous persons be considered selfish and egotistical outcasts or mature protagonists and the most valuable members of a community? What are the domains for exercising autonomy, and what are appropriate periods of life to do this?

The relationships between Culture and human autonomy are dialectical. This means that the symbolic-linguistic environment is absolutely necessary for the emergence and development of symbolic mental representations, and cultural practices in the form of formal education and training are crucial for teaching children how to use these mental representations properly. As these representations develop, a person acquires the power to distance him or herself psychologically, not only from a physical environment but also from the symbolic environment that enables his or her autonomy. When people reach an advanced level of autonomy, they acquire power of resistance to and ability of changing these cultural influences and demands. Different cultures have various ideologies about how to deal with autonomous people and with autonomy as a phenomenon. They may either facilitate or prohibit them. But these different ideologies have nothing to do with the understanding of the nature of psychological autonomy, which remains an evolved natural propensity of any healthy individual.

CONCLUSION

Eudaimonic living and high psychological well-being are achievable goals for any individual. One of the fundamental conditions for reaching these states is the presence of self-determined motivation, which includes autonomous and intrinsic motivation. These forms of motivation should regulate people's lives as well as particular forms of their daily activities. In order for people to be healthy and happy, they have to be psychologically free: free from being the puppets of their own unreflected desires and motivational urges, from uncritically accepting political, religious and ideological indoctrinations, and from blindly following expectations of others. This freedom, and the human psychological autonomy that is built on it, is grounded in a person's deep understanding of his or her own fundamental psychological needs, in developing in a self-determined manner his or her own values and goals, and in acknowledging and respecting needs and goals of other people. Psychological autonomy brings people eudaimonic happiness and well-being because only autonomous people have a full access to their inner worlds, and exercise a well-reflected understanding of physical and social worlds around them; only autonomy provides conditions for the promotion of life in its fullest forms and for experiencing the eudaimonic pleasure that comes with this promotion. Self-determination theory is a psychological theory that provides an elaborated account of motivational and social conditions that promote or thwart the manifestation and functioning of human autonomy. These motivational factors include harmonious satisfaction of the basic psychological needs for autonomy, competence and relatedness; relative dominance of the intrinsic life-goals and aspirations over the extrinsic ones, and relative prevalence of the self-determined forms of motivation, mostly autonomous (integrated and identified), over the controlled forms. Distal and proximal social conditions, which are arranged along the dimensions of horizontality and verticality of social relations, comprise the social context that either facilitates or hinders emergence and functioning of autonomy. The culture of horizontality is built on the values and practices of trust, respect, equality, tolerance and willingness to share. It is represented in the distal relations as liberal democracies, and social capital and social cohesion. In the proximal social relationships, this form of culture is known as autonomy supportive relations, authoritative and democratic parenting, and relations that support basic psychological needs. Culture of verticality propagates values and practices of control, power, obedience and loyalty. In the distal social arrangements, it manifests itself in dictatorial and autocratic political governance and in various social networks and structures that are built around hierarchies of status and power. On the more proximal social level, this culture is known as controlling relationships and authoritarian parenting. There are reciprocal relations among social contexts, self-determined individuals, and their well-being and happiness. Self-determined individuals are not only influenced by their social environments, but they also actively participate in changing them and making them more favorable for their own and other people's healthy functioning. Also, healthy motivation not only determines positive well-being outcomes, eudaimonic happiness, health, and success, but happy and healthy individuals also have a tendency to develop more advantageous motivation in themselves and in others. Dynamic and dialectical relations among these three components are the key to understanding people's good life and flourishing.

REFERENCES

Amabile, T. M. (1983). *The social psychology of creativity.* New York: Springer-Verlag.

Archer, M. S. (1996). *Culture and agency: The place of culture in social theory*. Cambridge, UK: Cambridge University Press.

Archer, M. S. (2000). *Being human: The problem of agency.* Cambridge: Cambridge University Press.

Assor, A., & Kaplan, H. (2001). Mapping the domain of autonomy support: Five important ways to enhance or undermine students' experience of autonomy in learning. In A. Efklides, J. Kuhl & R. M. Sorrentino (Eds.), *Trends and prospects in motivation research* (pp. 101-120). Boston, MA: Kluwer Academic Publishers.

Assor, A., Kaplan, H., Kanat-Maymon, Y., & Roth, G. (2005). Directly controlling teacher behaviors as predictors of poor motivation and engagement in girls and boys: The role of anger and anxiety. *Learning and Instruction, 15*(5), 397-413.

Baer, J., Kaufman, J. C., & Baumeister, R. F. (Eds.). (2008). *Are we free? Psychology and free will.* Oxford: Oxford University Press.

Bakhtin, M. (1984). *Problems of Dostoevsky's poetics*. Minneapolis: University of Minnesota Press.

Bargh, J. A. (2008). Free will is un-natural. In J. Baer, J. C. Kaufman & R. F. Baumeister (Eds.), *Are we free? Psychology and free will.* (pp. 128-154). Oxford: Oxford University Press.

Bargh, J. A., & Chartrand, T. L. (1999). The unbearable automaticity of being. *American Psychologist, 54*(7), 462-479.

Benson, C. (2001). *The cultural psychology of self: Place, morality and art in human worlds.* London: Routledge.

Berger-Smith, R. (2000). *Social cohesion as an aspect of the quality of societies: Concept and measurement.* (No. 14). Mannheim: Centre for Survey Research and Methodology.

Bergsma, A., Poot, G., & Liefbroer, A. C. (2008). Happiness in the garden of Epicurus. *Journal of Happiness Studies, 9*, 397-423.

Bobzien, S. (1998). *Determinism and freedom in Stoic philosophy.* Oxford: Oxford University Press.

Buber, M. (1970). *I and thou.* New York: Charles Scribner's Sons.

Carver, C. S., & Baird, E. (1998). The American dream revisited: is it *what* you want or *why* you want it that matters? *Psychological Science, 9*, 289-292.

Cheng, C.-y. (2004). A theory of Confucian selfhood: Self-cultivation and free will in Confucian philosophy. In K.-l. Shun & D. B. Wong (Eds.), *Confucian ethics: A comparative study of self, autonomy, and community* (pp. 124 -142). New York: Cambridge University Press.

Chirkov, V. I. (2010). Dialectical relationships among human autonomy, the brain, and culture. In V. I. Chirkov, R. M. Ryan & K. M. Sheldon (Eds.), *Human autonomy in cross-cultural contexts: Perspectives on the psychology of agency, freedom, and well-being* (pp. 65-92). Dordrecht: Springer.

Chirkov, V. I., Ryan, R. M., & Sheldon, K. M. (Eds.). (2010). *Human autonomy in cross-cultural contexts: Perspectives on the psychology of agency, freedom, and well-being.* Dordrecht: Springer.

Chirkov, V. I., Lebedeva, N. M., Molodtsova, I., & Tatarko, A. (in press). Social capital, motivational autonomy, and health-related behavior in Canadian and Russian youth. In D. Chadee & A. Kostic (Eds.), *Social psychological dynamics.* Trinidad, W.I.: University of West Indies Press.

Chirkov, V. I., Safdar, S., de Guzman, J., & Playford, K. (2008). Further examining the role motivation to study abroad plays in the adaptation of international students in Canada. *International Journal for Intercultural Relations, 32*, 427-440.

Chong, K.-c. (2003). Autonomy in the Analects. In K. Chong, S. Tan & C. L. Ten (Eds.), *The moral circle and the self: Chinese and western approaches* (pp. 269-282). Chicago: Open Court.

Christman, J. (2009). *The politics of persons: Individual autonomy and socio-historical selves.* Cambridge, UK: Cambridge University Press.

Coleman, J. S. (1988). Social capital in the creation of human capital. *American Journal of Sociology, 94*, 95-120.

Cooper, J. M. (2003). Stoic autonomy. In E. F. Paul, F. D. Miller Jr. & J. Paul (Eds.), *Autonomy* (pp. 1-29). Cambridge, UK: Cambridge University Press.

Cote, J. E., & Levine, C. G. (2002). *Identity formation, agency, and culture: A social psychological synthesis.* Mahwah, NJ: Lawrence Erlbaum Associates.

de Botton, A. (2004). *Status anxiety.*: Penguin.

Deacon, T. W. (1997). *The symbolic species: The co-evolution of language and the brain.* New York: Norton.

Deci, E. L., Eghart, H., Patric, B. C., & Leone, D. R. (1994). Facilitating internalization: The self-determination theory perspective. *Journal of Personality, 62*(1), 119-142.

Deci, E. L., & Ryan, R. M. (1985). *Intrinsic motivation and self-determination theory of human behavior.* New York: Plenum.

Deci, E. L., & Ryan, R. M. (2000). The "what" and "why" of goal pursuits: Human needs and the self-determination of behavior. *Psychological Inquiry, 11*(4), 227-268.

Deci, E. L., & Ryan, R. M. (Eds.). (2002). *Handbook of self-determination research.* Rochester, NY: The University of Rochester Press.

Dennett, D. C. (1986). *Elbow room: The varieties of free will worth wanting.* Cambridge, MA: The MIT Press.

Dworkin, G. (1988). *The theory and practice of autonomy.* Cambridge, UK: Cambridge University Press.

Elvin, M. (1985). Between the earth and haven: Conceptions of the self in China. In M. Carrithers, S. Collins & S. Lukes (Eds.), *The category of the person: Anthropology, philosophy, history* (pp. 156-189). Cambridge, UK: Cambridge University Press.

Engstrom, A., & Whiting, J. (Eds.). (1996). *Aristotle, Kant, and the Stoics: Rethinking happiness and duty.* Cambridge, UK: Cambridge University Press.

Erikson, E. H. (1964). *Insight and responsibility: Lectures on the ethical implications of psychoanalytic insight.* New York: W. W. Norton & Company.

Feldman, F. (2004). *Pleasure and the good life: Concerning the nature, varieties and plausibility of hedonism.* Oxford Clarendon Press.

Frankfurt, H. G. (1971). Freedom of the will and the concept of a person. *The Journal of Philosophy, 68*(1), 5-20.

Frey, B. S., & Stutzer, A. (2000). Happiness prospers in democracy. *Journal of Happiness Studies, 1*(1), 79-102.

Frie, R. (2008). *Psychological agency: Theory, practice, and culture.* Cambridge, MA: The MIT Press.

Fromm, E. (1941). *Escape from freedom.* New York: Farrar & Rinehart.

Gagne, M., & Deci, E. L. (2005). Self-determination theory and work motivation. *Journal of Organizational psychology, 26*, 331-362.

Giri, A. K. (2000). Rethinking human well-being: A dialog with Amartya Sen. *Journal of International Development, 12*, 1003-1018.

Grolnick, W. S. (2003). *The psychology of parental control: How well-meant parenting backfires.* Mahwah, NJ: Lawrence Erlbaum Associates.

Grolnick, W. S., Ryan, R. M., & Deci, E. L. (1997). Internalization within the family: The self-determination theory perspective. In J. E. Grusec & L. Kuczynski (Eds.), *Parenting and children's internalization of values* (pp. 135 - 161). New York: Wiley.

Grootaert, C., & van Bastelaer, T. (2001). *Understanding and measuring social capital: A synthesis of findings and recommendations from the Social Capital Initiative.* Washington, DC: The World Bank.

Gruen, A. (2007). *The betrayal of the self: The fear of autonomy in men and women.* Berkeley, CA: Human Development Books.

Guyer, P. (2000). *Kant on freedom, law, and happiness.* Cambridge, UK: Cambridge University Press.

Guyer, P. (2003). Kant on theory and practice of autonomy. In E. F. Paul, F. D. Miller & J. Paul (Eds.), *Autonomy* (pp. 70 - 98). Cambridge, UK: Cambridge University Press

Habermas, J. (1979). *Communication and the evolution of society.* Boston, MA: Beacon Press.

Habermas, J. (1990). Justice and solidarity: On the discussion concerning stage 6. In T. E. Wren, W. Edelstein & G. Nunner-Winkler (Eds.), *The moral domain: Essays in the ongoing discussion between philosophy and the social sciences* (pp. 224-252). Cambridge, MA: The MIT Press.

Habermas, J. (2003). *The future of human nature.* Cambridge, UK: Polity Press.

Hagger, M. S., & Chatzisarantis, N. L. (2007). *Intrinsic motivation and self-determination in exercise and sport.* Champaigne, IL: Human Kinetics.

Haworth, L. (1986). *Autonomy: An essay in philosophical psychology and ethics.* New Haven, CT: Yale University Press.

Heider, F. (1958/1982). *The psychology of interpersonal relations*: Psychology Press.

Horney, K. (1950). *Neurosis and human growth.* New York: Norton.

Inglehart, R. (2000). Culture and democracy. In L. E. Harrison & S. P. Huntington (Eds.), *Culture matters: How values shape human progress.* (pp. 80-97). New York: Basic Books.

Inglehart, R., & Oyserman, D. (2004). Individualism, autonomy, self-expression: The human development syndrome. In H. Vinken, J. Soeters & P. Ester (Eds.), *Comparing cultures: Dimensions of culture in a comparative perspective.* (pp. 74-96). Leiden: Brill.

Inglehart, R., & Welzel, C. (2005). *Modernization, cultural change and democracy: The human development sequence.* Cambridge, UK: Cambridge University Press.

Kagan, J. (2004). The uniquely human in human nature. *Daedalus, 133*(4), 77-88.

Kasser, T. (2002). Sketches for a self-determination theory of values. In E. L. Deci & R. M. Ryan (Eds.), *Handbook of self-determination research.* Rochester, NY: University of Rochester Press.

Kasser, T., & Ryan, R. M. (1993). A dark side of the American dream: Correlates of financial success as a central life aspiration. *Journal of Personality and Social Psychology, 65*(3), 410-422.

Kasser, T., & Ryan, R. M. (1996). Further examining the American dream: Differential correlates of intrinsic and extrinsic goals. *Personality and Social Psychology Bulletin, 22*, 280-287.

Kohlberg, L., Boyd, D. R., & Levine, C. G. (1990). The return of stage 6: Its principle and moral point of view. In T. E. Wren (Ed.), *The moral domain: Essays in the ongoing discussion between philosophy and the social science.* (pp. 151-181.). Cambridge, MA: The MIT Press.

Libet, B., Freeman, A., & Sutherland, K. (Eds.). (1999). *The volitional brain: Towards a neuroscience of free will.* Thorverton, UK: Imprint Academic.

Markus, H. R., & Kitayama, S. (2003). Models of agency: Sociocultural diversity in the construction of action. *Nebraska Symposium on Motivation, 49*, 1-57.

Martin, J. (2008). Perspectival selves and agents: Agency within sociality. In R. Frie (Ed.), *Psychological agency: Theory, practice, and culture* (pp. 97-116). Cambridge, MA: The MIT Press.

Martin, J., Sugarman, J., & Hickinbottom, S. (2009). *Persons: Understanding psychological selfhood and agency.* New York: Springer.

Martin, J., Sugerman, J., & Thompson, J. (2003). *Psychology and the question of agency.* Albany, NY: State University of New York Press.

Maslow, A. (1968). *Toward a psychology of being.* (2 ed.). Princeton, N.J.: Van Nostrand.

Mauss, M. (1985). A category of human mind: The notion of person; the notion of self. In M. Carrithers, S. Collins & S. Lukes (Eds.), *The category of the person: Anthropology, philosophy, history* (pp. 1-25). Cambridge, UK: Cambridge University Press.

May, H. (2010). *Aristotle's ethics: Moral development and human nature*. London: Continuum.

McCrone, J. (1999). A bifold model of free will. In B. Libet, A. Freeman & K. Sutherland (Eds.), *The volitional brain: Towards a neuroscience of free will* (pp. 241 - 259). Thorverton, UK: Imprint Academic.

Mele, A. R. (2001). *Autonomous agents: From self-control to autonomy*. Oxford: Oxford University Press.

Murphy, N. C., & Brown, W. S. (2007). *Did my neurons make me do it? Philosophical and neurobiological perspectives on moral responsibility and free will*. Oxford: Oxford University Press.

Niemiec, C. P., Lynch, M. F., Vansteenkiste, M., Bernstein, J., Deci, E. L., & Ryan, R. M. (2006). The antecedents and consequences of autonomous self-regulation for college: A self-determination theory perspective on socialization. *Journal of Adolescence, 29*, 761-775.

Niemiec, C. P., Ryan, R. M., & Deci, E. L. (2009). The path taken: Consequences of attaining intrinsic and extrinsic aspirations in post-college life. *Journal of Research in Personality, 43*(291-306).

Oshana, M. (2003). How much should we value autonomy? In E. F. Paul, F. D. Miller & J. Paul (Eds.), *Autonomy* (pp. 99 - 126). Cambridge, UK: Cambridge University Press

Patrick, H., Knee, C. R., Canevello, A., & Lonsbary, C. (2007). The role of need fulfillment in relationship functioning and well-being: A self-determination theory perspective *Journal of Personality and Social Psychology, 92*, 434-457.

Paul, E. F., Miller, F. D., & Paul, J. (Eds.). (2003). *Autonomy*. Cambridge, UK: Cambridge University Press

Reeve, J., & Jang, H. (2006). What teachers say and do to support students' autonomy during a learning activity. *Journal of Educational Psychology 98*(1), 209-218.

Reis, H. T., Sheldon, K. M., Gable, S. L., Roscoe, J., & Ryan, R. M. (2000). Daily well-being: The role of autonomy, competence, and relatedness. *Personality and Social Psychology Bulletin, 26*(4), 419-435.

Rogers, C. (1961). *On becoming a person: A therapist's view of psychotherapy*. Boston, MA: Houghton Mifflin Company.

Ryan, R. M. (1995). Psychological needs and the facilitation of integrative processes. *Journal of Personality, 63*, 397-427.

Ryan, R. M., Chirkov, V. I., Little, T. D., Sheldon, K. M., Timoshina, E., & Deci, E. L. (1999). The American dream in Russia: Extrinsic aspirations and well-being in two cultures. *Personality and Social Psychology Bulletin, 25*(12), 1509-1524.

Ryan, R. M., & Connell, J. P. (1989). Perceived locus of causality and internalization: Examining reasons for acting in two domains. *Journal of Personality and Social Psychology, 57*, 749-761.

Ryan, R. M., & Deci, E. L. (2000). Self-determination theory and the facilitation of intrinsic motivation, social development, and well-being. *American Psychologist, 55*(1), 68-78.

Ryan, R. M., & Deci, E. L. (2001). On happiness and human potentials: A review of research on hedonic and eudaimonic well-being. *Annual Review of Psychology, 52*, 141-166.

Ryan, R. M., Huta, V., & Deci, E. L. (2008). Living well: A self-determination theory perspective on eudaimonia. *Journal of Happiness Studies 9*, 139-170.

Ryan, R. M., Sheldon, K. M., Kasser, T., & Deci, E. L. (1996). All goals are not created equal: An organismic perspective on the nature of goals and their regulation. In P. M. Gollwizer & J. A. Bargh (Eds.), *The psychology of action: Linking cognition and motivation to behavior* (pp. 7-26). New York: Guilford.

Ryff, C. D., & Singer, B. H. (2008). Know thyself and become what you are: A eudaimonic approach to psychological well-being. *Journal of Happiness Studies, 9*, 13-39.

Sanderson, A. (1985). Purity and power among the Brahmans of Kashmir. In M. Carrithers, S. Collins & S. Lukes (Eds.), *The category of the person: Anthropology, philosophy, history* (pp. 190-216). Cambridge, UK: Cambridge University Press.

Schmuck, P., Kasser, T., & Ryan, R. M. (2000). Intrinsic and extrinsic goals: Their structure and relationship to well-being in German and U. S. college students. *Social Indicators Research, 50*(2), 225-241.

Searle, J. R. (2010). *Making the social world: The structure of human civilization.* Oxford: Oxford University Press.

Sen, A. (1999). Democracy as a universal value. *Journal of Democracy, 10*(3), 3-17.

Sheldon, K. M. (2002). The self-concordance model of healthy goal striving: when personal goals correctly represent the person. In E. L. Deci & R. M. Ryan (Eds.), *Handbook of self-determination research* (pp. 65-86). Rochester, NY: The University of Rochester Press.

Sheldon, K. M., & Niemiec, C. (2006). It's not just the amount that counts: Balanced need satisfaction also affects well-being. *Journal of Personality and Social Psychology, 91*, 331-341.

Sheldon, K. M., Ryan, R. M., Deci, E. L., & Kasser, T. (2004). The independent effect of goal contents and motives on well-being: it's both what you pursue and why you pursue it. *Personality and Social Psychology Bulletin, 30*(4), 475-486.

Sheldon, K. M., Ryan, R. M., & Reis, H. T. (1996). What makes for a good day? Competence and autonomy in the day and in the person. *Personality and Social Psychology Bulletin, 22*, 1270-1279.

Skinner, B. F. (1971). *Beyond freedom and dignity.* New York: Knopf.

Soanes, C., & Stevenson, A. (Eds.). (2008). *Concise Oxford English dictionary* (11 ed.). Oxford: Oxford University Press.

Tremblay, R. (2010). *The code of global ethics: Ten humanistic principles.* Amherst, NY: Prometheus Books.

Uyl, D. D. (2003). Autonomous autonomy: Spinoza on autonomy, perfectionism, and politics. In E. F. Paul, F. D. Miller & J. Paul (Eds.), *Autonomy* (pp. 30 - 69). Cambridge, UK: Cambridge University Press.

Vansteenkiste, M., Lens, W., & Deci, E. L. (2006). Intrinsic versus extrinsic goal-contents in self-determination theory: Another look at the quality of academic motivation. *Educational Psychologist, 41*(1), 19-31.

Vansteenkiste, M., Ryan, R. M., & Deci, E. L. (2008). Self-determination theory and the explanatory role of psychological needs in human well-being. In L. Bruni, F. Comim & M. Pugno (Eds.), *Capabilities and happiness* Oxford, UK: Oxford University Press.

Vansteenkiste, M., Simons, J., Lens, W., Sheldon, K. M., & Deci, E. L. (2004). Motivating learning, performance, and persistence: the synergistic effects of intrinsic goal contents and autonomy-supportive context. *Journal of Personality and Social Psychology, 87*(2), 246-260.

Veenhoven, R. (2000). Freedom and happiness: A comparative study in forty-four nations in the early 1990s. In E. Diener & E. M. Suh (Eds.), *Culture and subjective well-being* (pp. 257-288). Cambridge, MA: A Bradford Book.

Vygotsky, L. S. (1978). *Mind in society: The development of higher psychological processes.* Cambridge, MA: Harvard University Press.

Vygotsky, L. S. (1986). *Thought and language.* Cambridge, MA: MIT Press.

Wallis, K. C., & Poulton, J. L. (2001). *Internalization: The origin and construction of internal reality.* Buckingan, UK: Open University Press.

Waterman, A. S., Schwartz, S. J., & Conti, R. (2008). The implications of two conceptions of happiness (hedonic enjoyment and eudaimonia) for the understanding of intrinsic motivation. *Journal of Happiness Studies, 9,* 41-79.

Williams, G. C. (2002). Improving patients' health through supporting the autonomy of patients and providers. In E. L. Deci & R. M. Ryan (Eds.), *Handbook of self-determination research* (pp. 233-254). Rochester, NY: University of Rochester Press.

Williams, G. C., & Deci, E. L. (1996). Internalization of biopsychosocial values by medical students: A test of self-determination theory. *Journal of Personality and Social Psychology, 70,* 767-779.

In: Motivation, Consciousness and Self-Regulation
Editor: D. A. Leontiev, pp. 127-138

ISBN: 978-1-61324-795-2
© 2012 Nova Science Publishers, Inc.

Chapter 9

HARDINESS AS THE EXISTENTIAL COURAGE TO TURN STRESSES INTO GROWTH OPPORTUNITIES

Salvatore R. Maddi
University of California, Irvine

ABSTRACT

The chapter conceptualizes hardiness as the existential courage that facilitates being able to turn stresses from potential disasters into growth opportunities. In this explanation, life is assumed to be an inherently stressful phenomenon, involving ongoing developmental requirements, which get added to imposed megatrends. In all of this, the hardy attitudes and skills involve not only surviving, but thriving. This leads to enhanced performance, health, and subjective fulfillment. Furthermore, this chapter summarizes relevant research, which supports the position, and has led to validated procedures for hardiness assessment and training.

Keywords: Hardiness, existential courage, stresses, performance, health

INTRODUCTION

The emerging theme of positive psychology (Seligman, & Csikszentmihalyi, 2000), has emphasized happiness, as shown in such traits as optimism (Sheier, & Carver, 1985) and subjective well-being (Pavot, & Diener, 1993). Recently, courage has been added to positive psychology (Maddi, 2006), as mere happiness is insufficient in understanding how people can deal well with stressful circumstances. From the vantage point of existential psychology, this chapter elaborates theoretically and empirically on courage, as it facilitates the search for meaning.

THE NATURE OF LIVING

According to existential psychology, life is, by nature, continuously changing, and therefore a stressful phenomenon (Frankl, 1963; Graber, 2004; Kierkegaard, 1954; Maddi, 1996, 2004a; May, Angel, & Ellenberger, 1967). A major source of this stressful change is the developmental process. Development begins with the birth trauma, when we are pushed out of our mother's womb, into an environment with bright lights and loud noises, and are slapped on the back by a physician, so that we have to begin breathing for ourselves. As the days go on, we must learn to eat with our mouths, recognize the words the people around us are using to communicate with us, accept the regulations of sleeping and waking, and cry when we need something. Just as we are getting a bit socialized, we must begin regularly leaving the home into which we were born, in order to start schooling. We cry when our mother's drop us off at the unfamiliar environment, and find ourselves interacting with peers and teachers we know nothing about. The rules and regulations are new to us, and we must figure out how to behave, who to be friendly with, and what to learn. This process of change continues through middle and high school, and leads to the requirement that we consider what our adult lives will be like. What kind of career will we have, who will we date, and what does this all mean, now that we are becoming more distant from our families of origin? Will we go to college, or not? If we go, what shall we major in, and do we work on finding someone to partner with in establishing a family of reference? Who are we, anyway? Then, once we have started a career, and a family of reference, we need to get involved in taking care of our spouses, and helping our children go through this entire process of development. As we get even older, we struggle to learn how to stay healthy, and what to do to prepare for our inevitable deaths, and that of those around us.

As if these developmental stressors were not enough, there are also stressful megatrends imposed on us by changes taking place in our societies and environments. Examples that we have encountered in our time include the breathtakingly rapid technological advances that have led to our telecommunications industry, the related shift toward an information industry, the outsourcing of jobs abroad, shifts in requirements of job performance, economic downturns, and the threat of global warming. It seems to many people that nothing is stable and predictable anymore.

According to existential positions (Frankl, 1963; Kierkegaard, 1954; Maddi, 1996, 2004a;), the changing (and therefore stressful) nature of living requires that we continually make decisions as to what we think and do with regard to interacting with the world. Specifically, existentialists emphasize this interaction with others, social institutions, the environment, and ourselves (in the sense of an internal dialogue). This interaction with the world involves a continual process of making decisions as to what is going on, what to do, and how to feel. Although these decisions have a wide variety of content, they all have the same form, namely, decisions can be made either for the future, or the past. Decisions for the future involve perceiving experiences and resulting directions as new, whereas decisions for the past involve imposing what one already knows on experiences and directions.

The existentialists emphasize that making decisions for the future is the way to grow in wisdom and fulfillment, whereas making decision for the past has a stultifying effect. But, deciding for the future brings ontological anxiety (Frankl, 1963; Kierkegaard, 1954; Maddi, 2004a), because one is entering unpredictable and uncharted paths. One might think that choosing the past would be less troubling. Instead , choosing the past brings ontological guilt (the sense of missed opportunity), the accumulation of which results in emptiness and meaninglessness. So, for existentialists, the best answer is to choose the future as often as possible, so that one continues to grow and feel fulfilled. In this, the attitudes of existential courage are critical, because they help in tolerating ontological anxiety, so that the future-oriented decisions that facilitate growth and development can be made.

HARDINESS AS EXISTENTIAL COURAGE

We have conceptualized hardiness as three attitudes that together constitute existential courage (Maddi, 2004b, 2006). Specifically, these attitudes are the 3Cs of commitment, control, and challenge. If you are strong in commitment, you believe that, no matter how stressful things get, you are best off staying in close contact with the people and events in your life. It seems like a loss to pull back into isolation in hopes of protecting yourself from what might happen. If you are strong in control, you believe that, no matter how complex things get, you need to continue to have an influence on the outcomes going on around you. It seems like pulling back into passivity and powerlessness is just giving up, rather than living fully. If you are strong in challenge, you believe that life is by nature continually changing and stressful, but that is an opportunity to grow from what you learn by seeing what you can make of the given circumstances. It seems like a waste of life to just wish for and try to have easy comfort and security instead. In order to have existential courage, it is not enough to just be strong in one, or even two of these attitudes; you need all three.

It is the interaction between the 3Cs together that constitute the strength and motivation to do the hard work of choosing the future and learning from that experience, in order to turn changing and stressful circumstances from potential disasters into growth opportunities. Specifically, strong levels of the 3Cs should lead to low levels of painful emotions (e.g., anxiety, anger, fear, depression), even though you are addressing, rather than avoiding, the stressful circumstances. This is because the courage constituted by the 3Cs leads you to accept stress as natural, and not let it interfere with your social and environmental interactions. Furthermore, strong levels of the 3Cs should motivate you to do the hard work of problem-solving (rather than avoidance), coping, socially-supportive (rather than conflictful) interaction with others, and facilitative (rather than indulgent, undermining) self-care. Doing this hard work should result in hardiness leading to enhanced performance, health, and a sense of fulfillment and meaningfulness.

In contrast, an absence of the existential courage of hardiness will lead to a respone to changing and stressful circumstances of denial and avoidance , or exaggeration and striking out (Maddi, 2004b, 2006). Instead of looking to the future, and learning from the resulting experiences, you will be insisting on maintaining your conventionalism and what is already assumed to be the truth of experience. In this pattern, you will likely engage in avoidant or aggressive (rather than problem-solving) coping, avoidant or conflictful and retaliatory (rather than socially-supportive) interactions with others, and undermining (rather than facilitative) self-care techniques. This destructive pattern will also lead to experiencing painful and disruptive emotions (however much you may be trying to avoid them), an undermining of performance and health, and an increasing sense of missed opportunities and meaninglessness.

RESEARCH ON HARDINESS AS EXISTENTIAL COURAGE

In the last 30 years, considerable research on the relationship of hardiness to performance, health, and the sense of meaning and fulfillment has been done, in various settings and around the world (Maddi, 2002). As will be reviewed here, the findings of this research process have been largely supportive of the position elaborated above: that hardiness is the existential courage that facilitates personal development and growth.

The Illinois Bell Telephone Project

The first findings concerning hardiness emerged from the 12-year longitudinal project we conducted at Illinois Bell Telephone (IBT), in Chicago, IL (Maddi, 1987; Maddi & Kobasa, 1984). Begun in 1975, this project followed central employees at IBT, during the stressful period starting before, and continuing after the U.S. Government's deregulation of the telephone industry in 1981. Prior to that time, the telephone industry had been regulated in order to provide good and inexpensive service to citizens. I was a consultant for IBT in the early 1970s, and it was becoming apparent that deregulation would take place in order to spur the competition that would result in the US making strides in the new telecommunications industry provoked by the initial development of the internet. Thus, it seemed to me that, from a research perspective, the coming deregulation would serve as an effective natural experiment to see what the effects of a major stressful change would be on employees theretofore in a stable and predictable work environment.

Thus, every year from 1975 through 1987, we collected extensive psychological, performance, and health data from 450 IBT supervisors, managers, and decision-makers. Used for this purpose were yearly psychological interviews and test batteries, medical examination data, and job evaluations. There was lots of evidence that the 1981 deregulation of the telephone industry was a major upheaval for IBT. The company became preoccupied with the dramatic changes it needed to make in order to take a competitive approach, after all those years when its bottom line was unimportant. One year after the deregulation, the number of employees in the company had dropped nearly 50%. In 1982, we asked the people in our sample what it was like to work in the transforming company. One manager verbalized the disaster all were experiencing very well, when he reported that he had worked for 10 different supervisors in that one year. They were in and out the door, and did not know what their subordinates were doing. He, too, insisted that he did not know what he was doing. His was a common experience among the members of our sample.

In the six years following the 1981 disaster, two-thirds of the managers in our sample showed significant signs of the undermining of their performance, health, and sense of meaning and fulfillment. There were heart attacks, anxiety and depression disorders, violence in the workplace, divorces, and suicides. There were also dramatic statements about how terrible the upheaval was on their family and work interactions, and on their sense of what life was all about. But, the other third of sample was resilient, in not only surviving the upheaval, but thriving on it. If they remained at IBT, they rose to the top of the transitioning company. If they were downsized out, they tended to use their experience to either start their own companies, or become central in other companies that were forming in the new telecommunications industry.

In order to get a full picture of the long-standing differences between the two-thirds of the sample that fell apart, and the one-third that thrived, we compared the data on them collected in the six years before the upheaval. In this comparison, what we found was that all along, the one-third of our sample that responded resiliently to the upheaval had shown clear signs of (1) higher hardiness attitudes of commitment, control, and challenge, (2) higher hardiness skills of problem-solving coping, socially-supportive interactions with others, and effective self-care, and (3) lower anxiety and depression. Indeed, these differences between the two subgroups persisted even after the upheaval.

The voluminous findings of the IBT project were depicted in the Hardiness Model, which is shown in Figure 1. This model indicates that stress may be either acute (i.e., unexpected changes) or chronic (i.e., continuing conflicts between what you want and what you get). Acute and chronic stresses accumulate and, if they are not reduced, provoke strain (i.e., mental and physical arousal resulting from perceived dangers). At the physical level, strain involves increased hormonal levels of cortisol and adrenalin. If the Strain level is not reduced, it may be strong and long enough to deplete you of resilience resources, resulting in breakdowns into physical symptoms (e.g., nausea, sleep difficulties, loss of concentration and memory), psychological symptoms (e.g., anxiety, depression, anger, loss of meaning), and performance difficulties (e.g., inability to meet deadlines, decline in self-esteem and effort, cognitive and energy difficulties). As depicted in the model, these breakdowns may be influenced by your inherited physical vulnerabilities.

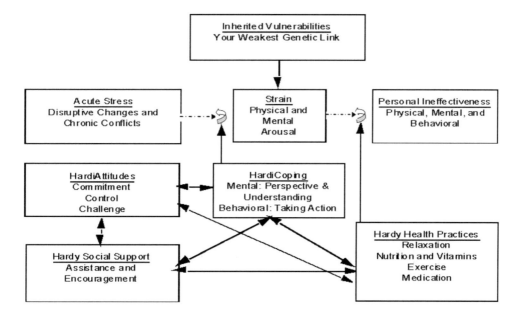

Figure 1. The Hardiness Model for Performance and health Enhancement, ©Copyright 1986-2004.

The good news depicted in the Hardiness Model involves the boxes at the bottom of the figure. Specifically, the Hardiness attitudes of commitment, control, and challenge together provide the courage and motivation to do the hard work of Transformational (problem-solving) Coping, Activistic (socially-supportive) Interactions with others, and Beneficial Self-Care. Beneficial Self-Care helps avoid breakdowns by lowering the strain provoked by stress (in such ways as moderating sweet and fatty foods, and alcohol intake). But, Self-Care alone is not enough to maintain performance and health, as it does not really resolve the stressful circumstances imposed on you. The most effective path to resilience involves a combination of Transformational Coping and Socially-Supportive Interactions, which help in avoiding Breakdowns by decreasing the stressfulness of circumstances through taking actions that help in resolving the particular stresses involved.

Subsequent Hardiness Research

Subsequent research has tended to confirm the hypotheses that hardiness maintains and enhances health under stressful circumstances. In stressful work and social contexts, ranging from life-threatening military combat and peacekeeping missions (e.g., Bartone, 1999), to firefighting (Maddi, Harvey, Resurreccion, Giatras, & Raganold, 2007), and the culture shock of immigration (e.g., Kuo & Tsai, 1986) or work missions abroad (e.g., Atella, 1989), through everyday work or school pressures and demands (e.g., Maddi, 2002), the buffering effect of the courage and motivation constituted by hardiness attitudes is shown in decreasing mental and physical symptoms.

Evidence is also indicating that hardiness attitudes lead to enhancement of performance under stress. For example, there was a positive relationship of hardiness to subsequent (1) basketball performance among varsity players (Maddi, & Hess, 1992), (2) success rates in officer training school for the Israeli military (Florian, Milkulincer, & Taubman, 1995; Westman, 1990), and in firefighter training in the U.S. (Maddi, et al., 2007), (3) transformational leadership among West Point military cadets (Bartone & Snook, 1999), (4) retention rate among college students (Lifton, Seay, & Bushke, 2000), and (5) speed of recovery of baseline functioning following disruptive culture shock (e.g., Atella, 1989; Kuo & Tsai, 1986).

There are also research findings concerning the mechanisms whereby hardiness attitudes (as existential courage and motivation) lead to turning stresses from potential disasters into performance and health advantages. In an experiential sampling study (Maddi, 1999), participants were paged at random to comment on their ongoing activities. What emerged was a positive relationship between hardiness and (1) involvement with others and events (commitment), (2) the sense that the activities had been chosen and could have been avoided (control), and (3) the positive process of learning from what was going on (challenge). Several studies (Maddi, 1986, 1994, 1997, 2002; Maddi, Wadhwa, & Haier, 1996; Weibe, & McCallum, 1986) show that, as expected, hardiness is positively related to problem-solving coping, socially-supportive interactions, and beneficial self-care efforts. Consistent with these findings are others showing that hardiness is associated with viewing stressful circumstances as more tolerable (Ghorbani, Watson, & Morris, 2000; Rhodewalt, & Zone, 1989), and avoiding excessive physiological arousal (Allred, & Smith, 1989; Contrada, 1989) and negative emotions (Maddi, 2002; Maddi, Harvey, Khoshaba, Fazel, & Resurreccion, 2009a).

Further, the findings of another study (Maddi, Khoshaba, Harvey, Fazel, & Resurreccion, 2011) show a positive correlation between hardiness and measures, from a test of existential approaches to meaning (Langle, Orgler, & Kundi, 2003), of accurate perceptions of ongoing situations, recognition of one's evaluative reactions to these ongoing situations, recognition of the choices one is making, and emphasis on carrying out one's developed plans and decisions.

Also, over the years, the measurement of hardiness has improved through research. The original questionnaire measure, the Personal Views Survey (PVS), was met with early criticisms that (1) it might not be a unitary characteristic, and (2) was little more than the opposite of negative affectivity or neuroticism (Funk & Houston, 1987; Hull, Van Treuren, & Virnelli, 1987). In response, the PVS was quickly supplanted by the Second Edition (PVS II), and then Third Edition (PVS III), and this ameliorated both problems (cf., Maddi, 1997; Maddi & Khoshaba, 2001). As expected, the PVS II and III characteristically yield estimates of the 3Cs of hardiness that are positively interrelated in all populations studied (e.g., Maddi, 1997;, Maddi & Hess, 1992; Maddi & Khoshaba, 1994). There are also studies showing that the PVS II and III are not redundant with negative affectivity or neuroticism (Maddi & Khoshaba, 1994; Maddi, Khoshaba, Harvey, Lu, & Persico, 2002). In particular, the negative relationship between hardiness and clinical scales on the Minnesota Multiphasic Personality Inventory, Second Edition (MMPI 2) persisted when negative affectivity was controlled. Furthermore, hardiness was not only negatively related to neuroticism, but positively related to the other four factors on the NEO-FFI. And, all five factors (of this five-factor model) together accounted for only a small amount of the hardiness variance. In addition, the findings of a recent methodological study (Sinclair & Tetrick, 2000) counter both early criticisms by confirming that, as expected, the 3Cs are best regarded as related subcomponents of a higher order hardiness factor, and that this factor is empirically distinct from negative affectivity or neuroticism.

Now, there is an even shorter version of the hardiness test, the PVS III-R, which contains the 18 most reliable and valid items from the 30 in the earlier PVS III. The first study using this most recent test (Maddi, Harvey, Khoshaba, Lu, Persico, & Brow, 2006) shows that the 3Cs and total score on the PVS III-R are highly correlated with, and show similar reliability to those on the PVS III. Continuing the process of contruct validation, the study shows that hardiness as measured by the PVS III-R is negatively related to repression, and positively related to both innovative behavior and success in entrepreneurial consulting. The second study using the PVS III-R (Maddi, Harvey, et al, 2009a) shows that, as expected in college students, hardiness is (1) positively related to positive attitudes toward school and self, (2) negatively related to depression, anxiety, and hostility, and (3) unrelated to socially-desirable responding.

Comparative Analysis Studies

The available findings seem to show that hardiness is a factor in enhancing performance and health, and protecting against painful emotions and meaningless. It is important, therefore, to determine the relative effectiveness of hardiness by comparison to other personal characteristics that may also be helpful in turning stresses to advantages. As summarized below, the three comparative studies currently available suggest that the existential courage measured by hardiness is more effective than happiness or religiousness in provoking problem-solving coping, moderating painful emotions, or enhancing performance.

The first such comparative analytic study (Maddi, & Hightower, 1999) utilized multiple regression analyses in comparing hardiness and optimism in their relative relationships to both problem-solving and avoidance coping. Although hardiness and optimism showed a significant positive correlation with each other, the regression analysis procedure purified each variable of shared variance with the other. Across two undergraduate and one adult sample, the results showed that hardiness exhibited stronger relationships, positively with problem-solving and negatively with avoidance coping, than did optimism.

Another comparative analytic study (Maddi, Brow, Khoshaba, & Vaitkus, 2006) compared hardiness with religiousness in their relationship to depression and anger in a sample of U.S. Army officers. Once again, the multiple regression analysis approach used purified hardiness and religiousness for their significant positive relationship, and showed that hardiness, and not religiousness, was negatively related to depression and anger. This suggests that it is the existential courage of hardiness, rather than the spiritual hopes of religiousness, that protect against negative emotions.

Yet another study (Maddi, Harvey, Khoshaba, Fazel, & Resurreccion, 2011) finds that hardiness is positively correlated with the variables of satisfaction with life (Pavot & Diener, 1993), spiritual well-being (Bufford, Paloutzian, & Ellison, 1991), and life regard (Battista & Almond, 1973) in samples of undergraduates. But, regression analyses using these personality characteristics as independent variables show that hardiness is the best predictor of performance, in the form of subsequent GPA at graduation.

Hardiness Training

There is also a procedure for helping people grow in hardiness, called HardiTraining (Khoshaba & Maddi, 2001; Maddi, 1987). Consistent with hardiness theory, this approach emphasizes assisting trainees in problem-solving coping, socially-supportive interactions, and beneficial self-care, all the while using the feedback from these efforts to deepen the hardiness attitudes of commitment, control, and challenge. The approach includes precise narrative and many related exercises that the trainee is to use in the process of transforming his/her ongoing life stresses into growth opportunities. Also basic are both inspirational and negative examples of how others have performed, and checkpoints during which the trainee reports on his/her efforts to the trainer. Evidence is exhibiting that this training procedure is effective not only in increasing hardiness attitudes and skills, but also in enhancing performance and decreasing illness symptoms for working adults (Maddi, 1987; Maddi, Kahn, & Maddi, 1998) and college students (Maddi, Khoshaba, Jensen, Carter, Lu, & Harvey, 2002; Maddi, Harvey, Khoshaba, Fazel, & Resurreccion, 2009b).

Hardiness assessment and training is clearly useful for individuals who want to improve their being-in-the-world, and for organizations that want to improve their workforces (Khoshaba & Maddi, 2001; Maddi, 2002; Maddi & Khoshaba (2001). The increasing turbulence of our times has led not only businesses and colleges, but also military, police, firefighters, and legal organizations to include our hardiness assessment and training procedures into their efforts to select and develop their personnel. This is happening not only in the U.S., but also in various European, Asian, African, and North and South American countries. Available on the internet for either individuals or organizations is the HardiSurvey III-R (www.HardinessInstitute.com) for assessment, and the HardiTraining Program (www.HardiTraining. coursehost.com). The HardiSurvey III-R incorporates measures of both hardiness attitudes and skills, and produces a comprehensive report concerning the courage and capabilities of the individual in dealing effectively with stresses. The HardiTraining Program puts the individual through the narrative, exercises, examples, and checkpoints, in a training process that facilitates learning the attitudes and skills that yield efforts to turn stresses from potential disasters into growth opportunities.

CONCLUSIONS

Conceptually and empirically, there is evidence for hardiness as the existential courage and motivation needed to turn stressful circumstances from potential disasters into growth opportunities instead. It appears that hardiness is a learned aspect of personality that facilitates the inherent human tendency to search for meaning, and enhance performance and health, regardless of circumstances. The implication is that an absence of learned hardiness is an important vulnerability, leading to reactions to changing, stressful experiences by denial and avoidance, or exaggeration and striking out. Presently, there are adequate procedures for hardiness assessment and training that are useful in teaching, counseling, and consulting.

REFERENCES

Allred, K. D., & Smith, T. W. (1989). The hardy personality: Cognitive and physiological responses to evaluative threat. *Journal of Personality and Social Psychology, 56,* 257-266.

Atella, M. (1989). *Crossing boundaries: Effectiveness and health among Western managers living in China.* Unpublished doctoral dissertation, University of Chicago.

Bartone, P. T. & Snook, S. A. (1999, May). *Cognitive and personality factors predict leader development. In U. S. Army cadets.* Paper presented at 35th International Applied Military Psychology Symposium (IAMPS), Florence, Italy.

Battista, J., & Almond, R. (1973). The development of meaning in life. *Psychiatry, 36,* 409-427.

Bufford, R. K., Paloutzian, R. F., & Ellison, C. W. (1991). Norms for the Spiritual Well-Being Scale. *Journal of Psychology and Theology, 19,* 56-70.

Contrada, R. J. (1989). Type A behavior, personality hardiness, and cardiovascular responses to stress. *Journal of Personality and Social Psychology, 57,* 895-903.

Florian, V., Milkulincer, M., & Taubman, O. (1995). Does hardiness contribute to mental health during a stressful real life situation? The roles of appraisal and coping. *Journal of Personality and Social Psychology, 68,* 687-694.

Frankl, V. E. (1963). *Man's search for meaning.* New York, NY: Simon and Schuster.

Funk, S. C., & Houston, B. K. (1987). A critical analysis of the hardiness scale's validity and utility. *Journal of Personality and Social Psychology, 53,* 572-578.

Ghorbani, N., Watson, P. J., & Morris, R. J. (2000). Personality, stress, and mental health: Evidence of relationships in a sample of Iranian managers. *Personality and Individual Differences, 28,* 647-657.

Graber, A. V. (2004). *Victor Frankl's Logotherapy* (2nd ed.). Lima, Ohio: Wyndham Hall Press.

Hull, J. G., Van Treuren, R. R., & Virnelli, S. (1987). Hardiness and health: A critique and alternative approach. *Journal of Personality and Social Psychology, 53,* 518-530.

Khoshaba, D. M., & Maddi, S. R. (2001). *HardiTraining.* Irvine, CA: Hardiness Institute.

Kierkegaard, S. (1954). *Fear and trembling and the sickness unto death* (trans. by Walter Lowrie). Princeton, NJ: Princeton University Press.

Kuo, W. H., & Tsai, Y. (1986). Social networking, hardiness, and immigrants' mental health. *Journal of Health and Social Behavior, 27,* 133-149.

Langle, A., Orgler, C., & Kundi, M. (2003). The Existence Scale: A new approach to assess the ability to find personal meaning in life and to reach existential fulfillment. *European Psychotherapy, 4,* 157-173.

Lifton, D. E., Seay, S., & Bushke, A. (2000). Can student hardiness serve as an indicator of likely persistence to graduation? Baseline results from a longitudinal study. *Academic Exchange,* 73-81.

Maddi, S. R. (1986). Existential psychotherapy. In J. Garske, & S. Lynn (Eds.), *Contemporary psychotherapy* , pp. 191-219. New York, NY: Merrill Publishers.

Maddi, S. R. (1987). Hardiness training at Illinois Bell Telephone. In J. P. Opatz (Ed.), *Health Promotion Evaluation*, pp. 101-115. Stevens Point, WI: National Wellness Institute. New York, NY: Wiley.

Maddi, S. R. (1997). Personal Views Survey II: A measure of dispositional hardiness. In C. P. Zalaquett, & R. J. Woods (Eds.), *Evaluating stress: A book of resources* pp. 293-310. New York, NY: University Press.

Maddi, S. R. (1999). The personality construct of hardiness, I: Effect on experiencing coping and strain. *Consulting Psychology Journal, 51,* 83-94.

Maddi, S. R. (2002). The story of hardiness: Twenty years of theorizing, research, and practice. *Consulting Psychology Journal, 54,* 173-185.

Maddi, S. R. (2004a). Existential psychology. In W. E. Craighead & C. B. Nemeroff (Eds.) *The concise Corsini encyclopedia of psychology and behavioral sciences* (3rd. Ed.). Hoboken, NJ: Wiley, pp. 344-345.

Maddi, S. R. (2004b). Hardiness: An operationalization of existential courage. *Journal of Humanistic Psychology, 44,* 279-298.

Maddi, S. R. (2006). Hardiness: The courage to grow from stresses. *The Journal of Positive Psychology, 1,* 160-168.

Maddi, S. R. & Hess, M. (1992). Hardiness and success in basketball. *International Journal of Sports Psychology, 23,* 360-368.

Maddi, S. R. & Hightower, M. (1999). Hardiness and optimism as expressed in coping patterns. *Consulting Psychology Journal, 51,* 95-105.

Maddi, S. R. & Khoshaba, D. M. (1994). Hardiness and mental health. *Journal of Personality Assessment, 63,* 265-274.

Maddi, S. R. & Khoshaba, D. M. (2001). *Personal Views Survey III-R: Test development and internet instruction manual.* Irvine, CA: Hardiness Institute.

Maddi, S. R., & Kobasa, S. C. (1984). *The hardy executive: Health under stress.* Homewood, IL: Dow-Jones Irwin.

Maddi, S. R., Kahn, S., & Maddi, K. L. (1998). The effectiveness of hardiness training. *Consulting Psychology Journal, 50,* 78-86.

Maddi, S. R., Wadhwa, P., & Haier, R. J. (1996). Relationship of hardiness to alcohol and drug use in adolescents. *American Journal of Drug and Alcohol Abuse, 22,* 247-257.

Maddi, S. R., Brow, M., Khoshaba, D. M., & Vaitkus, M. (2006). The relationship of hardiness and religiosity in depression and anger. *Consulting Psychology Journal, 58,* 148-161.

Maddi, S. R., Harvey, R. H., Khoshaba, D. M., Fazel, M., & Resurreccion, N. (2009a). The personality construct of hardiness, IV: Expressed in positive cognitions and emotions concerning oneself and developmentally-relevant activities. *Journal of Humanistic Psychology, 49,* 295-305.

Maddi, S. R., Harvey, R. H., Khoshaba, D. M., Fazel, M., & Resurreccion, N. (2009b). Hardiness facilitates performance in college. *The Journal of Positive Psychology, 4,* 566-577.

Maddi, S. R., Harvey, R. H., Khoshaba, D. M., Fazel, M., & Resurreccion, N. (2010). The personality construct of hardiness, V: Relationships with the construction of existential meaning in life. In preparation.

Maddi, S. R., Harvey, R. H., Khoshaba, D. M., Fazel, M., & Resurreccion, N. (2011). The relationship of hardiness and other related variables to college performance. Journal of Positive Psychology, in press.

Maddi, S. R., Harvey, R. H., Resurreccion, R., Giatras, C. D., & Raganold, S. (2007). Hardiness as a performance enhancer in firefighters. *International Journal of Fire Service Leadership and Management, 1,* 3-9.

Maddi, S. R., Harvey, R. H., Khoshaba, D. M., Lu, J. L., Persico, M., & Brow, M. (2006). The personality construct of hardiness, III: Relationships with repression, innovativeness, authoritarianism, and performance. *Journal of Personality, 74,* 575-598.

Maddi, S. R., Khoshaba, D. M., Harvey, R. H., Lu, J. H., & Persico, M. (2002). The personality construct of hardiness, II: Relationships with measures of psychopathology and personality. *Journal of Research in Personality, 36,* 72-85.

Maddi, S. R., Khoshaba, D. M., Jensen, K., Carter, E., Lu, J. H., & Harvey, R. H. (2002). Hardiness training for high-risk undergraduates. *NACADA Journal, 22,* 45-55.

May, R. , Angel, E., & Ellenberger, H. F. (1967). *Existence.* New York, NY: Simon & Schuster.

Pavot, W., & Diener, E. (1993). Review of the Satisfaction With Life Scale. *Psychological Assessment, 5,* 164-172.

Rodewalt, F., & Zone, J. B. (1989). Appraisal of life events, depression, and illness in hardy and nonhardy women. *Journal of Personality and Social Psychology, 56.* 81-88.

Seligman, M.E.P., & Csikszendtmihalyi, M. (2000). Positive psychology: An introduction. *American Psychologist, 55,* 5-14.

Sheier, M.F., & Carver, C.S. (1985). Optimism, coping, and health. Assessment and implications of generalized outcome expectancies. *Health Psychology, 4,* 219-247.

Weibe, D. J., & McCallum, D. M. (1986). Health practices and hardiness as mediators in the stress-illness relationship. *Health Psychology, 5,* 435-438.

Westman, M. (1990). The relationship between stress and performance: The moderating effect of hardiness. *Human Performance, 3,* 141-155.

In: Motivation, Consciousness and Self-Regulation   ISBN: 978-1-61324-795-2
Editor: D. A. Leontiev, pp. 139-171   © 2012 Nova Science Publishers, Inc.

Chapter 10

PERSONALITY DETERMINANTS OF SUBJECTIVE WELL-BEING IN OLD AGE: CROSS-SECTIONAL AND LONGITUDINAL ANALYSES

Frank Halisch, Ulrich Geppert

Max Planck Institute for Human Cognitive and Brain Sciences
Department of Psychology, Munich

ABSTRACT

Theories of aging consider subjective well-being (SWB) as a global indicator of sane psychological adjustment to life tasks and for successful aging. The present study is concerned with (a) SWB, (b) various personality variables, and (c) the influence these personality determinants have on SWB in old age. Participants were 259 females and 134 males ranging from 63 to 84 years of age at the first measurement wave. The sample was subdivided into three age cohorts: 63 to 68 (n=139), 69 to 72 (n=133), and 73 to 84 years (n=121). Three hundred and twenty-five participants were re-interviewed almost five years later.

SWB is usually conceived of having a cognitive as well as an affective component, both of which were assessed. Personality variables included personal agency (self-efficacy, externality, hopelessness), motive dispositions (achievement, power, affiliation), coping strategies (accommodative flexibility, assimilative persistence), goal variables (goal commitment, goal attainability, goal probability), and subjective health perception.

Results confirmed findings of SWB research, according to which SWB is at a rather high level, even in old age. Males indicated greater life-satisfaction and more positive affective well-being than females. The predictor variables formed a coherent pattern of four factors: (1) Assertiveness (persistence, achievement and power motives), (2) goals (commitment, attainability, probability, (3) flexibility, subjective health, (low) hopelessness, (low) externality, and (4) affiliation motive. Self-efficacy had equal substantial loadings on both the assertiveness and flexibility factors. This means that individuals with a strong sense of efficacy have both assimilative and accommodative coping strategies at their disposal. The association of subjective health with flexibility shows that individuals who are capable of adjusting their aspirations to age-related constraints feel less impaired by health restrictions. Gender differences relate to higher personal agency (self-efficacy, low hopelessness, low externality) and higher assertiveness (persistence, achievement, power) of males. However, there were no gender differences concerning accommodative flexibility and subjective health, and males and females were equally highly committed to their goals. There were distinct age-related changes: Personal agency, assertiveness and goal probability decreased, but the decline only began in the middle-age cohort and was mostly pronounced in the oldest cohort (age 78 upwards). The phase after entry into retirement was characterized by a rather high stability of personality, whereas a terminal decline occurred only in the oldest age. These results support the differentiation between a "third" and "fourth" age. Generally, goal commitment increased and subjective health decreased during the interval between the two measurement points.

Regression analyses on the impact of the predictor variables on SWB revealed (low) hopelessness as being the main predictor of both life satisfaction and affect. Beyond that, cognitive and affective well-being were influenced by *different* predictors. Self-efficacy and flexibility had the highest impact on life satisfaction, especially in the youngest age cohort. However, in the oldest cohort, the most influential predictor of life satisfaction was the success probability of attaining personal goals. Affective well-being, in contrast, was mainly influenced by subjective health perception in all cohorts.

Longitudinal analyses revealed that during the five-year interval, our participants' life satisfaction *increased*, whereas affective well-being *decreased*. These differing developmental trends could be explained by different predictor variables. Again, feelings of hopelessness had a detrimental effect on both changes in cognitive as well as in affective well-being. Beyond that, the increase in life satisfaction was mainly due to the ability to flexibly adjust one's own aspirations to reduced resources and, therefore, strive for achievable goals. The decrease in affect, in contrast, was primarily caused by poor subjective health.

Keywords: Subjective well-being, old age, personal goals, personal agency, self-efficacy, coping strategies, motive dispositions, subjective health, developmental changes in personality

INTRODUCTION

Increasing life expectancy is a well-known fact—at least in Western countries. The future of our society will be characterized by a rising proportion of old and very old people. This development is characterized as being a demographic revolution, and it indeed presents a challenge to society, mainly for social policy but also for various scientific disciplines (e.g., medicine, sociology, psychiatry, and not least, psychology). Thus, a new conceptualization of aging and a new way of dealing with the aged is needed. The stated aim is a society in which people in *all* stages of life will have a fair chance of fruitful development and of living a fulfilled life.

Subjective well-being (SWB) is a core variable in research on aging; it is understood as a global indicator of sane psychological adjustment to life tasks and successful aging (P. B. Baltes & Mayer, 1999). SWB is an important component of the quality of life because it is based, in contrast to "objective" measures (e.g., income, socioeconomic status, marital status), on an individual's own appraisal. People react differently to the same circumstances and, therefore, SWB estimates rely on individual's own standards and signal their beliefs of what is important in their lives.

Although most aged people live in satisfactory life circumstances (at least in Germany, where this study was conducted), growing old entails the risk of impairments including reduced material resources, declining physical health and intellectual functioning, loss of intimates, social isolation, social dependency. Nevertheless, nearly all studies confirmed that life satisfaction shows no decline with age (Diener, Suh, Lucas, & Smith, 1999; Diener & Suh, 1998; Halisch & Geppert, 2000, 2001; Smith, Fleeson, Geiselmann, Settersten, & Kunzmann, 1999).

The discrepancy between objective life conditions and subjective well-being appraisal points to a well-known finding of well-being research generally, the "paradox of subjective well-being"(Staudinger, 2000). This paradox describes the fact that even under adverse circumstances (a) most people are happy, and (b) the empirical mean of SWB is usually in the positive range. It is an often-reported fact that objective life conditions and situations affect the level of SWB to a moderate degree only; even facing extreme events, people show few long-term changes in their SWB (Diener & Diener, 1996). Many studies have shown that this pertains to individuals, groups, or even nations—irrespective of real disadvantages or discrimination (Diener et al., 1999) —and it has repeatedly been proved that these findings cannot be explained as a methodological artifact (Staudinger, 2000).

In the light of these findings, the focus of SWB research has shifted from an initial quite popular *bottom-up approach* in which SWB is explained by circumstances, events, and contexts to a *top-down approach* in which the role of individual differences in personality is emphasized (Brief, Butcher, George, & Link, 1993; Feist, Bodner, Jacobs, Miles et al., 1995; Headey, Veenhoven, & Wearing, 1991; Heller, Watson, & Ilies, 2004). Bottom-up theories maintain that SWB is derived from a summation of pleasurable and unpleasant experiences. In other words, satisfaction and happiness result from having many specific moments of happiness in life and a happy individual is happy because he or she experiences many happy moments. Consequently, this theoretical perspective conceives of life satisfaction as the result of a summation of satisfaction in a number of particular domains (e.g., family life, marriage, financial situation, and housing).

Alternatively, top-down theories assume that people have a general propensity to interpret life experiences in either positive or negative ways, and this predisposition in turn colors their evaluation of life satisfaction. From a top-down perspective, our subjective interpretation of events, rather than the objective circumstances themselves, should be the primary influence on SWB. The main proposition of this approach is that stable personality characteristics determine levels of SWB. Individuals who are happy are happy because they enjoy life's pleasures and not primarily because they experience more of them in an objective sense. Despite pleasant or unpleasant circumstances, some individuals seem to be happy people and others, unhappy people.

In an extensive meta-analysis, Heller et al. (2004) came to the conclusion that both the person-centered and also the situation-centered approach have their merits, and the best model would be an integrative perspective combining features from both the top-down and the bottom-up perspective. They were able to show that although personality plays a key role, situational factors are also important, and according to their view, "personality places some limits (i.e., a reaction range) on the level of life satisfaction people can experience; within this broad range, changes in people's environments, perceptions, feelings, and behaviors can increase or decrease their level of satisfaction" (p. 593).

The Concept of Subjective Well-being

Subjective well-being is usually viewed as a concept consisting of three components, namely pleasant affect, unpleasant affect, and life satisfaction. According to Diener and Lucas (1999, p. 213), SWB "refers to people's evaluations of their lives. These evaluations include both cognitive judgments of life satisfaction and affective evaluations of moods and emotions." In this classification, *life satisfaction* represents a global cognitive evaluation or judgment of an individual's satisfaction with his or her life. It is an evaluative summary that people have of their lives. Moods and emotions, on the other hand, which together are labeled *affect*, represent people's on-line evaluations of events that occur in their lives. They are reflections of people's actual affective experiences.

Although the concept of life satisfaction is theoretically different from the amount of positive or negative affect a person experiences, life satisfaction and affect are nevertheless interrelated. When making estimates of life satisfaction, for example, people may rely on current mood as an indicator of their overall satisfaction, or they simply reflect on the amount of time they have spent in a happy versus an unhappy mood. On the other hand, current emotion theories suggest that cognitions play a major role in the experience of emotion. Therefore, cognitive evaluations of one's life may determine the amount of positive and negative affect an individual experiences. Findings of several studies established the convergent and discriminant validity of both components of SWB (Lucas, Diener, & Suh, 1996; Schimmack, Radhakrishnan, Oishi, Dzokoto, & Ahadi, 2002; Schimmack, Schupp, & Wagner, 2008). There is convincing evidence that SWB is a multidimensional construct with cognitive and emotional components that are related but neither philosophically nor empirically identical. Moreover, affect is not a unitary construct with positive and negative endpoints along a one-dimensional scale. Instead, positive and negative affect are two independent types of emotion that are correlated to a moderate degree only and sometimes show different relations with external variables (Bradburn, 1969; Diener & Emmons, 1984; Diener, Smith, & Fujita, 1995; Heyl, Wahl, & Mollenkopf, 2007).

Personality Determinants of Subjective Well-being

Literature reviews often conclude that personality is a stronger predictor of SWB than environmental factors (Diener & Lucas, 1999; Diener et al., 1999; McCrae, 2002). Heller et al. (2004, p. 575) summarize the findings of the top-down approach with the conclusion that "well-being is a product of internal or subjective processes (e.g. goals, temperament) rather than of objective external factors (e.g. income, education)." In contrast to personality variables, demographic variables, as, for example, income, marital status, job status or even objective health, usually correlate less than .20 with SWB (Diener, Lucas, & Scollon, 2006).

Personal Agency

In a meta-analysis of studies on personality traits and SWB, DeNeve and Cooper (1998) reported that the personality constructs relating to sense of control and personal agency were among the most potent personality correlates of subjective well-being. Individuals with a strong belief in controlling and mastering goals and tasks in their everyday lives probably feel happy and satisfied. Having a sense of control and personal efficacy has indeed consistently been shown to improve well-being through the life cycle (Bandura, 1997; Lachman, Rosnick, & Röcke, 2009). Peterson (1999) concluded that a sense of control is a key protective factor for SWB in the face of declining health and other losses in later life, and Berg, Hassing, McClearn, and Johansson (2006) showed that a sense of being in control of one's life is important for well-being, even for the oldest old.

There are three key personality variables related to personal control, namely self-efficacy, externality, and hopelessness. *Self-efficacy is* a well-known personal agency construct introduced by Bandura more than 30 years ago. It refers to an individual's perceptions about his or her own capabilities to organize and implement actions necessary to attain designated goals (Bandura, 1977, 1997). The cornerstone of self-efficacy is the expectation of being able to execute desired behaviors successfully. According to Bandura, self-efficacy is a prerequisite of well-being throughout the lifespan. In later life, which is characterized by a depletion of resources due to multiple losses, individuals with high self-efficacy manage rather easily to cultivate new relationships and engage in productive activities, both of which contribute to positive functioning and well-being. Recently, Charrow (2006) confirmed that self-efficacy is a strong predictor of SWB in old age.

Compared to self-efficacy, *hopelessness* and *externality* are broader expectancy constructs. Whereas self-efficacy is focused on domain-specific or even act-specific expectancy, hopelessness (Beck, Weissman, Lester, & Trexler, 1974), which bears a close resemblance to the dispositional optimism/pessimism construct by Scheier and Carver (1992), is related to generalized expectancies that good or bad things will happen in one's life. The construct of generalized externality is based on Rotter's concept of internal versus external locus of control (Rotter, 1966). Externality refers to a tendency to attribute important life events to external and, therefore, uncontrollable factors. Individuals with an external locus of control believe that luck and powerful others determine their fates. Holding negative expectations for the future (hopelessness or pessimism) and perceiving one's own development as mainly influenced by external factors that are beyond personal control (externality) have detrimental effects on subjective well-being (e.g., Queen & Freitag, 1978; Scheier & Carver, 1992).

Motive Dispositions

A large number of studies have proved the motive dispositions of achievement, power, and affiliation motives, known as the motive triad, play a prominent role in most human goal-directed behavior (J. Heckhausen & Heckhausen, 2008; McClelland, 1985). There is some evidence that in old age, the importance of both the achievement and the power motive diminishes (McClelland, Scioli, & Weaver, 1998) and that correlations with life satisfaction are only moderate (Jacob & Guarnaccia, 1997). However, motives exert a special indirect influence on SWB. Well-being is negatively affected when there is incongruence between implicit and self-attributed motives (Baumann, Kaschel, & Kuhl, 2005; Langan-Fox, Sankey, & Canty, 2009; Langens, 2007) or between motives and personal goals (Brunstein, Schultheiß, & Größman, 1998; Hofer, Chasiotis, & Campos, 2006). Halisch and Geppert (2001) related events their participants experienced within the last six months to motives and found that the absence of affiliation- and power-related events had a detrimental influence, and the presence of achievement-related events had a positive influence on SWB.

Coping

A third set of variables relates to self-regulatory mechanisms (J. Heckhausen, 1999; J. Heckhausen & Dweck, 1998) and coping strategies (Brandtstädter, Rothermund, & Schmitz, 1998; Brandtstädter, Wentura, & Rothermund, 1999). Becoming old has been described as a life task in which individuals have to adjust their goals and aspirations to age-related constraints and restrictions in order to maintain personal continuity and self-esteem. Brandtstädter and Renner (1990) distinguished two coping strategies that aim to eliminate distressing discrepancies between actual situations and desired self-states, namely *accommodative flexibility* and *assimilative persistence.* Accommodative flexibility (or flexible goal adjustment) describes a tendency to positively reinterpret initially adverse situations and to relinquish blocked goal perspectives easily. It aims to eliminate such discrepancies by adjusting personal goals and preferences rather than by changing the actual situation. Assimilative persistence (or tenacious goal pursuit), in contrast, refers to an individual's tendency to tenaciously pursue goals even in the face of obstacles. It aims to change an unsatisfactory situation so that it becomes compatible with desired self-definitions or identity goals. According to Brandtstädter, both strategies may operate simultaneously in a given situation. Several studies have proved the importance of accommodative and assimilative coping for successful aging (Brandtstädter et al., 1998; Brandtstädter et al., 1999; Heyl et al., 2007). Both strategies can have a positive influence on SWB, but one can assume that with increasing age, shifting from assimilative to accommodative coping will benefit SWB.

Goals

Goal theories of human behavior maintain that setting and striving to achieve goals plays a central role in human development over the lifespan. Setting and pursuing future-oriented goals influence an individual's well-being, even in old age (Brunstein, Schultheiß, & Maier, 1999). Although there is some evidence that simply having valued goals can increase life satisfaction (Emmons, 1986), at present most researchers agree that high investment in the pursuit of personal goals does not necessarily produce positive well-being. According to Brunstein et al., (1999, p. 170) "… to achieve high levels of well-being, it is important for an individual to have both a strong sense of commitment to valued goals and a life situation that provides favorable conditions for the attainment of these goals." Accordingly, it is not sufficient to have goals, but goals have to be estimated by the individual as attainable. Moreover, Brunstein et al. (1998) showed that not all goals are equal in producing high SWB. Only progress in achieving goals that are thematically congruent with motive dispositions leads to high SWB. Adopting a method developed by Brunstein (1993), we asked our participants for goals they pursue and had them estimate their goal commitment, goal attainability, and goal probability.

Health

Finally, health seems to play an important role in SWB. There is, however, a remarkable discrepancy between the thinking of laypersons and the actual empirical results concerning the effects of health on SWB. No one would query the inclusion of health as an important factor, and we all know from talking with older people that health becomes even more important with age. Accordingly, Campbell, Converse, and Rodgers (1976), for example, found that health was rated by Americans as the most important factor in happiness. However, all pertinent studies revealed a surprisingly low correlation between health and SWB (cf. Diener et al., 2006). The key to explaining this puzzling fact is to take into account *subjective* health perception instead of objective health (Brief et al., 1993). Although subjective health certainly reflects objective health to some degree, it is also colored by individual interpretations (Pinquart, 2001). The crucial factor is the individual's perception and interpretation of health-related restrictions and not the objective health restrictions. Therefore, we added a measure of our participants' *subjective health perception* to the list of predictor variables.

To summarize, the present study is concerned with (a) subjective well-being in old age, (b) the role various predictor variables, namely personal agency variables (self-efficacy, externality, hopelessness), motive dispositions (achievement, power, affiliation), coping strategies (accommodative flexibility, assimilative persistence), goal variables (goal commitment, goal attainability, goal probability), and subjective health perception, play in explaining individual differences in subjective well-being, (c) changes in SWB as well as changes in the predictor variables after an interval of almost five years, and (d) the degree to which the predictor variables can explain age-related changes in SWB.

METHOD

The Study

The study is part of the extensive Munich Genetic Oriented Lifespan Study on differential Development (GOLD), started by Kurt Gottschaldt in 1937, with a sample of 180 mono- and dizygotic twins who were then about 11 years old (Weinert & Geppert, 1996, 1998; Weinert, Geppert, Dörfert, & Viek, 1994; see also Geppert & Halisch, in press). The participants who survived World War II were studied repeatedly in several measurement waves. For a follow-up study (named *measurement wave 1* in the following) conducted between 1995 and 1999, the original sample was extended with new pairs of twins of 63 to 84 years, giving a total of 393 participants altogether. In order to conduct cross-sectional analyses, the sample was divided into three age cohorts (Table 1). After an interval of almost five years, the participants were re-interviewed (*measurement wave 2*). This time, the sample was reduced to 325 participants (116 males and 209 females).

Table 1. Males and females, median age and age range of the three age cohorts

	Age cohorts		
	1	2	3
Males	63	45	26
Females	76	88	95
Median age	66;8	70;10	75;9
Age range (years; months)	63;8 – 68;11	69;0 – 72;11	73;2 – 84;4

In the GOLD study, a wide array of cognitive, emotional, motivational, social, and socio-economic variables was employed, and owing to the different measurement waves over a period of more than 60 years and the special sample of twins, it provides a valuable data pool for various developmental and genetic questions. The present chapter focuses on a portion of the study only and is not concerned with heredity analyses (for that see Geppert & Halisch, in press). Due to its design, the study allowed (a) cross-sectional as well as (b) longitudinal analyses of developmental changes.

Measures

Subjective Well-being

As mentioned above, SWB is usually conceived of having three components: a primarily cognitive element, *life satisfaction,* and two emotional elements, *positive* and *negative affect.*

Life Satisfaction

To assess life satisfaction, we used the Satisfaction with Life Scale (Diener, Emmons, Larsen, & Griffin, 1985), in which the participants are requested to indicate their agreement/disagreement with five statements (e.g., "In most ways, my life is close to ideal," "If I could live my life over, I would change almost nothing") on a seven-point scale (1=*strongly disagree* to 7= *strongly agree*).

Affective Well-being

Positive and negative affect were measured with the Affect Balance Scale (Bradburn, 1969). Sample items (four statements for positive and negative affect, respectively) included, for example: "During the past two weeks, did you ever feel pleased about having accomplished something?" "During the past two weeks, did you ever feel depressed or very unhappy?" Response choices were *yes/no.*

Personal Agency

Self-Efficacy

Self-efficacy was assessed via a questionnaire in which competence beliefs and internal control beliefs were aggregated to a self-efficacy score (Greve, Anderson, & Krampen, 2001; Krampen, 1991). The scales consisted of eight items each. Participants were instructed to agree or disagree on a six-point scale with statements that describe competence and control beliefs (e.g., "In unclear or dangerous situations, I always know what to do." = *competence belief.* "When I make plans, I am almost certain to make them work." = *internal control belief.*)

Externality

The externality measure is comprised of a scale for social externality (attribution to other persons) and one for fatalistic externality (attribution to good or bad luck or fate) (Greve et al., 2001; Krampen, 1991). Participants had to indicate their agreement/disagreement (six-point scale) with eight items for social externality (e.g., "I feel like what happens to me in my life is mostly determined by powerful people.") and eight items for fatalistic externality (e.g., "Often there is no chance of protecting my personal interests from bad luck happenings.")

Hopelessness

For the measurement of *hopelessness*, we employed the widely used Beck Scale that assesses the degree to which individuals hold negative expectations towards their futures (Beck et al., 1974; German version by Krampen, 1994).

Motives

The achievement, power, and affiliation motives were assessed by the Personality Research Form (Jackson, 1984; German version by Stumpf, Angleitner, Wieck, Jackson, & Beloch-Till, 1985).

Coping

To assess the coping strategies of *assimilative persistence* and *accommodative flexibility*, we used a questionnaire developed by Brandtstädter and Renner (1990). The participants had to indicate their agreement/ disagreement with 15 items for each measure on a five-point scale (e.g. "I can be very obstinate in pursuing my goals," "The harder a goal is to achieve, the more desirable it often appears to me" = *assimilative persistence*. "I usually recognize quite easily my own limitations," "I can adapt to changes in a situation quite easily" = *accommodative flexibility*).

Goals

We measured the goal variables of *goal commitment, goal attainability* and *goal probability* by adopting a technique developed by Brunstein (1993). The participants were asked for goals they pursue within the next six to twelve months. After having listed their goals, they indicated the two goals most important to them, and then they rated each of these along a number of goal variables. All judgments were made on a seven-point scale, with endpoints labeled *completely disagree* and *completely agree*. The *commitment* scale consisted of six statements (e.g., "No matter what happens, I will not give up this goal"). The *attainability* scale was also comprised of six statements (e.g., "I have many opportunities in my everyday life to work on this goal"). Finally, the participants estimated the *probability* of reaching the goal on a percentage scale from 0% to 100%.

Subjective Health

We constructed an index of *subjective health perception* based on the participants' estimates of their own states of health using three questions: (1) "How would you estimate your health at the moment?" five-point scale: 1=*very bad*, 5=*very good*. (2) "Is your state of health worse or better than five years ago, or has it remained unchanged?" Response choices were *worse, unchanged, better*. (3) "How strongly do your health problems impede you in living your life?" Response choices were *not at all, a little, very strongly*. The scores were z-transformed, and the mean of the three z-scores yielded the subjective health perception index.

RESULTS

Cross-Sectional Analyses

The first part of the results section is concerned with (a) our participants' SWB, (b) individual differences in the predictor variables, and (c) the influence that these variables had on SWB measures at measurement wave 1.

Subjective Well-being

Table 2 shows the intercorrelations of cognitive and affective well-being measures, and Figure 1 depicts the indicators of SWB as a function of age and gender. Life satisfaction, positive and negative affect were correlated in the expected way to a moderate degree (Table 2). This is completely in line with general findings of well-being research: The three components of subjective well-being are interrelated but, nevertheless, clearly distinct from each other.

Table 2. Intercorrelations of well-being measures

		Affect	
		positive	negative
Life satisfaction		.37	-.37
Affect	positive	-	-.45
	negative		-

Before looking at age and gender differences in SWB, first, an inspection of Figure 1 shows that life satisfaction and affective well-being scores were generally rather positive. The mean of the life satisfaction score was a full scale-point beyond the midpoint (4) in the positive range. The same effect became clearly evident in the affect scales, too. On average, our participants indicated an elated mood much more often than a depressed mood.

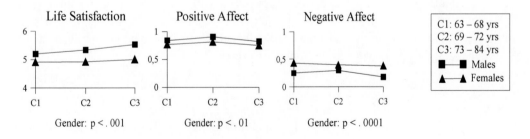

Figure 1. Subjective well-being as a function of age cohort (C1, C2, C3) and gender.

Two-way ANOVAs (age cohort x gender) revealed that males, as compared to females, were much more satisfied with their lives and showed more positive and less negative affect. There was no evidence of an age-dependent increase or decrease, either in cognitive or in affective well-being. Satisfaction with life seemed to increase from cohort 1 to cohort 3, especially in males, but this tendency was far from significant.

Predictor Variables

Table 3 depicts the zero-order correlations of the predictor variables. Self-efficacy was negatively correlated with externality and hopelessness and was positively related to all other variables, with the exception of the affiliation motive and subjective health perception.

Table 3. Zero-order correlations of the predictor variables

	2	3	4	5	6	7	8	9	10	11	12
1. Self-efficacy	-.33	-.41	.35	.38	.17	.41	.46	.23	.34	.24	
2. Externality		.35	-.14	-.17		-.32	-.28	-.18	-.25	-.17	
3. Hopelessness			-.27	-.30	-.13	-.39	-.32	-.19	-.38	-.23	-.23
4. Achievement				.46		.20	.65	.14	.15		
5. Power					.18	.18	.52	.17	.15		
6. Affiliation											
7. Flexibility							.21	.17	.24		.18
8. Persistence								.25	.20		
9. Goal commitment									.47	.33	
10. Goal attainability										.47	
11. Goal probability											
12. Subjective health											

All reported coefficients p < .01; bold coefficients p < .0001.

Externality and hopelessness were quite strongly correlated but were negatively correlated with nearly all other variables. Amongst the motives, the achievement and power motives were intercorrelated to a substantial degree, and both were positively correlated with self-efficacy and especially with assimilative persistence. Both were negatively correlated with hopelessness. The affiliation motive was not associated with any other variable substantially.

Accommodative flexibility and assimilative persistence were positively interrelated to a small degree. Both were correlated in the *same* way with self-efficacy, externality and hopelessness. However, there was a clear difference in the correlations with the achievement and power motives. Persistence was correlated with achievement and power, yet flexibility was not.

The goal parameters[1] of goal commitment, goal attainability, and goal probability were interrelated to a substantial degree. This means that participants who are committed to their goals mostly estimate the attainability and probability of reaching these goals rather high. The goal variables were correlated with the personality variables to a moderate degree—positively with self-efficacy and negatively with externality and hopelessness. Both coping strategies correlated marginally with goal commitment and goal attainability but not with goal probability.

---

[1] In the analyses of measurement wave 1 mean scores of the participants' first and second goal were computed for goal commitment, goal attainability and goal probability.

Finally, Table 3 reveals that subjective health perception had virtually no relation with the other variables. There were only two fairly small correlations: Increased hopelessness went together with diminished health perception, and accommodative flexibility seemed to have a slight positive influence on subjective health.

Table 4. Varimax-rotated principal components of the predictor variables

	Factor 1	Factor 2	Factor 3	Factor 4
Self-efficacy	**.51**	.27	**.46**	.04
Externality	-.23	-.25	**-.50**	-.38
Hopelessness	-.27	-.25	**-.66**	-.12
Achievement	**.80**	-.00	.07	.02
Power	**.77**	.08	.04	.14
Affiliation	.16	.10	.05	**.87**
Flexibility	.15	.13	**.72**	-.13
Persistence	**.85**	.11	.12	-.06
Goal commitment	.16	**.73**	-.03	-.15
Goal attainability	.08	**.79**	.23	.07
Goal probability	-.01	**.75**	.10	.13
Subjective health	-.21	-.15	**.65**	.22

Eigenvalues > 1; percentage explained: 62.1.

The variables were subjected to a principal component analysis (varimax-rotation), which resulted in a clear four-factor solution. The factor loadings are presented in Table 4. Factor 1 was made up of accommodative persistence, the achievement and the power motives (loadings > .77). Factor 2 is a "goal factor" with loadings (> .73) by goal commitment, goal attainability, and goal probability. Factor 3 consisted of a combination of assimilative flexibility, low hopelessness, and subjective health perception (loadings >. 65), and—to a lesser extent—low externality (loading =.50). Factor 4 had only one distinct loading (.87) by the affiliation motive. Of special interest is self-efficacy, which had substantial loadings on factor 1 (.51) as well as on factor 3 (.46).

Figures 2 to 5 depict the personal agency variables, motive dispositions, coping styles, and goal parameters as a function of age and gender. Two-way ANOVAs (age cohort x gender) were computed for each variable. There were pronounced gender differences in self-efficacy and hopelessness (Figure 2): Males were characterized by higher self-efficacy and lower hopelessness than females. A significant increase in externality could be observed with age, but this trend is qualified by an age x gender interaction. For females, externality continuously rose with age whereas for males a curvilinear effect took place: After an initial decrease from cohort 1 to cohort 2, a strong increase in externality occurred in cohort 3.

There were also clear gender differences in the achievement and power motives (Figure 3): Males were much more achievement and power motivated than females. These differences became even more pronounced with age as the age x gender interactions show. Differences in the affiliation motives were comparatively weak. The age x gender effect is attributed solely to an increase in the affiliation motive for males in cohort 3 and a concomitant decrease for females.

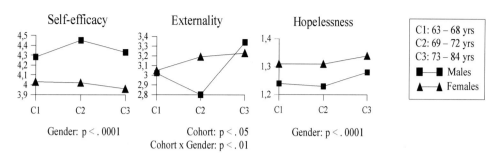

Figure 2. Personal agency variables as a function of age cohort (C1, C2, C3) and gender.

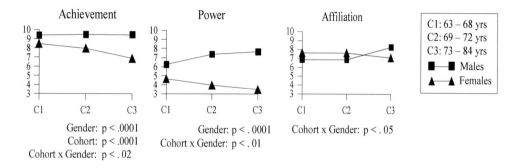

Figure 3. Motive dispositions as a function of age cohort (C1, C2, C3) and gender.

No age or gender differences could be found in accommodative flexibility (Figure 4). Assimilative persistence, on the other hand, diminished with age, and males were more persistent than females.

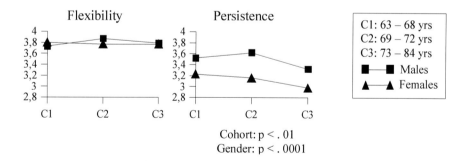

Figure 4. Coping strategies as a function of age cohorts (C1, C2, C3) and gender.

Finally, substantial gender differences were found for goal attainability and goal probability but not for goal commitment (Figure 5). Males estimated the attainability and the probability of reaching their goals higher than females. However, no age-related differences were found with respect to the goal parameters. Individuals of all ages pursued important personal goals. The degree of commitment, goal attainability and goal probability did not change with age, although there seemed to be a slight increase in goal probability in the oldest age group.

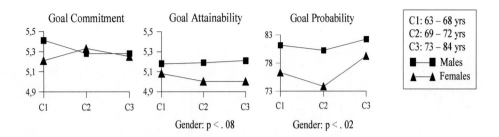

Figure 5. Goal variables as a function of age cohort (C1, C2, C3) and gender.

Concerning the participants' subjective health perception, no significant gender or age effects could be found (Figure 6). A tendency towards lower subjective health in the oldest age cohort did not reach significance.

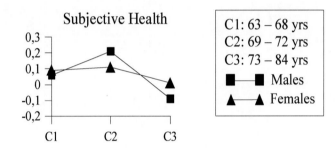

Figure 6. Subjective health perception as a function of age cohort (C1, C2, C3) and gender.

Predictors of Well-being

The following analyses are concerned with the influence the various predictors had on SWB. Looking first at life satisfaction, the correlations (Table 5) show that particularly self-efficacy but also flexibility, goal attainability, and goal probability went together with high life satisfaction scores. Hopelessness, in particular, and also externality were negatively corre-lated with life satisfaction. There were only weak but nevertheless positive correlations between the achievement, power, and affiliation motives and life satisfaction. Concerning affective well-being, the pattern of correlations was comparable, but the coefficients were generally lower. For subjective health perception, in contrast, the correlations with the affective well-being scores were notably higher than the correlation with life satisfaction.

As the predictor variables were intercorrelated to a considerable extent (Table 3), we conducted multiple regression analyses to estimate the influence each predictor had on cognitive and affective well-being (Table 6). Since conceptual differences between positive and negative affect are not the focus of the present paper, an affect-balance score was computed for affective well-being (positive minus negative affect scores).

Self-efficacy was the most powerful predictor of life satisfaction. Nearly equally important was low hopelessness. All other variables did not play a significant role in explaining the variance of life satisfaction scores. Concerning affective well-being, quite a different picture emerged. Hopelessness, and to a minor extent self-efficacy, were still important, but subjective health perception, which played absolutely no role in explaining life satisfaction, was by far the most powerful predictor of affective well-being.

Table 5. Correlations of predictor variables with SWB-measures

	Life satisfaction	Affect	
		positive	negative
Self-efficacy	**.42**	**.25**	**-.28**
Externality	**-.20**	**-.19**	.15
Hopelessness	**-.46**	**-.42**	**.28**
Achievement	**.18**	.20	-.16
Power	.14	.14	-.13
Affiliation	.15		
Flexibility	**.30**	.21	**-.18**
Persistence	.15	.20	-.16
Goal commitment			
Goal attainability	**.28**	**.25**	-.14
Goal probability	**.24**	.16	**-.21**
Subjective health	**.17**	**.32**	**-.28**

All reported coefficients p < .01; bold coefficients p < .0001.

Table 6. Regression analyses of predictors of life satisfaction and affect balance

Life satisfaction			Affect balance		
Predictors	ß	p <	Predictors	ß	p <
Self-efficacy	.30	.0001	Subjective health	.27	.0001
Hopelessness	-.27	.0001	Hopelessness	-.21	.0001
Persistence	-.11		Self-efficacy	,15	.01
Goal probability	.10		Goal commitment	-.13	.05
Affiliation	.08		Goal probability	.11	.05
Goal commitment	-.07		Goal attainability	.09	
Achievement	.07		Achievement	.05	
Goal attainability	.07		Externality	-.03	
Power	-.06		Affiliation	-.02	
Flexibility	.06		Persistence	.02	
Subjective health	.05		Power	.00	
Externality	.02		Flexibility	.00	

Note. R=.55, p < .0001   *Note.* R=.54, p < .0001.

Computing the same analyses within the three age cohorts revealed quite different age-related results. Table 7 depicts the correlations of predictor variables and SWB scores within the cohorts, and Tables 8 and 9 show the results of the respective regression analyses.

The impact of self-efficacy and hopelessness on life satisfaction was mainly present in the youngest cohort (Table 8). Hopelessness was still a predictor of life satisfaction in the middle-age cohort but to a moderate degree only in the oldest cohort. Similarly, the impact of self-efficacy diminished with age and was negligible in the oldest cohort. In the youngest cohort, in addition, accommodative flexibility played a moderate role. Flexibly adjusting one's own aspirations to situational constraints obviously had a beneficial effect on life satisfaction. Tenaciously pursuing personal goals (assimilative persistence), however, had, if any, a detrimental influence. In the oldest age group, these variables no longer played a role. Instead, a predictor variable that was completely unimportant in the two younger groups became prevalent, namely, goal probability. Goal probability was almost the only predictor of life satisfaction in the oldest old.

Table 7. Correlations of predictor variables with SWB-measures within age cohorts

Predictors	Life satisfaction			Affect balance		
	63–69 yrs	69-73 yrs	73-84 yrs	63–69 yrs	69-73 yrs	73-84 yrs
Self-efficacy	**.51**	**.41**	**.31**	**.35**	.29	.29
Externality	**-.33**	-.30		**-.30**		
Hopelessness	**-.51**	**-.51**	**-.34**	**-.49**	**-.42**	-.28
Achievement		.21		.23	.24	
Power				.26		
Affiliation						
Flexibility	**.46**	.25		**.37**		
Persistence		.25			**.30**	
Goal commitment						
Goal attainability		**.35**	**.34**		**.39**	
Goal probability			.47	.23	.25	
Subjective health		.22		**.37**	.27	**.40**

All reported coefficients p < .01; bold coefficients p < .0001.

Table 8. Regression analyses of predictors of life satisfaction within age cohorts

63-69 yrs			69-73 yrs			73-84 yrs		
Predictors	ß	p <	Predictors	ß	p <	Predictors	ß	p <
Self-efficacy	.38	.0001	Hopelessness	-.32	.002	Goal prob.	.38	.0001
Hopelessness	-.37	.0001	Self-efficacy	.23	.05	Hopelessness	-.22	.05
Flexibility	.24	.01	Subj. health	.18	.05	Externality	.17	
Persistence	-.17		Affiliation	.18	.05	Commitment	-.16	
Attainability	-.13		Attainability	.18		Self-efficacy	.14	
Subj. health	-.09		Power	-.10		Attainability	.13	
Power	-.07		Externality	-.08		Achievement	.12	
Affiliation	.06		Achievement	.06		Persistence	-.07	
Achievement	.04		Goal prob.	-.05		Affiliation	-.07	
Externality	.03		Persistence	-.04		Flexibility	-.03	
Goal prob.	.02		Flexibility	-.03		Subj. health	.02	
Commitment	.01		Commitment	-.01		Power	.01	

Note: R = .66; p < .0001   *Note*: R=.64; p < .0001   *Note*. R = .58; p < .0001

The predictors of affective well-being were also different within the age cohorts (Table 9). As was the case for life satisfaction, hopelessness played a prominent role in explaining affective well-being, but only in the two younger age groups. Concerning the other predictor variables, a completely different picture emerged. Self-efficacy was fairly negligible in explaining affective well-being scores, but subjective health perception, a factor that did not play any role in predicting life satisfaction, had a prominent impact on affective well-being. In the oldest age cohort, only subjective health could predict affective well-being to a significant degree.

Table 9. Regression analyses of predictors of affect balance within age cohorts

63-69 yrs			69-73 yrs			73-84 yrs		
Predictors	ß	p <	Predictors	ß	p <	Predictors	ß	p <
Hopelessness	-.30	.001	Attainability	.38	.0001	Subj. health	.37	.0001
Subj. health	.21	.05	Hopelessness	-.26	.01	Self-efficacy	.27	.05
Goal prob.	.18	.05	Subj. health	.20	.05	Externality	-.16	
Commitment	.18	.05	Persistence	.20		Goal prob.	.11	
Power	.17		Power	-.14		Commitment	-.09	
Attainability	-.14		Commitment	-.09		Flexibility	-.08	
Self-efficacy	.13		Self-efficacy	.08		Hopelessness	-.06	
Flexibility	.10		Externality	.08		Achievement	.06	
Achievement	.10		Affiliation	.07		Persistence	-.04	
Persistence	-.08		Achievement	.07		Attainability	-.03	
Externality	-.06		Goal prob.	.04		Affiliation	-.02	
Affiliation	-.05		Flexibility	-.02		Power	.02	
Note: R = .65; p < .0001			*Note*: R=.65; p < .0001			*Note:* R = .49; p < .01		

Longitudinal Analyses

The following part of the results section (a) presents findings of changes in SWB and in the predictor variables from measurement wave 1 to measurement wave 2 and (b) is concerned with the question to what degree the predictor variables can explain changes in cognitive and affective well-being within the five-year interval.[2]

Subjective Well-being

Table 10 depicts the intercorrelations between the SWB measures at waves 1 and 2. The findings of wave 2 were in line with those of wave 1 (Table 2): The well-being measures were correlated but by no means identical. Of special interest are the retest stabilities. The table shows a remarkably high stability coefficient for life satisfaction, which is within the range reached by personality measures (Table 11, below). For the affect scores, in contrast, the stability coefficients were much lower and did not surpass the inter-score correlations.

Figure 7 depicts the age trends for the SWB components. Two-way repeated measurement ANOVAs (age cohort x measurement wave) were conducted for each measure. Our participants' life satisfaction increased significantly within the five-year interval. However, positive affect decreased. This effect seemed to be more pronounced in the two older cohorts. For negative affect, the results were not so clear. It decreased in the youngest cohort, remained stable in the middle age cohort, and increased in the oldest cohort, but none of these effects reached significance. Hence, there were no significant effects for the affect-

---

[2] There were, again, main effects for gender at wave 2. However, since there were virtually no interaction effects of gender with age or measurement wave, and since gender was not the focus in present analysis, results on gender were omitted in the following analyses.

balance score, although especially in the oldest cohort, resultant affect notably decreased. In sum, we have the somewhat puzzling effect that *life satisfaction increased* while *affective well-being*, especially positive affect, *decreased* during the same period.

Table 10. Inter-score correlations / retest stability of SWB-measures

			Life satisfaction	Affect positive	Affect negative
Wave 1	Life satisfaction		**.69**	.30	-.28
	Affect	positive	.33	**.29**	-.17
		negative	-.31	-.17	**.40**
Wave 2	Life satisfaction		-	.44	-.34
	Affect	positive		-	-.41
		negative			-

Bold = stability coefficients.

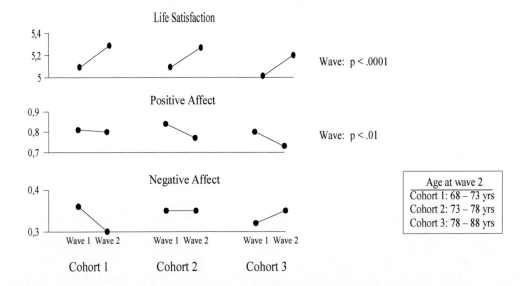

Figure 7. Subjective well-being in three age cohorts at both measurement points.

Predictor Variables

Table 11 reveals remarkably high test-retest correlations (= stability coefficients) for personal agency variables, motives dispositions, and coping strategies. In contrast, test-retest correlations for goal commitment, goal attainability, and goal probability were much lower.[3] Goal variables refer to specific actual goals and do not have the quality of a personality dimension. Subjective health perception lay somewhat in between. Obviously, subjective health perception was not as stable as personality variables but was influenced by situational factors to a greater degree.

---

[3] As a substantial portion of participants indicated only one goal at measurement wave 2 for the following analyses, only goal variables of the first goal were used.

Table 11. Test-retest correlations of predictor variables

		Measurement wave 2
	1. Self-efficacy	.72
	2. Externality	.66
	3. Hopelessness	.63
	4. Achievement	.72
	5. Power	.81
Measurement wave 1	6. Affiliation	.74
	7. Flexibility	.66
	8. Persistence	.76
	9. Goal commitment	.20
	10. Goal attainability	.30
	11. Goal probability	.17
	12. Subjective health	.48

Most of the predictor variables were also subject to age changes (Figures 8 to 12). For each variable, separate two-way repeated measurement ANOVAs (age cohort x measurement wave) were computed. For self-efficacy, only a weak effect of measurement wave but significant effects of cohort and cohort x wave interaction could be found (Figure 8).

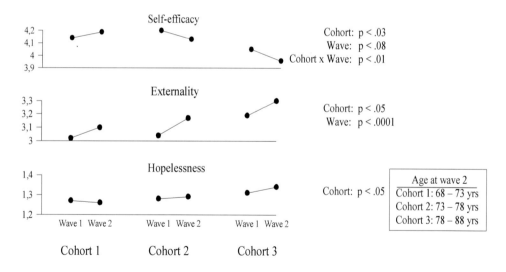

Figure 8. Personal agency variables in three age cohorts at both measurement points.

This was due to the youngest age group in which an *increase* in self-efficacy took place. From cohort 2 on there was a clear *decrease* and, overall, self-efficacy was lowest in the oldest cohort. External control beliefs and hopelessness increased (the latter falling short of significance). For both variables, the highest scores were found in the oldest cohort. Looking at the three personal agency variables together, it seems striking that changes took place beginning in the middle-age cohort and were most pronounced in the oldest cohort. This form of developmental trend—relative stability in the young old but decline in the oldest old—was also found in most of the other personality variables.

The achievement and power motives declined with age (Figure 9). But again, as was the case for personal agency, this decline began in the middle-age cohort only, whereas in the youngest cohort, both motives remained quite stable. For the affiliation motive, no age-related effect could be detected, although there seemed to be a decline in the oldest old.

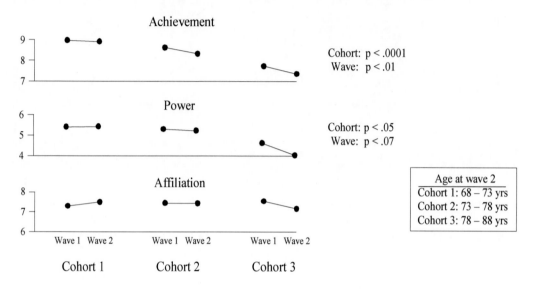

Figure 9. Motive dispositions in three age cohorts at both measurement points.

Both coping styles also revealed a significant decline with age (Figure 10). Assimilative persistence decreased markedly and was lowest in the oldest cohort. For accommodative flexibility, a decreasing effect also took place.

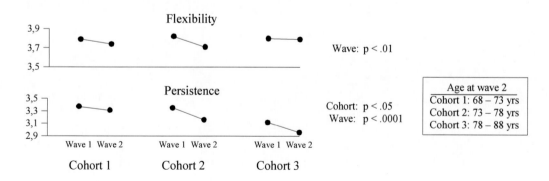

Figure 10. Coping strategies in three age cohorts at both measurement points.

For the goal variables, pronounced wave effects were found (Figure 11). The participants' commitments to their most important goals increased, but at the same time, the goal attainability and especially the probability of goal realization were estimated lower than before. Finally, subjective health perception clearly decreased in the five-year interval (Figure 12).

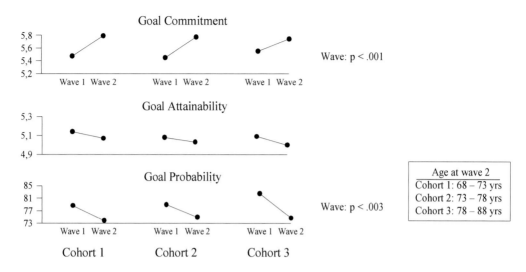

Figure 11. Goal variables in three age cohorts at both measurement points.

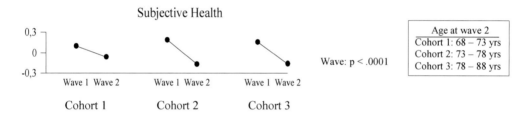

Figure 12. Subjective health perception in three age cohorts at both measurement points.

Table 12. Partial correlations of predictor variables with changes in SWB**

	Life satisfaction*	Affect *	
		positive	negative
Self-efficacy		**.22**	
Externality		-.17	
Hopelessness	**-.31**	**-.50**	**.30**
Achievement		.17	
Power		.18	
Affiliation		.13	
Flexibility	.19	**.25**	
Persistence		.15	
Goal commitment			
Goal attainability		.18	
Goal probability	.17	.19	-.15
Subjective health		**.32**	**-.26**

Note: All reported coefficients p < .01; bold coefficients p < .0001.
* Difference scores: wave 2 – wave 1.
** controlling variables: SWB-measures at wave 1.

Predictors of Changes in Subjective Well-being

To estimate the impact the predictor variables had in explaining changes in SWB from wave 1 to wave 2, we computed difference scores of SWB measures (wave 2 measures minus wave 1 measures) and conducted partial correlations between predictor variables and SWB measures, controlling for baseline values of SWB measures at wave 1 (Table 12).

Changes in life satisfaction correlated negatively with hopelessness and positively with flexibility and goal probability. A similar pattern was found for the affect measures; changes in positive affect were additionally correlated with self-efficacy. This means that the cognitive and emotional components of SWB were influenced by the personality variables in the *same* direction and the puzzling fact of differing age trends in cognitive and affective well-being could not be explained by personality predictors. However, the findings concerning subjective health perception open a new avenue for interpretation. Subjective health was substantially correlated with changes in affective well-being, that is, feelings of restrictions due to ill health dampened the affect balance. In contrast, subjective health had no effect on changes in cognitive well-being whatsoever.

In a second step, we performed regression analyses of the SWB difference measures to estimate the impact each predictor variable had in explaining age-related changes in SWB. To control for baseline levels, the SWB scores at wave 1 were added to the list of predictors. Not surprisingly, the baseline values of SWB accounted for a great portion of variance in both analyses (Table 13). Following that, hopelessness was the most powerful (= detrimental) predictor of changes in cognitive as well as in affective well-being. In the case of life satisfaction, accommodative flexibility added a moderate amount to the explanation of variance. But self-efficacy, which was a very powerful impact factor for life satisfaction in the cross-sectional analyses (Table 6), had no effect at all in predicting *changes* in life satisfaction. The results concerning affective well-being (here, the affect-balance score was again used) showed a different picture. In contrast to life satisfaction, the only variable that added a significant value was subjective health perception.

Table 13. Regression analyses of predictors variables of changes in SWB

Life satisfaction*	ß	p <	Affect balance*	ß	p <
Satisf. (wave 1)	-.52	.0001	Affect (wave 1)	-.73	.0001
Hopelessness	-.30	.0001	Hopelessness	-.35	.0001
Flexibility	.14	.02	Subjective health	.22	.0001
Goal probability	.11		Flexibility	.08	
Externality	.10		Achievement	.08	
Persistence	.08		Persistence	-.07	
Self-efficacy	-.06		Goal probability	.05	
Achievement	-.06		Goal commitment	-.03	
Affiliation	.05		Goal attainability	.02	
Power	-.02		Power	-.02	
Subjective health	.02		Externality	.01	
Goal attainability	.01		Self-efficacy	-.00	
Goal commitment	.00		Affiliation	-.00	
Note. R = .51, p < .0001			*Note.* R = 72, p < .0001		

* Difference scores: wave 2 – wave 1.

CONCLUSIONS

At the beginning of our conclusions, we would like to make two caveats. Firstly, the sample consisted of monozygotic and dizygotic twins, but we disregarded this fact in our analyses (for genetic analyses, see Geppert & Halisch, in press). Secondly, most of our participants were quite fit. They easily managed to travel to Munich, to stay at a hotel for a week and to undergo lengthy testing at our institute. One has to be careful in generalizing our results to aged people who may not be as physically or as mentally able. Bearing these limitations in mind, our data, nevertheless, yielded some impressive results concerning personality variables and subjective well-being in old age.

Personality Variables

The personality variables formed a coherent and plausible pattern of four factors. From our view, two aspects are of special interest. First, the coping strategies of assimilative persistence and of accommodative flexibility were correlated to a moderate degree, but nevertheless, each was the leading variable of two independent factors. Assimilative persistence formed a factor of assertiveness together with the achievement and the power motive. Accommodative flexibility, on the other hand, was associated with low hopelessness and low externality, and, in particular, with good subjective health. Brandstädter and colleagues (Brandstädter & Renner, 1990; Brandstädter et al., 1998; Brandstädter et al., 1999) have consistently pointed out that the processes of assimilation and accommodation are functionally antagonistic but not mutually exclusive. Our results corroborate this assumption. Second, self-efficacy was not unambiguously attached to one factor. Instead, it had nearly equal loadings on the persistence as well as the flexibility factor. Obviously, individuals with a high sense of control and efficacy can use *both* strategies in the same way. High self-efficacy by no means simply implies assimilative efforts that aim to achieve and maintain desired outcomes. Confronted with the fact that, in old age, it becomes increasingly difficult to counteract losses and diminishing resources, individuals with high self-efficacy can also flexibly adjust their ambitions to situational constraints and "downgrade" their goals and aspirations. In our opinion, it would be misleading to argue that such lowering of aspirations would also inevitably damage feelings of self-efficacy. In expectancy-value theories, e.g. Atkinson's risk taking-model (1957, 1964) or Heckhausen's self-evaluation model (H. Heckhausen, 1991), success in tasks of moderate difficulty (= subjective success probability) yields the optimal self-evaluative outcome consequences. The key factor for subjective success probability is competence. Only tasks that are within the individual's span of competence, that is tasks neither too easy nor too difficult, provide a well-adjusted balance of self-evaluative consequences. A lowering of goals, when confronted with the experience that even great effort is in vain can contribute to a positive self-evaluative balance and thus *enhance* self-efficacy. In this line of argumentation, it appears comprehensible to maintain that—depending on situational demands—individuals with high self-efficacy have both assimilative as well as accommodative coping strategies at their disposal.

High negative loadings of hopelessness and externality on the flexibility factor also confirm Brandstädter's notion that accommodative strategies should not be confused with hopelessness or depression (Brandtstädter et al., 1998). In contrast, in the model of assimilative and accommodative coping feelings of hopelessness rather reflect difficulties in shifting from assimilative to accommodative coping. Of equal interest is the fact that subjective health perception was associated with accommodative flexibility. We have pointed out that health is an important factor in successful aging, but instead of objective health, it is *subjective* health perception that plays the decisive role. According to our findings, accommodative and assimilative coping processes have a prominent impact on subjective health. Rigidly pursuing personal aspirations in spite of external resistance can lower subjective health but lowering one's own aspirations can obviously help to re-interpret situational constraints and alleviate the negative effects of health restrictions. Subjective health is not only a matter of objective health but also a consequence of accommodative coping processes. Similarly Pinquart (2001, p. 420) concluded "that older adults have higher abilities to adapt their criteria of perceived health to deteriorating objective health so that the age-associated growing number of objective health problems has only limited influence on health perception." Individuals who are able to adjust their ambitions to what is possible obviously feel influenced to a lesser degree by health restrictions.

In addition to persistence and flexibility, a third factor was made up of the goal variables. Individuals who were highly committed to their goals were mostly convinced that they could attain these goals and estimated the probability of reaching them as rather high. Again, self-efficacy comes into play: Individuals with high self-efficacy tended to pursue goals that they themselves consider to be within their own control. This result is in accordance with the relation of self-efficacy and accommodative coping processes, as discussed above.

Our data concerning gender differences corroborate the results found so far (Feingold, 1994). Males were characterized by a greater sense of personal agency (self-efficacy, low hopelessness, low externality), and higher assertiveness (persistence, achievement motive, power motive) compared to females. Furthermore, although males and females were equally committed to their goals, males estimated the attainability and the probability of achieving their goals at a significantly higher level. In the light of these rather pronounced differences, it is of special importance that we did not find any gender difference in accommodative flexibility and subjective health perception. Males and females are equally able to adjust their ambitions to situational constraints, and their subjective interpretation of their own health does not differ.

The central topic of the present paper is related to developmental changes in old age. The range of our sample spans from 64 years (at wave 1) to almost 90 (at wave 2). This means that at the time of the first measurement, a sizable portion of participants had reached retirement age (a few were still working). Entry into retirement has been described as a life task in which occupational involvements have to be replaced with other purposeful activities (Havighurst, 1960, 1972; Neugarten & Hagestad, 1976). Retired people can no longer derive satisfaction from occupational pursuits or raising a family but have to find new ways to lead rewarding lives (cf. Rapkin & Fischer, 1992). Accordingly, their goals mostly refer to traveling, intellectual tasks (e.g. learning a new language), or supporting grandchildren (Halisch, in press). At the other end of the age range, our oldest participants inevitably approached the phase of senescence and frailty. They had probably reached their limits of cognitive functioning or were even in a phase of terminal decline, and they had to face the fact of a limited future time perspective. This final stage of life has been described as the "fourth age"—in contrast to the "third age" of the young old reaching the phase of retirement (P. B. Baltes & Smith, 2003).

To reflect these "multiple ages of old age," we divided our sample into three age cohorts. The cross-sectional analyses revealed only a few differences between age cohorts. Assimilative persistence and the achievement motive decreased from cohort 1 to cohort 3, while externality increased. Remarkably, we found no significant cohort differences in subjective health, although it seemed to be lowest in the oldest cohort. There were also no age differences concerning the goal variables. Of course, the longitudinal analyses are more convincing, and these analyses show that most of the predictor variables were subject to distinct age-related changes. Personal agency clearly diminished with age: Self-efficacy decreased, whereas externality and hopelessness increased. In the same way, the achievement motive, the power motive and assimilative persistence showed a distinct decline. Careful inspection of the respective graphs, however, reveals that these developmental changes occurred only in the older participants (beginning at about 73 years of age) and were most strongly pronounced in the oldest (78 upward). In cohort 1, self-efficacy actually seemed to increase. In accordance with the concept of a third and a fourth age (P. B. Baltes & Smith, 2003), these results confirm that the first years of retirement age (cohort 1) are characterized by a relative stability of personal agency, sense of control, and assertiveness. A noticeable decline only begins later and reaches its lowest level in the oldest old. Accommodative flexibility also diminished with age but, compared to the other personality variables, to a much lesser degree. The mean levels of flexibility in cohort 1 and cohort 3 were nearly identical. Obviously, accommodative adaptation processes stay alive until the oldest age.

It is particularly noticeable that the decline in agency and assertiveness had no effect on goal commitment. Although our participants indicated fewer goals at wave 2 than at wave 1, their commitment to their most important goals increased with age. But at the same time, the probability of successfully achieving this goal decreased. This result can possibly be interpreted as the individual's acceptance of a realistic view of their own remaining strengths and possibilities. Finally, in accordance with all scientific as well as naïve theories of aging, subjective health perception demonstrated a strong decline.

Subjective Well-being

Our data are in line with general findings of research on SWB. First, life satisfaction is correlated with both emotional measures of SWB (.37 with positive affect and -.37 with negative affect). These correlations are within the range reported by Lucas et al. (1996), for example, and since the coefficients reach only a moderate degree, they corroborate the assumption that the cognitive and affective components are distinct constructs (cf. also Schimmack et al., 2008). The correlation between positive and negative affect (-.45) slightly exceeded the coefficients reported by Lucas et al. (1996), but the difference was not great enough to cast doubt on the independence of both types of affect. Theoretical and empirical independence of components of SWB is a precondition for analyzing different developmental trends and searching for different predictors (see below). Second, as to the level of SWB, the results confirm that elderly people are mostly satisfied with their lives (e.g., Diener & Suh, 1998). On the average, our participants' life satisfaction as well as their affective well-being were at a rather high positive level.

Numerous studies have addressed the question of gender differences in SWB. Although the results are somewhat inconsistent, it was mostly found that for women, life satisfaction is lower and affect is more negative than for men (cf. M. M. Baltes, Freund, & Horgas, 1999; Tesch-Römer, Motel-Klingebiel, & Tomasik, 2008). In a meta-analysis of 300 empirical studies, Pinquart and Sörensen (2001) found that this is also true in late adulthood, and our data corroborate these findings. We found comparable gender differences in all components of SWB. Usually this is attributed to different living conditions of men and women, to women's poorer financial resources, or their higher risk of being widowed or having health problems. But, in a cross-cultural study on gender differences and SWB, Tesch-Römer et al. (2008) came to the conclusion that opportunity structures and the availability of resources that are relevant to goal-directed behavior is probably the crucial factor. Our data provide a supplementary explanation: We found that males had higher self-efficacy scores than females and adhered to personal goals of higher attainability and probability. In accordance with findings of other studies (e.g., Brunstein, 1993, 1999), we showed that pursuing attainable goals enhances feelings of subjective well-being (Halisch & Geppert, 2001). In our view, this is one main reason why males indicated a greater satisfaction with life and a more positive affect balance than females.[4]

The long-term analyses revealed distinctly different stability coefficients for cognitive and affective SWB measures. The stability of life satisfaction (.69) came close to the stability reached by personality variables. The stabilities of the affect measures were much lower (.29 for positive affect and .40 for negative affect). Diener et al. (2006) reported similar stability coefficients of SWB measures. Life satisfaction is a kind of retrospect, a cognitive summary evaluation of one's life, and is much less affected by situational influences than the affect measures, which are rather indicators of one's actual mood. In addition, Diener et al. (2006) showed that the stability of positive affect declined with longer time periods, whereas the stability of negative affect remained at the same relatively high level. They put forward the idea that "these findings suggest that stable individual baselines might be more characteristic of negative affect than positive affect. However, [...] life satisfaction was most stable" (p. 308). These results also indicate that the different components of SWB can develop into different directions.

In the cross-sectional comparisons, we found no differences in SWB between age cohorts but the longitudinal analyses evinced clear and at first view somewhat puzzling results. Life satisfaction significantly *increased* in the five-year interval between the two measurement waves, whereas positive affect *decreased* during this time and was lowest in the oldest age cohort at measurement wave 2. For negative affect, there was no clear age effect, although the data suggest a curvilinear development: In the youngest age cohort, negative affect diminished, but in the oldest cohort, it increased from wave 1 to wave 2. Therefore, the affect balance clearly decreased in the oldest age cohort. In our view, this result again supports the assumption that affective well-being, compared to life satisfaction, is more sensitive to situational influences and impairments due to aging processes.

---

[4] A post hoc analysis of covariance supports this assumption. The gender differences in life satisfaction and positive affect completely disappeared in an ANOVA controlling for self-efficacy as a covariate. The gender differences in negative affect also diminished but were still significant. The latter result could be interpreted by females' greater emotional intensity and their greater willingness to disclose negative emotions (Diener, Sandvik, & Larsen, 1985; Nolen-Hoeksema & Rusting, 1999).

Recently, Gerstorf and colleagues (Gerstorf, Ram, Estabrook et al., 2008; Gerstorf, Ram, Röcke, Lindenberger, & Smith, 2008) analyzed the data of deceased participants of two large-scale longitudinal studies. They showed that a mortality-related model explains individual differences in changes in life satisfaction better than an age-related model. This means that not chronological age but the proximity of death plays the decisive role. At some point not far from death, a terminal decline takes place: Both the individuals' functioning and well-being deteriorate quite rapidly. Gerstorf and colleagues only reported data on life satisfaction and not on affective well-being, and we can, therefore, only speculate at this point: Possibly the decline in affect in our oldest cohort can be interpreted as a first sign of approaching death.[5]

Predictors of Subjective Well-being

The present findings concerning the personality determinants of subjective well-being are completely in line with the top-down approach (Heller et al., 2004): Personality variables influence individual differences in SWB in old age. Generally—this comes as no surprise—hopelessness had a strong dampening influence on all components of SWB. Individuals who hold negative expectations towards their future negatively estimated their actual mood (affective well-being) and were dissatisfied with their lives (cognitive well-being). Additional determinants, however, were different (a) for different components of SWB and (b) for different age phases.

The cross-sectional analyses of measurement wave 1 revealed that the cognitive and affective components of SWB were influenced by the personality variables in different ways. Concerning life satisfaction, the results proved an often-stated but less frequently empirically tested (Charrow, 2006, Lachman et al., 2009) influence of self-efficacy. Elderly individuals who believe they have abilities allowing them to exercise influence on their lives are usually satisfied with their lives. Moreover, the correlations between personality variables and life satisfaction showed that, generally speaking, a sense of high personal agency (high self-efficacy, low hopelessness, low externality) combined with the ability to transform one's own aspirations flexibly to life constraints (accommodative flexibility) and therefore to pursue goals with high attainability and success probability were of high benefit for life satisfaction. The correlational pattern as to the affect measures was comparable, but the coefficients were much lower. The deciding variable was subjective health perception: Subjective health had a strong impact on affective well-being but was of only minor importance for life satisfaction. The regression analyses also confirmed that life satisfaction and affective well-being were influenced by different predictors. Self-efficacy was the most powerful predictor of life satisfaction, whereas subjective health perception had the strongest influence on affective well-being. Obviously, compared to life satisfaction, affective well-being is much more sensitive to actual and situational determinants such as health.

To detect possible age-related differences, we conducted the same analyses separately for the three age cohorts. Although there were no age-related differences in levels of cognitive and affective well-being, the predictor variables were different within the age cohorts. The major role of self-efficacy in life satisfaction only realized in the youngest cohort and was

---

[5] In fact, the individuals who passed away before measurement 2 (n=39) indicated lower positive affect and higher negative affect than the rest of the sample at wave 1, but the differences did not reach significance.

attenuated with age; self-efficacy completely lost its importance in the oldest cohort. In the youngest cohort, the ability to flexibly adjust one's own aspirations (accommodative flexibility) additionally had a positive influence, whereas tenaciously pursuing personal goals (assimilative persistence) had, if at all, a detrimental influence. This underscores the importance of accommodative adaptation processes to secure personal continuity and integrity in age (Brandtstädter et al., 1998). In the oldest cohort, on the other hand, the variable goal probability, which had virtually no effect in the younger cohorts, came into play. The probability of reaching one's most important goal was by far the strongest predictor of life satisfaction in the oldest old. Here, all other factors played a subordinate role only. It has repeatedly be shown that striving for achievable personal goals can enhance SWB (Brunstein, 1993; Brunstein, 1999; Halisch & Geppert, 2001), but this result emphasizes a special point: Obviously, when confronted with the diminishing time yet to be lived, it is of increasing importance whether one still sees a chance of realizing personal goals or not.

The analyses of the predictors of affective well-being corroborated the general influence of subjective health perception in all cohorts, but the impact became increasingly stronger with age. In the oldest cohort, it was by far the most important determinant of individual differences in affective state.

We found that the cognitive and affective components of SWB moved in different directions from wave 1 to wave 2 (see above): Life satisfaction *increased,* whereas positive affect (and hence the affective balance of positive and negative affect) *decreased.* The regression analyses showed that these different developmental trends could be partly explained by the predictor variables we employed. First, hopelessness had a great impact on changes in SWB as a whole. But beyond that, different predictors again came into play. Flexibility in goal adjustment and a high success probability of desired goals led to an enhancement of life satisfaction. Again, the special role of a shift to accommodative processes in age becomes obvious. Individuals who can lower their aspirations to meet age-related constraints and therefore strive for achievable goals continue to have high life satisfaction. In contrast to life satisfaction, the decline in affective well-being could not be explained by personality and goal variables. Instead, subjective health perception was the only factor that had an impact on the decrease in affect. Feelings of restrictions due to ill health reduced the affect balance. However, subjective health had no effect on changes in cognitive well-being whatsoever. To underscore the key point: The perception that one's own health is poor impaired affective well-being, but the perception of being in good health did not increase life satisfaction. On the other hand, flexibility in goal adjustment was beneficial with respect to the increase in life satisfaction but did not account for changes in affective well-being.

In general, we can draw the following three conclusions about subjective well-being in old age. First, personality variables influence SWB to a great extent. Secondly, the personality determinants of SWB are different for the various components of SWB, and, finally, they are also different for different age phases.

ACKNOWLEDGEMENTS

We gratefully acknowledge the assistance of Rolf Brekenkamp and Rosie Wallis in improving the English text.

REFERENCES

Atkinson, J. W. (1957). Motivational determinants of risk-taking behavior. *Psychological Review, 64*(6), 359-372.

Atkinson, J. W. (1964). *An introduction to motivation.* Princeton, NJ: Van Nostrand.

Baltes, M. M., Freund, A. M., & Horgas, A. L. (1999). Men and women in the Berlin Aging Study. In P. B. Baltes & K. U. Mayer (Eds.), *The Berlin Aging Study: Aging from 70 to 100* (pp. 259-281). New York, NY, USA: Cambridge University Press.

Baltes, P. B., & Mayer, K. U. (1999). *The Berlin Aging Study: Aging from 70 to 100.* New York, NY, US: Cambridge University Press.

Baltes, P. B., & Smith, J. (2003). New frontiers in the future of aging: From successful aging of the young old to the dilemmas of the fourth age. *Gerontology, 49*(2), 123-135.

Bandura, A. (1977). Self-efficacy: Toward a unifying theory of behavioral change. *Psychological Review, 84*(2), 191-215.

Bandura, A. (1997). *Self-efficacy: The exercise of control.* New York, NY: Freeman.

Baumann, N., Kaschel, R., & Kuhl, J. (2005). Striving for unwanted goals: Stress-dependent discrepancies between explicit and implicit achievement motives reduce aubjective well-being and increase psychosomatic symptoms. *Journal of Personality and Social Psychology, 89*(5), 781-799.

Beck, A. T., Weissman, A., Lester, D., & Trexler, L. (1974). The measurement of pessimism: The Hopelessness Scale. *Journal of Consulting & Clinical Psychology, 42*(6), 861-865.

Berg, A., Hassing, L., McClearn, G., & Johansson, B. (2006). What matters for life satisfaction in the oldest-old? *Aging & Mental Health, 10*(3), 257-264.

Bradburn, N. M. (1969). *The structure of psychological well-being.* Chicago, Ill.: Aldine.

Brandtstädter, J., & Renner, G. (1990). Tenacious goal pursuit and flexible goal adjustment: Explication and age-related analysis of assimilative and accommodative strategies of coping. *Psychology & Aging, 5*(1), 58-67.

Brandtstädter, J., Rothermund, K., & Schmitz, U. (1998). Maintaining self-integrity and efficacy through adulthood and later life: The adaptive functions of assimilative persistence and accommodative flexibility. In J. Heckhausen & C. S. Dweck (Eds.), *Motivation and self-regulation across the lifespan* (pp. 365-388). New York, NY, USA: Cambridge University Press.

Brandtstädter, J., Wentura, D., & Rothermund, K. (1999). Intentional self-development through adulthood and later life: Tenacious pursuit and flexible adjustment of goals. In J. Brandtstädter & R. M. Lerner (Eds.), *Action & self-development: Theory and research through the lifespan.* (pp. 373-400). Thousand Oaks, CA: Sage.

Brief, A. P., Butcher, A. H., George, J. M., & Link, K. E. (1993). Integrating bottom-up and top-down theories of subjective well-being: The case of health. *Journal of Personality and Social Psychology, 64*(4), 646-653.

Brunstein, J. C. (1993). Personal goals and subjective well-being: A longitudinal study. *Journal of Personality and Social Psychology, 65*(5), 1061-1070.

Brunstein, J. C. (1999). Persönliche Ziele und subjektives Wohlbefinden bei älteren Menschen [Personal goals and subjective well-being among older adults]. *Zeitschrift für Differentielle und Diagnostische Psychologie, 20*(1), 58-71.

Brunstein, J. C., Schultheiß, O. C., & Gräßman, R. (1998). Personal goals and emotional well-being: The moderating role of motive dispositions. *Journal of Personality & Social Psychology, 75*(2), 494-508.

Brunstein, J. C., Schultheiß, O. C., & Maier, G. W. (1999). The pursuit of personal goals: A motivational approach to well-being and life adjustment. In J. Brandtstädter & R. M. Lerner (Eds.), *Action & self-development: Theory and research through the lifespan* (pp. 169-196). Thousand Oaks, CA: Sage .

Campbell, A., Converse, P. E., & Rodgers, W. L. (1976). *The quality of American life: Perceptions, evaluations, and satisfactions.* New York, NY: Russell Sage Foundation. .

Charrow, C. B. (2006). Self-efficacy as a predictor of life satisfaction in older adults. *Dissertation Abstracts International, 67*(1-A), 292 (UMI No. 3200607).

DeNeve, K. M., & Cooper, H. (1998). The happy personality: A meta-analysis of 137 personality traits and subjective well-being. *Psychological Bulletin, 124*(2), 197-229.

Diener, E., & Diener, C. (1996). Most people are happy. *Psychological Science, 7*(3), 181-185.

Diener, E., & Emmons, R. A. (1984). The independence of positive and negative affect. *Journal of Personality and Social Psychology, 47*(5), 1105-1117.

Diener, E., Emmons, R. A., Larsen, R. J., & Griffin, S. (1985). The Satisfaction with Life Scale. *Journal of Personality Assessment, 49*(1), 71-75.

Diener, E., & Lucas, R. E. (1999). Personality and subjective well-being. In D. Kahneman, E. Diener & N. Schwarz (Eds.), *Well-being: The foundations of hedonic psychology* (pp. 213-229). New York, NY: Russell Sage Foundation.

Diener, E., Lucas, R. E., & Scollon, C. N. (2006). Beyond the hedonic treadmill: Revising the adaptation theory of well-being. *American Psychologist, 61*(4), 305-314.

Diener, E., Sandvik, E., & Larsen, R. J. (1985). Age and sex effects for emotional intensity. *Developmental Psychology, 21*(3), 542-546.

Diener, E., Smith, H., & Fujita, F. (1995). The personality structure of affect. *Journal of Personality and Social Psychology, 69*(1), 130-141.

Diener, E., Suh, E. M., Lucas, R. E., & Smith, H. L. (1999). Subjective well-being: Three decades of progress. *Psychological Bulletin, 125*(2), 276-302.

Diener, E., & Suh, M. E. (1998). Subjective well-being and age: An international analysis. In K. Schaie & M. P. Lawton (Eds.), *Annual review of gerontology and geriatrics: Focus on emotion and adult development* (Vol. 17, pp. 304-324). New York, NY: Springer Publishing Co.

Emmons, R. A. (1986). Personal strivings: An approach to personality and subjective well-being. *Journal of Personality and Social Psychology, 51*(5), 1058-1068.

Feingold, A. (1994). Gender differences in personality: A meta-analysis. *Psychological Bulletin, 116*(3), 429-456.

Feist, G. J., Bodner, T. E., Jacobs, J. F., Miles, M., et al. (1995). Integrating top-down and bottom-up structural models of subjective well-being: A longitudinal investigation. *Journal of Personality & Social Psychology, 68*(1), 138-150.

Geppert, U., & Halisch, F. (Eds.). (Report, in press). *Persönlichkeitsentwicklung über die Lebensspanne. Die Münchener genetisch orientierte Lebensspannenstudie zur differentiellen Entwicklung (GOLD) [Personality development over the lifespan. The Munic genetically oriented lifespan study on differential development (GOLD)].*

Gerstorf, D., Ram, N., Estabrook, R., Schupp, J., Wagner, G. G., & Lindenberger, U. (2008). Life satisfaction shows terminal decline in old age: Longitudinal evidence from the German Socio-Economic Panel Study (SOEP). *Developmental Psychology, 44*(4), 1148-1159.

Gerstorf, D., Ram, N., Röcke, C., Lindenberger, U., & Smith, J. (2008). Decline in life satisfaction in old age: Longitudinal evidence for links to distance-to-death. *Psychology and Aging, 23*(1), 154-168.

Greve, W., Anderson, A., & Krampen, G. (2001). Self-efficacy and externality in adolescence: Theoretical conceptions and measurement in New Zealand and German secondary school students. *Identity: An International Journal of Theory and Research, 1*(4), 321-344.

Halisch, F. (in press). Persönliche Ziele und subjektives Wohlbefinden als Kern adaptiver Altersanpassung [Personal goals and subjective well-being as core processes of adaptiaion to old age] In U. Geppert & F. Halisch (Eds.), *Persönlichkeitsentwicklung über die Lebensspanne. Die Münchener genetisch orientierte Lebensspannenstudie zur differentiellen Entwicklung (GOLD) [Personality development over the lifespan. The Munic genetically oriented lifespan study on differential development (GOLD)].*

Halisch, F., & Geppert, U. (2000). Wohlbefinden im Alter: Der Einfluss von Selbstwirksamkeit, Kontrollüberzeugungen, Bewältigungsstrategien und persönlichen Zielen. Ergebnisse aus der Münchner GOLD-Studie [Well-being in old age: The influence of self-efficacy, control beliefs, coping strategies and personal goals. Results from the Munic GOLD Study]. In J. Stiensmeier-Pelster, F. Försterling & L. Silny (Eds.), *Kognitive und emotionale Aspekte der Motivation [Cognitive and emotional aspects of motivation].* (pp. 121-152). Göttingen: Hogrefe.

Halisch, F., & Geppert, U. (2001). Motives, personal goals and life satisfaction in old age: First results from the Munich Twin Study (GOLD). In A. Efklides, J. Kuhl & R. Sorrentino (Eds.), *Trends and prospects in motivation research* (pp. 389-409). Dordrecht: Kluwer.

Havighurst, R. J. (1960). Life beyond family and work. In E. W. Burgess (Ed.), *Aging in Western societies* (pp. 299-353). Chicago: Chicago University Press.

Havighurst, R. J. (1972). *Developmental tasks and education* (3 ed.). New York, NY: David McKay.

Headey, B., Veenhoven, R., & Wearing, A. (1991). Top-down versus bottom-up theories of subjective well-being. *Social Indicators Research, 24*(1), 327-349.

Heckhausen, H. (1991). *Motivation and action.* Berlin: Springer Verlag.

Heckhausen, J. (1999). *Developmental regulation in adulthood: Age-normative and sociostructural constraints as adaptive challenges.* New York, NY: Cambridge University Press.

Heckhausen, J., & Dweck, C. S. (1998). *Motivation and self-regulation across the lifespan.* New York, NY: Cambridge University Press.

Heckhausen, J., & Heckhausen, H. (Eds.). (2008). *Motivation and action* (2nd ed.). New York, NY: Cambridge University Press.

Heller, D., Watson, D., & Ilies, R. (2004). The Role of Person Versus Situation in Life Satisfaction: A Critical Examination. *Psychological Bulletin, 130*(4), 574-600.

Heyl, V., Wahl, H.-W., & Mollenkopf, H. (2007). Affective well-being in old age: The role of tenacious goal pursuit and flexible goal adjustment. *European Psychologist, 12*(2), 119-129.

Hofer, J., Chasiotis, A., & Campos, D. (2006). Congruence Between Social Values and Implicit Motives: Effects on Life Satisfaction Across Three Cultures. *European Journal of Personality, 20*(4), 305-324.

Jackson, D. N. (1984). *Personality research form* (3 ed.). Port Huron: Research Psychologists Press.

Jacob, M., & Guarnaccia, V. (1997). Motivational and behavioral correlates of life satisfaction in an elderly sample. *Psychological Reports, 80*(3, Pt 1), 811-818.

Krampen, G. (1991). *Fragebogen zu Kompetenz- und Kontrollüberzeugungen [Inventory on competence and control beliefs].* Göttingen: Hogrefe.

Krampen, G. (1994). *Skalen zur Erfasung von Hoffnungslosigkeit (H-Skalen) [Hopelessness Scale].* Göttingen: Hogrefe.

Lachman, M. E., Rosnick, C. B., & Röcke, C. (2009). The rise and fall of control beliefs and life satisfaction in adulthood: Trajectories of stability and change over ten years. In H. B. Bosworth & C. Hertzog (Eds.), *Aging and cognition: Research methodologies and empirical advances* (pp. 143-160). Washington, DC, US: American Psychological Association; US: American Psychological Association.

Langan-Fox, J., Sankey, M. J., & Canty, J. M. (2009). Incongruence between implicit and self-attributed achievement motives and psychological well-being: The moderating role of self-directedness, self-disclosure and locus of control. *Personality and Individual Differences, 47*(2), 99-104.

Langens, T. A. (2007). Congruence between implicit and explicit motives and emotional well-being: The moderating role of activity inhibition. *Motivation and Emotion, 31*(1), 49-59.

Lucas, R. E., Diener, E., & Suh, E. (1996). Discriminant validity of well-being measures. *Journal of Personality & Social Psychology, 71*(3), 616-628.

McClelland, D. C. (1985). *Human motivation.* Glenview, IL: Scott, Foresman.

McClelland, D. C., Scioli, A., & Weaver, S. (1998). The effect of implicit and explicit motivation on recall among old and young adults. *International Journal of Aging & Human Development, 46*(1), 1-20.

McCrae, R. R. (2002). The maturation of personality psychology: Adult personality development and psychological well-being. *Journal of Research in Personality, 36*(4), 307-317.

Neugarten, B. L., & Hagestad, G. O. (1976). Age and the life course. In R. H. Binstock & E. Shanas (Eds.), *Handbook of aging and the social sciences* (pp. 35-55). New York, NY: Van Nostrand.

Nolen-Hoeksema, S., & Rusting, C. L. (1999). Gender differences in well-being. In D. Kahneman, E. Diener & N. Schwarz (Eds.), *Well-being: The foundations of hedonic psychology* (pp. 330-350). New York, NY: Russell Sage Foundation.

Peterson, C. (1999). Personal control and well-being. In D. Kahneman, E. Diener & N. Schwarz (Eds.), *Well-being: The foundations of hedonic psychology* (pp. 288-301). New York, NY: Russell Sage Foundation.

Pinquart, M. (2001). Correlates of subjective health in older adults: A meta-analysis. *Psychology and Aging, 16*(3), 412-426.

Pinquart, M., & Sörensen, S. (2001). Gender differences in self-concept and psychological well-being in old age: A meta-analysis. *Journals of Gerontology: Series B: Psychological Sciences & Social Sciences, 56B*(4), P195-P213.

Queen, L., & Freitag, C. B. (1978). A comparison of externality, anxiety, and life satisfaction in two aged populations. *Journal of Psychology: Interdisciplinary and Applied, 98*(1), 71-74.

Rapkin, B. D., & Fischer, K. (1992). Personal goals of older adults: Issues in assessment and prediction. *Psychology and Aging, 7*(1), 127-137.

Rotter, J. B. (1966). Generalized expectancies for internal versus external control of reinforcement. *Psychological Monographs: General & Applied, 80*(1), 1-28.

Scheier, M. F., & Carver, C. S. (1992). Effects of optimism on psychological and physical well-being: Theoretical overview and empirical update. *Cognitive Therapy and Research, 16*(2), 201-228.

Schimmack, U., Radhakrishnan, P., Oishi, S., Dzokoto, V., & Ahadi, S. (2002). Culture, personality, and subjective well-being: Integrating process models of life satisfaction. *Journal of Personality and Social Psychology, 82*(4), 582-593.

Schimmack, U., Schupp, J., & Wagner, G. G. (2008). The influence of environment and personality on the affective and cognitive component of subjective well-being. *Social Indicators Research, 89*(1), 41-60.

Smith, J., Fleeson, W., Geiselmann, B., Settersten, R. A., Jr., & Kunzmann, U. (1999). Sources of well-being in very old age. In P. B. Baltes & K. U. Mayer (Eds.), *The Berlin Aging Study: Aging from 70 to 100* (pp. 450-471). New York, NY, USA: Cambridge University Press.

Staudinger, U. M. (2000). Viele Gründe sprechen dagegen, und trotzdem geht es vielen Menschen gut: Das Paradox des subjektiven Wohlbefindens. [Many reasons speak against it, yet many people feel good: The paradox of subjective well-being]. *Psychologische Rundschau, 51*(4), 185-197.

Stumpf, H., Angleitner, A., Wieck, T., Jackson, D. N., & Beloch-Till, H. (1985). *PRF-D. Personality research form - German version.* Göttingen: Hogrefe.

Tesch-Römer, C., Motel-Klingebiel, A., & Tomasik, M. J. (2008). Gender differences in subjective well-being: Comparing societies with respect to gender equality. *Social indicators research, 85*(2), 329-349.

Weinert, F. E., & Geppert, U. (1996). *Genetisch orientierte Lebensspannenstudie zur differentiellen Entwicklung (GOLD). Report Nr. 1: Planung der Studie [Genetic oriented lifespan study of differential development (GOLD). Report No 1: Plan of the study].* München: Max-Planck-Institut für Psychologische Forschung.

Weinert, F. E., & Geppert, U. (1998). *Genetisch orientierte Lebensspannenstudie zur differentiellen Entwicklung (GOLD). Report Nr. 2: Erste Ergebnisse der Studie [Genetic oriented lifespan study of differential development (GOLD). Report No 2: First results].* München: Max-Planck-Institut für Psychologische Forschung.

Weinert, F. E., Geppert, U., Dörfert, J., & Viek, P. (1994). Aufgaben, Ergebnisse und Probleme der Zwillingsforschung. Dargestellt am Beispiel der Gottschaldtschen Längsschnittstudie [Tasks, results, and problems of twin research. Illustrated by Gottschaldt's longitudinal study]. *Zeitschrift für Pädagogik, 40*(2), 265-288.

In: Motivation, Consciousness and Self-Regulation   ISBN: 978-1-61324-795-2
Editor: D. A. Leontiev, pp. 173-186   © 2012 Nova Science Publishers, Inc.

Chapter 11

MOTIVATIONAL FOUNDATIONS OF LEARNING: IMPLICATIONS FOR A RELATIONAL EDUCATIONAL PRACTICE

M. V. Abreu, M. P. Paixão
University of Coimbra, Portugal

ABSTRACT

Nuttin's critique of Thorndike's *Law of Effect* made a substantial contribution to the experimental study of motivation and its influence on learning and performance. The studies stimulated by this critique contributed much to Nuttin's formulation of his Relational Theory of human motivation and personality, a conceptual framework that can be used to analyze the main shortcomings of the traditional educational practice, both at macrosystem and at microsystem levels. This traditional educational system reproduces high rates of school dropouts and underachievement, as well as persistent emotional problems. The authors propose an alternative view on educational practice based on the ideas of task tension and of instrumental dynamic functioning proposed by J. Nuttin.

Keywords: Law of Effect, Relational Theory of motivation and personality, learning, educational system

INTRODUCTION

The academic work of Joseph Nuttin was centered upon three major domains of psychology: *learning, motivation and personality*. Nuttin's contributions to each of these domains are closely interconnected; they constitute a global theory of human behavior. This integrated vision of psychological activities originates in Husserl's phenomenological conception of the intentionality of consciousness (Nuttin, 1955), which was influential at the Institute of Philosophy at the University of Louvain. In psychology, the leading protagonist of that influence was Albert Michotte, Director of the Laboratory of Experimental Psychology of the above-mentioned Institute, where Nuttin received his scholarly training and started his experimental laboratory research. It was, indeed, by suggestion of Michotte that Nuttin started a wide program of experimental studies envisioning the clarification of the problem of the relation between learning and motivation.

In this chapter, we intend to underline the motivational implications of Nuttin's relational theory of motivation and personality for the organization of the educational system. Thus, in the first part of the chapter, we will briefly point out Nuttin's contributions regarding that issue and present our laboratory studies, which were carried out following the controversy between Greenwald (1966) and Postman (1966) about the relevance of Nuttin's experimental results. In the second part of the text, we will discuss our main practical applications based on Nuttin's cognitive-dynamic approach of human behavior, specifically in the area of education and career counseling.

NUTTIN'S CRITIQUE OF THE THEORETICAL LAW OF EFFECT

The research carried out by Nuttin on learning, in particular on serial selective human learning, is to be considered in the context of the theoretical and experimental generalization from animal learning research to human learning research made by Thorndike (1931; 1968). In contrast to the zoo-centric view of human behavior developed by Thorndike, Nuttin emphasized that learning is a complex process of behavioral change, mediated by a cognitive structuring of information from three main sources: a) the stimuli of the learning situation; b) the responses given by the individual; c) the positive or negative outcomes implied by each response. The cognitive structuring of these different kinds of information is influenced by the motivation to learn, functioning as a persistent tension to improve the achievement in future learning tasks (e.g., to obtain more successful responses on future trials than on past ones). Thus, Nuttin was a systematic opponent of the connectionist conceptions and anti-cognitivist explanations of learning defended by Thorndike.

In fact, according to connectionist conceptions, learning is a process of acquiring associations or connections between stimuli (S) and responses (R). In the process of acquiring a habit, the result or outcome following the response has a decisive role: a positive result (*reward*) increases the strength of the connection between the stimuli and that response; on the contrary, a negative result (*punishment*) produces the opposite effect, or an emotionally disturbing effect that inhibits the S-R connection. According to Thorndike's theoretical law of effect, the differential effect of results on the strength of connections is processed in a direct and automatic way, that is, without the mediation of cognitive activities, such as remembering the responses and/or the results. In a learning situation, more frequent repetition of rewarded responses as compared to punished ones is explained by stronger connections of those responses with the corresponding stimuli.

Nuttin questioned the validity of this *theoretical explanation* proposed by Thorndike (1911, 1932, 1949), although he acknowledged the *empirical law of effect*: in fact, selective learning situations produce a higher repetition of the responses on the test-trials evaluated as correct by the experimenter on the acquisition-trials. What Nuttin criticized was the *theoretical hypothesis* explaining the superior strength of rewarded S-R connections as compared to punished ones. He developed an alternative hypothesis. The higher frequency of correct responses would be due not to the reinforcing effect of rewards but rather to the motivation to learn or to perform well. Aiming to demonstrate empirically the weakness of the automatic reinforcement hypothesis and the value of his alternative cognitive-motivational explanation, Nuttin planned and executed a wide program of experimental research, using selective human learning as Thorndike did.

However, when testing the validity of Thorndike's hypothesis about the superiority of the *strength of rewarded connections* over the *strength of punished connections*, Nuttin faced a methodological problem. How could he measure the strength of the connections, either rewarded or punished, in such a way that he would be able to compare them in a non-biased condition? Thorndike used the frequency of the rewarded and non-rewarded answers in the test-trial as a measure of the *strength* of the connections of the responses with the correspondent stimuli. Since the rewarded responses were more frequently repeated, it was inferred that the strength of the rewarded responses was also higher than that of the punished ones. But, as Nuttin suggested, if the strength of the punished connections is equal to the strength of the rewarded connections, the higher repetition of the rewarded responses might be explained by the activation of another modality of strength: the one that arises from the intrinsic motivation to learn based on the individuals' commitment to the goal of progressively improving the performance of the proposed task. To perform the task well, individuals had to repeat the responses previously marked as correct and avoid the repetition of the incorrect responses.

However, using the performance of responses in the test-trial as the measure of the strength of connections created a methodological bias, since it favored the repetition of the rewarded responses in relation to the repetition of punished ones that individuals, in a learning situation, would avoid repeating. For this reason, in order to be able to measure and compare the strength of punished and rewarded connections in equal motivational conditions, Nuttin proposed to change the nature of the variable used by Thorndike. Instead of the performance on the test-trial, Nuttin began to use guided memory or cued recall of both rewarded and punished responses. In the test-trial, after recording the responses performed to the stimuli of the experimental list, the experimenter asked the participants to recollect the response they had given to each stimulus on the acquisition-trials. The data showed that in learning situations, the rewarded responses were much better remembered than the punished ones.

These results could be explained by the influence of the *persisting task tension* on memory, revealed in the research of Bluma Zeigarnik (1927), under the supervision of Lewin. The motivation to learn enhanced the memory of the responses previously considered correct in comparison to the punished responses, and subsequently, performance. The point was to create an experimental situation in which the persisting task tension would be neutralized. Nuttin named situations of this kind *closed task situations*, to distinguish them from learning situations qualified as *open task situations*. As a matter of fact, in closed task situations, the activity proposed to the participants was presented as requiring just one presentation of a series of stimuli or one trial; in this way, no expectation of having to face a new trial with the same activity was implied. In the course of the experiment, a response, which was to be given to each stimulus, was qualified by the experimenter as "right" or "wrong". The task was considered to be completed when the last response to the last item of the series was given and the result was announced. In contrast to what happens in learning situations, in which individuals expect to improve the performance in future trials, in closed task situations, the motivation to perform well is confined to the current activity alone. Nuttin found that in closed tasks—where rewards and punishments fulfilled only controlling function rather than informative one, which is salient in open task situations (cf. Ryan & Deci, 2000)—the memory of rewarded responses did not differ from the memory of the punished ones. In other words, in the absence of persistent motivation for the improvement of the performance the superiority of the mnemonic reproduction of the rewarded responses cannot be observed. The data obtained led him to think that the superiority observed in the selective learning situations could be due to a specific dynamic factor that is absent in closed task situations, that is, the persistent tension to achieve the desired goal. In the methodological design conceived by Nuttin and consistent with his thesis, it was necessary to verify the effect of the persisting task tension on the recall of information in experimental conditions *per se*, separated from the effect of performance feedback. In fact, the data obtained showed that the same information is better remembered in conditions of persisting task tension. This is the way motivation affects cognitive processes such as information retention and reproduction.

DISCUSSIONS ON NUTTIN'S CRITIQUE

The experiments carried out by Nuttin included several variations, and their results were published in the 1940s (Nuttin, 1942; 1947a; 1947b; 1949). The description and global analysis of these results was presented in his book *Tâche, Réussite et Échec: Théorie de la conduite humaine (Task, success and failure: a theory o human behavior)* (1953); this book represents a historical mark in the European psychology, since it contains the theoretical-experimental basis of the most consistent attack against the concept of automatic reinforcement as the explanation of learning in general. The results of Nuttin's research on human learning in Europe were very similar to the results obtained by Tolman (1932; 1966) on animal learning in the USA. However, Nuttin's research did not have the impact it deserved, certainly not in the United States. In 1953, the scientific community was not yet ready to accept the cognitive interpretations or, more precisely, the cognitive-motivational interpretations of learning. Generally, behaviorist and neo-behaviorist conceptions were admissible. Hulls' theory, which was formalized in his *Principles of behaviour* (1943) as a hypothetical-deductive system, was widely referred to as "the" scientific research paradigm in psychology. On the other hand, Skinners' supposed "a-theoretical" conception of operant conditioning reinforced the anti-cognitivist trend in the explanation of learning by defending the thesis of the "automatic, direct and unavoidable reinforcement" of S-R connections produced by rewards (Skinner, 1950).

In this historical context, it's not surprising that Greenwald (1966), with the "cognitivist revolution" already ongoing (Baars, 1986), commented that the theoretical and experimental work of Nuttin was not as widely known in the United States as it should be.

In his answer addressed to Greenwald, Postman (1966) rejected the critique of negligence by American researchers concerning the conceptions and experiments of Nuttin, explaining its weak diffusion by the fact that Nuttin did not use performance as a measure of learning, while this was the measure used by Thorndike. According to Postman, by using the cued recall of responses, Nuttin restrained the amplitude of his experiments; as Postman pointed out, the law of effect was a law of *performance* rather than a law of *learning*. However, by the end of the paper, Postman acknowledged the relevance of Nuttin's conceptions and left open the possibility of reviewing his position under certain conditions: *"If and when Nuttin's hypotheses are tested under conditions which bear directly on the law of effect, the picture may change"* (Postman,1966, p.387). Postman's critique of Greenwald's position focused on the difference of the measures used by Thorndike and Nuttin, without re-evaluating the theoretical and methodological reasons that justified Nuttin's choice of cued recall as the measure for selective learning rather than the performing the responses. In spite of that, Postman's final warning constituted a challenge in relation to the complementarity of the measures used by Thorndike and Nuttin. It was this challenge that Abreu accepted when he decided to undertake a research project that grew in the context of the Greenwald-Postman polemic. In fact, this controversy generated a large number of theoretical and experimental studies aiming to clarify some unsolved questions about the relations between motivation, memory and learning (Marx,1967; Nuttin & Greenwald,1968; Buchwald, 1969; Longstreth, 1970; d'Ydewalle, 1973, 1976; d'Ydewalle & Eelen, 1975; d'Ydewalle & Buchwald, 1976).

METHODOLOGICAL INNOVATIONS: THE DEPLOYMENT OF THREE INDICATORS OF SELECTIVE LEARNING

Responding to the challenge proposed by Postman, Abreu planned a series of three experiments in which he used experimental situations similar to the ones used by Thorndike and Nuttin and in which he measured, on the test-trials, three kinds of variables: the repetition of responses (*performance*), the mnesic reproduction of responses (*cued recall of responses*) and the mnesic reproduction of the feedback (*cued recall of results*) that followed each response in the acquisition-trial (Abreu, 1978). Here, we briefly present only the third one.

The experiment was conducted with a group of 60 university students (30 males and 30 females) distributed randomly over two different motivational conditions: a closed task condition and an open task condition.

To induce the *closed task condition*, the activities to be performed during the experiment were presented to the individuals as pertaining to the study of the students' capacity in a modality of extra-sensory perception (ESP). For this purpose, the individuals were shown a list of 20 words (adjectives such as: shining, fast, eloquent, etc.) knowing that each word on the list had been randomly associated to a number from 1 to 10. After presenting each word for five sec., the individual had to choose a number from 1 to 10. Immediately after each "guessing-response," the experimenter would classify it as a correct ("right") or an incorrect ("wrong") response. The instructions, read to the individuals, explained that the information given after each response would allow each participant, at the end of the task, to form a global impression of his/her capacity on this modality of perceptive activity.

To induce *the open task condition*, the experiment was presented as having the goal of studying learning processes. The individuals' tasks consisted of learning the number that had been randomly associated to each item of a list of 20 words. The instructions were similar to those in the closed task situation, but with important differences in the final part. After the description of the practical procedures to execute the task, the individuals were told by the experimenter that, once the presentation of the first list of words was finished, new trials would follow with the same list of words in the same order, until the number of correct answers reached the learning criterion set by the experimenter. In fact, in each experimental condition, two presentations of the list were carried out: the first one (acquisition-trial) and the second one (test-trial). In this last one, the responses given by the participants after the presentation of the words were not followed by the announcement of the result (right/wrong). After the experimenter had registered the responses (which allowed for the comparison with the responses given during the first trial), the individuals were asked to recall the responses that they had previously given and also to reproduce the result that had been announced. In this way, three measurements related to learning were obtained: the response, the recalled responses and the recalled results.

The experimental data were analyzed at two different levels. First, the main purpose was to check if the measures of the three dependent variables differed in the two motivational conditions. Second, we compared the recall results depending on the different patterns of mnesic availability. Finally, we tested the predictions based on the alternative hypotheses concerning the relations between performance and mnesic availability.

The results of the first level of analysis showed that all the three dependent variables varied significantly across the two motivational conditions. In fact, in a *closed task* situation, the repetition rate for rewarded responses was somewhat higher than the punished ones, but the difference was not significant. In the *open task* situation, the difference between the repetition rates for correct and incorrect responses was, however, significant ($t=2.29$, $p<.02$). Parallel to this, in the *closed task* condition, the difference in recall of rewarded and punished responses was also not significant. However, in the *open task* situation, the difference in favor of correct responses was again significant ($t=1.92$, $p<.05$). *Regarding the recall of the responses' results* in the *closed task situation*, the difference between results evaluated as "right" and the ones evaluated as "wrong" was again not significant. On the contrary, in the *open task situation*, Abreu found a significant increase in the number of recalled punishments in comparison to the recall of the rewards ($t=1.75$, $p<.05$).

The obtained results do not confirm the hypothesis of the automatic reinforcement that predicted a higher rate of repetition of the rewarded responses as compared to the punished ones, independently of the motivation. The predicted increase was not observed in the closed task situation but only in the open task situation, where the persisting motivation for the task performance and the expectation of improvement of the performance in future trials were present. In addition, a significant difference between the repetition and recall of the rewarded responses relative to the punished ones was only observed in the open task situation. That was due rather to a decrease in the number of repetition and recall of the punished responses than to an increase of the repetition and recall of the rewarded responses, as compared to the results in the closed task situation. This decrease in repetition and recall of the punished responses in the open task situation is related to the increase of the recall of the negative results that was also observed on this situation.

The second level of analysis focuses on the relations between performance (or repetition of responses) and the mnesic availability of the responses and their results. In this case, *four patterns of mnesic availability* were considered: i) *pattern of total mnesic availability,* in which the individuals remembered correctly the responses and the corresponding results; ii) *pattern of partial mnesic availability (of the response),* in which the individuals remembered correctly the responses but not the corresponding results; iii) *pattern of partial mnesic availability (of the result),* in which the individuals remembered incorrectly the responses but correctly recalled the corresponding results; iv) *pattern of mnesic unavailability,* in which individuals failed to remember both the responses and the results. Based on the opposing *performance* theories (the automatic reinforcement of rewards theory and the theory of mediating cognitive-motivational processes), several predictions were made concerning the differences of repetition of the rewarded and the punished responses that were registered under the different patterns of cognitive-mnesic availability. The analysis of the results showed a systematic conformity with the predictions that resulted from the theory of mediating cognitive-motivational processes. In all the mnesic patterns taken into account and, specifically, in the total *mnesic availability* patterns *versus* the total *mnesic unavailability* ones, the data obtained revealed that the higher level of repetition of the rewarded responses in relation to the punished ones could only be observed in the former and was absent in the latter.

The experimental results allowed the following conclusions: 1) the increased repetition of the rewarded responses relative to the repetition of the punished responses used as a criterion of selective learning (in the sense given by the defenders of direct and automatic effect of rewards, e.g., Thorndike and Postman) is not independent of the motivational conditions, since it does not occur in the closed task situation; 2) the increased repetition of the rewarded responses relative to the repetition of the punished ones observed in open task situations depends on the availability of the conjoint recall of responses and results, meaning that selective learning is mediated by processes of cognitive-mnesic structuring; 3) the negative outcomes (punishments or errors)— through a process of discriminatory retention of the information they carry—fulfill an important selective role in the open task situation, a role that does not exist in the closed task situation.

Having taken into account the methodological conditions required as necessary by Postman, Abreu supplemented the measures of selective learning (memory of responses) used by Nuttin, with measures of the repetition of responses (performance) that Thorndike and the defenders of the theoretical law of effect used. The results demonstrated that rewards do not bear an automatic impact on the selective performance of responses; the impact might be attributed to the temporal persistence of the individuals' intentions or goals to improve, in the subsequent trials, the activities they were engaged in. On the other hand, goal persistence in open task situations seems to direct attention to the informative role errors play in learning tasks.

Considering that in the above-mentioned experiments the hypotheses originating from the two opposing theoretical conceptions were in identical refutability conditions, according Poppers' methodological recommendations (1974) to the experimental test of theories, the obtained results allowed the rejection of the direct and automatic reinforcement of rewards hypothesis, and justified the choice of Nuttins' cognitive-motivational approach.

FROM THE RELATIONAL THEORY OF HUMAN BEHAVIOR TO A RELATIONAL MODEL OF PSYCHO-SOCIAL PRACTICE

Besides its theoretical value, which is grounded in the experimental validity of its explanation for selective learning and performance, the cognitive-dynamic theory of human behavior formulated by Nuttin has also significant potentialities for developing practical activities, namely in educational and vocational development settings.

In this section, we will discuss three examples highlighting the relevance of the relational theory of human motivation for the elaboration of more efficient educational strategies and for the resolution of persistent problems in academic contexts.

The first example reports the formulation of a *motivational strategy for persistent school learning* (Abreu, 2001, 2005). This formulation has been progressively developed across two action-research studies carried out in order to prevent school underachievement (Abreu, 2005). Within these studies, the researchers proposed a series of teachers' training interventions aiming to promote a qualitative renewal of teaching methods. This broad motivational strategy is composed of seven distinct steps that are closely interrelated:

1. *Formulating,* at the beginning of the teaching process, *the training objectives or the goals to be reached at the end of the process*, indicating the temporal length between the beginning and the end (representing the temporal span), and thus creating a future time perspective. The presentation of the goals is carried out in operational terms, focusing on the behavioral changes that are expected to occur at the level of conceptual restructuring (knowledge), at the level of technical competences (skills) and at the level of self-awareness, meta-cognition and personal development (attitudinal level);

2. *Briefly presenting the intervening activities* to be developed and the didactic instruments to be used in the course of the training process—both by the teachers and the students—and which are essential to reach the proposed training goals;

3. *Characterizing the activities to be developed by the teachers*, describing them as activities supporting the effort of the students in the organization of their learning, and presenting the role of the teacher as equivalent to that of a coach;

4. *Identifying the activities involved in the students' learning process*, pinpointing the factors and conditions that facilitate its organization;

5. *Restructuring the training or teaching-learning activities as open task situations* requiring problem-solving strategies;

6. *Applying modalities of "dynamic and formative evaluation,"* focused on the performance of activities that are similar to the operations that allow the achievement of the training goals, rather than summative evaluation procedures;

7. *Integrating personal self-awareness into the progressive construction of life/career projects.*

This "motivational strategy" is an interactive didactic instrument, since it requires the collaborative involvement of teachers, students and psychologists. The psychologists' activities focus on the training of meta-cognition and on efforts intended to help students to build a useful career project (Duarte, Paixão & Lima, 2010; Paixão, 2004). This "motivational strategy" has been used in teachers' and psychologists' training and has been integrated in school underachievement prevention programs, in combination with other psycho-pedagogic activities.

The organization of *school underachievement prevention programs* is the second example of transference from Nuttins' cognitive-dynamic approach of human behavior to the level of practical educational interventions. School underachievement, specifically in the 12 to 17 age group, reaches very high rates in Portuguese basic and secondary schools. It is a source of serious concern because of the waste it represents and, mostly, because of the negative psycho-social impact that systematic failure may have on the students, with the risk of stigmatization and social exclusion. In the light of the relational theory of human motivation and personality, academic failure must be conceived as the result of a complex network of personal, interpersonal and institutional variables and not as the predominant result of individual psychological shortcomings or handicaps. In this context, an action-research program to prevent school underachievement (or, more constructively, to promote academic success) was organized and implemented in three eighth-grade classes (in three secondary schools in Coimbra), composed by students delayed two years in school, due to school failure (Abreu, 1986, Abreu et al., 1988).

In a very brief description, we may say that the program articulated activities involving *teachers, the researcher psychologist, students and their parents,* aiming at the enhancement of a more effective and consistent network of interpersonal relations and at a convergent configuration of more positive expectations. Among the activities developed with the teachers, a special emphasis was given to the *students' linguistic competences development program,* mainly in the specific domains of language comprehension and expression, either written or verbal. Among the activities developed with the students, we should emphasize the relevance of the *cognitive development program* (focusing on attention, perceptive structuring, memory organization, reasoning, problem solving) and of the *promotion of career management skills.* Other, less intensive interventions, which involved meetings with the students' parents, also took place. The evaluation of this intervention program required a quasi-experimental design, where the outcomes of the experimental group (the underachieving students) were compared to those of an equivalent control group. These outcomes involved both the academic achievement results of the students and the evolution of their logical thinking skills, as measured by Longeot (1975). The data obtained showed that the academic results of the students who had previously experienced a high failure rate were not lower than those observed in the control group. Similarly, the data from the Longeot test showed a significant increase in the logical thinking skills from the first to the second application in the experimental group, which was not observed in the control group. Thus, we can conclude that the relational program of school success promotion showed positive effects both in the academic achievement domain and in the development of logical thinking processes.

The outcomes of the action-research study just briefly described confirmed that it is possible to warrant educational success for all students and to promote the development of individual cognitive potentialities. In order to reach this, *one important methodological condition should be accomplished*, that is planning and acting within a relational and integrative framework. In fact, this relational and integrative approach concerning psychological intervention practices is more adequate to the dynamic and holistic organization of human behavior than the "individualistic" or "solipsistic" traditional approaches.

The demonstration of this programs' efficacy encouraged the conception of an interactive and relational model of the educational system based on Nuttin's Relational Theory of Human Behavior. The *interactive and relational model of the educational system* (Abreu, 1996) allows a systemic view and a dynamic-structural analysis of the complex network of *actors, functional structures and goals* that are influential within the school system. Besides its intrinsic value at a conceptual level, the "relational and integrative model of the educational system" also bears a practical value as a useful instrument for identifying topological sources of practical problems or functional difficulties within the system.

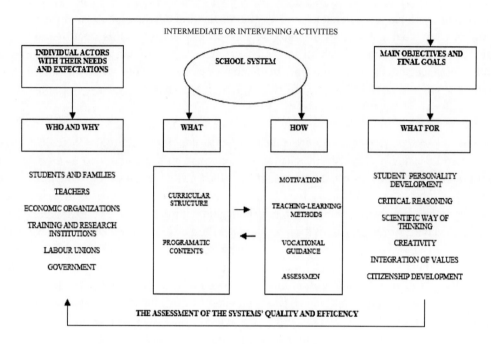

Figure 1. Relational and integrative model of the educational system.

TOWARD A GENERAL RELATIONAL MODEL OF EDUCATIONAL PRACTICE

Figure 1 presents the structure of the model, where its fundamental components, as well as the structural relations between them, are indicated. First of all, in the left column (*Who / Why*) are indicated the *actors*, with their motives, values and expectations, conceived as psychological forces supporting the organization of intermediate activities oriented towards the realization of valuable *goals*. Between the actors and their long-term objectives or end-goals, a diversity of intervening structures, instruments and activities is considered, as represented in the central columns (*What*) and (*How*). The *What* column concerns the curricular organization and the knowledge contents of the different subject matters. In the *How* column are situated the motivational strategies, the teaching and learning methods, the school guidance activities, and the main evaluation procedures. Finally, the *What For* column identifies the final goals to be reached by the school system. The formulations of the educational end-goals differ across countries, but are very similar in its contents, the main points being: the development of the students' personality, as well as the development of their logical thinking, their critical reasoning, creativity, autonomous decision making, and integration of personal values.

Two examples illustrate the instrumental value of the model in detecting important dysfunctions in the educational system functioning.

The first one regards the increasing dissatisfaction/de-motivation of teachers and students originating in the focus of school practice around performance tests and exams. This dissatisfaction is evident in the high rates of school dropouts, increasing acts of indiscipline and violence, as well as symptoms of depression and anxiety (Esteve, 1992; Jesus, 1995). The problem here seems to rely on the fact that some intermediate variables considered in the *What* column (e.g., assessment of students' achievement via written tests or exams) assumes, within the school system, a final goal statute. In fact, instead of being perceived as a means (thus bearing a regulating function within the learning process) towards a valued end— cognitive, emotional and social development of the students—they are conceived as end-tasks with no instrumental value, once the repetition and reproduction of learning materials by the students becomes the only criterion which must be taken into account to evaluate "the goodness-of-fit" of the activities to be developed or implemented by the main actors (teachers, students, managers, etc.) operating within the school system.

The second example of the utility of the relational model as a structural source that enables the identification of a practical problem in the educational system is the recognition that the failure of the main school reforms that have been implemented in Portugal in the last years relies on the fact that they strongly favor teaching/learning contents over teaching/learning processes. In fact, these reforms have been primarily centered on *contents* and have been neglecting the renewal of the learning and teaching *processes*. And this focus on program contents rather than valuing the processes of personal and cultural development makes the main reason for their failure, a fact that is highlighted both by Bruner (1996) in a psychological perspective and by Tedesco (1999) in a sociological perspective.

It is important to point out two other characteristics of the model: i) by situating school as a *mediating and instrumental structure*, the model does not view it as a closed system, with a final and unchangeable organization. On the contrary, school must be conceived as an *open system*, in which the network of relationships between its structural components is in a persistent tension towards improvement; ii) the model can be used as a conceptual map either on the level of *macroscopic analyses*, which involve the system in the totality of its internal and external relations, or on the level of *microscopic analyses*, which embrace some of its specific components, such as the network of relations established in the classroom within the teaching/learning process.

CONCLUSION

Considering the teaching and learning tasks as intentional activities, Nuttin's relational theory of human behavior is capable of facilitating a renewal of the traditional educational practice mostly based on behaviorist assumptions similar to the ones proposed by Thorndike. In the context of this traditional educational practice, examinations and final grades are conceived as the main goals to be reached via the performance of repetitive and routine tasks. The qualitative renewal of the traditional educational practice is based on a strategy that suggests setting educational goals in operational terms as the starting point of the learning process. The whole educational system can be analyzed through this relational lens that clearly defines the main actors, the complex net of mediating activities to be developed in order to reach the valued end goals (e.g., personality development) towards which the educational system is oriented.

The new organization of the learning process during basic and secondary schooling addresses the following aspects: identification of general and specific training goals in each educational step or cycle, definition of these training goals and clarification of the instrumental and regulatory function of students' evaluation procedures, acceptance of comprehensive functions associated with the teaching activity (e.g., training students in problem-resolution and decision-making skills, enhancement of curiosity and observational skills, etc.), and the conception of learning as a personal change process in the areas of knowledge, skills, competencies and attitudes. Psychological interventions in school contexts that are based on the Relational Theory of human behavior must thus extend beyond the diagnosis and treatment of underachievers to the promotion of healthy developmental trajectories, where the elaboration of life projects is articulated with the facilitation of academic achievement.

REFERENCES

Abreu, M. V. (1978; 1999). *Tarefa Fechada e Tarefa Aberta. Motivação, aprendizagem e acção*. Coimbra, Imprensa da Universidade.

Abreu, M.V. (1986). Para uma nova teoria dos interesses. *Biblos, vol. LXVII*, 217-229.

Abreu, M.V., Leitão, L.M., Santos, E.R. & Paixão, M.P. (1988). Mobilização de potencialidades de desenvolvimento cognitivo e promoção do sucesso escolar. *Psychologica 1,* 1-26.

Abreu, M. V. (1996). *Pais, professores e psicólogos. Contributos para o desenvolvimento de uma prática relacional*. Coimbra, Coimbra Editora.

Abreu, M. V. (2001). Desenvolvimento vocacional e estratégia de motivação para aprendizagens persistentes, *Psychologica, 26,* 9-26.

Abreu, M. V. (2005). Para além dos exames: Contributos para recolocar os exames na sua função de meio instrumental e não de fim primordial do ensino e da aprendizagem. *Revista Portuguesa de Pedagogia, 39*(2), 51-78.

Baars, B. J. (1986). *The cognitive revolution in Psychology*. New York, The Guildford Press.

Bruner, J. (1996). *The culture of education*. Cambridge, Harvard University Press.

Buchwald, A. M. (1969). Effects of "right" and "wrong" on subsequent behavior: a new interpretation. *Psychological Review, 76,* 132-143.

Duarte, M.E., Paixão, M.P. & Lima, M.R. (2007). Perspectives on counseling psychology: Portugal at a glance. *Applied Psychology: An International Review, 56*(1), 119-130.

d'Ydewalle, G. (1973). Time perspective and learning in open and closed tasks, *Psychologica Belgica, 13,* 139-147.

d'Ydewalle, G. (1976). Recall of "right" and "wrong" responses as a function of instructions for intentional learning and task familiarization, *Psychological Report, 38,* 619-624.

d'Ydewalle, G. & Buchwald, A. M. (1976). Effects of "right" and "wrong" as a function of recalling either the response or the outcome, *Journal of Experimental Psychology: Human Learning and Memory, 2,* 728-738.

d'Ydewalle, G. & Eelen (1975). Repetition and recall of "right" and "wrong" responses in incidental and intentional learning, *Journal Experimental Psychology: Human Learning and Memory, 104,* 429-441.

Esteve, J. (1992). *O mal-estar docente.* Lisboa, Escher.

Greenwald, A. (1966). Nuttin's neglected critique of the law of effect, *Psychological Bulletin, 65,* 199-205.

Hull, C. L. (1943). *Principles of behavior. An introduction of behavior theory.* New York, Appleton-Century-Crofts.

Jesus, S. (1995). *A motivação para a função docente.* Aveiro, Estante Editora. (2ª ed., 2000. *Motivação e formação de professores.* Coimbra, Quarteto).

Longeot, F. (1975). *L'échelle de développement de la pensée logique.* Issy-les –Molineaux, EAP.

Longstreth, L. E. (1970). Test of the law of effect using open and closed tasks, *Journal of Experimental Psychology, 84,* 53-57.

Marx, M.H. (1967).Analysis of spread of effect: A comparison of Thorndike and Nuttin. *Psychological Bulletin,* 67, 413-415.

Nuttin, J. (1942). De finaliteit in het menselijk handelen en het connectionisme. Een studie nopens de wet van het effect. *Tijdschrift voor Philosophie, 4.* 235-268.

Nuttin, J. (1947a). La loi de l'effet et la finalité du comportement, in *Miscellanea Psychologica A. Michotte.* Louvain, Publications Universitaires, 611-633.

Nuttin, J.(1947b). Respective effectiveness of success and task-tension in learning. *British Journal of Psychology,* 38, 49-55.

Nuttin, J. (1949). "Spread" in recalling failure and success. *Journal Experimental Psychology, 39,* 690-699

Nuttin, J. (1953). *Tâche, réussite et échec: Théorie de la conduite humaine.* Louvain, Publications Universitaires.

Nuttin, J. (1955). Consciousness, Behavior and Personality, *Psychological Review, 62,*349-355.

Nuttin, J. & Greenwald, A. (1968).*Reward and punishment in human learning.* New York, Academic Press.

Paixão, M.P. (2004). Insucesso escolar e perda: Transformar os riscos em oportunidades para a mudança contextual e o crescimento pessoal . *Psychologica, 35,* 147-165.

Popper, K. (1974). *The logic of scientific discovery.* London: Hutchinson.

Postman, L. (1966). Reply to Greenwald. *Psychological Bulletin, 65,* 383-388.

Ryan, R. M. & Deci, E.L. (2000). Intrinsic and extrinsic motivations: Classic definitions and new directions. *Contemporary Educational Psychology, 25,* 54-67.

Skinner, B.F. (1950). Are theories of learning necessary? *Psychological Review,*57,193-216.

Tedesco, J.C. (1999). *O novo pacto educativo.* Vila N. de Gaia, Fundação M. Leão.

Thorndike, E.L. (1911). *Animal Intelligence.* New York, Macmillan.

Thorndike, E.L. (1932). *The Fundamentals of Learning.* New York, Teachers College.

Thorndike, E.L. (1949). *Selected writings from a connectionist's psychology.* New York, Appleton-Century-Crofts.

Tolman, E.C. (1932). *Purposive behavior in animals and men.* New York, Appleton-Century-Crofts.

Tolman, E.C. (1966). *Behavior and psychological man.* Berkeley, Univ. of California Press.

Zeigarnik, B.(1927). Ueber das behalten von erledigten und unerledigten Handlungen. *Psychologischen Forschungen, 9,* 1-85 (On finished and unfinished tasks, *in* W.D. Ellis, *A source book of gestalt psychology*. London, Routledge & Kegan Paul, 1959).

PART 4. CULTURAL MEDIATION OF MOTIVATIONAL PROCESS

In: Motivation, Consciousness and Self-Regulation
Editor: D. A. Leontiev, pp. 189-207

ISBN: 978-1-61324-795-2
© 2012 Nova Science Publishers, Inc.

Chapter 12

MOTIVATIONAL DIALOGUE AS THE CORE OF THE SELF-DETERMINATION PROCESS

Catherine Patyayeva
Moscow State University

ABSTRACT

The aim of this chapter is to propose a model of the self-determination process, based on the cultural-historical view on human motivation. Before describing the model itself, the author elaborates the main ideas about human motivation, originated in the framework of cultural-historic approach in the broad sense of the term. Higher forms of motivation (such as self-determination and will) are understood as specific 'motivational abilities' which can be acquired in some social and educational environments but not in others. Relying on the concepts of P. Janet, L.S. Vygotsky, M. M. Bakhtin and B. F. Porshnev, the author considers the motivating speech influence to be the universal 'building block' of the complex social motivating systems, shaping our motivations in a very high degree. An act of speech influence can lead either to simple obedience/disobedience or it can start a real motivational dialogue. The latter is seen as a process in which new motives, desires and decisions emerge. Motivational dialogue can be internalized; in such a case, it is considered to be the real core of the self-determination process. So, creating a 'dialogical environment' is regarded as the main path for developing the self-determination ability in children.

Keywords: Cultural-historical approach, human motivation, speech, dialogue, self-determination

INTRODUCTION

The idea of self-determination conceals a hidden paradox. On one hand, the self-determined action is a *determined* one, i.e. it has some 'proper' driving forces. On the other hand, these driving forces are somewhat mysterious: they are neither external stimuli nor internal (bodily) states and needs, the origin of determination being that obscure *self*, the very existence of which is so often questioned. What is this enigmatic 'self'? Is it 'something', or 'somebody', or just some 'language game' in the vein of the later Ludwig Wittgenstein? There are many possible ways to answer these questions, and every answer will entail different approaches to a tremendous practical problem closely related with the idea of self-determination: the problem of developing the ability for self-determination in young people (and here, one more question arises: is such a development at all possible?). The aim of this chapter is to propose a model of the self-determination process, based on the cultural-historical view on human motivation, which can be used as the foundation for developing practical training programs, fostering the ability for self-determination. Before describing the model itself, we shall elaborate the main ideas about human motivation, originated in the framework of cultural-historic approach in the broad sense of the term.

So, first of all, the three main paradigms of understanding human motivation will be discussed: the dualistic, the naturalistic and the cultural-historical ones. Then we shall analyze the socio-cultural motivating systems and the intra-personal motivations brought about by them. After that, we shall turn our attention to the motivational function of speech and to the motivational dialogue, which, from the author's point of view, is the real core of the self-determination process. And finally, we shall discuss how to develop the ability for self-determination in young people and how the modern school system hinders such a development.

THREE PARADIGMS OF UNDERSTANDING HUMAN MOTIVATION

From the epoch of Socrates and Plato and till the end of the 18th century, the main concept of human behavior was *dualistic*. On one hand, human beings were seen to be driven by natural impulses such as hunger or sexual attraction, on the other hand, they were considered to possess free will and to be capable to act freely, reasonably and with full responsibility. So, it was decided that the human being is 'composed of' body and soul (and/or spirit). The soul was deemed to possess free will from the very beginning and was considered to be the source of all 'higher" human motives (also called spiritual ones), such as the aspirations for good, for justice, for freedom and many others. And the body was seen as the source of all 'inferior' motivations, including hunger, thirst and sexual desire, but also greed, atrocity, envy and other 'mortal sins'. So, according to the dualistic view, humans have two types of motives – physical and spiritual – and two types of motivating processes: on one hand, the pressure of bodily needs and other 'inferior' impulses, and on the other hand, free will, self-determination and rational decision.

Throughout history a lot of thinkers have been disputing the dualistic position, and from the middle of the 18th century, when the famous „*L'homme machine*" by J. O. Lamettrie was published, the idea of strict determinism has been gaining more and more popularity. According to this idea, human behavior is motivated only by 'natural forces' like any mechanic device, the only difference being our lack of knowledge of the relevant forces. So, the second approach to human motivation was born – the *naturalistic* one. In the 19th century, this view flourished under the influence of the huge development of natural sciences, and the concept of human behavior being motivated only by different instincts, needs and drives has become prominent. Later, in the first half of the 20th century, the partisans of this deterministic approach have succeeded in the full expulsion of will, reason and 'higher motivations' as such from the mainstream psychology, so that all human actions were considered to be simple or complex reactions to different inner needs and external stimuli. This situation did not last long. In the second half of that century, 'higher motivations' began coming back into psychology – but now under the guise of specific 'basic needs', which are innate, obligatory and universal. The most well-known examples of such 'higher' basic human needs deemed to be innate and universal, are the need for self-actualisation (A. Maslow) and the need for self-determination (E. Deci and R. Ryan). So, the *need paradigm* has been shaped as the modern form of the naturalistic view on human motivation, and the capacity for self-determination has been understood as the highly developed form of the respective need.

But the concept of needs is not the only possible alternative to the dualistic view on human motivation. In the same 18th century, another concept of human motives has emerged – the cultural-historical one. In 1795, the illustrious *"Sketch for a Historical Picture of the Progress of the Human Mind"* by French philosopher and political scientist J.-A. Condorcet was published posthumously. Its author argued that the past revealed an order that could be understood in terms of the progressive development of human capabilities, including the capacity for moral action and self-determination. Condorcet introduced the idea of cultural tools that accumulate our mental achievements and help to pass them on from one generation to another. About the same time, his German colleague W. von Humboldt began to elaborate his views on the influence of culture (and language in particular) on the spiritual development of individuals. Both thinkers, alike their 'naturally oriented' contemporaries, have exceeded the bounds of the dualistic concept of human behavior, but in contrast to the latter, they took their cues not in the natural sciences but in history and other humanities. The cultural-historical approach has been actively developing throughout the 19th century, for example, by early K. Marx, W. Wundt and W. Dilthey. In the first decades of the 20th century, it yielded such seminal works as *"The Protestant Ethic and the Spirit of Capitalism"* by M. Weber (1905), *"What Social Objects Must Psychology Presuppose?"* (1910) and other papers by G. H. Mead, *"The Elementary Forms of Religious Life"* by E. Durkheim (1912), *"The Psychological Evolution of Personality"* by P. Janet (1929), *"Tool and Symbol in Child Development"* (1930) and other works by L.S. Vygotsky. But later, the cultural-historical approach was 'ousted' from the mainstream psychology by the proponents of the more naturalistic views and throughout the rest of the 20th century, the cultural-historical tradition of understanding the dynamics of human behavior was carried on mainly in the sociology, the cultural anthropology, the political science and in the study of culture, but hardly in the psychology of motivation.

Of course, the influence of culture and social situation on human motives is highly recognized in psychology. But it is usually conceptualized only as 'shaping' or even 'flavoring' of 'human natural needs' – while the cultural-historical tradition assumes that culture not only *shapes* some human motivations, but also *creates* a lot of new motives and motivational processes. It is very important that these motives and motivational processes – in contrast to 'universal needs' – are acquired by a person only in specific social, cultural and historical conditions and they cannot be acquired in a different social environment. Let us illustrate this difference by an example of a patient, described by Rollo May (1972) under the name of Mercedes. This lady was extremely submissive and resigned to her fate and had not shown even the slightest signs of any desire or capacity to make her own choices and decisions (she came for therapy in spite of herself, being sent by her husband's therapist). In other words, her behavior demonstrated the complete absence of any 'need for self-determination' – so, two or three therapists, working with Mercedes before R. May, decided she was 'incurable'. But if we see the desire for self-determination not as a manifestation of some universal and innate need, inherent in every person, if we see such a desire as a result of a more or less safe 'middle class' childhood, we would not be surprised if a person, who had grown up in much more severe conditions, shows no signs of the desire to make his or her own decisions. And working with such a person we would see such a desire not as a universal prerequisite of any therapeutic work, but rather as one of the possible goals of this work. This was the case with R. May, who undertook with Mercedes a series of literally *joint* acts of experiencing and decision-making – compensating lacunae of her childhood and helping her to become an autonomous person, capable to make her own decisions.

Thus, we have three main approaches to understanding and conceptualizing human motivation in contemporary psychology: the need paradigm, the dualistic one, and the cultural-historical one. (It should be mentioned, that the dualistic approach was re-introduced into modern psychology by many authors; for example it is realized in the concept of fundamental existential motivations by A. Längle (1999; 2011) or in the concept of spiritual aspirations by R. Emmons (1999)). There are at least two crucial questions, separating these three approaches – the problem of 'higher' motivations and the problem of 'free will' or 'self-determined' actions. According to the dualistic view, each person is free from the beginning and each has universal spiritual aspirations in addition to bodily needs. In other words, the capacity for self-determination is inherent to every person (or to every soul). As for the need paradigm, it gives two possible answers: either freedom is an illusion and human behavior is fully determined by organic needs and external stimuli, or humans are supposed to have some special innate 'quasibiological' needs for self-actualization, self-determination and the like. In the second case it is usually supposed that this specific need, being innate, can 'blossom out' only in some favorable conditions. And from the cultural-historical point of view, the ability for self-determination is an acquired one: any person can *become* free, but only if she or he gains some important psychological skills during her or his own life. Also, the cultural-historical position assumes that any person growing up in a certain society, becomes integrated in the social motivating systems of this society and acquires a lot of culturally determined motives and motivational processes. Let us consider this in detail.

SOCIAL MOTIVATING SYSTEMS: TOWARDS A CULTURAL-HISTORICAL THEORY OF HUMAN MOTIVATION

From the cultural-historical point of view, all of "the higher human capacities" are neither innate nor predetermined by human nature. They are seen as a result of cultural development of a person which includes not only regular education of any kind but also all sorts of spontaneous acquisition of human forms of behavior in the course of growing up in human environments (which includes family, peer groups, school friends, playing with toys, watching television, reading books, and so on). One more factor of the cultural development of a person is his or her own activities seeking to master different skills and abilities. Higher forms of human motivation – such as free will, making choices and decisions, self-motivation and self-determination – are not an exception. They are also seen as a result of cultural development of a person in the course of spontaneous socialization, regular education and autonomous activity. So, according to this view, in different societies and different social and cultural strata, we can find not only different forms of universal motivations, but also really different needs, motives, motivational processes and 'motivational abilities'. And while a lot of people acquire such 'higher motivational abilities' spontaneously and without efforts (this is the case with the most children from prosperous and educated families), others (for example, a lot of children from the under-privileged sections of the population and from the under-privileged nations) should be taught these abilities purposefully – or otherwise they would be submitted to the influences of other people and social institutions and would not be able to stand on their own feet and to make their own choices and decisions.

It is very important to note that acquiring higher motivational processes and abilities is a much more complex process than being taught arithmetic or even mastering logical thinking. The cultural development of a person is taking place in the course of his or her everyday life in specific social and cultural environments. And each such environment can be seen as Lewin's psychological "field" with lots of positive and negative valences. Or, in other words, as specific motivating systems, urging us to some course of behavior. Let us take a look at these systems in detail.

Social and Cultural Motivating Systems

Within the cultural-historical paradigm, the profound dependence of human motivation on culture and society was conceptualized in two different ways. First of all, there are different cultural "means" and "tools" that can be used by individuals to motivate themselves (as well as other persons) to do something – such as a prayer urging a person to start an unpleasant or dangerous work or a dice helping to make a decision (Vygotsky, 1931). Such means and tools mediate the motivational process, and human will may be seen as a motivational process mediated by various cultural means and acts, such as dice, vows, rites, self-orders and lots of others (for example, see Vygotsky, 1931; Ivannikov, 1990).

Next, there is a real socio-cultural 'universe', that envelops and surrounds a person, that nurtures and molds him or her. Such a 'universe' is composed of different social institutions, collective representations, social regulations, various narratives, ideals, symbols, layouts, etc. The 'social facts' of that sort can be seen not only as mediators of human motivations, but also as the ultimate sources of some of our actions. For example, things, places and persons we consider to be 'sacred' often urge us to accomplish certain acts, and our behavior in such cases may have no other motivational sources except the 'sacredness' of the thing or person in question. The phenomenon of sacredness was thoroughly investigated in the classical work by E. Durkheim (1912), who has shown how different societies – from the native Australian tribes to the European states of his time – produced various 'sacred' things, persons and ideas. One of the most striking examples is the sacredness of state as such: Durkheim (1912, 1915) has analyzed the processes of worshipping the state during the French revolution of 1789-1793 and also during World War I in Germany. As he died in 1917, he could not have seen the most notorious state cults of the 20th century – the sacralization of state neither in the Soviet Union, nor in the Nazi Germany nor in the Maoist China. Some decades later, the investigation of state cults as well as of various sectarian cults has gained greater popularity and it was shown, for example, by R.J. Lifton's works (1961), that the motivational power of cult ideas may well exceed the power of 'ordinary' human needs and motivations.

The main difficulty in understanding the influence of different socio-cultural "universes' on human motivation is their utmost complexity: they include such heterogeneous 'elements' as social institutions, types of discourse, special buildings, codes of laws and regulations and so on. To refer to such a socio-cultural 'universe', disposing us to certain actions and demanding from us certain behaviors, I will use M. Foucault's term 'dispositif' below (see Foucault, 1994).

Socio-cultural dispositifs differ from cultural means (such as dice or a prayer) in three ways. First of all, means, being 'the things of culture', are some*thing* we use, whereas dispositifs are rather some*where*, they are specific socio-cultural 'spaces' or systems, inside which we find ourselves. In the second place, we use different cultural means voluntarily (so we are the '*origins*' using different means), but we may be '*pawns*' inside various dispositifs. And thirdly, using means is a form of *mediating* our motivation, while dispositifs are not only mediating, but also *motivating* systems.

The Structure of a Dispositif

The idea of social creation of many human motives is much older than the term 'dispositif', or device, coined by M. Foucault. We can trace it in the analysis of bureaucracy in K. Marx's early works, in M. Weber's "etoses" or "spirits" of traditionalism, Protestantism and capitalism, in "collective representations" of the French sociological school or K. Lewin's "social field". As far as I can judge, the most all-embracing account of the structure of some prominent dispositifs of Western civilization – from the *traditional spirit* closely associated with Catholicism through various *protestant systems of practical ethics* to the *spirit of capitalism* – was given by Max Weber (1905).

Describing these "cultural spirits" or dispositifs, Weber reveals at least five groups of elements for each of them. The first element is belongingness of an individual to a certain group of people: to a community, a Church, a circle of *electi* and so on. In other words, every dispositif presupposes differentiation of people into those who are "friends", "members of our society" or "the faithful" and those who are "enemies", "strangers" or "infidels". This belongingness is felt as the supreme value, so that the threat of expulsion from the community is a very strong motivating factor. In the second place, there is the collection of social roles in a given society, and the hierarchy of these roles: for example, there are bishops, priests and laymen, proprietors, managers and hired workers, and so on. And each role position is associated with certain prescriptions, determining what a person should do and what he or she should not do. Thirdly, there are collective representations about Good and Evil and about the highest purposes that every member of a given society should strive for. For all Christian dispositifs, the highest aim is the salvation of the soul, for the classical capitalist dispositif – making money and increasing the profits, for the socialist dispositif – constructing of a just and fair society and so on. In his work, M. Weber has most convincingly shown that such lofty purposes for the members of respective societies were being the most real and extremely emotionally charged everyday motives. The fourth group of a dispositif's elements is compiled from different daily practices, rites and procedures, in whole constituting the common way of life in a given society. Such daily practices are built traditionally or rationally, and they are supposed to be in accordance with the highest goals of a given society and its images of Good and Evil. Each dispositif works out its own system of prescriptions and principles of behavior, leading to the respective highest goal. Such are, for example, the church discipline or the rules of compliance with one's professional vocation. Daily practices of this sort always have their own sets of inner psychological rewards and punishments (the feeling of satisfaction, pangs of conscience and so on). And, lastly, the fifth part of each *system of practical ethics* (M. Weber) or *dispositif* (M. Foucault) is the system of external and internal social control with specific sanctions (rewards and punishments) for the 'proper' and 'improper' behavior. In religious dispositifs, external sanctions may be ranging from simple reproach to being not allowed the Holy Communion or even expulsion from the community; in the ripe capitalist dispositif, the most natural sanctions are monetary fines and bonuses.

Cultural Development of a Child as His or Her Getting Implanted into Culture and Society

Living in a given society, each child literally "grows into" its dispositifs and internalizes a great deal of social motivating influences. Some of them can become "his own" needs and motives, as for example, the well-studied achievement motivation – we have to recall in this connection, the classical work of D. McClelland, showing the visible development of the rate of achievement motivation in different societies in the course of history.

"Growing into" some dispositif, the child joins in with all its "elements". First of all, he or she becomes a member of different groups – family, gender, ethnic, religious ones and so on. And s/he gets accustomed to identify himself or herself with the group and to feel his or her belonging to it as a value. At the same time, s/he acquires different social roles and interiorizes all corresponding prescriptions and social norms, determining what s/he should and should not do. Also, s/he adopts all of the collective representations of his or her group and society, including the set of supreme goals and values. So, his or her behavior is becoming to be determined by various ideas of *The sacred*, *Justice*, *Freedom*, *Greatness* and the like. Of course, s/he assimilates as well all of the daily practices and routines of his or her culture and society with their own sets of psychological rewards and punishments. And s/he, certainly, becomes subjected to different forms of external and internal social control, getting appropriate rewards and punishments for his or her "good" and "bad" behavior.

But, taking all of this into account, how is the *self*-determination at all possible? In order to answer this question, we should now turn to the function of speech in the process of social motivation.

SPEECH INFLUENCE AS A SEPARATE MOTIVATIONAL FORCE

A lot of psychologists, including P. Janet, L.S. Vygotsky, J. Lacan and B.F. Skinner, have insisted on the idea that the basis of the social motivating influences is constituted by human speech. For example, P. Janet considered speech to be the foundation of all the "higher psychological functions" and believed verbal commands to be the first form both of speech and of specifically human motivation. His ideas were carried on by L.S. Vygotsky, who has shown the genesis of human will as a result of interiorizing of two various types of speech: on one hand, words of adults addressed to the child and on the other hand, the child's own words addressed to adults. When these two types of speech are united inside one person, they give birth to the will as such (Vygotsky, 1930, 1931).

Some decades later, Russian historian and psychologist B.F. Porshnev has continued the work of Janet and Vygotsky. He has collected a lot of data, showing that motivating other people to do something was the very first historical function of emerging speech, and that the first historical form of human speech had been a simple suggestion (Porshnev, 1969, 1974). It means that the first words were orders and commands, loaded with huge suggesting power – the residues of this epoch being the inflammatory speeches of charismatic orators, as well as military commands, hypnotic suggestion, and the very first words of babies, which are not so much designating something but urging an adult to come to the baby and to help him.

According to B.F. Porshnev, the first forms of suggestion were not quite articulate, being weakly differentiated complexes of gestures and specific sounds (we can get the rough idea of them, looking at gestures of little babies and enthusiastic orators as well as at stimulating gestures of apes). Later on, the "proper" words appeared, and commands took the familiar form of verbal orders. So the immediate speech motivating influence was born, constituting the first form of social motivation.

The evolution of this speech motivation went in two directions: first of all, speech inducement was becoming more and more *complicated* and along with simple commands and orders a lot of new forms of speech motivating have appeared: impersonal prescriptions, parables, stories of heroes (becoming the examples for everyday imitating), general principles and ethical ideas and so on. The second line of development was constituted by the process of *internalization* of speech inducements: commands, persuasions and ideas of other persons as well as impersonal prescriptions, myths and ideologies were becoming the subject's own inner commands, arguments and convictions.

Taking as the point of departure Janet's conception of historical evolution of personality (1926, 1929) and Porshnev's ideas of speech genesis (1966, 1974), we can understand the main stages of speech motivating as follows. First comes the hypothetical prehistoric stage of not quite articulate suggestion. It should be noted here, that from the very beginning, people differed according to the degree of suggestiveness of their speech – some were more energetic and assertive and easily induced their fellows to fulfill their will, others were more timid and uncertain, so that hardly anybody obeyed them. The remnants of this stage in modern man are assertiveness, charm and 'natural charisma' – as well as other 'paraverbal' components of speech.

Then, the phase of articulated verbal commands and first symbols comes. These first symbols can be divided into two types: one being the symbols of a group and of belonging to the group (such as totems, flags, tattooing, Christian cross, special clothes and so on) and the other – the symbols of status and power within the group (staff of a tribal leader, scepter, military shoulder straps and the like). Symbols of belonging indicate the circle of "we" in opposition to "others". People get used to trusting those belonging to "us", listening to them, to fulfill their requests, to accept their offers and proposals, and not to trust "them", strangers. So, at this stage, the group as such – as a socio-cultural entity – emerges, as well as the identification of an individual with the group. The symbols of status and of power serve to differentiate people within the group, to distinguish between authorities and regular members of the group. And a person gets accustomed to obey just to authorities marked by specific symbols, from a tribal chief to modern policeman or the head of state, and to command those having lower status in the group hierarchy than himself. In such a way, over the net of immediate interpersonal influences and pressures "superimposes" the system of social roles, each role having the corresponding "symbol of duties". At this level of behavior (*pre-intermediate* according to P. Janet's concept), the motivating power of human words is quite explicit ("do this!").

Orders of chiefs and other authorities can be memorized and reproduced by ordinary people themselves, so gradually they can become *internalized self-orders*, representing, using Durkheim's words, "the voice of society within the individual". And children, while growing-up, pick up commands and instructions of adults and get used to saying these same commands and other words to themselves and to others. So, the system of internalized impersonal prescriptions and bans arises, including rules of behavior ranging from "sacred" tribal taboos to modern trends and principles of "good tone". The motivating power of such internalized speech of others (orders, commands, taboos, etc.) is also explicit.

At the next stage of cultural-historical development, *collective representations* (E. Durkheim, L. Levy-Brule) or *beliefs* (P. Janet) appear, i.e. simple or complex *statements about something supposed to be true*. For example: "We are the blessed people", "Boys never cry", "Noblemen have different blood than ordinary people", and so on. According to Janet, beliefs constitute the so called *intermediate* level of human behavior. The motivating influence of a belief can be conceived as follows: "boys never cry", so, if you want to be a "proper" boy, you should not cry. Prescription is related here to some desired identification: "if you want to be a ..., do this!" (in contrast to the bare prescription of the previous stage: "do this!"). Nowadays, such "motivating formulas" are widely used not only in the upbringing of young generations, but also in advertising, political propaganda and everyday life. Words and phrases are loaded in this case with *hidden* motivating power: they look like a simple description ("boys never cry"), while at the same time harboring a hidden prescription ("you should not cry, because you are a boy"). The process of motivating becomes "twofold": first comes identification ("you are a boy"), than the corresponding prescription ("you should not cry"). And identification usually is not limited with a given situation, but envelops a wide range of possible situations. So, *persuasion,* relying on beliefs, appears as a new form of social motivating (it may be called *duplex* motivating). Beliefs, as well as explicit commands, can be intermalized, becoming "one's own" self-descriptions, convictions, superstitions, ethnical prejudices, principles of behavior, representations of reality, slogans and so on. The system of social authorities becomes much more complex: along with people invested with power, there appear now various impersonal 'authoritative beliefs' such as sayings, proverbs, citations, and so on.

The next step in the erecting of socio-cultural motivating systems is marked by a transition from simple beliefs to *collective myths and stories* (mythology, epos, tales and other narratives, including preaching, admonition and propaganda). Stories marvelously broaden the scope of one's life and experience, creating virtual reality, common to all members of a group or a society as a whole (i.e. *collective con-science* in the verbatim sense of the term). In the center of each story there is a hero, whose deeds and adventures fascinate listeners and inspire them to imitate his behavior. And identification with heroes becomes a literally inexhaustible reservoir of social motivating: children are being taught to behave like their fathers, ancestors, epical and historical heroes, adults can often be persuaded to do something by a parable or some example. Each culture, each society creates its own collections of classical stories and heroes, which every person learns during the process of socialization.

Social motivating at this stage of cultural-historical development becomes still more complicated, it includes now at least three stages: telling the story (in other cases: recalling the story, reminding the story, inventing the story) – identification with the hero ('be like him') – corresponding prescription ("do this"). Classical example of this *triplex* motivating are the young *pioneer-heroes* of the Soviet epoch: first, the stories of "the feats" of 10-12-year-old pioneers[9] were made up, the most famous being that of Pavlik Morosov, than these stories were spread around through "Pyonerskaya Pravda" (a special pioneer newspaper) and the children were made enthusiastic about these "young heroes" and were taught to follow their example, and in the end such "feats" became widespread (Leontyeva, 2005). Within persuasion, relying on myths and other stories prescription becomes one step more hidden: the story invites us to enjoy the deeds and adventures of a hero, at the same time it is prompting us to admire the hero, to be like him and to imitate his behavior. Acknowledged heroes become one more kind of authority (as well as authors of popular stories), it is often enough now just to remind a person of some well-known hero (including various pop-stars and other public images) in order to make him behave in a desirable way. Stories we believe in, be it mythical, historical, religious or everyday ones, are also serving as a source of various upper goals and life scenarios of a given culture and society.

And finally, the most recent layer of socio-cultural motivating comes into being – that is the world of ideas, ideal goals and values, rationalized convictions and volitional actions (constituting the superior level of behavior according to P. Janet). The beginning of this rationalized motivating has been thoroughly reconstructed in the classical work of Max Weber (1905). At this level, the process of motivating acquires important new links, such as setting objectives, rational planning and volitional keeping up the performing of action in spite of fatigue, lassitude or reluctance. Here, the system of motivating becomes *fourfold*. It's first "story" usually avoids our attention: it consists in creating a system of ideas, goals, role positions, rewards and punishments, among the most common examples of such social systems being schools, factories, army and various organizations and corporations. From the perspective of a separate individual, this first stage of motivating is incorporating the individual into such a system, i.e. making him a member of the given social body – a pupil, an employee, a serviceman, and so on. The second phase, or "story", of the motivational process is putting tasks to persons turned into pupils, workers, officers, clerks and performers of all the other social roles. A teacher giving homework to her students, a head of the department setting his employees the task, a general defining the goal to his staff – all of them are exercising the second stage of rational social motivating. Then comes the third phase which consists of accepting the task and transforming it into a person's purpose (if necessary, this stage includes also planning and setting oneself intermediate aims). And the last, the fourth, story of rational motivating is made up of (self)-commands and volitional efforts to perform the task, resembling the simple orders of the early era of emerging speech ("do it!").

Thus, all of the components of social dispositifs – orders, role prescriptions, impersonal social norms, various collective representations, elevated ideas, lofty aims, ideal values, cultural scenarios of behavior, induced desires and so on – appear to be derivatives from

---

[9] i.e. members of mass children's organization in the Soviet Union which brought up children (from 9 to 14 years old) to be 'the true followers of V. I. Lenin'.

speech or from speech-dependant[10] images and symbols. Of course, there is a big problem of alloying and combining such socio-cultural motivation with different forms of need motivation. We may suppose that such alloying yields a great variety of social and cultural needs which are fundamentally different from basic 'instinctoid' needs in the sense of A. Maslow (1976) or E. Deci and R. Ryan (Ryan & Deci, 2000; Deci & Ryan, 2008)[11]. But, for the sake of simplicity, I will concentrate upon the speech motivating influence as such.

And now, having established this connection between socio-cultural motivating and speech, we can return to the question of the possibility of self-determination.

MOTIVATIONAL DIALOGUE AS THE PROCESS OF DETERMINING THE COURSE OF ACTION

Speaking and Being Spoken To

The act of speech influence has two different poles: the speaker and the listener, or, in other words, the person who speaks and the person who is spoken to, the person, who commands, and the person who obeys (or disobeys). The first tells what to do (be it a command, a request, a proposition, a hint or anything else), the second listens, understands and carries out the needed action. And while mastering speech habits, the child from the very beginning practices *both* operations: not only listening and obeying (or reacting in general), but also influencing the others: asking, begging, inviting, persuading, commanding and so on.

Both of these operations can be internalized: while growing up, a child takes in not only commands and other influences coming from adults, but also *his own acts of urging* other people to do something. According to Vygotsky, only a combination of both of these operations within one and the same person gives birth to the human will as such – when the child applies to himself the motivating influence, which *he has addressed earlier to adult,* for example, while asking him for something (Vygotsky, 1931). Thus, not social influences alone, but also a person's own acts of influence upon other persons become internalized. In other words, our "inner voice" is not only "the voice of society within an individual" (E. Durkheim), but also our own "social voice" telling other people to do something.

Emerging of a Dialogue

It is quite evident, that the person who is being spoken to does not always obey. She or he can react to a speech impact in a great number of different ways: in particular, s/he can not only obey or disobey, but also s/he can answer verbally: for example, s/he can put a question or explain the reasons why the fulfillment of a required action is impossible. And her/his answer can start the more or less extensive *dialogue,* i.e. to a sequence of speech replicas by two (or more) persons, where both partners in turn change role positions of the speaker and

---

[10] For example, most of human visual images are speech-dependant, implying some name or even some implicit story (be it a specific story of a given hero or some abstract "story of success (of love, of victory, etc.)".

[11] See, for example, the thorough examination of these 'basic social needs' in the classical work of M. Halbwachs (1913).

the listener and are supposed to understand each other, at least to some degree. From ancient times, dialogue has been regarded as the source of new understanding and new ideas. In more recent times, M. Bakhtin (1963) has shown that the very nature of human "self" is dialogic, that "self" can exist only in relation with others (Bakhtin, 1963; Holquist, 2002, p. 19).

There are many types of dialogue, differing in content and in the intentions of its participants. If both of them are trying to understand some difficult question, we will get a *truth-oriented* dialogue (or a scientific dialogue if they are also observing the rules of scientific discourse). If the interlocutors are trying to "resolve the idea", as, for example, Dostoevsky's heroes did, and the contents of the dialogue is the clash of ideas, the result will be an *ideological* dialogue. When one participant of a dialogue explains something to the other, the dialogue may be called *explanatory* or *pedagogical*, and if one of the partners unbosoms himself to the other, the dialogue would be called a *confessional* one, and so on. And when the intention of at least one of the speakers is to induce his partner to do something, we can speak about *motivational* dialogue. The latter would be discussed below in more detail, but first we should say a few words about Bakhtin's ideas of dialogue as the resource of human '*unfinalizability*', based on the analysis of Dostoevsky's works.

The Dostoevsky-Bakhtin's Conception of Dialogue and of Human 'Unfinalizability'

In his famous book "Problems of Dostoyevsky's Poetics", M. Bakhtin introduces three very important concepts, closely related to the problem of self-determination. First is the concept of the *unfinalizable* self: individual people cannot be finalized, completely understood, known, or fully characterized by any labels, including psychological ones (such as traits, types, complexes and so on). In all of his big novels, Dostoevsky had most energetically argued with the widespread[12] naturalistic view of human behavior as being strictly determined by physiological needs, social situations and psychological predispositions, so that it was considered to be possible to predict human actions and to manipulate a person, pulling the right strings. Based on Dostoevsky's works, Bakhtin develops the concept of an unfinalizability and principal unpredictability of the human being, possessing the ability to change most radically and contrary to any forecasts. In other words, every person is always "unfinished" and capable for essential changes and transformations.

The second idea is that of dialogue being "the mode of life" of human self – meaning both dialogue with other people and with one's own self. According to Bakhtin, no person can be regarded as isolated, everyone exists within the net of relationships between the self and others, everyone is influenced by others in an inescapably intertwined way, not merely in terms of how a person comes to be, but also in how a person thinks, acts and how a person sees him- or herself truthfully. And this incessant social intercourse, this continuous dialogue, appears to be the inexhaustible source of human freedom and unpredictable renewal: dialogue constitutes the special breeding-ground, giving birth not only to new understandings and ideas, but also to new decisions, motives and deeds. Dialogues of different types can yield new, diverse formations: ideological dialogue bears new truths and new understandings,

---

[12] In his time as well as in ours.

whereas motivational dialogue leads to the springing up of new intentions, new decisions and new deeds.

And the third very important concept is that of the *polyphonic* dialogue and *polyphonic* understanding of truth. Each character in Dostoevsky's work has his own truth and represents a voice that speaks for an individual self, distinct from others. And no one – including the author – possesses the *whole* truth or the *absolute* truth. The idea of polyphony implies that there are many voices, representing different points of view, different truths, all of them being necessary, mutually addressed and engaged to the context of a real-life event.

Taking all of this into consideration, dialogue appears to be some special *joint work* of unfinalizable individuals, yielding new understandings and new intentions, which would determine the future behavior of these individuals. Speaking only of motivational dialogue, we have to discuss two varieties of such: motivational dialogue with other people and inner motivational dialogue, the latter being dialogue with one's own self, where other people are often represented as ideal interlocutors.

Motivational Dialogue with other People

Dialogue may be seen as a third way besides obeying and disobeying some motivating influence. And the sequence of events in this case can be described as a six-staged motivational process, leading to some action, which may be the same one as was implied by the initial motivating influence, or may be totally different. The first stage is the motivating influence itself, i.e. command, request, norm, custom, prescription, proposal, setting a goal, making a hint, telling a story, throwing in an idea and so on. Then, at the second stage, the listener turns into the speaker: he neither simply obeys, nor disobeys, but answers verbally, be it asking some question, doubting the norm, objecting the proposal, arguing with the custom, suggesting some alternative, beginning a quarrel and so on. So, at this phase, some contradiction, collision or even conflict comes into being, creating specific tension between the interlocutors and turning them into opponents. The third stage consists in the searching for answers and producing different ideas, concerning the action in question and capable to resolve or to overcome the emerged contradiction and to relieve tension. Arguing, discussing, estimating ideas and working out agreements and compromises (sometimes also quarreling and swearing) makes up the contents of the fourth stage. At the fifth stage, the final decision is formulated and accepted – as a result of a compromise or due to the victory of some of the ideas, having occurred in the course of the argument. This decision can be a joint one, or it can be imposed by one partner on another one; in some cases, the decision can even be the rupture of relationships at all. And the sixth stage is the execution of the decided action.

Let us illustrate this sequence with a very simple everyday example of a father, taking a walk with his little daughter and prompting her to return home:

Father: Let's go home, it's time to do your homework (1).
Daughter: No, it's too early (2), I'll manage to do it in the evening (3).
F.: In the evening you were going to play with Robert (3, 4).
D.: The task isn't large today, I'll manage to cope with it in an hour (4).
F.: OK, one more half an hour and then we are going home without any discussion (5).
D.: OK. (5).

Such a motivational process should be called neither external determination, nor self-determination, it essentially differs from both of them. And since both partners are making their contributions to the final decision, the process deserves the name of a *joint* determination. It goes without saying that the order of individual operations is not always the same: argumentation can precede the search for new ideas, and proposed final decision can evoke strong opposition and return the whole process back to the beginning. In any case, dialogue proves to be the way out from external determination and the mode of inventing new intentions and decisions.

The principal model of joint determination is represented at Figure 1.

Of course, motivational dialogues in our life are often much more complex and sophisticated than the simplified example above. Such complicated cases of joint determination are often described in classical literature, especially in Dostoevsky's novels: we can remember, for instance, how a series of dialogues and discussions with the people around led Kirillov, a character from *Demons*, from an abstract idea of a "suicide for freedom" to committing a real suicide with no other reasons but the "idea of freedom".

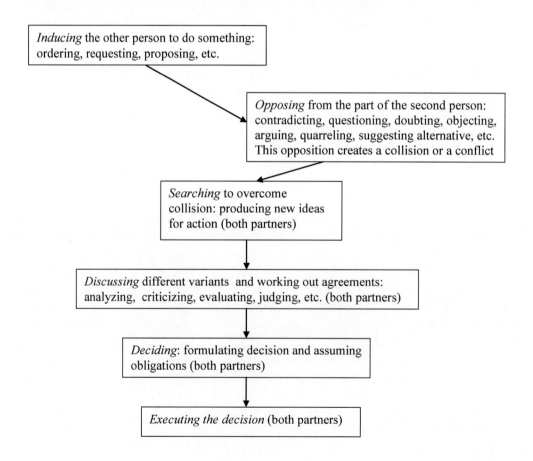

Figure 1. The principal model of joint determination.

Inner Motivational Dialogue as the Process of Self-determination

All of the steps and operations of a motivational dialogue can be internalized and fulfilled by one and the same individual speaking with himself, so that the motivational dialogue becomes an *inner* one. In this case, a person has to be able to cast doubt not only on social influences but also on his or her own desires and goals, to discuss and criticize his or her own ideas, to argue with him- or herself. And if the individual himself accomplishes all of the psychological work needed to determine the course of his or her future action, than we should acknowledge that he or she carries out the process of real self-determination, creating new intentions and decisions which have not existed prior to the dialogue with his or her own self. As an example, we can take another Dostoevsky's character, Rodion Raskolnikov, whose fatal decision to kill the old pawnbroker was growing up just in his inner dialogues. Let us remember that at the beginning of the motivational process, leading to his terrible deed, there happened to be someone's comment about the pawnbroker, overheard by Raskolnikov (i.e. external motivational influence). Then a series of inner dialogues, various events and trial actions take place, converting the idea into Raskolnikov's own decision taken on his own free will. Comparing these dialogues with the simple everyday ones, we can see a lot of new "elemental operations" emerging within the motivational process. Also, it becomes evident, that each stage of a self-determining dialogue may be dragged out for many days, weeks and even months. Let us take a look at two of Raskolnikov's inner dialogues. The first is taking place when Raskolnikov, coming out of the garret in which he lodged in order to visit the old pawnbroker for a "rehearsal" of an intended murder, is frightened to meet his landlady (whom he was hopelessly in debt) on the staircase (comments in square brackets point out the elementary motivational operations):

"I want to attempt a thing _like that_ and am frightened by these trifles," he thought, with an odd smile [*reflecting about his own behavior*]. "Hm... yes, all is in a man's hands and he lets it all slip from cowardice, that's an axiom [*pondering, applying general statement to the current situation*]. It would be interesting to know what it is men are most afraid of. Taking a new step, uttering a new word is what they fear most... [*reasoning*]. But I am talking too much [*judging his own behavior*]. It's because I chatter that I do nothing. Or perhaps it is that I chatter because I do nothing [*reasoning, discussing his own behavior*]. I've learned to chatter this last month, lying for days together in my den thinking... of Jack the Giant-killer [*reflecting about his own behavior*]. Why am I going there now? [*challenging himself*] Am I capable of _that_? [*challenging himself*] Is _that_ serious? [*challenging himself*] It is not serious at all [*retreating*]. It's simply a fantasy to amuse myself; a plaything! Yes, maybe it is a plaything [*calming himself*]." (Crime and punishment. Part 1. Chapter 1.).

The second inner dialogue takes place just after the "rehearsal", when Raskolnikov went out from the old woman's flat in complete confusion:

As he went down the stairs, he even stopped short, two or three times, as though suddenly struck by some thought. When he was in the street he cried out, "Oh, God, how loathsome it all is! [*moral judgement*] and can I, can I possibly [*accusing himself*].... No, it's nonsense, it's rubbish!"[*rejecting the intention*] he added resolutely. "And how could such an atrocious thing come into my head? [*wondering, accusing himself*] What filthy things my heart is capable of. Yes, filthy above all, disgusting, loathsome, loathsome!--and for a whole month I've been...." [*criticizing and accusing himself, swearing at himself*]

Now we can outline the principal model of the self-determination process (Figure 2).

In addition to the principal fact that all motivational operations are carried out here by one and the same person, there is one more essential difference from the process of the joint determination: the opposition with others is shifted here from the beginning of the motivational process to it's very end, to the stage of implementation of adopted decision. It should also be noted that a lot of intermediate variants between completely joint determined actions and entirely self-determined ones exist, since the degree of internalization may differ: some operations may become internalized, while others remain external.

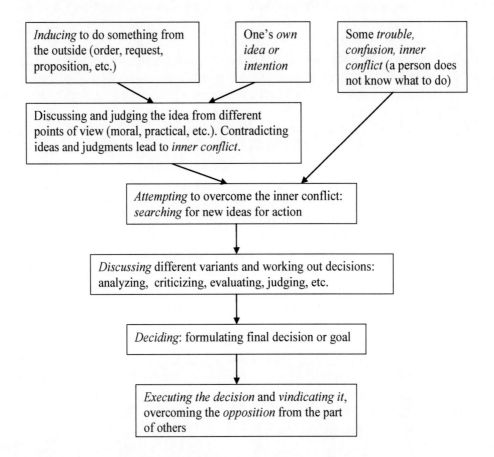

Figure 2. The principal model of the self-determination process.

At advanced levels of internalization, inner motivational dialogue often gets heavily reduced and becomes more compact and more concentrated, since inner speech as such being a curtailed and abbreviated form of speech (Vygotsky). In the end it may be reduced to a single word, for instance, to W. James's '*Fiat!*', or even to a barely noticeable volition.

DEVELOPING THE ABILITY FOR SELF-DETERMINATION

According to the general idea of development of all higher psychological abilities from their "inter-psychic" or social form (in other words, from an action, divided between two or more persons) to their "intra-psychic" or individual form (to an entirely individual psychic process) (Vygotsky), the most promising way of cultivating the ability for self-determination is organizing children's "life space" as a dialogical one. It means creating not only opportunities for discussing different questions, but, first and foremost, opportunities for joint determination of all of the important and difficult actions of children and continuously enlarging their experience of self-determination as they grow older. In other words, the period of education should become the time of acquiring a lot of skills necessary for motivational dialogues both with others and with oneself, such as doubting another's words, initiating discussion, proposing one's own ideas, listening to the other person, understanding his views and taking his opinions into account, criticizing someone's ideas, arguing, fighting for one's decision, evaluating one's own actions, and so on.

Proceeding from this idea, the author of the present chapter has devised a program for the self-determination training for school students, which included discussing the real problems of school life, searching for possible solutions and negotiating with the head teacher. The results have been hopeful, but at the same time, a fundamental obstacle to developing the ability for self-determination in students has been revealed, namely the shortage of 'life space' for real dialogue in 'the class-lesson' school system. The point is, that even a good teacher in the modern class-lesson system has to make the children do what the program prescribes: the teacher can discipline his pupils (or students) or fascinate them – but in most cases, there is no room for discussing what to do and what not to do. The teacher simply cannot afford motivational dialogues with his or her students, or else they would not master the school program. Of course, dialogues are possible in school, but mainly of other types: pedagogical, truth-oriented, sometimes even ideological ones. And motivational dialogues can usually take place only within very narrow bounds, for the most part, while discussing what to do after finishing school. As for other situations, in the majority of them, the children are obliged to fulfill the tasks and to answer the teacher's questions, but not to argue with the teacher or to cast doubt on his or her words. Thus, we should either accept the fact that the ability for self-determination will continue to be the property only of those lucky individuals, who have had a happy and safe childhood, or turn to severe critics of the school system as such (see, for example, Illich, 1971) and create an efficient alternative educational system.

CONCLUSION

Basing on the cultural-historical point of view, we can thus conceptualize the process of self-determination as the inner motivational dialogue, giving birth to new motives, intentions and decisions. In this case, the ability for self-determination can be understood as an acquired one, and the necessary intermediate stage while mastering the aptitude for self-determination appears to be the process of a joint determination of future actions in the course of motivational dialogues with other people. It seems to be highly desirable to make such external motivational dialogues a common practice at secondary schools, though the current "class-lesson" school system principally contradicts such a development. So, if we want the ability for self-determination to become a universal one, serious modernization of the current "class-lesson" school system seems to be the necessary pre-condition.

REFERENCES

Bakhtin, M.M. (1963). *Problemy poetiki Dostoyevskogo* (*Problems of Dostoyevsky's Poetics*). Moscow: Sovetskii pisatel. (English edition: Minneapolis: University of Minnesota Press, 1984).

Deci, E. L. & Ryan, R. M. (2008). Self-Determination Theory: A Macrotheory of Human Motivation, Development, and Health. *Canadian Psychology, 49* (3), 182–185.

Durkheim, É. (1912) *Les formes elementaires de la vie religieuse. Le systeme totemique en Australie.* (*The Elementary Forms of The Religious Life. The Totem System in Australia.*) Paris: PUF.

Durkheim, É. (1915) *" L'Allemagne au-dessus de tout ". La mentalite allemande et la guerre.* (*'The Germany Is Above All'. The German Mentality And The War.*) Paris: Armand Colin.

Emmons, R.A. (1999) *The Psychology of Ultimate Concerns : motivation and spirituality in personality.* New York; London: The Guilford Press.

Foucault, M. (1994) *Dit et ecrit. 1954-1988* (sous la direction de D.Defert et F.Ewald), en 4 volumes. Vol. III. (*Said and Written.1954-1988*) Paris: Gallimard.

Halbwachs, M. (1913) *La classe ouvrière et les niveaux de vie. Recherches sur la hiérarchie des besoins dans les sociétés industrielles contemporaines.* (Working Class And Levels of Life. The Hierarchy of Needs in Modern Industrial Societies) Paris : Félix Alcan.

Holquist, M. (2002) *Dialogism*. London, New York: Routledge.

Illich, I. (1971). *De-schooling Society*. New York: Harper & Row.

Ivannikov, V.A. (1990) *Psichologiya voli.* (*Psychology of Will*). Moscow: Moscow State Univ. Press.

Janet, P. (1926) *De l'angoisse à l'extase. Étude sur les croyances et les sentiments.* (*From Anxiety to Ecstasy. An Essay on Beliefs and Sentiments.*) *Vol. I.* Paris: Alcan.

Janet, P. (1929) *L'evolution psychologique de la personnalite. (The Psychological Evolution of Personality)* Paris: Edicion Chanine.

Längle, A. (1999) Die existentielle Motivation der Person. (The Existential Motivation of The Person.) *Existenzanalyse 16* (3), 18-29.

Längle, A. (2011). The Existential Fundamental Motivations Structuring the Motivational Process. In D. Leontiev (Ed.) *Motivation, consciousness, and self-regulation* (pp. 00-00). N.Y.: Nova Science Publishers.

Leontyeva, S. G. (2005) Zhisneopisanie pionera-geroya: tekstowaya tradiciya i ritualnyi kontekst (Life history of a pioneer-hero: text tradition and ritual context). In M.V. Ahmetova (Ed.), *Sovremennaya rossiyskaya mifologiya.* (*Modern Russian Mythology.*) (pp. 89-123) Moscow: RSHU-Publishers.

Lifton, R.J. (1961) *Thought Reform and the Psychology of Totalism: A Study of "Brainwashing" in China.* New York- London: W. W. Norton & Co.

Maslow, A. H. (1976). *The Farther Reaches of Human Nature*. Harmondsworth: Penguin.

May, R. (1972) *Power And Innocence*. New York: Norton.

Porshnev, B.F. (1966) *Socialnaya psychologia i istoriya* (*Social Psychology And History*). Moscow: Nauka.

Porshnev, B.F. (1974) *O nachale chelovecheskoy istorii* (*On The Beginning of Human History*). Moscow, Nauka.

Ryan, R. M. & Deci, E. L. (2000) Self-Determination Theory and the Facilitation of Intrinsic Motivation, Social Development, and Well-Being. *American Psychologist, 55* (1), 68-78.

Vygotsky, L.S. (1930) Orudie i znak v razvitii rebyonka. (English edition (1994): Tool and symbol in child development. In R. van der Veer & J. Valsiner (Eds.) *The Vygotsky Reader* (pp. 99-174). Oxford UK & Cambridge USA: Blackwell.)

Vygotsky, L.S. (1931) *Istoria razvitiya vysshih psihicheskih funkciy* (The history of development of higher psychological functions). First published: Vygotsky, L.S. (1960) *Razvitie vysshih psihicheskih funkciy.* Moscow: APN RSFSR. (English edition: Vygotsky, L.S. (1978) *Mind in society. The development of higher psychological processes.* Cambridge, MA; London: Harvard Univ. Press)

Weber, M. (1905) Die protestantische Ethik und der 'Geist' des Kapitalismus. (The Protestant Ethic and the Spirit of Capitalism.) *Archiv für Sozialwissenschaft und Sozialpolitik, 20* (1904), 1–54 und *21* (1905), 1–110.

In: Motivation, Consciousness and Self-Regulation
Editor: D. A. Leontiev, pp. 209-242

ISBN: 978-1-61324-795-2
© 2012 Nova Science Publishers, Inc.

Chapter 13

DEVELOPMENT OF MORAL FOUNDATIONS OF ACTION: THE ROLE OF THE NARRATIVE FUNCTION OF LANGUAGE

Eugene Subbotsky

Psychology Department, Lancaster University, UK

ABSTRACT

A theory is presented that highlights the narrative role of language in moral development. Two stages in moral development are distinguished: the stage when children can speak and memorize events but are not yet capable of cheating and the stage when they are capable of creating deceptive stories in order to protect themselves from punishment for non-compliance with moral rules. When children reach the second stage, they may encounter situations of free moral choice – the situations in which they can transgress on a moral rule and yet get away with this by presenting adults with a deceptive story. From the view of the presented theory, these kinds of situations are key for the emergence of the intrinsic moral motivation – motivation based on respect for moral rules rather than on the fear of negative consequences for non-compliance. Various scenarios of the development of this kind of moral motivation are considered, and experimental studies that aimed to test the theory are reviewed.

Keywords: Moral development, motivation, narrative function of language, deception

INTRODUCTION

Is children's deception a by-product of moral development that needs to be overcome, or can it play a positive role in this development? Isintrinsic, free of self-interest moral motivation an achievement of the mature mind only, or can it also be found in preschool children? When children comply with moral rules in the absence of direct surveillance, does it necessarily mean that moral values are internalized? Can children's development in the domain of cheating and deception be generalized to other aspects of the moral lives of children? Is it possible that different phenomena of moral life, such as moral identity, moral integrity, moral agency, moral hypocrisy and moral disengagement have a common developmental root? These and other issues debated by developmental researchers are raised in this article.

REALITY THAT CAN BE TAMPERED WITH

Among its many functions in children's cognitive development (Piaget, 1926/1959, 1932, 1951/1962; Vygotsky, 1987), language has a function whose importance for the moral development of the child remained relatively underestimated by theorists. This function is a "story-telling" or narrative function of speech. Indeed, as soon as the child acquires the capacity of "thinking through language" (i.e., sometime between 2 and 3 years of age), the child's behavior becomes "duplicated". From now on, not only is the child doing something, but he or she also knows and remembers that he or she is doing this. In other words, language becomes a medium for alternative (or represented) reality. This new reality, correctly or incorrectly, reflects the outer world, but its most important feature in the context of this article is that it can be intentionally distorted.

It is important to emphasize here that, unlike the child's growing capacity of executive control over other mental functions (such as thinking or social behavior - see Maccoby, 1980; Vygotsky, 1987), the process of "verbal duplication" of the child's behavior is not voluntary. It is not only that the child can duplicate his or her everyday behavior in his or her memory through language; the important point is that, from now on, the child cannot help doing this. This mental, internal "dubbing" is a necessary and unavoidable accompaniment of all conscious actions of a linguistic individual.[1]

There have been interesting attempts to interpret moral development as a partial result of the human ability to create narratives. Taking from Heidegger, Packer (1991) theorized that morality involves constructing one's new identity through narrations about oneself. Furthermore, Tappan (2006) argues that moral development involves "the experience of social communication and social interaction between speaking persons, engaged in ongoing dialogue with others…" (p.18). In order to preserve their identity as moral persons, individuals create a "life-story" about themselves, which is an ongoing narrative that explains to other individuals the reasons behind their actions in important events of their lives (McAdams, 1993). Research confirms that in their narratives, people often dismiss immoral things that they did in order to maintain their moral self-image (Pasupathi, Mansour & Brubaker, 2007). The important point the above theories make is that creating narratives can lead to building up the moral self-image yet it can also be used for justifying immoral actions and lies.The issue that remains to be studied is in what way the narrative function of language shapes the early stages of moral development.

The child's capacity of creating and telling narratives has been mainly investigated in the studies of autobiographical memory. The studies showed that young children can provide a good account of episodes of their past experiences (Hudson, 1990; Miller & Sperry, 1988; Nelson, 1989). At the same time, children's general memory abilities, as well as memory

---

[1] Some researchers argue that it is the narrative function of language that distinguishes humans from non-humans in the most cardinal way (see Carrithers, 1991).

about misleading or accurate narratives, increases with age (Templeton & Wilcox, 2000). Yet, it is not until 4 years of age that children become able to represent the views of other people in their narratives, thus contrasting what they know (think) about some events, and what others may know (think) about these events (Nelson, 1992; Perner, 1992). For example, Nicolopoulou and Richner (2007) analyzed 617 stories created by 3 to 5 year old children and found that in the 3-year-olds' stories, characters are represented by their physical and external features, whereas 4- and 5-year-olds increasingly attributed "agents" with mental states and mental representational capacities. The point I am going to make is that the capacity of creating narratives in which different points of view can be contrasted is a crucial prerequisite for the emergence of the new type of mind.

THE T-MIND AND THE TDT-MIND[2]

Sometime between the ages of 2 to 3 years, the child becomes an individual with a little "bug" in his or her head, and this bug is language. Whatever the child does, or thinks, or experiences at the moment, is now being recorded on the "portable tape recorder" of his or her verbal (narrative) memory. Through this taping, an original copy of the child's behavior is created. Of course, this copy is far from being perfect. When telling about past events, the child may forget or misinterpret something, and there can be other factors responsible for the loss of information (like the lack of attention, insufficiency of linguistic means, etc.). It was reported for instance that preschool children are vulnerable to misleading suggestions (Bruck&Ceci, 1999), and in certain cases children and adults claimed that they actually experienced events they only imagined or thought about (Belli, Schuman, & Jackson, 1997; Ceci, 1994). There is also a developmental progression between 3 and 6 years of age on both general memory abilities and abilities to report accurate or misleading narratives (Templeton & Wilcox, 2000).Nevertheless, if you ask a 3-year-old child to tell what he or she has been doing for the last few minutes, the child will come up with a more or less plausible story. Let me call this original story "the first tape", or simply the tape (T). This is not to say that young children's memory is a passive "imprinting" of information on the brain tissue, similar to that which happens in taping a sound on a tape recorder. All the above studies have shown that this process is more constructive and interpretive than the "tape" metaphor would suggest. Yet this metaphor is useful because it emphasizes the compulsory and involuntary nature of young children's memory. The changes in young children's memories that result from misunderstanding or misinformation are akin to "noises" on the tape of a tape recorder, rather than to deliberate amendments made with the purpose of misleading and deceiving others.

In everyday life, the usual function of the T is the same as that of verbal memory. Apart from storing, keeping and retrieving information, the T maintains the unity and consistency of the 'stream of consciousness' as it flows from the past to the future. There is, however, a class of situations when producing the T becomes insufficient for coping with reality. In these situations, the child anticipates that he or she would have to expose the T to other people, but for some reasons is unwilling to do so. Typically, such situations emerge when the child's

---

[2] These abbreviations stand for the mind without the capacity of cheating (the T-mind) and the mind with that capacity (the TDT-mind).

self-interests contradict the interests of other and more powerful individuals, and the child is aware of this.

In my analysis of these conflicting situations, I am going to skip trivial cases where the child is simply too small and immature to be able to control his or her actions. For example, if a 2-year-old child has a strong temptation to take a bite from a cake that was prepared for a party of guests and left on the table unattended, the child would hardly be able to restrain his or her impulse, and most adults are aware of that. If, however, the child is already capable of keeping his or her impulses under control, the child still has a chance of doing what he or she wants and getting away with this. For that to be possible, however, the child has to create a story for the "outer use" – a double tape (for instance, that it was a dog or another child who tried the cake).

In the view presented in this article, the capacity of creating the T-duplicates, which distort reality, is of fundamental importance for the child's moral development. With the creation of the T-duplicates, the child's mental space becomes doubled, or double-layered. In the first layer, the T, the events are stored as they occurred. As this process is compulsory and involuntary, it cannot be edited on purpose, even if the child does not want some events to remain in his or her memory. With the T-duplicate things are different. The child creates and edits the events, adjusting the T-story to his or her own needs. In the process of editing, the child replaces some events written on the T with different events, or changes some of their elements and their succession.

I'd like to emphasize that creating the T-duplicates is not the same thing as cheating. In everyday life, many of our lies happen unexpectedlyand without selfish intention. When my friend, in whose house I am enjoying a pleasant evening, suddenly asks if I like his new carpet, I might be tempted to say "yes, I do", even though I might not. When at a table a mother asks her 5-year-old daughter if she had washed her hands, the girl might say that she had whereas she actually hadn't. In contrast, the T-duplicate story is a deceptive story that is prepared in advance, with the intention to be used in the future in order to achieve a personal benefit.

Yet are young children cognitively sophisticated enough to develop a dual-process model that creating the T-duplicates involves? There is evidence that shows young and preschool children's capacity to manipulate imagined objects and reflect upon them, and that this capacity is more advanced than is usually assumed. For instance, Piaget (1962) argues that the capacity to symbolically represent things and sensibly manipulate symbolic representations is present in 3-year-old children. Piaget also gives multiple examples of 4- and 5-year-olds' imaginary stories in which children could consistently and for a long time manipulate complex imaginary objects. In a more recent work, Harris (2000) provided ample evidence for young children's precocious capacity to deal with the imaginary world. For example, in a game of pretence, 2-year-olds were shown to be able to imagine a chain of causal transformations of objects and describe their outcomes; they could also manipulate pretend, imagined objects in such a way that these object retained both physical and causal properties of the physical prototypes. Dias and Harris (1988) have shown that 6- and even 4-year-olds, under certain circumstances, are capable of drawing logically correct conclusions from semantically incorrect premises. Shultz, Wells, and Sarda (1980) reported that preschool children can distinguish between intentional and unintentional actions. In light of this and other existing evidence, the task demand of creating the T-duplicates does not seem particularly challenging.

To be able to create the T-duplicate, the child has to acquire two major capacities. First, the child has to believe that his or her mind is private, and the T cannot be read by other people directly from his or her mind (understanding the privacy of the individual mind). If the child has any doubts about this, then the creation of the T-duplicate has no point; this could only damage the child's image in the eyes of other people and aggravate the anticipated punishment. There is indirect evidence that the awareness of their minds' privacy appears in young children: even 3-year-olds were able to understand that, unlike perceived physical objects, imagined entities cannot be touched or seen by other people and can also be fantastic (Estes, Wellman & Woolley, 1989; Wellman & Estes, 1986).

Second, the child has to be able to view the situation through the eyes of other people, or to have some kind of "theory of mind" (ToM). Intense research has been done on children's understanding that others have mental states, such as desires, intentions, and beliefs. A central aspect of research on ToM was children's understanding of false beliefs. The concept of false beliefs stems from the distinction between mind and world and presents the mind as a representational device that sometimes gets things wrong (Dennett, 1979; Premack& Woodruff, 1978). Several tasks have been created to trace the development of preschoolers' false belief understanding. In the change of location task, children witness a character placing an object in one location and then leaving the room (Wimmer&Perner, 1983). In the character's absence, another character moves the object to a new location. Children are then asked where the first character will look for his or her object upon his or her return. Children younger than about 4 years of age typically state that the character will look for the object where it really is and not where the character presumably believes it to be (where he or she placed it last). Another task, the unexpected identity task, was designed to reduce task demands by dispensing with the narrative form. The children are presented with a "smarties" box and asked what they think is inside (Gopnik&Astington, 1988; Perner, Leekam, &Wimmer, 1987). After they answer, "smarties," the box is opened to reveal pencils. The box is then closed and children are asked "When you first saw the box, before we opened it, what did you think was in the box?" Typically, three-year-olds state "pencils," while older children correctly state "smarties." Summarizing extensive research on false belief tasks in a meta-analysis, Wellman, Cross, and Watson (2001) concluded that children's performance on these tasks improves dramatically from ages 3 to 5 years, from below-chance performance before 3 years and 5 months to above-chance performance after 4 years. This improvement is highly robust even in the face of various manipulations designed to simplify the task. There is some evidence that indicates understanding of false belief to be a uniquely human ability: children were able to succeed in both verbal and nonverbal false belief tasks, whereas no ape could succeed on nonverbal false belief tasks (Call &Tomasello, 1999). Recently, evidence has been reported that 15-month-old infants already possess (albeit in a rudimentary and implicit form) the ability to attribute false beliefs to an actor (Onishi&Baillargeone, 2005). Like the earlier reported kinds of "implicit knowledge" in infants, the nonverbal "understanding" of false beliefs cannot compete with older children's verbal understanding of false beliefs: in order to create the T-duplicates, children have to have verbal representations of other's false beliefs. Importantly, children's ToM performance is positively related to their language ability (Cheung, Hsuan-Chih, Creed, Ng, Wang & Mo, 2004; Lohman&Tomasello, 2003; Milligan, Astington, &Dack, 2007), inhibitory control (Carlson & Moses, 2001; Perner, Lang &Kloo, 2002), understanding pretence (Rosen, Schwebel& Singer, 1997), and deception (Carlson, Moses &Hix, 1998).

It is approximately at the age of 3 years that children also become capable of lying (Hala, Chandler & Fritz, 1991; Lewis, Stranger, &Sallivan, 1989; Polak& Harris, 1999; Perner, 1992; Sodian, Taylor, Harris &Perner, 1991). Talwar, Lee, Bala and Lindsay (2002) asked 3- to 7-year-olds not to peek at a toy while the children stayed alone in the room. Although the children promised not to peek, 82% of them peeked. When asked about whether they had peeked or not, 37% of 3-year-olds and 86% of children between 4 and 7 years of age lied. The majority of children were also able to identify an incorrect statement of a story character as lying. At the age of 5 years, children not only can effectively deceive, but they also can confidently detect lying in other people. Lee, Cameron, Doucetteand Talwar (2002) presented 3- to 6-year-olds with a story in which a protagonist made and implausible statement. They found that 3-and 4-year-olds tended to accept the claim, whereas 5- and 6-year-olds reported that the character committed a misdeed. Asendorf and Nunner-Whinkler (1992) reported that at the age of about 5 years, children are explicitly aware that they are expected not to violate moral rules. At the same time, it was found that cognitive moral understanding is not a good predictor of children's moral behavior: "Rather, an overwhelming majority of younger children will "happily" transgress in order to satisfy their own needs when these collide with known and well understood moral commands" (Nunner-Winkler, 1998, p.601).

It is important to emphasize that children's capacity for deception, which is of importance for this paper, is based on language and implemented through linguistic means, which makes it a specifically human ability. Indeed, non-human primates demonstrate a number of behaviors that function to deceive others, such as "tactical deception" of other animals (Whiten & Byrne, 1994) or using knowledge of what a human competitor can and cannot see to develop deceptive strategies for concealing their approach to contested food (Hare, Call &Tomasello, 2006). However, these non-verbal deceptive behaviors are no match to children's deception that operates on the basis of language. Behavioral deception in primates is confined to the presently unfolding events, whereas language based deception can also operate with events of the past and the future.

Having these capacities in his or her possession, the child is able to create a narrative in which the picture of past events is arranged in the way the child would like others to believe the events occurred. As a result, the child interprets the meaning of what other people do on the basis of the T-duplicate, and this meaning can be drastically different from (even opposite to) the meaning that these actions would have without the T-duplicate being involved. For instance, if the child says that the dog has eaten from the cake and is praised by the adults for not doing it himself or herself, the child must be aware that the praise is given to him or her not for the transgression (which is written on the T) but for his or her good behavior (which is presented to adults in the form of the T-duplicate and wrongly taken by them for truth).

With the acquisition of the capacity for creating edited duplicates intended for outer use, the child's mind becomes able to operate with two kinds of representational reality: the one that exists for private use (the T-reality) and the other that is used for presenting to the external social environment (the T-duplicated reality). I will call this kind of mind the T-doubled-T-mind (the TDT-mind), contrasting it to a simpler T-mind that precedes the TDT-mind. It has to be emphasized here that, although the TDT-mind requires the understanding of "false belief" and the privacy of the individual mind, it cannot be reduced to either of these capacities. The acquisition of the capacities for representation and meta-representation, as well as of making and telling narrations, are necessary but not sufficient conditions for the emergence of the TDT-mind. In this paper,I am going to show that (1) it is only when the child's representational mind becomes the TDT-mind, the child enters the space of free moral choice (SFC), and (2) entering the SFC is crucial for the development of a special kind of moral motivation – the intrinsic motivation based on the moral self-esteem.

THE TDT-MIND AND MORAL DEVELOPMENT

Let me start with the important distinction between the *rule-conforming moral behavior* and the *free moral action*. Suppose that a friend of mine, who lives in a foreign country, left with me some books that I promised to donate to the library for the public use. When I inspected the books and found them to be of no particular interest to myself, I fulfilled my promise and donated the books to the library. By so doing, I followed the moral rule of decency (to keep one's promises). The important feature of this action is that following the moral rule (my moral interest) also coincides with my self-interest (not to keep in my house the books that I do not need). Let me call this kind of behavior "the rule-conforming moral behavior".

Now, suppose that after I examined the books, I found them very interesting and important for my own work – the books that I would like to have permanently on my desk. In this case, my self-interest (to keep the books) is in contradiction with my moral interest (to fulfill my promise and donate the books to the library). Even now, if I donated the books to the library, I would still be in doubt of what made me do so – my intrinsic moral motivation or my hidden self-interest. Indeed, I might think that my friend could enquire if I had fulfilled his promise and donated the books, and he would be angry with me if I didn't do so.

Suppose, however, that I received sad news that my friend had tragically died in a car accident. Now I know for sure that I can keep the books that he left without anyone ever finding out about the promise that I gave to my friend. In other words, now I am completely free in my choice to either donate the books or keep them. It is only now that if I donated the books to the library, I could be sure that I committed a moral action – the action based on intrinsic moral motivation. In other words, by a "free moral action" I mean an action that includes three components: (a) it is committed in accordance with the moral rules; (b) in order to commit this action, I have to give up my self-interest; and (c) when committing this action, I am free from external or internal enforcement to comply with the moral rules. Importantly, component (c) includes anonymity, which means that I am free not to comply with the moral rule and still appear a moral person in the other people's eyes.

Perhaps, some readers would find this situation too rigorous and constrictive and away from the moral challenges of the everyday life. This, however, is not the case, because the above situation bears on important theoretical issues of moral development. Ever since the XVIII century's dispute between Immanuel Kant and Francis Hutcheson (Kant, 2005/1785), there is an ongoing discussion about the possibility of the autonomous, "free of self-interest" moral motivation in real humans (for the update, see Batson, 1990; Batson & Thompson, 2001: Blasi, 1983; Nucci& Lee, 1993). This dispute is far from being only academic since the existence of this kind of moral motivation proves the ability of a human individual to exercise free action and thus creates a psychological ground for juridical and political practices that are based on the presumption of an individual's freedom and personal responsibility.

On the basis of this definition, the development of a free moral action in a child includes the acquisition of three main psychological properties: the ability of inhibitory control, the knowledge of moral rules, and the development of appropriate moral motivation.

Although the precursors of inhibitory control can be traced in infants (Bruner, 1974), the proper ability to control one's actions appears at the age of 3 years (Diamond &Talor, 1996; Hughes, 1998). Like the case with the ToM development, a crucial step in the inhibitory control performance seems to occur between 3 and 4 years, and this improvement is significantly related to the performance on ToM tasks(Carlson & Moses, 2001).

Children beginusing social and moral rules as arguments in family disputes at the age of around 3 years (Dunn & Munn, 1987). Mostly, children spontaneously learn moral rules from their caregivers and older siblings, with adults only occasionally giving the children direct moral instructions (Edwards, 1980; 1987). Interestingly, even young children can distinguish moral transgressions (such as lying and stealing) from violations of social conventions; it is only with regard to moral transgressions that children refer to rights and welfare of others (Turiel, 1983). Both preschool (Smetana, 1981) and school age children (Nucci&Nucci, 1982; Smetana, 1981) react to moral transgressions differently from how they react to transgressions of conventional rules: moral transgressions are viewed as more serious offences then conventional transgressions. This capacity to verbally formulate moral rules crowns up the previous development, during which children acquire some intuitions about right and wrong, as they begin to react with distress and shame to their mishaps and wrongdoings (Cole, Barrett & Zahn-Waxler, 1992; Stipek, Gravinski& Kopp, 1990).

But the most important and psychologically interesting is the third process – the development of moral motivation in children. At the age of 2 years, children can show certain precursors of moral feelings (Cole et al, 1992). Reacting with particular emotions (like anxiety) in response to violations of prohibitions can be acquired quite early in life through reinforcement (Emde, Biringen, Clyman& Oppenheim, 1991). Yet, these reactions do not fundamentally differ from emotional responses of animal subjects as they are trained to behave in a certain way. By definition, the intrinsic moral motivation can only emerge (and work in the child's action) in a situation when the child has a free choice between following his or her self-interest (and, therefore, transgressing), and following moral rules.

The question arises, under what conditions can such situations occur in the everyday life of a child? Obviously, all the components that are necessary for a moral action must be present: (a) the child is aware of the moral rule and anticipates punishment for the transgression, (b) the child's self-interest makes the transgression attractive for the child, and (c) the child sees the opportunity to transgress while making others think that he or she did not transgress. While conditions (a) and (b) do not require the child's mind to be the TDT-mind, condition (c) does.

The crucial point to emphasize is that *there can be no free moral decision made if there is no opportunity to transgress and still appear to be a moral person in the other people's eyes.*In certain situations children can use their TDT-mind for deception and still go unpunished if, for example, they can relegate responsibility for their lies to other people or excuse these lies by circumstances (see Braginsky, 1970). This kind of cheating behavior, usually displayed in the studies of Machiavellianism is, however, of no interest for the purpose of this article, because it exposes the child as a liar and has no bearing on the development of intrinsic moral motivation. The opportunity to transgress anonymously can only appear if the child can create a story in which he or she did not transgress, present this story to other people and make them believe it. In this article, this kind of lying will be referred to as "negation of wrongdoing" lying. If the child's mind is the T-mind, the child can still transgress, but he or she can only do this in the anticipation (perhaps, unconscious and "conditioned" by previous experiences) of the forthcoming exposure and, most likely, punishment. That is why wrongdoings in toddlers are usually accompanied by frustration and anxiety (Cole et al., 1992; Stipek et al., 1990). When the child's mind becomes the TDT-mind, situations emerge in which the child is aware that he or she can get away with the "negation of wrongdoing" lying and, therefore, is free to transgress. In this paper, this class of moral conflict situations will be referred to as "the space of free choice" (the SFC) situations.

In the real life of a young child, in most situations of moral conflict only conditions (a) and (b) are implemented; as far as it concerns condition (c), the opportunity to create a feasible "negation of wrongdoing" story and make others believe it is a rare occasion for the child. Children of the young age are rarely left unsupervised, and in most cases transgressions leave traces and are easily detectable. For instance, in the "cake temptation" example, the child with the TDT-mind will hardly go for the transgression, as soon as he or she is already smart enough to understand that the "dog story" is not going to work. Since most real life situations of the young child are like that, the child with the TDT-mind would not transgress even if left alone and unobserved, or transgress and try to avoid punishment through making excuses of relegating responsibility to others (i.e., saying that he or she had been encouraged to try the cake by an older brother).

As the child grows older however, constant surveillance is lifted and the child increasingly finds herself in the SFC situations. Usually, children learn about the SFC situations by observing other children or story characters who successfully deceive others by creating the "negation of wrongdoing"lies and get away with this. On the basis of these observations (conversations) children become aware that there is for them an opportunity to do the same. When later finding themselves in such situations, children with the TDT-minds will try to create the "negation of wrongdoing"story. Having lied successfully for the first time, the child would then be less hesitant and find more and more opportunities to do so. The more efficient deceiver the child becomes, the larger the space of free moral choice gets. So, it is not an exaggeration to say that it is through deception and lying about their own behavior that children enters the space of free moral choice and moral responsibility[3].

It should not be surprising that the child who entered the SFC does not go for a moral choice straight away. In fact, if this were the case, there would be no need for development of intrinsic moral motivation. Indeed, if, by some miracle, children had an innate tendency (motive) to follow moral rules in the SFC situations, then they wouldn't have a free choice; rather, the children would follow moral rules in the same way animals follow their instincts. On this basis, one has to conclude that there could be no an opportunity for children to develop a moral action if they did not acquire the capacity to deceive. The stage of lying about their own behavior is the first and necessary stage in the development of free moral action in children.

---

[3] This is not to say that young children are exceptionally deceptive in a sustained way. As argued above, the opportunities to deceive anonymously are not so frequent.However, the significance of these opportunities for the development of intrinsic moral motivation is in contrast with their relatively small proportion among the whole number of situations of moral conflict. By analogy, involvement in a pretend play, especially with adults, is key for the development of children's imagination (Harris, 2000), yet for most children this kind of play is not an everyday experience and happens relatively infrequently.

As the TDT-mind develops and the SFC expands, the child creates two different images of himself or herself: one is the private image, and the other is the image presented for the outer world. In his or her private image, the child is a liar, and in his or her public image, the child is an honest individual. As soon as conformity to moral rules is positively evaluated by society and nonconformity is evaluated negatively, the child's private image acquires for the child an ambiguous meaning. The child may think of himself or herself as a smart and clever liar, yet he or she is aware that what he or she is doing is wrong. At the same time, the public image, due to positive social reinforcement, acquires a positive meaning in the child's eyes ("a good boy or girl").

So, in the beginning, a positive moral image of themselves is created by children with the TDT-mind as a protective shield against the pressure of society. This positive moral self-image can be viewed as an analogy to what Freud named "superego". There is, however, one important difference. According to Freud (1966), "superego" emerges as a result of the "introjection" of a parental image by a child, driven by the child's (mainly, a male child's) desire to resolve the "Oedipus complex" (the erotic drive the child has to his or her parent of the opposite sex). In this process, the child is viewed as a passive individual who is forced to let the external controller (the "superego") in his or her mind under the pressure of society. In contrast, the TDT-mind theory proposes that children of both sexes actively create their positive moral self-images; the driving force behind this is not the erotic need or the feeling of guilt, but the need of the children to protect their self-interests against the interests of the more powerful individuals (parents, caregivers).

Viewed in this way, the whole process of the development of the free moral action in the child is about when and how the positive moral self-image ceases being "the means to the ends" and becomes the "end in its own right". In other words, why and when do children become interested (motivated) to do what their positive moral self-images require them to do (that is, to go for the moral choices in the SFC situations)? It could be argued that preschool children are not capable of this kind or intrinsic moral motivation as long as it requires the development of moral self, which does not appear until the age of adolescence. On the contrary, as the "social domains" approach to morality emphasizes, the children's moral decisions vary across domains and are influenced by context (Nucci, 2002; Turiel, 2001).

However, I do not see a contradiction between the "context driven" moral motivation and the type of motivation based on the moral self-esteem. Rather, the situation in which a person has to make a moral decision while being free from internal and external enforcement is an extreme case of the "context dependent" moral judgment and behavior. The characteristic feature of this case is that here the space of free moral choice stands for the context. As was pointed out above, situations like that occur in the everyday life, and they can be reconstructed in experiment with the purpose of answering the important theoretical question whether autonomous, free of self-interest moral motivation is a late achievement only, as Blasi's (1983) theory would suggest, or it can be observed in children, at least in its rudimentary form.In my view, the latter possibility cannot be completely overruled. In order to be able to conform to a moral rule on the ground of respect to this rule, one does not have to be an expert on the metaphysics of morality. Rather, under certain circumstances, a simple knowledge that, in the eyes of loved caregivers, lying is a bad thing to do may motivate a childnot to lie. This goes along with the view that "moral reflection is a capacity available in different forms at all points in development and . . . people at all points in their social growth can evaluate social situations from a moral point of view" (Nucci, 2004, p.127).

Speaking theoretically, there can be at least three scenarios of under what circumstances this "reflective motivation" might appear in children. The first, and the simplest one, is the *"discipline internalization"* scenario. According to this scenario, sooner or later (and better sooner than later) adults discover the child's "negation of wrongdoing"lies and apply disciplinary measures. This would restore the child's rule-conforming behavior, but at the price of throwing the child out of the space of free choice and back in the space of externally controlled moral behavior. This scenario would reduce the problem of moral development to the process of elaboration and internalization of the means of external control and surveillance over the child's behavior.

Of course, the process of elaboration and internalization of adequate disciplinary techniques is an important issue of moral education (for the review, see Grusec&Goodnow, 1994). However, this process has one major limitation: what is called the "internalization of values" resulting from the application of disciplinary techniques is in fact the internalization of "external incentives to follow the values". Indeed, with cognitive development, children become more sophisticated in their capacity to anticipate the disciplinary consequences of their transgressions and learn to obey moral rules even at the absence of adults' surveillance. Yet they do this not because the moral values *per se* are important for them, but because they become more sensitive to the possible dangers of disciplinary consequences of moral transgressions. In fact, this process of internalization of surveillance is a cognitive elaboration of the rule-conforming motivation that appears in toddlers. What in toddlers exists in the form of emotional anticipation of the disciplinary consequences of a transgression, in older children becomes cognitively based anticipation. In both cases, the result of internalization is the rule-conforming moral behavior, rather than a free moral action. It is also possible that early forms of external moral motivation acquired through "social learning" (Bandura, 1969; Perry & Perry, 1983; Sears, Maccoby& Levin, 1957), and the later, cognitively mediated forms (Grusec&Goodnow, 1994; Kochanska, 1994) work together, making transgressions in the absence of apparent surveillance even more difficult for a child.

This is not to say that perfection and sophistication of the disciplinary techniques is unimportant for moral development. It is through the disciplining and external control that the child with the TDT-mind acquires the awareness of the positive value of moral norms, and the polarization between the child's private image and his or her public image grows. Yet, the role of disciplining for the development of moral action is only auxiliary. Disciplining provides a background, a foundation for the development of moral action, but it cannot make this action appear. Rather, the sophistication of disciplinary techniques does a good job of providing motivation for children's rule-conforming moral behavior. In an indirect way, the limited nature of disciplining is acknowledged by some authors who make a point that maintaining good and healthy relationships with children should be given priority over the goal of internalization, particularly if the cost of internalization is an increase in children's feelings of anxiety and guilt (Goodnow, 1992; Higgins, 1981, 1989). Another way to acknowledge a limited nature of internalization is emphasizing negative ramifications of cognitive development for moral conduct. Bandura, Barbarinelli, Caprara and Pastorelli (1996) argued that cognitive development, along with creating an invariant control system within a person that prompts the person to cherish moral values, also creates mechanisms by which self-sanctions can be disengaged from inhumane conduct. The authors studied 10 to 15 year old adolescents' proneness to moral disengagement (such as resort to moral justification, euphemistic labeling, advantageous comparison, displacement and diffusion of responsibility, distortion of consequences, and dehumanization of victim) and found high correlations between moral disengagement and delinquent behavior. Children who were prone to moral disengagement exhibited a higher level of interpersonal aggression and delinquent behavior than individuals who maintained a high level of moral agency.

The second possible scenario is the *"cognitive identification"*. It can be hypothesized that, as the number of occasions to achieve the child's goals through "negation of wrongdoing"cheating grows, so does the dissociation between the child's private image and his or her public image. In order to reduce this dissociation ("cognitive dissonance"), children identify themselves with the public self-images they have created, in the same way that children identify themselves with their gender roles (Bem, 1981; Kohlberg, 1966). This process of "cognitive identification" with the positive moral self-image (which the public image of the child is) can be facilitated by the child's learning about folk story characters that impersonate the good and bad behaviors, and by observing moral behavior of other people in the SFC situations.

Lastly, the third scenario is the *"emotional identification"*.Baumrind (1967) found that children who displayed most competent and mature social and moral behavior had loving, demanding and understanding parents. In contrast, restrictive, punitive and inaffectional parents mostly had disphoric and socially immature children. Although the connection between child-rearing practices and children's psychological development is a complex one and depends on children's individual differences (Kochanska, 1991; Kochanska, Kuczinski, &Radke-Yarrow, 1989; Lamb, 1982), the view prevails that parental warmth, cooperation and helping in treating their children, understanding children's needs and respect to the child's self-esteem facilitates children's moral development (Damon, 1988; Dunn, Brown, &Maquire, 1995; Higgins, 1989; Maccoby, 1980; Maccoby& Martin, 1983; Walker &Talor, 1991). It can be assumed that if children are treated in a trusting and loving way, if they have a fair share of their parents' time and personal attention to their needs, then the public image which is associated with the kind of a person the parentswould like the child to be, acquires an emotionally positive value for the children. As a result, each time when the child's "negation of wrongdoing"cheating is accepted "on trust" by a person whom the child loves and respects, the child can experience emotional discomfort and guilt for having deceived the person. Conversely, when at another time the child goes for a moral choice in the SFC situation, he or she can experience a positive feeling for meeting the parents'expectations. This "transfer of love" from the object of affection (the parents) to the moral norms (positive moral self-image) can later be generalized to include moral conduct with regard to other people.

In any of the above scenarios, the child has to develop a kind of moral motivation that is free from self-interest, something akin to what theorists called moral identity – the tendency to live consistent with one's moral self (Blasi, 1983; Colby & Damon, 1992). Yet, as some authors pointed out (Hardy & Carlo, 2005; Nucci, 2004), the moral identity theory only accounts for the intrinsic moral motivation that emerges in young adulthood. The question that remains open is whether people of earlier ages can develop intrinsic moral motivation. Some data suggested that autonomous moral motivation in adolescents could emerge prior to moral identity development (Pratt, Hunsberger, Pancer, &Alisat, 2003). As this paper proposes, there are no grounds to reject the idea that even preschool children, in certain circumstances, can develop intrinsic moral motivation based on moral self-esteem and moral self-respect; after all, at the age of 6 children have awareness of moral norms, relate those norms to their own behavior, and have other prerequisites of autonomous morality, such as understanding theory of mind (see *The T-mind and the TDT-mind*).[4]

In this scenario, it is important not to confuse the feeling of trust and love that drives the child's emotional identification with his or her positive moral self-image and the feeling of empathy that is considered to be an emotional underpinning of moral development (Eisenberg & Miller, 1987; Hoffman, 1988; Smith, 1966). Empathy can indeed make a person comply with moral rules even in the absence of surveillance or pressure of social environment (Batson, 1990), yet it is a biologically predisposed emotion and promotes the development of rule-conforming moral behavior rather than a free moral action. For the purpose of the analysis chosen in this paper, only those situations of moral conflict have been selected in which transgressions cause minimal harm to other people and are unlikely to evoke the feeling of empathy in the child.

TESTING THE TDT-MIND THEORYIN CHILDRENIN THE SITUATION OF A FREE MORAL CHOICE

In order to test the TDT-mind theory, an experimental paradigm was needed that met the criteria of the SFC-situation. First, in this situation, children must be aware that not only are they not under surveillance, but also that there is no way for other people to find out about their moral transgression (anonymity). Second, children must be aware that, if they transgressed, the consequences of the transgression for other people would be negligible (freedom from empathy). This would eliminate the possibility for the feeling of empathy to contaminate the freedom of the child's choice. Third, children should be explicitly alerted to the fact if they complied with the game rules, there might be a price to pay (awareness of consequences of being moral). This would eliminate the possibility that children might abstain from violation of the game rules and still hope that they will be externally rewarded for doing this. Fourth, children must be made aware that if they violated the game rules, they would be questioned about what they did when they were left alone (anticipation of having to cheat). This is needed in order to rule out the possibility that children transgress in the hope they will not be asked questions about their transgression. Fifth, the children must be aware that if they unintentionally transgressed on the game rules, they would have the chance of correcting themselves, thus avoiding questioning and having to cheat (disengagement of inhibitory control failures from moral transgressions). This condition disengages violations that resulted from insufficient inhibitory control from violations that are committed on purpose.

---

[4]This is not to say that in preschool children their intrinsic moral motivation is the same as the one based on moral identity in adults. Rather, intrinsic motivation in preschoolers should be viewed as an early and rudimentary form of the intrinsic moral motivation that later develops in adults. The authority of loved parents, which underlies the children's respect to moral norms, in adults can be replaced by the authority of God.After all, according to the two dominant religions of the Western world, Judaism and Christianity, the basic moral rules ("the Ten Commandments") were received by Moses directly from God.Despite today we view these rules not as divinely given, but as a set of useful conventions worked out by our societies, some people still voluntarily obey moral rules in the absence of surveillance, although obeying these rules involves sacrificing their personal interests (Batson & Thompson, 2001). This suggests that, subconsciously, people might still believe that the Ten Commandments are God's imperatives, even though consciously they may consider themselves not to believe in God.

In research, two main paradigms were used for studying deception in children. One paradigm (the "pointing paradigm") was employed for examining "strategic deception" – the children's capacity to make others believe false information. For instance, Sodian (1991) asked 3-year-olds to point to an empty location in order to deceive a "robber" as to where "a treasure" was hidden. Russell, Mauthner, Sharpe &Tidswell (1991) used a "window task", by asking children to point to the empty box to deceive a competitor as to whereabouts of the chocolate. This paradigm is a version of the ToM task, rather than a task on compliance with moral rules. As long as deception of this kind is not about children's own behavior and is not directly related to moral development, these studies will not be considered here.

The other (the "temptation-resistance") paradigm have been used in order to study the "negation of wrongdoing"type of deception in children. Lewis, Stanger and Sullivan (1989) asked children to sit in a chair with their back to a small table and told that the experimenter was going to put out a surprise toy. The children were instructed not to peek, after which the experimenter left the room and the children's behavior was videotaped through a one-way mirror. On return, the experimenter asked the child if he or she had peeked, and the negative response of the child who had peeked was counted as deception.Arsendorf and Nunner-Whinkler (1992) developed a version of this paradigm. In their study, children were encouraged to guess what kind of animal the experimenter hid under a scarf. After three unsuccessful trials, the experimenter left the room, and the child's behavior was videotaped from behind a one-way mirror. Immoral behavior was defined as violating the rule (i.e., peeping under the scarf) and subsequently denying this in the post-test interview. Polak and Harris (1999) added a control condition to a modified Lewis et al.'s (1989) paradigm. In the prohibition condition, children were asked not to touch a toy in the experimenter's absence, and in the permission condition, they were told that they could touch a toy. The higher rate of denial in the prohibition condition than in the permission condition ruled out the possibility that in the prohibition condition children lied unintentionally. Kochanska, Murray, Jacques, Koenig and Vandergeest (1996) employed experimental scenarios based on the same principle: children were either prohibited to do some actions (i.e., touch some objects on the shelf) or asked to complete a task in a certain way and then left unsupervised. For example, in the Animal Game, the child was asked to identify three animals hidden under the cloth by touching with a tip of a finger but without looking under the cloth. In the Bird Game, the child was asked to select "Magic birds" marked by a sticker on the bottom from among a large number of birds, being allowed to touch no more than two. Finally, in the Dart Game, the child had to throw five darts into a ring on the floor placed very far away, not being allowed to leave a confined space outlined on the floor. Violations of these prohibitions were qualified as transgressions. In all these versions of the temptation-resistance paradigm, only the first (anonymity) and the second (freedom from empathy) criteria of the SFC situation were met, albeit sometimes inconsistently (for instance, in Lewis et al.'s study a mother remained in the room sitting with her back to the child). None of the above studies included a pre-test interview that alerted children to the fact that the game might become impossible to win if the agreed rules are complied with (awareness of consequences of being moral). It was therefore possible that some children transgressed on the rules (i.e., peeked) and still hoped that they would get the praise for the correct "guessing". In none of the studies were children alerted to the perspective of being questioned about their performance if they did not comply with the rules (anticipation of having to cheat). The most important disengagement of inhibitory control failures from deliberate moral transgressions (analyzed in more detail later in this paper) was not provided as well. Because of this, once children transgressed on the game's rules (i.e., peeked), then there was no way that they could avoid either lying or acknowledging that they broke the rules. This made it possible that children violated the game rules involuntarily and then were bound to lie in order to cover their transgressions. In other words, the earlier studies of cheating behavior dealt with children's unintentional cheating, rather than with their capacity to use their TDT-minds for creating and presenting the T-duplicates about their behavior.

In order to meet all the three criteria of the SFC situation, a new version of the temptation-resistance paradigm was developed – the "bucket and balls" (B&B) task. In the warming up session, children were taught to perform a manual task – to transfer three ping-pong balls from a bucket into a jar using a special L-shaped shovel, without touching the balls with their hands (for the original research reports, see Subbotsky, 1983, 1993). The correct performance on this task required some training, but it was quite manageable even for 3-year-olds, as long as the bottom of the L-shaped shovel was slightly concave.

In the first experimental condition (verbal behavior in an imaginarysituation), children were individually told a narrative of a character (a boy) who was instructed by an adult to do the task. The character was promised a praise only if he successfully completed the task. If the task remained uncompleted or was completed in the wrong way (moving the balls with the hands), the character was told that he would not be given the praise. The adult then left the room and allowed the boy to work on the task unsupervised. The character tried hard to do the task right but failed. He then decided to transfer the balls with his hands and, when the adult returned, said that he had done the task in the right way. The adult said "Good boy", gave the character his praise and the boy returned to his classroom. Participants were asked to repeat the story and then to judge the character's actions and say what would they do in his place.

This condition was multipurpose. First, it tested whether the children were aware about the rules of decency and honesty and considered these rules to be directives for their own behavior. Second, the children were given hints (a) that the task they had been trained on can be impossible to win, (b) that abstaining from a violation of the task's rules might have a price to pay (not getting the praise), and (c) that violating the task's rules would have to be backed by cheating if the character wanted to win the praise.

In the second condition (free choice, no direct surveillance) children were individually offered the opportunity to do the task and left alone in the room. The child's behavior was observed through a screen, of which the child was unaware. Soon, the child discovered that it was impossible to transfer the balls with the scoop, because an identical but slightly convex scoop surreptitiously replaced the concave scoop used in the training session. The differences between the B&B paradigm and paradigms used in the earlier research are summarized in Table 1.

Minding the distinction between moral and conventional rules (Nucci&Nucci, 1982, Smetana, 1981; Turiel, 1983), I would like to emphasize that, as in other experimental paradigms used in the studies of "negation of wrongdoing"lying, the B&B situation involves both types of rules. Whereas the rule "not to touch the balls with one's hands" is a social convention between a child and an experimenter, the rule "not to lie" when asked about whether the transfer had been made in the right way is a moral rule, because saying that something was done in a way it actually wasn't is a distortion of truth. The methodical advantage of the B&B task over the earlier version of the "resistance to temptation" paradigm is that, in the B&B task, violation of the conventional rule (i.e., moving the balls with the hands) is disengaged from violation of the moral rule (i.e., cheating to an adult): even if a child unintentionally touched or moved the balls with his or her hands, he or she still had the opportunity to undo the action and thus avoid being questioned about the way he or she completed the task.

On the base of the TDT-mind theory it was expected that children with the T-minds would move the balls with their hands, and then acknowledge this to the experimenter (Group 1). Children with the TDT-minds would make attempts to transfer the balls with their hands, thus preparing the basis for the "negation of wrongdoing" story, but then they would split into three groups.

Table 1. The differences between the tasks earlier employed for testing children's deception about their own behavior and the B&B task

	Earlier employed	**The B&B task**
Awareness that complying with task's ruleswill entail personal cost	Not provided	Provided
Awareness that violation of task's ruleswill have to be backed by cheating	Not provided	Provided
Inhibitory control componentand moral choice component	Not disengaged	Disengaged

Children who lacked intrinsic moral motivation would either leave the balls in the jar and lie to the experimenter (Group 2), or return the balls into the bucket and tell they could not manage (Group 3). This latter group would do this not because they went for a moral choice (what it superficially looks like), but because of the fear that their transgression and lying would be somehow discovered by the experimenter. The internalized (or imaginary) external control provides that these children comply with the game's rules. The fourth group of children would show the same pattern (attempting transgression and then returning the balls into the bucket), but for a different reason: they would be driven by intrinsic moral motivation not to cheat. Lastly, the fifth group of children would not even try to touch the balls with their hands, thus showing both the high level of inhibitory control and intrinsic moral motivation. These predictions are summarized in Table 2.

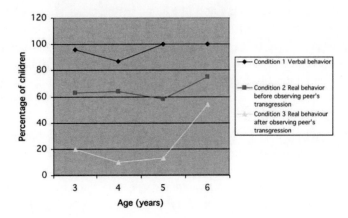

Figure 1. Percentage of children who complied with the moral rule in the B&B task as a function of age and experimental condition.

Table 2. Expected patterns of children's behavior in the B&B task

Behavioral pattern	TDT-mind				
	Absent	Present			
		Intrinsic moral motivation			
		Absent		Present	
	Group 1	Group 2	Group 3	Group 4	Group 5
Move the balls with their hands	v	v	v	v	
Move the balls back to thebucket and leave them there			v	v	
Cheat to the experimenter		v			
Acknowledge moving the balls with their hands	v				
Don't touch the ballswith their hands					v

Participants were 136 children from a suburb in Moscow, aged 3 years to 6 years 11 months and coming from mixed socioeconomic background. Only a few 3-year-olds displayed the T-mind pattern of behavior (Group 1). They were excluded from the subsequent analysis. The results of the performance of children with the TDT-minds in conditions 1 and 2 of the experiment are shown in Figure 1 (upper and middle lines).

As predicted, in condition 1, nearly all children disapproved of the character's actions because he broke his promise and lied. All these children also told that they would not try to touch the balls with their hands and lie. In condition 2, almost all children in some way attempted to use their hands in order to "help the scoop". On average, around 60 percent of children in all age groups either left the balls in the bucket or brought them back to the bucket from the jar. The rest of the participants moved the balls from the bucket into the jar with the help of their hands and lied to the experimenter (Group 2). There were no marked gender differences observed.

In order to separate between the group of children with the TDT-mind who did not lie *because the internalized external control (surveillance)* prevented them from doing so (Group 3 in Table 1), and the group who displayed a similar pattern of behavior because they had *intrinsic moral motivation* (Group 4 in Table 1), each child who observed the moral rules in Condition 2 (including those of Group 5) participated in Condition 3 of the experiment. In this condition, a target child was left in the room with another child (the model, a former transgressor) who was asked to perform this task one more time. Sometime during the performance, the model moved the balls with his or her hands and, on the experimenter's return, lied. The model was then given the praise and sent back to the classroom. After that, the target child was offered an opportunity to give the task "another try" and left alone in the room.

The purpose of this procedure was to free the target child from the internalized (imaginary) external control. If, in the second condition, the child was anticipating that the adult would somehow find out about his or her transgression and so decided not to lie, now the child was sure that the adult would accept his or her version of the events presented in the

T-duplicate. This means that in Condition 3, children were free from the imaginary (internalized) surveillance. If the child with the TDT-mind, after observing the other child's transgression left undetected, moves the balls with his or her hands and denies doing so, then the child can be viewed as the one who, in his or her previous behavior, was driven by the internalized surveillance. If, however, the child still complies with the rules of the game, then the child can be classified as the one who has intrinsic moral motivation.

Eighty-one children, who belonged to the TDT-mind category and did not transgress in Condition 2 of the experiment, participated in Condition 3. The results (Figure 1, bottom line) showed that the percentage of children who did not transgress dropped significantly in all age groups, but the oldest one. This effect *demonstrates that even if children comply with moral rules in a situation in which direct surveillance is absent, this does not necessarily mean that the children have intrinsic moral motivation.* A significant increase in the number of children who opted for the moral choice in the SFC situation was observed among 6-year-olds as compared to younger children, but there were no significant differences between the numbers of such children found among 3-, 4-, and 5-year-olds.[5]

Interestingly, in concordance with the "social domain" theory, when the same children who cheated on the B&B task were tested in other situations in which an immoral choice could bring negative consequences for others, the children behaved differently. For instance, in the "distributive justice" situation in which a child had to distribute a prize of two attractive objects between himself or herself and the partner with the option to keep both objects, around 50% of 4- and 5-year-olds shared the prize. Similarly, in another situation where partner's interests were involved – helping versus not helping a partner – children complied with the moral rule significantly more frequently than in the B&B situation (Subbotsky, 1993). This improved performance can be explained by the fact that in these situations children's intrinsic motivation was helped by additional factors, such as moral emotions (empathy) and external control. Indeed, in the situations where peers' interests were involved, children's partners were not passive observers of the child's behavior; rather, most of them actively encouraged the child to help or share. This explanation of the contrast between children's performance on the B&B task and their performance on helping and sharing tasks receives support in the fact that when the experimenter remained in the room, almost none of the children aged 3 to 6 years cheated on the B&B task. On the other hand, when children of the same age groups were given an opportunity to anonymously donate to a good cause, the percentage of children who donated was about the same as in the B&B task (around 14%), despite the fact that in the pre-test interview 80% of children said that they would donate. Interestingly, Batson, Kobrynowicz, Dinnerstein, Kampf, and Wilson (1997) reported that when adults were given an opportunity to anonymously take advantage of their position in the situation of distributing unequally attractive tasks between themselves and their partners, only about 20 percent of participants complied with the rule of fairness, though the majority of non-compliers later acknowledged that what they had done was wrong. The authors explain the participants' immoral behavior by "moral hypocrisy"-- a special motive according to which "individuals want to appear moral while, if possible, avoiding the cost of actually being moral" (Batson & Thompson, 2001, p.54). Further research showed that many participants initially want to be truly moral (i.e., to maintain their "moral integrity"), but this intention is

---

[5] This experiment was reproduced in Czechoslovakia with Slovak children and yielded similar results (Pozar&Subbotsky, 1984).

overpowered by stronger self-interested motives ("overpowered integrity") (Batson, Tsang, & Thompson, 2000). In the B&B task, children showed similar patterns of behavior: some of those who had promised to comply with the game's rules, violated the rules immediately after the adult left the room, waited for the adult to come back and lied without hesitation ("moral hypocrisy"), whereas other children two or three times moved the balls forth and back with their hands before they decided to lie, thus showing a pattern consistent with the "overpowered integrity". The above data suggest that children's behavior in the B&B situation can be generalized to more common aspects of moral lives of children and adults, such as donation or distributional justice.

In other words, it can be assumed that in moral domains other than cheating, the TDT-mind works in a similar way: when confronted with a moral challenge in the SFC situations, people with the TDT-mind but with no intrinsic moral motivation don't comply with moral rules if their non-compliance remains anonymous, and subsequently deny non-compliance. In the non-SFC situations of moral challenge, many people still don't comply with moral rules, but in order to excuse their immoral behaviors they use mechanisms other than creating the "negation of wrongdoing"stories. Bandura (1999, 2002) provided a detailed description of those mechanisms, such as moral justification of reprehensible conduct, diffusion of responsibility, minimizing detrimental effects and consequences of immoral acts, and dehumanization of victim.

Still, up to 20% of younger children and 46% of 6-year-olds in this study complied with the game rules, indicating that they were driven by intrinsic moral motivation. This kind of motivation can be viewed as the beginning, or an early form of what in the social cognitive theory is called "moral agency" – a mechanism through which "moral reasoning is translated into actions through self-regulatory mechanisms rooted in moral standards and self-sanctions" (Bandura, 1999, p.2). According to Bandura (1991), neither moral thinking nor cognitive conflict can provide a link between moral reasoning and conduct; for such a link to be possible, moral agency must emerge. In the course of moral development, the emergence of moral agency can provide gradual substitution of external sanctions and demands by symbolic and internal moral motivation. However, the mechanisms for the exercise of agency that social cognitive theory provides (such as "self-belief of efficacy", "goal representations", "anticipated outcomes" – Bandura, 1989) are properties of the mature mind. The question remains open as to what kinds of mechanisms can underlie operation of moral agency in its early stages of development, including preschool and elementary school children. The TDT-mind theory suggests a possible answer to this question.

Regarding children's rule complying behavior in the B&B situation, this behavior was obviously not motivated by external demands. The feeling of empathy could not drive their actions either as soon as all the children were aware that the experimenter had the whole bag full of postage stamps. The explanation that in these children external control simply was more strongly internalized than in other children looks unlikely as well. After witnessing the peer's "negation of wrongdoing"cheating behavior that the adult takes for truth, children of this age understand that they too can deny wrongdoings and get away with this. This implies that the internalized surveillance can no longer keep the children from lying. The most likely explanation of children's non-cheating behavior in this situation is that the children identified themselves with their positive moral self-images. The fact that this identification was most evident among 6-year-olds is consistent with the recently reported data about a significant shift that occurs in children between the ages of 5 and 7. According to Lagattuga (2005), 7-

year-olds and adults attributed negative emotions to transgressors and positive emotions to people who comply with the rules that run against their desires significantly more frequently than did 4- and 5-year-olds. This data could signify that at the age of about 6 years children begin to identify themselves with their positive moral self-images, and this makes them increasingly aware that they would feel bad if they were to go against the rules albeit in a situation in which their transgression is likely to remain unnoticed. Studies of children's autobiographical memory also suggest: it is only since 6 years of age that children's mental representational abilities and their eyewitness memory could be considered to be similar to that of adults (Templeton & Wilcox, 2000).

The question still to be answered is which of the two possible mechanisms for this identification (the cognitive categorization mechanism or the emotional identification mechanism) is to be preferred? It is also possible that both mechanisms contributed in making the children go for a moral choice.

Indirect evidence for the cognitive categorization version comes from some children's controversial behavior – refusal of the praise. Some children who transgressed, deceived, and got the praise, suddenly refused to accept the praise (that resembles the so-called "phenomenon of a bitter candy" described earlier by A. N. Leontiev, 1977). This can be interpreted as a result of a cognitive clash between what the child knows he or she was doing (lying to an adult) and what he or she was getting (a praise for having done the task in the right way). In its full version, this phenomenon was observed only in a few children. Many children, however, displayed another pattern of behavior that could be viewed as a mild version of the above phenomenon. This was most children's unwillingness to remain in the experimental room after they deceived and got the praise. Even when they were encouraged by the experimenter to stay ("Let's read a book together", "Let's play some games"), the children were eager to leave the room as soon as possible, coming up with various excuses ("I need to go to the bathroom", "My friends are waiting for me"). This pattern of behavior (refusal of communication) was in sharp contrast to the children's behavior in the warm-up session when they were happy to stay in the experimental room as long as possible, as well as to the behavior of children who did not lie and who always wanted to stay in the room for some time.

In the literature, there is mixed evidence against and for the cognitive categorization scenario for the age involved in this study. Nunner-Whinkler and Sodian (1988) showed children a vignette featuring a child character that wants to steal his classmate's possession and then decided against this. When asked what the protagonist would feel, most 4- and 6-year-olds predicted that the protagonist would feel bad after following the rules because he failed to fulfill his desire. In contrast, a significantly smaller number of 8-year-olds made such a prediction. This and other research (Arsenio& Kramer, 1992; Barden, Zelco, Duncan, & Masters, 1980; Keller, Gummerum, Wang & Lindsey, 2004) showed that children younger than 8 years view rule breakers as happy and rule compliers as unhappy. The understanding that a rule breaker is likely to experience mixed emotions develops only in older children and adults. If, in the present study, the complying children cognitively categorized themselves with their positive moral self-images, then they should be expected to be able to predict that they would feel bad after breaking the moral rule. Yet, the above research shows no evidence that 3- to 6-year-old children are able to make such a prediction. However, a more methodologically advanced study showed that children as young as 4- and 5-years were yet sensitive to the fact that breaking a rule undermines the good feeling that results from fulfilling one's desire (Lagattuga, 2005).

The evidence for the emotional identification version, indirect as well, comes from a study in which various parenting styles were related to children's preferences to go for the moral or the self-interest choices in the B&B situation (Subbotsky, 1992, 1993). This study showed that most children whose parents showed the authoritarian-rejecting pattern of parenting style as assessed by a multi-factorial projective questionnaire (treating children in an emotionally cold way, making emphasis on punitive measures, devaluating children's achievements) cheated. In contrast, most children whose parents exhibited the subjectively favorable pattern (emphasizing positive emotions and trust, respecting children's needs, combined with posing reasonable demands on their achievements) opted for the moral choice. This was in concord with the data showing that parenting styles that stress respect of children's opinions and emotional support facilitates advanced moral reasoning in children (Walker &Hennig, 1999).

In order to test the "cognitive categorization" versus the "emotional identification" scenarios, an intervention study was conducted with two groups of children: 210 children aged from 3 to 5 years were in the younger group, and 220 children aged 5 to 7 years were in the older group (Subbotsky, 1993). In the pretests (the B&B task, Conditions 2 and 3), all the children broke the game rules and lied. Both groups were divided into six subgroups, with approximately equal numbers of participants in each. Children in these subgroups were then individually subjected to various kinds of intervention treatment, after which they were post-tested in the same B&B task.

In the first two intervention conditions (the "demonstration of a positive model" treatment), children were given an opportunity to observe another child (Condition 1) or an adult (Condition 2) performing the B&B task. On discovering that the task was impossible to fulfill, both the peer and the adult models opted for the moral choice. This treatment was expected to accentuate the cognitive dissonance between the participants' private and public images and prompt them to go for a moral choice in the subsequent retest.[6]

In Conditions 3, 4, and 5, children were involved in various treatments that accentuated the experimenter's trust and respect for their needs and their positive moral self-images. In Condition 3 the experimenter "forgave" the child's "mishap", in Condition 4 the child was asked to function in the role of a moral instructor for other children, and in Condition 5 the experimenter for two months systematically involved children in all sorts of emotionally positive interactions.Condition 6 was a control one – children in this group did not receive any treatment but were retested two months after the pretest.

The results indicated that in Conditions 1 and 2 (observation of a positive model) the number of children who made moral choices in the posttest increased only insignificantly as compared to the increase in the control groups. In contrast, Conditions 3, 4 and 5 yielded a significant increase in the number of moral choices. As predicted by the "emotional identification" scenario, in Condition 5 younger children showed an increase in the number of moral choices only if tested by the person who was involved in the emotionally positive interaction, but not if a stranger tested them. Unlike younger participants, older children

---

[6]In some studies of altruism, a positive effect of observing an altruistic model on children's prosocial behaviorwas reported(Bryan, 1971; Harris &Samerott, 1975; Wagner & Wheeler, 1969). In contrast to this study, however, in the studies of altruism children were tested in situations in which their choices could have been affected by the anticipated imaginative control and the feeling of empathy.

showed a significant increase in this type of behavior with regard to a stranger as well. This can be interpreted as an indicator that in older preschoolers the emotional identification with their positive self-images resulting from the intervention was transferred from the person who conducted the intervention (the figure of children's affection) to a stranger. Viewed in general, the results of the intervention experiment are in favor of the emotional identification scenario. They supported the assumption that trust, forgiveness and respect to children's personal needs facilitate the process of children's identification with their positive moral self-images which results in the emergence of intrinsic moral motivation.

Another prediction that can be made on the basis of the TDT-mind theory of moral development concerns the relationships between moral behavior and inhibitory control (IC). In research, studying this relationship produced contradictive results. Kochanska et al. (1996) found that children who had high IC at an earlier time of testing (2.2-3.4 years) were more likely to resist the temptation to cheat at a later time of testing (3.5-4.6 years), thus demonstrating a positive relationship between IC and non-transgression on moral choice tasks.However, Carlson, Moses and Hix (1998) reported a positive relationship between IC and cheating in 3– and 4-year-olds on a deceptive task: children with high IC were more successful deceivers. Considering these data, it appears that IC skills are positively correlated with both compliance and non-compliance with moral rules.

In the light of the TDT-mind theory, the apparent contradiction between the above data can be explained. The explanation is that in the above studies, the tasks in which children were required not to cheat were not the SFC tasks; rather, those tasks tested children's capacity to inhibit the impulse of breaking a conventional rule. Obviously, in these kinds of tasks the children who have a better developed capacity for inhibitory control can be expected to show a stronger tendency to comply with the prohibition (i.e., of not going outside the confined space), than the children with less developed capacity for inhibitory control. Likewise, in the tasks that required children to cheat (i.e., inhibit the impulse to show to the box in which an object really is) children with better developed inhibitory control would again do better than children with less developed inhibitory control.

However, if the task were a free moral choice kind that allows children to deceive about their own behavior, then the direct link between children's capacity for IC and their performance on the moral task would no longer exist. The B&B task is just this kind of task. Unlike the moral choice tasks in which violation of a prohibition inevitably led to subsequent cheating, in the B&B task the children who violated the prohibition (i.e., touched the balls with their hands or even moved the balls into the jar) could still avoid lying by leaving the balls in the bucket or moving them back into the bucket. In other words, the B&B task enabled children to make their moral choice decision independently from their IC capacity. This enables one to explore children's level of IC and their moral motivation as two independent "within" factors: the performance on the low-level IC component of the B&B task can be assessed by the number and latency of touches, and the performance on the high-level moral component of the same task can be assessed via the general patterns of behavior. For instance, on the higher-level component of this task (moral choice level), children who moved the balls with their hands as soon as they discovered that the shovel did not work, left the balls in the bowl and cheated were awarded the lowest moral motivation score of 0. These children demonstrated no conscious intention to comply with their verbal moral judgment.In contrast, children who did not touch the balls with their hands were awarded the highest score of 4. This behavioral pattern revealed that the child had no conscious intention of cheating.

All the other patterns of behavior received scores between 0 and 4: these patterns revealed various degrees of hesitation between compliance and non-compliance with the moral rule.

One further feature of the B&B task that distinguishes it from the moral choice tasks employed in earlier research is that in the B&B task the IC component is subordinate to the moral choice component and receives feedback from this component. If children, once they discovered that the balls could not be moved without violating the rule, decided that they would not go for deception, this decision made touching the balls unnecessary, thus enhancing children's resistance to the temptation of touching the balls. In other words, the children's decision on the *higher-level component* of the B&B task (i.e., intrinsic moral motivation) can affect their decision on the *lower-level component* of the B&Btask (i.e., inhibitory control). This up-down link may *allow children who acquired intrinsic moral motivation to override their impulse to touch the balls and perform well on the IC sub-level, even if their actual IC skills are relatively poor.*On this ground, it was predicted that (a) there will be no a significant correlation between children's performance on the higher-level of the B&B task and their performance on independent IC tasks, however, (b) there will be a significant correlation between the higher-level component of the B&B task (i.e., moral motivation) and the lower-level component of this task (i.e., inhibitory control).

In order to test these predictions, eighteen 4-year-old and twenty-one 5-year-old children attending schools at Lancaster (England) were tested on the B&B task and on the four IC tasks: *Rattle/Car Task, Day / Night Task, Cup / Saucer / Cube task, and Statues Task* (Harrison &Subbotsky, 2007). For instance, on the *Rattle/Car Task*, the child and the experimenter each had a rattle and a toy car. Children were first trained to imitate the experimenter's action that were performed in accord with the objects' usual functions (i.e., shaking the rattle, moving a car on the table – 20 actions altogether), and then the children were asked to switch to the "non-imitation game": they were asked to shake the car whenever the experimenter rolls her rattle across the table, and roll their rattle across the table whenever the experimenter shakes her car (20 test actions were then administered). Children's performance on both the lower- and higher-level components of the B&B task and on the IC tasks was rated in accordance with the standard scoring schemes.

In this study patterns of children's behavior were very similar to those in the study conducted earlier in Moscow. Out of the thirty-nine children tested, thirty-seven declared that they would not touch the balls with their hands. However, 54% of these children moved the balls with their hands and denied having done so. The rest of the children did not touch the balls with their hands, touched the balls but in the end left them in the bucket, or moved the balls in the bucket with their hands but returned them back into the bucket and left them there.

As predicted by the TDT-mind theory, there was a significant correlation between performance on the higher-level (moral motivation) component of the B&B task and the lower-level (inhibitory control) component of the same task, whereas all correlations between the higher-level component of the B&B task and independent IC tasks were not significant (Table 3). This supports our assumption that inhibitory control, along with other abilities, is a necessary condition for the development of the free moral action, but it cannot explain or predict the child' decision in the situation of free moral choice.

Table 3. Pearson correlations between scores on the two levels of the B&B task and the IC tasks

	RATCAR	DYNIGHT	CUPSAUC	STATUE	L2B&B
Level 1 B&B	**.150**	**.269**	**.090**	**.301**	**.870**
Sig. (2-tailed)	.363	.067	.585	.062	.001
Level 2 B&B	.129	.190	-.064	.139	1
Sig. (2-tailed)	.435	.246	.698	.398	.

It can also be expected that for children it would be easier to practically use their TDT-minds for deception than to understand the work of the TDT-mind if this work were presented to them as a narrative about deception. This expectation follows from the earlier reported data according to which children can demonstrate competence in a practical task, and yet cannot reason about the same task verbally. For instance, studies on children's metalinguistic awareness showed that young children spontaneously correct their speech errors, and yet do not possess the explicit knowledge necessary to answer questions on the rules of language correctly (Karmiloff-Smith, 1986).In order to examine this expectation, 5- and 8-year-old children were individually shown 4 pictures that presented a character performing the B&B task (Fig.2, top left), failed to do it in the right way (Fig.2, top right), moved the balls with her hands while being unobserved Fig.2, bottom left), and in the final episode was telling something to the adult (Fig.2, bottom right) (Honeyman, 2003). Participants were explained the rules of the game (like in the real B&B task) and then asked a series of questions in order to find out if they understood the nature of the TDT-mind.

For instance, when the child was shown Episode 4 (Fig.2, bottom right), he or she was asked "How does Mary think she moved the balls?" (understanding of the tape question), and "What is Mary telling the man about how she moved the balls? (understanding of the doubled tape question). Unlike 8-year-olds, 5-year-olds exhibited poor understanding of the "negation of wrongdoing"type of lying. For example, to the above questions most children answered that the character knew the true story (tape) but was telling the truth (uncorrected doubled tape), thus utterly missing the point that it made no sense for the character to move the balls with her hands and then acknowledge this to the adult. Provided that in earlier research more than 80% of 5-year-olds (and even 3-year-olds) deceived the experimenter on the B&B task, we concluded that in most children their capacity to create and use the "negation of wrongdoing" deceptive story in a practical B&B task is not accompanied with the understanding of the same type of lying when it is presented to the children in the shape of a narrative. These data also suggest that inferring the protagonist's deception about her own behavior (the "negation of wrongdoing"type of lying) from the protagonist's actions is a more difficult task than inferring the deception about external events from the protagonist's utterances which most 5-year-olds were able to do(Lee et.al., 2002; Wimmer&Perner, 1983).

A possible explanation of why it is more difficult to understand lying in the B& B situation than to lie in the real B&B situation is that the former requires more cognitive sophistication than the latter. Indeed, in order to deceive about their own actions in the practical situation, children only have to understand false beliefs of the first-order (i.e., that the person who is being deceived will have a false belief about the children's actions). In contrast, inferring the "negation of wrongdoing"lying from the protagonist's actions implies the grasp of second-order beliefs (i.e., beliefs about beliefs). Indeed, in order to infer that the girl in Figure 2 is lying, children have to understand that the girl believes that the adult she is lying to will have a false belief about her beliefs. This implies that a positive correlation should exist between understanding of the "negation of wrongdoing"deception and understanding of second-order beliefs.

In order to test these predictions, 5- and 6-year-old children were tested on the above "B&B understanding" task and on two second-order beliefs tasks ("ice-cream" and "birthday puppy") taken from Sullivan, Zaitchik and Tager-Flusberg's (1994) study (Ungen, 2004). As predicted, significant correlations were found between children's understanding of deception in the B&B task and their understanding of second-order beliefs.

Altogether, the above data suggest that children first start using their TDT-mind in order to lie about their own behavior, and only later do they become capable of reflecting upon their TDT-mind as the tool for deceiving others.

Figure 2. Drawings used in the understanding of the TDT-mind test.

THE DEVELOPMENTOF MORAL ACTION IN CHILDREN: A SUMMARY

According to the TDT-mind theory, the mind of an infant is a one-dimensional kind of mind. Although the cognitive world of a young infant appears to be rather complex (Bower, 1974; Onishi&Baillargeon, 2005), the infant's behavior remains "un-taped" in the infant's mind due to the lack of language.

The mind becomes the T-mind when the child develops the capacity to create simple narratives, which occurs approximately at the age of 2 – 2.5 years. Starting from this age, children become able to create simple stories that reflect, although imperfectly, the succession of events of their everyday lives. At the same time, children of this age acquire rudimentary notions of moral rules. Some of these notions come through the caregivers' demands, and others are absorbed from stories and other narratives with moral content (like "Snow White" and "Little Red Riding Hood"). At this stage, moral norms become personally significant for toddlers, as the children's emotional reactions to mishaps and transgressions show (Cole et al., 1992). Yet, due to the lack of an appropriate level of self-control and other cognitive prerequisites of the TDT-mind, children are not yet capable of using the knowledge about moral norms for creating T-duplicates.

The T-mind becomes the TDT-mind at some point between 3 and 4 years of age. At this age, children start enjoying a number of new cognitive achievements: a more powerful capacity for creating narratives, an increased level of self-control, and at 4 years – the capacity for representing views and false beliefs of other people. On the basis of these cognitive advances, children discover a new opportunity for themselves – to create a shield that could protect their self-interests if these interests conflict with the interests of individuals on whom the children depend (parents, caregivers). In this way, children become capable of and interested in creating special edited versions of their past behavior – the T-duplicates. From now on, the child's "story of life" splits into two parts: the T-story (a private image of himself or herself) and the T-duplicate story (an image created for the outer use). In those cases of the "conflict of interests" in which the child of 3-5 years of age thinks that he or she can transgress and still appear moral by presenting the adults with the T-duplicate story, the child would go for it. Through this, the child creates a positive moral image of him or herself but does not yet identify him or herself with this image. The split between the private and public images creates a special space in the child's mind – the space of free moral choice. In this space, the child is free to go for a moral option but chooses not to do so.

The next step in the development of the moral action comes at around 6 years of age, when there is a marked increase in the number of children who go for a moral option in the SFC situation. This can be a result of either cognitive categorization or emotional identification of the child with his or her positive moral self-image. Although the experimental data presented in this article are in favor of the "emotional identification scenario", the possibility of the "cognitive identification scenario" cannot be utterly overruled. For the "emotional identification" to work, it is necessary that the child's caregivers treat him or her in a trusting and loving way, respect the child's interests and his or her self-esteem, putting at the same time reasonable demands on the child's achievements. It is also important that the caregivers show their disapproval of deceptive behavior without being too directional and "pushing' in their disciplinary techniques and without making a special stress on surveillance and "unmasking" the child's deceptions. If the child is lucky enough to have this kind of treatment, then the trust and love to the caregiver is likely to be transferred to the child's positive moral self-image. The positive moral self-image that the child initially created in order to protect his or her self-interests, thus becomes the image with which the child identifies himself or herself. This results in the emergence of the first form of intrinsic moral motivation.

As far as it concerns the further development of intrinsic moral motivation in adolescents and adults, it is possible that children's identification with their positive moral self-images that initially occurs in the area of deception about their own behavior is later generalized to other areas of moral life, such as helping, sharing or donating. Together with the increasing cognitive mediation and appropriation, this process can gradually result in what in adults is called "moral identity" (Blasi, 1983, 1993; Colby & Damon, 1992), "moral integrity" (Batson & Thompson, 2001) and "moral agency" (Bandura, 1989, 1991). As a result of religious education, the authority of loved parents, which underlies the children's autonomous respect to moral norms, in adults can be replaced by the authority of God. Ever since the Kantian claim of the existence of the "categorical imperative", there has been an ongoing debate over why some people are able to act for the sake of "goodness itself". The popular answer to this difficult question by reference to evolutionary benefits of unselfish behavior (Dawkins, 1976, 2007; Stenger, 2007) has a plausible alternative in the hypothesis that, subconsciously, some people, including atheists, still believe that following "goodness itself" pleases God (Subbotsky, 2011).It is also possible that in some children's later life this identification with their positive moral self-image never occurs. These children can still grow into moral individuals, but in these individuals their compliance with moral rules needs support from external and internal incentives, such as empathy or surveillance; if these incentives are not strong enough, phenomena such as "moral hypocrisy", "corrupted integrity" (Batson & Thompson, 2001) or "moral disengagement" (Bandura, 1999, 2002) are likely to emerge. The evidence shows that, under certain conditions adolescents and adults violate moral rules (Bandura, 1999, 2002; Batson, Thompson, Sueferling, & Strongman, 1999; Batson & Thompson, 2001; Bersoff, 1999; Corey, 1937; Freeman &Aatov, 1960; Hartshorne & May, 1928/1930). It can be safely assumed therefore that the process of the individual's identification with his or her positive moral self-image is never complete.

In conclusion, I would like to emphasize that the TDT-mind theory illuminates only one line in the child's moral development – the emergence of the first form of intrinsic moral motivation and the role that the narrative function of language plays in it. Other lines of moral development go in parallel: the development of moral motivation as a function of social domains (Grusec&Goodnow, 1994; Nucci, 2001; Turiel, 1998, 2002), the cognitive elaboration of empathy (Hoffman, 1988), and the development of various motives of prosocial behavior (Eisenberg &Fabes, 1998). In other words, the moral development of a child is a complex process that can only be accounted for in a wide range of interdisciplinary studies. Nevertheless, I believe that the development of the free moral action can be viewed as a prototypical case for the development of intrinsic moral motivation in other domains of moral functioning. In perspective, the TDT-mind theory can account for the common developmental root of a range of phenomena (such as moral agency, internalization of moral values, moral integrity, moral identity, as well as moral hypocrisy, corrupted integrity, and moral disengagement) that currently are viewed and studied as separate entities.

REFERENCES

Arsenio, W., & Kramer, R. (1992). Victimizers and their victims: Children's conception of mixed emotional consequences of moral transgressions. *Child development*, 63, 915-927.

Bandura, A. (1969). Social-learning theory of identificatory processes. In D. A. Goslin (Ed.), *Handbook of socialization and research.* Chicago: Rand McNally.

Bandura, A. (1989). Human agency in social cognitive theory.*American Psychologist*, 44, 1175-1184.

Bandura, A. (1991). Social cognitive theory of moral thought and action. In W. M. Kurtines& J. L. Gewirtz (Eds.) *Handbook of moral behavior and Development*. Volume 1: Theory. (pp. 45-101). Hillsdale, New Jersey: Erlbaum.

Bandura, A. (1999). Moral disengagement in the perpetration of inhumanities.*Personality and Social Psychology Review*, 3, 193-209.

Bandura, A. (2002). Selective moral disengagement in the exercise of moral agency.*Journal of Moral Education,* 31, 101-119

Bandura, A., Barbarinelli, C., Caprara, G. V., &Pastorelli, C. (1996). Mechanism of moral disengagement in the exercise of moral agency. *Journal of Personality and Social Psychology*, 71, 364-374.

Bandura, A., & Walters, R. H. (1964). *Social learning and personality development.* New York, Toronto and London: Holt.

Barden, R. C., Zelco, F. A., Duncan, S. W., & Masters, J. C. (1980).Children's consensualknowledge about the experiential determinants of emotions.*Journal of Personality and Social Psychology,* 39, 968-976.

Batson, D. S. (1990). How social an animal? The human capacity for caring.*American Psychologist,* 45, 3, 336-346.

Batson, C. D., Kobrynowicz, D., Dinnerstein, J. L., Kampf, H.C., & Wilson, A. D. (1997). In a very different voice: Unmasking moral hypocrisy. *Journal of Personality and Social Psychology,* 72, 1335-1348.

Batson, C. D., Thompson, E. R., Sueferling, G., Whitney, H. & Strongman, J. A. (1999). MoralHypocrisy: Appearing moral to oneself without being so. *Journal of personality andSocial Psychology.*77(3) 525-537.

Batson, C. D., & Thompson (2001). Why don't moral people act morally? Motivational considerations. *Current Directions in Psychological Science*, 10, 54-57.

Batson, C. D., Tsang, J., & Thompson, E. R. (2000). *Weakness of will: Counting the cost of being moral.*Unpublished manuscript, University of Kansas, Lawrence.

Baumrind, D. (1967). Child care practices anteceding three patterns of preschool behavior. *Genetic Psychology Monographs,* 75, 43-88.

Belli, R. F., Schuman, H. & Jackson, B. (1997). Autobiographical misremembering: John Dean is not alone. *Applied Cognitive Psychology,* 11, 187-209.

Bem, S. L. (1981). Gender schema theory: A cognitive account of sex-typing. *Psychological Review,* 88, 354-364.

Bersoff, D. H. (1999). Explaining unethical behavior among people motivated to act prosocially. *Journal of Moral Education*, 28, 4, 414-428.

Blasi, A. (1983). Moral cognition and moral action: A theoretical perspective. *Developmental Review*, 3, 178-210.

Blasi, A. (1993). The development of identity: Some implications for moral functioning. In G.G.Noam&T.E.Wren (Eds.).*The moral self* (pp.99-122). Cambridge, MA: MIT Press.

Bower, T. G. R. (1974). *Development in infancy.* San Francisco: Freeman.

Braginsky, D. D. (1970). Machiavellianism and manipulative interpersonal behavior in children.*Journal of Experimental Social Psychology,* 6, 77-99.

Bruck, M., &Ceci, S. J. (1999).The suggestibility of children's memory.*Annual Review of Psychology*, 50, 419-439.

Bruner, J. (1974). *Beyond the information given*. London: George Allen &Unwin Ltd.

Bryan, J. H. (1971). Model effect and children's imitative altruism.*Child Development,* 42, 6, 2061-5.

Call, J., &Tomasello, M. (1999). A nonverbal false belief task: The performance of children and great apes. *Child Development*, 2, 381-395.

Carlson, S. M., & Moses, L. J. (2001). Individual differences in inhibitory control and children's theory of mind.*Child Development*, 72, 1032-1053.

Carlson, S. M., Moses, L.J. &Hix H. R. (1998). The role of inhibitory processes in youngchildren's difficulties with deception and false-belief.*Child Development.* 69 (3), 672-691.

Carrithers, M. (1991). Narrativity: Mindreading and making societies. In A. Whiten (Ed.), *Natural theories of mind: Evolution, development and simulation of everyday mindreading.* Oxford, England: Basil Blackwell, pp.317-331.

Ceci, S. J. (1994). Repeatedly thinking about a non-event: Source misattribution amongpreschoolers. *Consciousness & Cognition: An International Journal*, 3, 388-407.

Cheung H., Hsuan-Chin, C., Creed, N., Ng, L., Wang, S. P., & Mo, L. (2004). Relative roles of general and complementation language in theory-of-mind development: Evidence fromCantonese and English. *Child Development*, 75, 1155-1170.

Colby, A., & Damon, W. (1992). *Some do care: Contemporary lives of moral commitment.*New York, NY: Free Press.

Cole, P. M., Barrett, K.C., & Zahn-Waxler, C. (1992). Emotion display in two-year-olds during mishap.*Child Development,*63, 314-324.

Corey, S. M. (1937). Professed attitudes and actual behavior. *Journal of Educational Psychology,* 38, 271-280.

Damon, W. (1988). *The moral child.*New York: Free Press.

Dawkins, R. (1976). *The Selfish Gene.* Oxford: Oxford University Press.

Dawkins, R. (2006). *The God Delusion*. London: Transworld Publishers.

Dennett, D. C. (1979).*Brainstorms.*Hassocks, England: Harvester.

Diamond, A., & Taylor, C. (1996). Development of an aspect of executive control: Development of the abilities to remember what I said and to "Do as I say, not as I do." *Developmental Psychobiology,* 29, 315-334.

Dias, M., & Harris, P. L. (1988). The effect of make-believe play on deductive reasoning. *BritishJournal of Developmental Psychology,* 6, 207–221.

Dunn, J., Brown, J. R., &Maquire, M. (1995). The development of children's moral sensibility: Individual differences and emotion understanding. *Developmental Psychology,* 31, 649-659.

Dunne, J. & Munn, P. (1987). Development of justification in disputes with mothers and siblings.*Developmental Psychology,* 23, 791-798.

Edwards, C. P. (1980). The development of moral reasoning in cross-cultural perspective. In R. H. Munroe & B. B. Whiting (Eds.), *Handbook of cross-cultural human development*, New York: Garland Press.

Edwards, C. P. (1987). Culture and the construction of moral values.A comparative ethnography of moral encounters in two cultural settings. In J. Kagan& S. Lamb (Eds*.), The emergence of morality in young children,* Chicago: University of Chicago Press, pp.123-151.

Eisenberg, N., &Fabes, R. A. (1998). Prosocial development. In W. Damon, & N. Eisenberg (Eds.), *Handbook of child psychology, 5th edition, Volume 3: Social, emotional and personality development.* New York: John Wiley & Sons, Inc., pp.701-778.

Eisenberg, N., & Miller, P. A. (1987). The relation of empathy to prosocial and related behaviors.*Psychological Bulletin,*101, 1, 91-119.

Estes, D., Wellman, H. M., and Woolley, J. (1989). Children's understanding of mental phenomena.In H. Reese (Ed.), *Advances in child development and behavior* (pp.41-86). New York:Academic Press.

Emde, R. N., Biringen, Z., Clyman, R. B. & Oppenheim, D. (1991). The moral self of infancy:Affective core and procedural knowledge. *Developmental Review,*11, 251-270.

Freeman, L. C., &Aatov, T. (1960).Invalidity of indirect and direct measures of attitude towardscheating.*Journal of Personality,* 38, 443-447.

Freud, S. (1966). *Introductory lectures on psychoanalysis.* New York: LiverightPublishers Co.

Goodnow, J. J. (1992). Analyzing agreement between generations: Do parents' ideas have consequences for children's ideas? In I. E.Sigel, A. McGillicuddy-DeLisi, & J. J. Goodnow(Eds.), *Parental belief systems* (pp.293-317). Hillsdale, NJ: Erlbaum.

Gopnik, A., &Astington, J. W. (1988). Children's understanding of representational change and itsrelation to the understanding of false-belief and the appearance-reality distinction.*Child Development,*59, 26-37.

Grusek, J. E., &Goodnow, J. J. (1994). Impact of parental discipline methods on child's internalization of values: A reconceptualization of current points of view. *Developmental Psychology,*30, 1, 4-19.

Hala, S., Chandler, M., & Fritz, A. (1991). Fledgling theories of mind: Deception as a marker of 3year olds' understanding of false belief. *Child Development,* 62, 83-97.

Hardy, S. A., & Carlo, G. (2005). Identity as a source of moral motivation.*Human Development,* 48, 232-256.

Hare, B., Call, J. &Tomasello, M. (2006). Chimpanzees deceive a human competitor by hiding.*Cognition,* 101, 495-514.

Harris, P. (2000). *The work of the imagination.* Malden, Massachusetts: Blackwell.

Harris, M. B., &Samerott, G. (1975). The effects of aggressive and altruistic modeling on subsequent behavior.*Journal of Social Psychology,* 95, 2, 173-182.

Harrison, J., &Subbotsky, E. (2007) Preaching and practicing morality: The relationship between moral judgment, inhibitory control and children's moral action (*unpublished manuscript*). Psychology Department, Lancaster University, UK

Hartshorne, H., & May, M. A. (1928-1930). *Studies in the nature of character. Volume 1: Studies in deceit.* New York: Macmillan.

Higgins, E. T. (1981). The 'communicative game': Implications for social cognition and persuasion.In E. T. Higgins, C. P. Herman, & M. P. Zanna (Eds.), *Social Cognition: Vol.1. The Ontariosymposium* (pp.343-392). Hillsdale, NJ: Erlbaum.

Higgins, E.T. (1989). Continuities and discontinuities in self-regulatory and self-evaluative process: A developmental theory relating self and affect. *Journal of Personality,*57, 407-444.

Hoffman, M. L. (1988). Moral development. In M. N. Bornstein & M. E. Lamb (Eds.),*Developmental psychology: And advanced textbook.* New Jersey, Hillsdale: Erlbaum, pp. 497-541.

Honeyman, G. (2003). *Children's understanding of the intentional nature of moral transgression.*Dissertation of Bsc (hon) in psychology. Psychology Department, Lancaster University.

Hudson, J. A. (1990). The emergence of autobiographic memory in mother-child conversations.In R. Fivush& J. A. Hudson (Eds.), *Knowing and remembering in young children.* New York: Cambridge University Press.

Hughes, C. (1998). Executive function in preschoolers: Links with theory of mind and verbal ability.*British Journal of Developmental Psychology*, 16, 233-253.

Karmiloff-Smith, A. (1986). From meta-processes to conscious access: Evidence from children'smetalinguistic and repair data. *Cognition, 23*, 95-147.

Keller, M., Gummerum, M., Wang, X., & Lindsey, S. (2004). Understanding perspective and emotions in contract violation: Development of deontic and moral reasoning. *Child Development,* 74, 614-635.

Kochanska, G. (1991). Socialization and temperament in the development of guilt and conscience.*Child Development,* 62, 1379-1392.

Kochanska, G. (1994). Beyond cognition: Expanding the search for the early roots of internalizationand conscience. *Developmental Psychology,* 30, 20-22.

Kochanska, G., Kuczynski, L., &Radke-Yarrow, M. (1989). Correspondence between mothers' selfreported and observed child-rearing practices. *Child Development,*60, 56-63.

Kochanska, G., Murray, K., Jacques, T. Y., Koenig, A. L. &Vandergeest, K. A. (1996).Inhibitorycontrol in young children and its role in emerging internalisation.*Child Development*, 67, 490-507.

Kohlberg, L. (1966). A cognitive-developmental analysis of children's sex role concepts and attitudes. In E.E. Maccoby (Ed.), *The development of sex differences.* Stanford, CA:Stanford University Press.

Lagattuga, K. H. (2005). When you shouldn't do what you want to do: Young children'sunderstanding of desires, rules, and emotions. *Child Development*, 76, 713-733.

Lamb, M. E. (1982). What can 'research experts' tell parents about effective socialization? In E.Zigler, M. E. Lamb, & I. L. Child (Eds.), *Socialization and personality development.* Oxford:Oxford University Press.

Lee, K., Cameron, C. A., &Talwar, V. (2002).Fantoms and fabrications: Young children's detectionof implausible lies. *Child Development*, 2002, 73, 1688-1702.

Leontiev, A. N. (1977). Dejatel'nost'. Soznanije. Litchnost'. (Activity. Consciousness. Personality).Moscow: Politizdat.

Lewis, M., Stranger, C., & Sullivan, M. W. (1989).Deception in 3 year olds. DevelopmentalPsychology, 25, 439-443.

Lohmann, H., &Tomasello, M. (2003). The role of language in the development of false beliefunderstanding: A training study. *Child Development,* 74, 1130-1144.

Luria, A. R. (1971). *Mozgcheloveka in psikhicheskijeprotzessy (Human brain and psychologicalprocesses),* Vol.2, Moscow: Pedagogica Publ.

Luria, A. R., &Subbotsky, E. V. (1978). ZurFrühenOntogeneze der SteuerdenFunktion derSprache. In: *Die Psychologie des 20 Jahrhunderts,*Zürich: Kinder Verlag, pp.1032-1048.

Maccoby, E. E. (1980). *Social development. Psychological growth and the parent-child relationship.*New York: Harcourt Brace.

Maccoby, E. E., & Martin, J. A. (1983). Socialization in the context of the family: Parent-childinteraction. In P. H. Mussen (Series Ed.) & E. M. Hetherington (Vol.Ed.), *Handbook of child psychology: Vol.4. Socialization, personality, and social development* (4th ed., pp.1-101). New York: Wiley.

McAdams, D. P. (1993).*The stories we live by: Personal myths and the making of the self.* New York: NY: Guilford Press.

Miller, P. J., & Sperry, L. L. (1988). Early talk about the past: the origins of conversational stories ofpersonal experience. *Journal of Child Language,* 15, 292-315.

Milligan, K., Astington, J. W., &Dack, L. A. (2007). Language and theory of mind: Meta-analysisof the relation between language ability and false-belief understanding. *Child Development,*78, 622-646.

Nunner-Whinkler, G., Sodian, B. (1988).Children's understanding of moral emotions.*ChildDevelopment,* 59, 1323-1338.

Nunner-Winkler, G. (1998).The development of moral understanding and moral motivation.*International Journal of Educational research*, 27, 587-603.

Nelson, K. (Ed.)(1989). *Narratives from the crib.* Cambridge, MA: Harvard University Press.

Nelson, K. (1992). Emergence of autobiographical memory at age 4.*Human Development,*35, 172-177.

Nucci, L. (2001). *Education in the moral domain.* Cambridge, England:Cambridge University Press.

Nucci, L. (2004). Reflections on the moral self-construct. In D. K. Lapslay& D. Narvaez (Eds.),*Moral development, self and identity* (pp.111-132). Mahwah, NJ: Erlbaum.

Nucci, L. P., &Nucci, M. S. (1982). Children's responses to moral and social conventionaltransgression in free-play setting.*Child Development,* 53, 1337-1342.

Nucci, L., & Lee, J. (1993). Morality and personal autonomy.In G. G. Noam & T. E. Wren (Eds.).*The moral self* (pp.123-148). Cambridge, MA: MIT Press.

Onishi, K. H., &Baillargeon, R. (2005). Do 15-month-old infants understand false beliefs? *Science,* 308, 255-258.

Packer, M. J. (1991) Interpreting stories, interpreting lives: Narrative and action in moraldevelopment research. *New Directions in Child Development,* 34, 63-81.

Parker, S. T. (1990).Origins of comparative developmental evolutionary studies of primate mentalabilities. In S. T. Parker & K. R. Gibson (Eds.), *Language and intelligence in monkeys and apes:Comparative developmental perspectives* (pp. 3-64)*.* New York: Cambridge University Press.

Pasupathi, M., Mansour, E., & Brubaker, J. R. (2007). Developing a life story: Constructing relationsbetween self and experience in autobiographical narratives. *Human Development*, 50, 85-110.

Perner, J. (1992). Grasping the concept of representation: Its impact on 4-year-olds' theory of mindand beyond. *Human Development,* 35, 146-155.

Perner, J., Lang, B., &Kloo, D. (2002). Theory of mind and self-control: More than a commonproblem of inhibition. *Child Development*, 73, 752-767.

Perner, J., Leekam, S. R., & Wimmer, H. (1987). Three-year-olds' difficulty with false belief: The casefor a conceptual deficit. *British Journal of Developmental Psychology*, 5, 125-137.

Perry, D. G., & Perry, L. C. (1983). Social learning, causal attribution, and moral internalization. InJ. Bisanz, G. L. Bisanz, & R. Kail (Eds.), *Learning in children: Progress in cognitivedevelopment research* (pp.105-136). New York: Springer-Verlag.

Piaget, J. (1926/1959). *The language and thought of the child.*3rd edition. London: Routledge&Kegan Paul.

Piaget, J. (1932). *The moral judgment of the child.* London: Routledge&Kegan Paul.

Piaget, J. (1951/1962). *Play, dreams, and imitation in childhood.* London: Routledge&Kegan Paul.

Polak, A., & Harris P. L., (1999).Deception by young children following non-compliance.*Developmental Psychology*, 2, 561-568.

Pozar, L., &Subbotsky, E. (1984). Experimentál nyvyskumnie kotory chmoralny chcértosobnosti deti (An experimental study of some moral characteristics in children).*Zbornikkatedryspecialnej a liecebnejpedagogiky,*PadagogickeyFakulty, University Komenskego, X, pp.9-20.

Pratt, M. W., Hunsberger, B., Pancer, S. M., &Alisat, S. (2003). A longitudinal analysis of personal value socialization: Correlates of moral sel-ideal in adolescents. *Social Development,* 12, 563- 585.

Premack, D., & Woodruff, G. (1978). Does the chimpanzee have a theory of mind?*Behavior andBrain Sciences,*4, 515– 526.

Rosen, C. S., Schwebel, D. C., & Singer, J. L. (1977). Preschoolers' attribution of mental states in pretense.*Child development*, 68,6, 1133-1142.

Russell, J., Mauthner, N., Sharpe, S., &Tidswell, T. (1991).The "windows task" as a measure of strategic deception in preschoolers and autistic subjects.*British Journal of Developmental Psychology,* 9, 331-349.

Sears, R. R., Maccoby, E. E., & Levin, H. (1957). *Patterns of childrearing.* Evanston, IL: Row, Peterson.

Shultz, T. R., Wells, D., &Sarda, M. (1980). The development of the ability to distinguish intended actions from mistakes, reflexes, and passive movements.*British Journal of Social and Clinical Psychology,* 19, 301–310.

Smetana, J. G. (1981). Preschool children's conceptions of moral and social rules.*Child Development*, 52, 1333-1336.

Smith, A. (1966). *The theory of moral sentiments.* New York: Kelley.

Sodian, B. (1991).The development of deception in young children.*British Journal of Developmental Psychology,* 9, 137-188.

Sodian, B., Taylor, C., Harris, P. L., &Perner, J. (1991). Early deception and the child's theory of mind: False traits and genuine markers. *Child Development,* 62, 468-483.

Stenger, V. J. (2007). *God, the failed hypothesis: How science shows that God does not exist.* New York: Prometheus Books.

Stipek, D. J., Gralinski, J. H., & Kopp, C. B. (1990). Self-concept development in toddler years.*Developmental Psychology,* 26, 972-977.

Subbotsky, E. V. (1983). Shaping moral action in children. *Soviet Psychology,* 22, 1, 56-71.

Subbotsky, E. V. (1992). Moral socialization of the child in the Soviet Union from birth to age seven. In J. L. Roopnarine, & D. B. Carter (Eds.), *Parent-child socialization in diverse cultures. Annual Advances in Applied Developmental Psychology,* Vol.5, Norwood, NJ: Ablex Publishing Corporation, pp.89-105.

Subbotsky, E. V. (1993). *The birth of personality.The development of independent and moralbehavior in preschool children.* New York - London: Harvester Wheatsheaf.

Subbotsky, E. V. (1995). The development of pragmatic and non-pragmatic motivation.*HumanDevelopment*, 38, 217-134.

Subbotsky, E. (2011). The magic of today: Is the belief in magic fundamental to our minds?*Personality and Social Psychology Review* (under review)

Talwar, V., Lee, K., Bala, N., & Lindsay, R. C. L. (2002). Children's conceptual knowledge of lyingand its relation to their actual behaviors: Implications for court competence examinations. *Law and Human Behavior*, 26, 395-415.

Tappan, M. B. (2006). Moral functioning as mediated action.*Journal of Moral Education*, 35, 1-18.

Templeton, L. M. & Wilcox, S. A. (2000). A tale of two representations: The misinformation effectand children's developing theory of mind. *Child Development*, 71, 402-416.

Turiel, E. (1983). *The development of social knowledge: Morality and convention.* Cambridge,England: Cambridge University Press.

Turiel, E. (2002). *The culture of morality.* Cambridge, England: Cambridge University Press.

Turiel, E. (1998). The development of morality. In W. Damon, & N. Eisenberg (Eds.), *Handbook of child psychology, 5th edition, Volume 3: Social, emotional and personality development.* New York: John Wiley & Sons, Inc., pp.863-932.

Ungen, S. (2003). *Children's understanding of moral transgression in relation to second orderbeliefs.*MSc Dissertation. Psychology Department, Lancaster University.

Vygotsky, L. S. (1987). *Thinking and speech.* In: The Collected Works of L. S. Vygotsky, Vol.1,New York: Plenum.

Wagner, C., & Wheeler, L. (1969). Model, need, and cost effects in helping behavior. *Journal ofPersonality and Social Psychology,* 12, 2, 111-116.

Walker, L. J., &Hennig, K. H. (1999). Parenting style and the development of moral reasoning.*Journal of Moral Education,* 28, 3, 359-374.

Walker, L. J., & Taylor, J. H. (1991). Family interactions and the development of moral reasoning.*Child Development,* 62, 2, 64-283.

Wellman, H. M., Cross, D., & Watson, J. (2001). Meta-analysis of theory-of-mind development: Thetruth about false belief. *Child Development*, 72, 655–684.

Wellman, H. M., and Estes, D. (1986). Early understanding of mental entities: a re-examinationofchildhood realism. *Child Development,* 57, 910-923.

Wimmer, H., &Perner, J. (1983). Beliefs about beliefs: Representation and constraining function ofwrong beliefs in children's understanding of deception. *Cognition,* 13, 103-123.

Whiten, A., & Byrne, R. W. (1988). Tactical deception in primates.*Behavioral and Brain Sciences*, 11, 233-273.

In: Motivation, Consciousness and Self-Regulation
Editor: D. A. Leontiev, pp. 243-269

ISBN: 978-1-61324-795-2
© 2012 Nova Science Publishers, Inc.

Chapter 14

FLOW EXPERIENCE IN INTERNET-MEDIATED ENVIRONMENTS

Alexander E. Voiskounsky

Psychology Department, Lomonossov Moscow State University

ABSTRACT

This chapter presents a review of the current literature on theoretical and empirical studies of flow experience (or optimal experience) within Internet-mediated environments. The concept of flow as introduced by Csikszentmihalyi is described, the parameters characterizing optimal forms of experience are discussed, as well as data collection methods which are most often used to measure flow. The particular Internet-mediated environments connected with the studies of optimal experience and thoroughly reviewed in the chapter include online (1) shopping, (2) learning, (3) game playing, and (4) interaction. A brief overview of the projects in the field, initiated and performed by the author and his colleagues, is also presented.

Keywords: Positive psychology, flow experience, intrinsic motivation, experience sampling method, cyberpsychology, web applications, online learning, video game playing, virtual shopping, online interaction, mimetic flow

INTRODUCTION

Discussing the means and sources of human mental development, psychologists discovered the fundamental role of *mediation* based on the use of instruments: material tools, signs and semiotic systems. Since genuinely human forms of behavior are mediated by culture-related signs, investigation of mediated behavior is traditional for the Vygotskian approach. By the end of the 20th century, it became evident that computer facilities and networked computers were becoming crucial in mediating human behavior. More precisely, computers and web/Internet-related social services mediate our *interactions and relations, playing and recreation, learning and exploration, working behavior and shopping, negotiations and gambling,* etc.

Mediation is a universal principle. Taking this principle into account, one is free to investigate human behavior mediated by computers and the Internet in terms of particular psychological theories. This chapter deals with the theory of *flow* experience, which is a part of positive psychology. *Flow experience is discussed within the context of computers/Internet mediated behavior.* The chapter presents an extensive literature review, including the author's previous work in the field.

Flow experience is also called an *optimal* form of experience. The two terms will be used interchangeably. Some main ideas and concepts of the optimal experience are introduced in the chapter, followed by the methods which are specific for this field of study and practice. The optimal experience is connected with intrinsic motivation, which is distinguished from extrinsic motivation.

The chapter is then rubricized according to the major types of Internet-mediated behavior, such as marketing and shopping, learning and teaching, recreation (namely, online, computer and video gaming), and interaction; less elaborated dimensions, such as psychological rehabilitation by means of new immersive technologies, illicit penetrations into the cyberspace environments and computer security regulations, and usability testing to adapt web sources to target populations, will not be discussed. The selection of sections is largely dependent on the amount of the allocated publications in the field. The publications deal with the principles and methods of positive psychology, and refer to the growing research field of the Internet-related human behavior. Alongside with strictly psychological works, publications in a number of neighboring fields are collected and discussed, including such fields as computer science, human-computer interaction, marketing, media science, education (mostly, e-education), business and management, sociology, social work, law and information security, culture studies, medicine and rehabilitation, usability and design, etc.

Lastly, a brief description of the studies in which the author is affiliated is presented. The chapter characterizes various directions of studies and provides a perspective of academic and practical work related to the optimal experience and done within the environments dealing with the use of computers and the Internet.

OPTIMAL EXPERIENCE, ALSO KNOWN AS FLOW EXPERIENCE

The most promising perspectives within the positive psychology in our context seem to be the Self-Determination theory developed by Deci and Ryan (1985) and the optimal experience theory developed by Csikszentmihalyi (2000/1975; 1990, etc.). Both theories are intensely used in the field of computers/Internet-mediated behavior: scholars (e.g., Chang & Wang, 2008; Jung et al., 2009; Lu et al., 2009; Roca & Gagne, 2008; Rodriguez-Sanchez et al., 2008; Thatcher et al., 2008; Wang et al., 2008) make their best to take advantage and use well-established methods in the rapidly developing environments dealing with the Internet applications. In fact, the practice of usage of such methods in the studies related to human behavior (such as interaction, exploration, problem solving, gameplaying, shopping, etc.) in computers/Internet-related environments started shortly before the positive psychology acquired an institutional status (Ghani & Deshpande, 1994; Hoffman & Novak, 1996;

McKenna & Lee, 1995; Rotto, 1994; Trevino & Webster, 1992 – to name just a few early studies).

This chapter is devoted exclusively to the optimal experience theory, widely known also as flow experience. The history and some current studies related to flow experience in the computer/Internet environments was recently reviewed (Voiskounsky, 2008); the current chapter follows the earlier review with an updated presentation of the relevant studies and an extended emphasis on the methods of measurement of flow experience.

The feeling of finding oneself – mentally – in the midst of a torrent of liquid (especially running water) is not totally alien to psychological theory, taking into consideration such traditional terms as the stream of consciousness or the flight of ideas. Mihaly Csikszentmihalyi introduced the notion of flow after he interviewed hundreds of people, and each time when respondents showed a real devotion to any sort of work (mostly professional or hobby, and often hard and risky work), their reports contained a common element – a metaphoric description of a sensational experience for which Csikszentmihalyi (2000/1975) could have hardly chosen a name other than *flow*. Indeed, almost every respondent mentioned "flowing from one moment to the next, in which he is in control of his actions, and in which there is a little distinction between self and environment, between stimulus and response, or between past, present, and future" (Csikszentmihalyi, 2000/1975, p. 36). Flow (both habitual and rarely occuring) was reported to happen irrespectively of the type of the work: be it spiritual or mundane, creative or routine, unique or known to almost everyone, individual or team-work, rarely or regularly performed.

Csikszentmihalyi and his followers found that respondents never report of flow happening (and it is indeed a sort of an artistic happening!) when they feel relaxed: on the contrary, to experience flow a person needs to be genuinely and deeply involved in the preferred type of work. When the working environments include the use of information and communication technologies, work engagement is believed to be a "predisposition" for experiencing flow (Rodriguez-Sanchez et al., 2008). People report that they experience flow when they perform their work to the utmost and get a positive result: Csikszentmihalyi and other scholars call it a *peak* performance. The necessity to achieve success, even quite moderate, explains the need to acquire, prior to experiencing flow, some competence in performing the work, not necessarily very high. Respondents always describe flow as associated with *enjoyment*, this feeling being characteristic of flow; throughout the lifespan they tend to remember such happenings quite well, sometimes decades after the experience itself. Within the positive psychology paradigm, this sort of experience is called *optimal experience*.

Both the Self-Determination theory and the theory of optimal experience stand as theories of *intrinsic* motivation. Various types and models of intrinsic motivation have been described (Csikszentmihalyi, 2000/1975; Keller & Bless, 2008; Malone & Lepper, 1987; Ryan & Deci, 2000) and widely exploited while designing computer/Internet applications, as well as in the practice of self-regulation, management, education, etc. An intrinsically motivated *process* is self-rewarding, while its *results* might be (at least partly) irrelevant. In the optimal experience context, a process, or a sequence of intermediate goal-directed efforts performed in order to achieve the desired result is often reported to be much more pleasing and self-rewarding than the result itself, when and if it is gained (Csikszentmihalyi, 1990; 2000/1975). Optimal experience has been called (Csikszentmihalyi, 2000/1975) *autotelic* (from Greek: self + goal), it means that the goal of doing some work is just the act of doing it, regardless of whether external rewards will follow.

While an intrinsically motivated work may bring enjoyment, *exotelic* work and extrinsic motivation may bring *pleasure* which is, in the optimal experience context, a somewhat passive and relaxing feeling, compared to enjoyment. No doubt, the achievement of pleasure, and respectively the extrinsic motivation (in the form of monetary bonuses or increases of power) have always been an incomparably strong stimulus of diverse human activities. Positive psychology suggests, nevertheless, that neither intrinsic stimuli nor enjoyment should be underestimated; successive managers try to combine the two types of motivation to stimulate the employees. In adopting new online services, such as instant messaging, both types of motivation are shown to correlate tightly (Lu et al., 2009). While distinguishing, in the cyberspace context, (1) intrinsic hedonic *enjoyments* and (2) extrinsic utilitarian *interests,* Huang (2006) adds that both the enjoyments and the interests need to be presented in the future in the scholar and practical procedures. Intrinsic motivation is considered vital not only in such areas as education, psychology or management: for example, experts in robotics are making their best to work out formal models describing intrinsic motivation in order to use them in robotic studies (Oudeyer & Kaplan, 2007).

CHARACTERISTICS OF FLOW

As a result of theoretical and empirical analysis, Csikszentmihalyi (1990; 2000/1975 etc.) distinguished the following major characteristics of flow: *clear and distinct objectives; temporary loss of self-consciousness; distorted sense of time; actions merging with awareness; immediate feedback; high concentration on the task; high level of control over the task; balance (precise matching) between the available skills and the task challenges; full satisfaction while doing work which is worth doing for its own sake.* As it is stated in a review paper, "these factors may not be the only ones that contribute to flow, but Csikszentmihalyi identifies them as the most commonly exhibited ones" (Finneran & Zhang, 2005, p. 83).

This set of characteristics and their applicability in the cyberspace environments has been discussed more than once. Diverse views on the theme reviewed elsewhere (Voiskounsky, 2008) include the following statements: (1) these characteristics are not rigorous enough and need to be thoroughly operationalized, (2) empirical evidences confirm that at least some of these characteristics are in close agreement to what has been stated in several independent studies, and (3) additional characteristics have been suggested for consideration as specific for the cyberspace environments. We will not discuss points 1 and 2 since no important new material has been published on the theme, compared to what was presented earlier (Voiskounsky, 2008). As for point 3, the commonly suggested additional characteristics include (though are not restricted to) *presence*, or "mediated perception of an environment" (Hoffman & Novak, 1996, p. 61) – respondents often formulated it as a feeling of "being in a somewhat different place, possibly sharing this place with other people" (Chen et al, 1999; Hoffman & Novak, 1996; Novak & Hoffman, 1997; Pace, 2004; Skadberg & Kimmel, 2004; Seah & Cairns, 2008; Takatalo et al., 2008a) – and *interactivity* which distinguishes new responsive media from traditional media (Chang & Wang, 2008; Choi et al., 2007; Chen et al., 1999; Nakatsu et al., 2005; Novak & Hoffman, 1997; Novak et al., 2000; Polaine, 2005;

Wu & Chang, 2005). The whole variety of characteristics which were introduced in diverse studies, with antecedents and consequences of the flow experience, are presented elsewhere, often in a table form (Finneran & Zhang, 2005; Hoffman & Novak, 2009; Siekpe, 2005). As it has been recently formulated, "to date, the flow concept has undergone a first generation of understanding and testing" (Ilsever et al., 2007, p. 5).

While additional characteristics are being suggested, one would find few empirical studies in which all of the characteristics stated by Csikszentmihalyi have been selected and measured. As it has been noted, "not all of them are needed ... to give users the experience of Flow" (Chen, 2007, p. 32); in result, "no two researchers seem to measure flow in the same way" (Hoffman & Novak, 2009, p. 8). Indeed, a particular set of characteristics indicating flow in Internet-mediated environments seems to be problem-, instruction- and competence-specific, and are very likely dependent on particular interfaces and software applications; thus it has been suggested to distinguish diverse *"flow dialects"*, or "possibly numerous sets of flow characteristics" (Voiskounsky, 2008, p. 79). That means that one should differentiate particular versions of flow experience. In this context, Zwick and Dholakia (2007) point out that "the current model of flow needs to be revised to account for variations in the intensity with which consumers experience flow" (p. 33), and conclude that from a marketing perspective, "the level of flow differs depending on the activity in which the consumer is engaged" (ibid.). At the same time, it is important to note that "measuring only a few dimensions... may be misleading because we may miss some important ingredient" (Hektner et al., 2007, p. 96).

Whatever "flow dialect" is accepted in any particular project, just one of Csikszentmihalyi's findings has been intensely and universally exploited – namely, that experiencing flow means working at the utmost or, in a more specific terminology, it means that the available *skills* balance the complexity of goals, i.e. the chosen *task challenges*, provided that both the challenges and the tasks are not simplistic but rather high. Observations and experiments show that flow is placed at the cutting edge of one's skills, and it is a moving target: almost any increase in the acquired skills impels, in order to save the precise matching, to an appropriate extension of the challenges, and reciprocally, a choice of the greater challenges demands an update of the available skills.

The balance of task challenges and skills, provided that scores for the both are high enough (for details see: Hektner et al., 2007, pp. 93-96), is universally accepted as a major characteristic and an antecedent of flow (Hoffman & Novak, 1996; Pearce & Howard, 2004). The opposing views are not numerous. Some authors, for example, failed to find the skills/challenges ratio as a significant parameter of flow experience (Skadberg & Kimmel, 2004), while still others reported that participants may get confused when asked to determine their level of the skills and/or the task challenges (Chen et al., 1999; Shin, 2006) or remind them that activities such as online shopping do not demand highly-developed skills (Zwick & Dholakia, 2007). A recently published book contains a warning, saying that "a balance of high challenge and high skill defines the *conditions* where optimal experience is most likely to occur, but does not necessarily describe the *experience* of flow. Experientially, flow is characterized not only by a balance of challenges and skills but also by deep concentration, loss of self-consciousness, and deep engagement. ... So one must decide whether the research question would be better addressed using indicators of the conditions for flow or the experience of flow" (Hektner et al., 2007, p. 46). This warning has to be considered within the research community; at the same time, creation and measurement of conditions for optimal forms of experience is an invaluable practice, since optimal experience presents a sound basis for personal growth.

Scholars have made laborious efforts, including expeditions to faraway locations, trying to find out whether parameters of flow experience may turn out to be culture dependent; comparative studies are traditional in the field (Moneta, 2004; Pedrotti et al., 2009; Seligman & Csikszentmihalyi, 2000). Cross-cultural studies in Internet-mediated environments are definitely under-represented, as it is stated elsewhere (Voiskounsky, 2007a; Voiskounsky, 2008). It would be incorrect to say that there are no studies done within populations other than speakers of English (the majority of studies in the field were done in Australia, Canada, Great Britain, New Zealand, and the USA – too numerous to cite) or Chinese: additionally to the studies held in Taiwan (e.g., Chang & Wang, 2008; Chiou & Wan, 2006; Chou & Ting, 2003; Fu et al., 2009; Hsu & Lu, 2004; Liao, 2006; Wan & Chiou, 2006; Wan & Chiou, 2007; Wu & Chang, 2005), some studies are now being held in the mainland China (Lu et al., 2009) and in Singapore (Wang et al., 2008). Geographical variety can be presented as follows: the studies have been carried out within such populations as Korean online gamers (Choi & Kim, 2004; Kim et al., 2005; Lee & Kwon, 2005) and learners (Shin, 2006); German-speaking video gamers (Schultheiss, 2007) and learners (Konradt & Sulz, 2001; Konradt et al., 2003; Tzanetakis & Vitouch, 2001; Vollmeyer & Rheinberg, 2006); Russian online gamers (Voiskounsky et al., 2004; Voiskounsky et al., 2005) and hackers (Voiskounsky & Smyslova, 2003a, 2003b); Scandinavian information technologies users – speakers of Swedish (Jegers, 2006; Montgomery at al., 2004; Nacke & Lindley, 2008; Sharafi et al., 2006), Finnish (Pilke, 2004; Takatalo et al., 2008a; Takatalo et al., 2008b), Norwegian (Heidman & Sharafi, 2004), and Danish (Andersen & Witfelt, 2005); Israeli online chatters (Shoham, 2004); Internet users from the South Africa (Thatcher et al., 2008); Brasilian gamers (Fernandez, 2007) and journalists making use of online services (Manssour, 2003); Turkish children playing social games (Inal & Cagiltay, 2007); Spanish college students and civil employees using information technologies (Rodriguez-Sanchez et al. 2008; Sicilia & Ruiz, 2007); Swiss online gamers (Weibel et al., 2007). Although the abovementioned studies were carried out in different countries, none of them deal with a comparative study: as it was stated (Voiskounsky, 2007a; Voiskounsky, 2008), cross-cultural studies of optimal experience in Internet-mediated environments is a vacant and promising research area.

DATA COLLECTION METHODS

On one hand, the data collecting methods measuring flow experience in Internet-mediated environments are borrowed from the methods practiced outside the field and include surveys (both paper and pencil, and online), interviews and semi-structured interviews, open-ended and closed questionnaires, focus groups and group discussions (based for example on narratives describing particular flow-related cases), estimations of the frequency of occurrence of selected parameters which are close to the optimal forms of experience (Chen, 2006; Chen et al, 1999; Davis & Wong, 2007; Li & Browne, 2006; Manssour, 2003; Novak et al., 2000; Pace, 2004; Pearce et al., 2005; Pilke, 2004; Rettie, 2001; Shoham, 2004; Wang et al., 2008). On the other hand, a more specific method, namely the Experience Sampling Method, is widely used and is described in this section. The data collecting methods are also discussed in several recent publications (Finneran & Zhang, 2005; Hektner et al., 2007; Voiskounsky, 2008).

A frequently employed method of measuring flow experience both in and outside of the cyberspace is *surveying*. Surveys are administered within particular populations of computers/web users: junior/high-school/college students, web-shoppers, video/computer/online gamers, web-sites visitors, etc. Surveying is a *retrospective* method: a respondent is asked questions concerning his or her recently achieved or habitual experience, for example, on the application of a new software product, on problems with an online search, or on a visit to a specific web-site. In retrospective questioning, some important details stay non-reflected: as Brosnan and Goodison (*date not specified*) mention, "reports of flow elements ... relate to the whole session and this loses details of how moments of flow might relate to moments of learning and details of design" (p. 15).

Beginning with the earliest studies and up to now, scholars intensely employ self-report scales to measure flow (Chen et al., 1999; Ghani & Deshpande, 1994; Novak et al., 2000; Trevino & Webster, 1992), "so as to capture the subjective state while minimizing interference" (Huang, 2006, p. 393). Huang distinguishes two self-report variations: the first consists of presenting certain brief descriptions of flow events, while respondents "provide personal examples of flow events and rate these events", or "rate the overall flow experienced while using the Web" (ibid.); the second variation measures the flow components by the use of Likert-type statements or bipolar semantic differential scales. The two variations follow the difference between a qualitative and a quantitative study. While the latter type of studies is more numerous, an example of a qualitative study is described by Chen and his colleagues (1999): the respondents (pre-selected and/or self-selected) had to recognize first whether they have ever had flow-like experiences (a description taken from the writings of Csikszentmihalyi and presented to them in brief excerpts) while using Web applications; second, those respondents who did acknowledge such experiences provided descriptions of "the contextual and situational conditions that existed when they encountered these experiences in their Web activities" (Chen et al., 1999, p. 595); lastly, content analysis of the descriptions was done resulting in the selection of the likely factors and activities favoring flow events, possible casual relationships, etc. In building up a grounded theory of the web-related flow experiences on a qualitative basis, Pace (2004) started with the semi-structured in-depth interviews and then turned to theoretical sampling, aimed "to maximize opportunities for exploring emerging concepts" (p. 334), namely: performed procedures of open, theoretical, and selective coding, of sorting data, and finally, of writing the grounded theory and of its verification.

Other than verbal measures of flow are rare; for example, Nacke and Lindley (2008) report an attempt to work out a behavioral measure: while playing a shooter videogame, participants have to move through three virtual "rooms": to pass these rooms means to take first a low-level, then a middle-level and finally the highest-level task challenge; thus, the challenges evidently change and can be graduated while the gamer's competence (skill level) presumably does not change much during the study.

Prior and parallel to measuring flow, academics and practice-oriented scholars usually administer psychological tests and marketing questionnaires, register behavioral parameters and the participants' effectiveness in performing the required activity. A trend towards a technology-rich research design includes, for example, eye-tracking which is believed to identify immersion, which is close to presence, the latter has been added to the flow characteristics as an indicator saying that the "awareness of the frustrations of everyday life is removed," and that "the sense of the duration of time is altered" (Kearney & Pivec, 2007). The immersion as a component of presence has been investigated by Takatalo and his colleagues (2008a). In this technology-rich work, the parameters of flow were studied in a 3D CAVE-type immersive environment: the participants' task was to search and identify unusual objects while wandering within a virtual house and perceiving computer-generated visual, acoustic and haptic signals. As Hoffman and Novak (2009) confess, "the rapid explosion of Web-based virtual worlds (e.g. Second Life, There.com, Active Worlds, The Sims Online) presents an exciting and accessible fertile environment for the study of flow" (p. 17).

Apart from traditional data collecting methods, like surveys or interviews, and specific methods, like the abovementioned virtual reality systems usage, there is an intensely applied method inherently connected with the flow experience analysis. It is the *Experience Sampling Method* (ESM) which proved to be a highly accurate method of collecting data in naturalistic environments and widely used both within and outside the positive psychology studies (Csikszentmihalyi & Larson, 1987; Gaggioli, 2005; Gaggioli et al., 2003; Hektner et al., 2007). The ESM procedure involves participants' agreement or will (1) to fill in an experience sampling sheet provided by a scholar, and (2) to perform it continuously many times a day, during weeks or sometimes months. The idea is that while filling in such a sheet, a participant self-reports the characteristics of his or her actual experience; particular self-reports are believed to be less biased (compared to one-time question-answering) due to a tendency to present socially desirable views. As a rule, the particular booklet (usually it is the same sheet each time, at least within the particular study, although there may be diverse research plans) corresponds to the goals of a specific study and combines both open-ended and scaled questions. The moments to complete it throughout a day are selected on a random basis; thus, the participants have to be informed (signaled) of the recurrent moment to complete the sheet. Here is where the technologies enter the ESM procedure.

Numerous reports and recommendations are available (Barrett & Barrett, 2001; Conner Christensen et al., 2003; Hektner et al., 2007) about the use of beeping pagers, pre-programmed wristwatches, SMS or e-mail messages, palmtop computers and PDAs, mobile phones, as well as software packages (see for example an open source program for a Palm at: http://www.experience-sampling.org/). Three types of signaling schedules are differentiated (Barrett & Barrett, 2001, p. 178; Hektner et al., 2007, p. 40): *interval-contingent sampling* (regular, e.g. hourly intervals for self-reporting the current activities), *event-contingent sampling* (self-reports need to be completed following a specific event; since the schedule of events in interest is hardly predictable, it has been found reasonable to give regular signals just to remind participants of their responsibilities), and *signal-contingent sampling*, which is the most typical and involves signaling at random moments over the time of the study (most often, several days or weeks). After collecting hundreds of reports, the scholars restore realistic itinerary and timing of various day-long activities employed by a certain group of participants.

Unlike political, clerical, industrial and financial leaders or world-known celebrities whose secretaries schedule the bosses' daily activities, ordinary people are rarely aware of the precise timing of their activities in the day/week/month/year span. This is most often true even for those who write diaries, including online blogs: the content is, as a rule, more significant than time management – registration of time given to diverse sorts of daily activities. Exceptions are unique; such an exception was a Russian biologist Alexander

Lubischew (1890-1972). As an entomologist and expert in biological systematics, theory of evolution, history of science and mathematical statistics, he had broad interests including science, philosophy, classical and modern fiction. This universal scholar spent his whole life in a Russian province, he was not eligible to lecture at the best universities since he did not share vulgar materialist dogmas dealing, for example, with the evolution of species; obviously not being able to criticize the Darwinian theory or the Marxist views on the history of science openly, he used to describe his ideas in personal letters to several correspondents; at times these letters acquired public interest within an "invisible college" of competent colleagues.

Lubischew invented and decades-long kept following a unique system of *time management*: every day during all his adult life he registered the time span devoted to diverse activities, such as the main scientific work, organizational work, attendance of professional committees and meetings, interactions with relatives and colleagues, reading (and preparing concise abstracts, often with critical reviews) scientific books and papers in Russian and in foreign languages, reading fiction, watching movies and performances, writing letters, length of business travels and time on public transport, etc. The accuracy of registration was 5 to 10 minutes; Lubischew made for himself monthly and yearly reports on time management, he was able to plan time to be given in the next year (and several years running, too) to all types of his work, and quite often the accuracy of planning his activities was surprisingly good with a variance which did not exceed one per cent.

Lubischew believed that time given to time management was not a waste time: this system was his personal support in adjusting his life activities and planning productive creative work. In fact, he was both creative and productive – although his list of publications contains about 70 items, his archive exceeds 12 thousand typewritten pages. His life and his time management system was described in a biography book by a renowned novelist Daniil Granin; to the best of our knowledge, the book written in Russian was never translated into other languages.

Useful or not, time management is not widely practiced, and the Experience Sampling Method is adapted to learn the participants' diverse daytime activities, including those which are likely to provide conditions for experiencing flow. The use of stand-alone computers is restricted to the time during which the respondents work with computers, apart from other activities; the use of mobile technologies for signaling and registering self-reports bring minor problems such as theft or discharge of batteries (Hektner et al., 2007). But in cases when the study plan is limited to human experiences in the Internet-mediated environments, the ESM is well-adapted for computers and/or online applications. Starting to survey online participants in the 1990s (Chen et al., 1999), Chen (2006) reports that he has constructed a web version to substitute the random-time beeper and the ESM sheet to fill in by pop-ups at the monitor screen which activate the questionnaire items. After the questionnaire is filled in, its content is forwarded to the researcher's remote database: in result, "the on-line ESM tool proved to be reliable and valid" (Chen, 2006, p. 232). This methodology is believed to foster investigations of the optimal experience in cyberspace. O'Broin and Clarke (2006) report developing a technology in which students click the special icon (and fill in a form that appears on the monitor) each time they believe "the conditions of flow have changed"; it is expected that an ESM-like computerized method helps the students provide replies to the questions while the learning conditions are still fresh in their mind.

FLOW EXPERIENCE STUDIES CORRESPONDING TO THE PARTICULAR TYPES OF THE INTERNET-MEDIATED ENVIRONMENTS

An ad hoc classification of content-dependent types of environments of the flow experience has been suggested elsewhere (Voiskounsky, 2008). The particular studies are further discussed in the current chapter following the abovementioned classification scheme, with several exceptions. The exceptions refer to non-elaborated types of environments within the optimal experience context: (1) the illicit behavior in the virtual environments, (2) usability evaluation, referring to design of both web-sites and applied software items, including, for example, online games, and (2) the applications of the flow methodology in the studies and practice of psychological rehabilitation. Since only few new papers in the abovementioned fields have been published, these dimensions will not be discussed in the current chapter.

VIRTUAL SHOPPING

The number of studies related to online shopping, i.e. consumer and marketing dimensions of the optimal experience theory and practice, is growing parallel to the advance of online trade and the increase of e-stores. Numerous empirical studies show that unlike a traditional offline consumer, an e-shop visitor is, at the same time, a computer/Internet user, and thus his or her consuming behavior is partly determined by the shopper-friendly design of the shopping website: "The more confident and comfortable consumers feel with the Web site, the more likely it is that they will enjoy it" (Koufaris, 2002, p. 218). The consumer's skills in the use of computers and in carrying out an explorative search throughout the Web is a no less important parameter, as well as his or her readiness to thoroughly explore various online shops to get a better price and/or a better-quality product. Since the skills are believed to be a meaningful parameter, and the existence of task challenges is inherent of web consumption, the idea of measuring the optimal experience parameters seems promising (Hoffman & Novak, 1996).

Purchases in the e-shops can be subdivided into planned and unplanned (i.e. impulsive), or goal-directed and experiential (Novak et al., 2003). An important e-marketing parameter can be associated with unplanned purchases, namely with the likeability of returns to the particular e-store or trading e-portal. There is a stable tendency to combine flow experience with e-loyalty, or increased likelihood of a return to an e-shop or to a marketing website (Ilsever et al., 2007; Luna et al, 2003; Smith & Sivakumar, 2004).

Trying to acquire marketing advantages, both scholars and practitioners are making continuous efforts aimed at finding a place for flow experience in the overall consumption behavior. The major idea is to find particular interdependencies between (1) flow characteristics, (2) traditional behavioral and marketing parameters, and (3) indicators of the web-shop visitors' skills in order to develop a hierarchy of the first-order and the higher-order dimensions in the field (Hoffman & Novak, 1996; Huang, 2006; Korzaan, 2003; Koufaris, 2002; Siekpe, 2005; Zwick & Dholakia, 2007).

In an influential study Novak, Hoffman and Duhachek (2003) found that, contrary to what was expected, flow experience did not regulate either experiential purchases or intentions to return a purchase at a particular web-store. As Rettie (2001) formulates it, "flow is more likely to occur when they have a specific task than when they are just surfing for fun" (p. 109). Koufaris (2002) was not able to connect flow experience with unplanned buys; besides, he states that we should collect data on the first-time customers who might be able to visit the particular marketing website and make a planned purchase: "A future study that captures actual new customers would be able to better explain the factors behind customer acquisition and planned purchasing" (p. 218). Following Koufaris, Korzaan (2003) reported of a positive impact of flow experience on e-shopping attitudes and purchase intentions; such an impact has also been partly confirmed in the study of Luna and his colleagues (2003). Fairly useful recommendations have been carried out, aimed at lessening negative influences of the existing e-shops upon the visitors and customers, and at perfecting the dynamic design and the usability of the would-be e-marketing sites (Huang, 2006; Pace, 2004; Rettie, 2001; Siekpe, 2005; Wan et al., 2008). As Hoffman and Novak (2009) formulate, "those who experience flow, seek, at a minimum, ease of use in Web shopping. It may be the case that for some consumers, under some conditions, a compelling online experience may offer an alternative to seeking the lowest price" (p. 21).

Online consuming is not restricted to visits to e-shops; more and more often it includes an explorative search over the Web – and possibly the experience of flow (Mathwick & Rigdon, 2004). Explorative searches can be further subdivided into utilitarian (e.g. "During my shopping trip I tried to find the shortest and most rapid way to buy the CD player") and hedonic (e.g. "This online shopping trip was truly a joy") search style, and flow has been shown to influence the latter but not the former (Sénécal et al., 2002). Marketers should be aware that flow experience influences an interest to an e-shop and an intention to visit it repeatedly, as well as fosters a through-the-site navigation, though parameters of flow do not necessarily influence an interest to e-shop products (Sicilia & Ruiz, 2007). In a qualitative study, Zwick and Dholakia (2007) start with a puzzle question, noting that "it is not clear how a market environment may be capable of inducing flow in loyal customers" (p. 28) and go on insisting that flow experience should not be taken as a "yes/no" dichotomy – instead, these authors define flow states as "the experiential result of transitioning between behavioral modes" (p. 32), and finally, present a model with levels of flow classified by a changing intensity of the optimal experience; besides, they are developing a model of "repeated flow" which depends mostly on web-site characteristics and in a lesser extent on the traits of particular consumers.

To conclude, the particular dimension of the optimal experience related to rather obscure specified characteristics of the specific websites which were to be visited and revisited by participants in the empirical studies, is worth being investigated and discussed. Certainly, flow cannot be taken as the only psychological or even the only motivational parameter influencing web navigation and choice of specific web-sites as appropriate or acquiring negative attitudes toward "inappropriate" web-sites. Quite a number of website visitors' psychological parameters are being studied parallel to flow, including, for example, personality characteristics such as intro/extraversion, need for cognition, neuroticism, locus of control (Amichai-Hamburger, 2005; Amichai-Hamburger et al., 2007) or parameters connected with culture specifics and cognitive style (Dong & Lee, 2008; Luna et al., 2002). In the area of the flow-related studies, some additional recommendations for web designers are given, such as the application of light colors and music to influence visitors' positive moods, or making use of different rhetoric constructions for visitors with low and high scores of the "need for cognition" (Li & Browne, 2006).

In the prognostic section of their paper, Hoffman and Novak (2009) make an attempt to draw the scholars' attention to the rapidly coming new sources of the economic activity in Internet-mediated environments. They find perspectives in virtual worlds such as Second Life with its social contexts (including pets and avatars, as well as numerous people, who are often eager to interact), realistic 3D environments, sense of place, and possibly haptic gadgets, since "the construct of the need for touch (…) would be expected to be an important antecedent of flow in virtual worlds" (Hoffman & Novak, 2009, p. 16). The role of matching skills and task challenges will be increasing in the new coming environments: the same authors predict that "skill acquisition and the seeking out of new challenges is a dynamic process which evolves over long periods of time in developing mastery in a virtual world, and the feedback role of flow in motivating the consumer to develop greater skills and seek greater challenges is a particularly important topic of study" (p. 18). In a prognostic context, Gaggioli (2005) shows how optimal experience can be realized in the would-be responsive embedded environments qualified as ambient intelligence. Flow experience characterizing the Second Life visitors has been recently studied by Faiola and Smyslova (2009).

VIRTUAL LEARNING

The educational applications of the optimal experience methodology, both in the traditional and in the Internet-related environments, are intensely investigated. The web learning aspects related to the flow experience were mentioned and discussed already in the early 1990s (Webster et al., 1993). Referring to this study, Hoffman and Novak (1996) mention that "learning is a reasonable outcome of the flow state" (p. 64). Since that, the flow-related e-learning dispositions and outcomes have been studied in a number of works (Chan & Ahem, 1999; Choi et al., 2007; Davis & Wong, 2008; Konradt & Sulz, 2001; Konradt et al., 2003; Pearce et al., 2005; Shin, 2006). Generally speaking, flow experience is a significant predictor of the learners' satisfaction with the teaching courses (Finneran & Zhang, 2003; Shin, 2006). The process of learning has been found to be effective under the following conditions: "As expected, flow experience had a positive impact on people's learning. People experiencing flow while browsing the Web site were more likely to respond positively about their increased knowledge about the place presented" (Skadberg & Kimmel, 2004, p. 415). Moreover, Skadberg and Kimmel add that "flow experience was found to be the largest contributor to increased learning" (p. 418).

It should be noted, though, that the increase of knowledge may partly depend on the students' prior knowledge in the field (Konradt & Sulz, 2001; Konradt et al., 2003). The scholars make their best to present "significant interdependent relationships" between the parameters of e-learning, flow experience, and students' attitudes towards e-learning; the learning outcomes are considered to be fruitful with flow experience, the latter corresponds with the attitudes towards e-learning and takes the central position in the model of the e-learning process that has been worked out (Choi et al., 2007).

Distance education is a promising perspective for all of those engaged in the practice of teaching, and a new challenge for scholars engaged in the organization of the distant learners' optimal forms of experience. New teaching technologies should be capable of "gradually increasing the challenges to promote students to increase their levels of skills to cope" (Brosnan & Goodison, *date not specified*), which is not an easy task. Liao (2006) reports of a study in which a possible impact of the types of the interactions available in the distance learning paradigm on the flow experience was measured. Of the three interaction types investigated (i.e., learner-learner, learner-instructor and learner-interface), the former one did not relate significantly to flow, while the latter two types turned out to be related to flow. O'Broin and Clarke (2006) report of an adaptive utility: they "developed a mobile teaching assistant tool that helps plan learning sessions for individual students: when one or more conditions of flow are absent, the tool can suggest modifications to the session so that the conditions may once again be present." More and more sophisticated applications of the optimal experience theory in the educational practice of the hypermedia use can be expected to follow (Konradt & Sulz, 2001; Konradt et al., 2003).

Any positive effects of the flow experience upon a learner's task, Pearce and Howard (2004) state, should be differentiated from the possibly interfering effects which may originate in the use of artifacts related to virtual environments: these artifacts (such as web pages, simulation models, etc.) start to compete for a learner's attention. Davis and Wong (2008) report that some specific flow-related parameters, such as time distortion and presence, are negatively correlated to effective online learning, probably because students' "minds become so distracted and absorbed that they cannot concentrate on their primary goal, which is learning" (p. 118-119). Chan and Ahem (1999) warn that the selection of unnecessarily complex ways to present the content items may be distracting. Moreover, it is recommended to avoid rigid procedures in tutoring and instead provide the learners with the maximum of autonomy and flexibility, including, for example, free navigation within the educational software (Konradt et al., 2003).

The "virtual learning" dimension is on the rise, irrespectively of the numerous tough problems inherent for this area of study. The reason is simple enough: the scholars believe that "without any effort to induce learners' flow experience, it will be difficult to achieve high effectiveness in e-learning" (Choi et al., 2007, p. 238).

COMPUTER/VIDEO/ONLINE GAME PLAYING

Playing various computer games is an emblematic characteristic of the first decade (and very likely, the coming decades, too) of this century and the last decades of the previous century. Total gaming symbolizes a new *generation gap*, since the new generations, unlike the earlier generations, for example, *baby boomers* in the USA, have grown up more or less immersed in computer/video/online games; moreover, the growing numbers of adults go on playing familiar and/or newly-produced games. Thus, gamers as well as former gamers have a lot in common as a group, and this fact seems to be sufficient to change the would-be traditions in doing business, in arranging private matters, probably in politics and certainly in decision-making (Beck & Wade, 2004). No wonder, the fast growing body of the optimal experience studies is devoted to gaming. For example, Mathwick and Rigdon (2004) report that in experiencing flow, the students in the process of doing explorative work (e.g., search of information, which is a part of web-consuming behavior) may get so fully immersed in the online activity that the latter is being transformed into a sort of a play.

The playing sessions, related to all sorts of computer, video and online games, including the MMORPGs (Massively Multi-player Online Role-Playing Games), are a popular area of flow related investigations (Chen, 2007; Chen & Park, 2005; Chiou & Wan, 2006; Choi & Kim, 2004; Chou & Ting, 2003; Hsu & Lu, 2004; Kim et al., 2005; Jegers, 2006; McKenna & Lee, 1995; Sweetser & Wyeth, 2005; Voiskounsky et al, 2005; Wan & Chiou, 2006; Wang et al., 2008). Such parameters as the game design, including well-organized feedback, and the appropriateness of the gamers' goals were shown to be important for the occurrence of flow (Choi & Kim, 2004). Characteristics of flow have been found effectively realized in a gaming environment for computer learning courses adapted for the students of a primary and secondary school (Andersen & Witfelt, 2005).

At the same time, it was stated that gamers, at least inexperienced ones, although capable of experiencing flow, may not be sure if their skills fit the task demands. This is evident in case the plan of the study provides an automatic adjustment of the task complexity to the available skills (Keller & Bless, 2008) – thus adaptive computer games might be the most welcomed and profitable. Moreover, empirical efforts aimed at developing a procedure of inducing flow are based on the use of video games such as Tetris (Moller et al., 2010).

Flow has been found to be one of the most reliable predictors of the players' acceptance of a new online game (Hsu & Lu, 2004); moreover, Chen (2007) suggests an adaptive strategy of a game design, which would let diverse players experience flow in their own personal way and thus, let them enjoy the game. A kind of an enjoyment related to a flow experience is supposed to be the major factor explaining the fact that certain text-only (i.e., lacking graphics) multi-player role-playing games (namely, MUDs, or Multi-User Dungeons) remain attractive for the numerous players over several decades (McKenna & Lee, 1995; Voiskounsky et al., 2008). This conclusion is proved to be true, taken samples of Russian (Voiskounsky et al., 2004; Voiskounsky et al., 2005), French (Voiskounsky et al., 2006a; Voiskounsky et al., 2006b), American (Faiola & Voiskounsky, 2007) and Chinese (Voiskounsky et al., 2008) gamers. That means, flow experience is universally attractive and may be considered among the major explanatory principles of the lasting popularity of certain games. For example, the earlier games are poorer in design but may turn out to be preferred thanks to their structure or narrative. Choi and Kim (2004) come to a close conclusion: they report that gamers continue playing online games due to the effects of optimal experience.

Gackenbach (2008) reports of correlations between flow experience and parameters of game structure, such as sound, graphics, background and setting, duration of game, rate of play, advancement rate, use of humor, control options, winning and losing features, character development, multi-player features, and game dynamics. The author describes correlations between the two abovementioned sets of parameters; for example, the highest scores of game dynamics have been found to "interfere" with flow, while moderately lower scores are highly predictive of flow.

Many studies involve multi-user games such as MMORPGs: flow experience is found to correlate significantly with the social interactions during the playing sessions (Chen & Park, 2005; Kim et al., 2005; McKenna & Lee, 1995; Voiskounsky, 2008). Not surprisingly, the gamers estimate their interactions with other gamers rather high, while they take "machine interactivity" for granted: human interactivity is shown to be "a sufficient condition for the flow experience of players" (Kim et al., 2005, p. 89). Choi and Kim (2004) show that flow states depend on "effective interaction" with the game management system and on "pleasant social interactions" with other players. The former depends on the appropriateness of goals and operators, and on feedback, and the latter depends on the appropriateness of tools and places for communication. The authors conclude that "more recently developed online games should be included in future research..." (ibid., p. 22), and indeed, production of online games is evidently on the rise.

Lee and Kwon (2005) indicate that the characteristics of flow tell nothing about game-related achievements; thus, one may suppose that gamers interested in achievements and gamers interested in flow (plus social interactions and/or social cognition) represent different types of gamers. The 'achievers' may be disposed to following self-determined goals (game missions) or, on the contrary, the goals determined by the leaders or senior gamers; scholars conclude that "more studies involving game structures and in-game behavior must be conducted to find out why the experience of flow, behavioral regulations, and affect differ among gamers" (Wang et al., 2008, p. 43). One should keep in mind that there is a sample of MMORPG gamers who seek neither flow nor achievements; instead, from a longitudinal perspective, they report of the states like 'escapism' and 'relaxation' as their motivation for playing (Schultheiss, 2007), or of 'diversion' as a chance to avoid stress or responsibilities, to kill time, or because there is nothing else to do (Sherry, 2004).

Technology-rich research methodology is entering the area of flow-related game playing studies. For example, an eye-tracking method was applied (Kearney & Pivec, 2007) to identify the players' states of immersion, which is hypothetically closely connected with the in-game flow states. The authors conclude: "Eye tracking techniques alone cannot be used to identify player immersion because of the varying screen design and game type. However, eye tracking can be used during the design phase to create an interface that minimizes eye movement and increases the potential concentration at the same time" (ibid.). Nacke and Lindley (2008) report of a behavioral measure of flow experienced while playing a shooter game. The three levels of the game environment stand for the differences in task challenges a successful gamer takes, and since the level of the available skills is about the same during the game session, the skills/challenges fitness (and thus, the non-flow/flow states) can be graduated. Flow has been measured (by means of a questionnaire) in a virtual reality setting: the participants wearing stereo glasses had to move in a CAVE-type system in a virtual five-bedroom house with virtual (computer generated) images projected on the walls. The same participants had to solve the quests presented in the visual mode; among the main purposes of the study was the investigation and description of the "Presence-Flow Framework" (Takatalo et al., 2008a). This study was given a special note by Hoffman and Novak (2009) when they discuss the most promising ways "toward a variety of new emerging areas" (p. 16) in the study of optimal experience in Internet-mediated environments.

Sweetser and Wyeth (2005) and Jegers (2006) introduce a GameFlow model. This model of computer gaming is presumably based on the characteristics of flow and includes such constructs as 'social interaction' and 'immersion' – the latter is an advanced version of "presence." The methodology of optimal experience has already proved to be essential for the immersive style of playing. Seah and Cairns (2008) differentiate presence and immersion and insist that "immersion is a precursor of flow": though there are often no clear challenges in a game, a player may stay immersed, and even more, game conditions often provoke negative feelings, while flow experience is a definitely positive state. Lemay (2007) introduces a theoretical model of flow experienced in gameplaying, and a pattern language which will be supposedly helpful for game designers. Wan and Chiou (2007) find that in the future the optimal experience methodology can be applied in advanced studies of the MMORPG gamers' intrinsic and extrinsic motivation.

The model proposed by Fernandez (2007) includes the notion of fun experienced while playing. One of the attempts to split the cognitive and the emotional components of flow experience, based on the reports given by a large sample of gamers (N > 2,000), was undertaken by Finnish scholars. They report that competence (plus control over the game) leads to a pleasurable experience, while in order to attain an enjoyable experience, a gamer requires challenges (plus an emotional arousal); the authors conclude that "this combination makes enjoyment more intensive and a stronger emotion as compared to pleasure" (Takatalo et al., 2008b, p. 41). Thus, the distinction between enjoyment and pleasure, introduced by Csikszentmihalyi decades ago, has proved to be correct.

Generally speaking, the flow-related approach to the study of the computer, video and online gamers' behavior is certainly fruitful.

INTERACTION

The studies of the optimal experience related to the mediated forms of Internet-mediated interaction are not numerous. They refer to chatting, instant messaging (IM), journalistic work and web-media enjoyment (Chang & Wang, 2008; Lu et al., 2009; Luna et al., 2002; Manssour, 2003; Nakatsu et al., 2005; Sherry, 2004; Shoham, 2004). Scholars empirically show the importance of flow experience, interpreted as a model of intrinsic motivation, in explaining the attitudes towards the adoption of new computer-mediated environments, and specifically, the environments which include interactive technologies such as the instant messaging and/or the mobile services (Chang & Wang, 2008; Lu et al., 2009); interactivity is one of the major factors (Wu & Chang, 2005). In case the extrinsic motivation is examined parallel to the intrinsic one, the two types of motivation are reported to effect differently: "Intrinsic motivational factors have a more powerful effect than extrinsic factors in building positive attitudes to IT [Information Technology]" (Chang & Wang, 2008, p. 2352). The users of instant messaging interactional services are reported to be "concerned about both extrinsic and intrinsic motivation. They not only expect a useful and easy-to-use IM platform, but also want to have fun and enjoy a flow experience" (Lu et al., 2009, p. 37).

Pleasure and enjoyment frequently accompany processes of media consuming; flow is inherently connected to the latter but not to the former. As Sherry (2004) notes, "although not originally designed as an explanation of media enjoyment, flow theory resonates with reports of media enjoyment and fits the experience well" (p. 331).

In considering the newest forms of entertainment, active experience is believed to be preferable for getting enjoyment (Nakatsu et al., 2005). The process of consuming traditional media is, on the contrary, most often a passive process; consequently, it is pleasurable and needs to be distinguished from the optimal (enjoyable) forms of experience (Kubey & Csikszentmihalyi, 2002). "TV watching … leads to the flow condition very rarely," as Csikszentmihalyi (1990, p. 83) reasonably mentioned. With the advance of mobile TV, though, this conclusion may turn out to be premature (Jung et al., 2009): parameters of flow experience are shown to impact the adoption of this rising service, and the content of mobile TV is shown to impact flow experience; the scholars define content as "a consumer's assessment that programs are applicable (relevance), up-to-date (timeliness), and sufficient (sufficiency)" (Jung et al., 2009, p. 125). In the optimal experience context, Sherry (2004) states that flow can be interpreted as a condition when the content of the media fits the individual ability to interpret the messages.

Shoham (2004) distinguishes the "flow-like" experience of the chat-rooms visitors, and proves that this type of experience provides the participants (i.e., chatters) with the means and instruments they need to manage and possibly enhance their self-images. Manssur (2003) finds it possible to discuss flow states which take place when journalists work distantly. Flow states are recognizable in the behavior of musical improvisers during jam-sessions, which obviously represent a specific type of an interactional environment (Dubnov & Assayag, 2005). All of these types of optimal experiences are hardly specific for the cyberspace environments: "If we want to identify the match between perceived challenges and required skills, the answer is probably not related to the Web technology itself or to the chatting environment but to the behavior of interacting with others" (Chen et al., 1999, p. 590).

The interactional services are the oldest among the cyberspace environments: the first online services were Fido, e-mail or Usenet, i.e. purely interactive media. They keep developing in a good tempo – just to mention such services as blogging, mobile telecommunications, instant messaging, social networks, photo and video sharing, Internet telephony, or webcasting. Evidently, human interactions are capable of numerous forms of optimal experience. Nevertheless, the number of studies dealing with flow experience in Internet-related environments does not correspond to the amount of mediated communications and their role in modern culture. Hopefully, this disbalance will be leveled in the nearest future. Meanwhile, it is worth reminding that there are some flow experience studies on the patterns of mediated social interactions between the online gamers (see the previous section). These studies partly compensate relative shortages of empirical studies referring to the optimal experience accompanying the usage of interactive services within the Internet-mediated environments.

A BRIEF DESCRIPTION OF THE AUTHOR'S PROJECTS

The author is involved in several projects aimed to investigate the specifics of flow experience in the cyberspace environments. These projects are briefly described in the current section.

It is an often expressed view that flow experience is closely correlated with the Internet addictive behavior, or as it is often labeled, problematic Internet use or Internet abuse/misuse. This view is questioned (Voiskounsky, 2007b; 2008; 2010) on theoretical basis: following Massimini and Delle Fave (2000), one should distinguish flow experience from a so-called *mimetic flow* – the latter refers to negative types of behavior, such as the intake of drugs, passive leisure activities or abuse of technological artifacts, including computers and computer games. The psychological nature of mimetic flow is argued to be entirely dissimilar with the enjoyable nature of optimal experience. Thus, the Internet abuse or addiction, on one hand, and flow experienced while using the Internet, have different inner psychological structures; this theoretical statement is being empirically verified (this work is in progress).

While the methodology of optimal experience is applied in the usability context (as described in: Voiskounsky, 2008), Smyslova and Voiskounsky (2009) suggest diverse ways to perform usability testing in order to promote the initiation of parameters characteristic of the intrinsic motivation and flow experience on the part of the users of particular software products. Intrinsic motivation, it is argued, would be responsible for long-term usage of new (or newly updated) software products, and experience-sampling methodology is promising in checking whether the products are properly used, and hence, in what direction the users' motivation is developing. This research field is competitive: should a reasonable recommendation (aimed, for instance, to improve a game interface, to update a usability checking procedure, to optimize Web navigation, etc.) emerge, excellent opportunities will be open for both academics and practitioners alike.

In a cross-cultural study of online gamers, a questionnaire was validated for application within the samples of Russian (Voiskounsky et al., 2004; Voiskounsky et al., 2005), French (Voiskounsky et al., 2006a; Voiskounsky et al., 2006b), Chinese (Voiskounsky et al., 2008) and American (Faiola & Voiskounsky, 2007) gamers; in result, flow experience was shown to be a major factor for all of the samples; additionally, it was found that certain culture specifics should be given attention (Voiskounsky, 2007a). Flow experience was suggested to explain the reasons of popularity of particular multi-user games, namely those which might be called old-fashioned and which lack modern principles of game design.

In a study of illicit forms of the cyberspace related behavior in the optimal experience context, a dynamic model of computer hackers' motivational development was worked out (Voiskounsky & Smyslova, 2003a; Voiskounsky & Smyslova, 2003b). The major finding is the following: both poorly and highly qualified hackers report of flow experience, while those who have moderate qualification in the use of information technologies only rarely report optimal forms of experience. This empirical result is promising in attempts to reduce the number of qualified hackers: dynamics of their motivational development might push them to turn into computer security experts instead of progressing in hacking activities (Voiskounsky, 2004).

CONCLUSION

The field of optimal experience studies is a developing problem area within psychology (especially positive psychology) and the neighboring disciplines both in academia and in practice. Human beings find themselves immersed in the rapidly growing number of Internet-mediated environments. In fact, Internet-related flow studies belong to various areas of knowledge. These areas include psychology, cyberpsychology, computer science, education, human-computer interaction, communication and media science, marketing, business and management, culture studies, sociology, social work, law, usability and design, security studies, rehabilitation and medicine, etc. All of these studies rely on a steady-based methodology of optimal experience.

The variety of research directions makes a reviewer's task not easy. Having different backgrounds, scholars put forward diverse models of flow experience, presumably the most easy-to-build and/or the most effective from the perspective of the discipline they belong to. At the same time, the scholars who are active in this field get interested in what is being discussed and particularly where the mainstream of the current studies is. This chapter might be viewed from this angle. Last but not least, the studies related to the optimal experience applications in Internet-mediated environments are capable to contribute to the discipline that might be referred to as its point of departure, i.e. positive psychology.

ACKNOWLEDGEMENTS

Research was supported by the Russian Foundation for Humanities, project 11-06-00647.

REFERENCES

Amichai-Hamburger, Y. (2005). Personality and the Internet. In: Amichai-Hamburger, Y. (Ed.), *The social net: Human behavior in cyberspace* (pp. 27-55), Oxford University Press, New York, NY.

Amichai-Hamburger,Y., Kaynar, J., & Fine, A. (2007). The effects of need for cognition on Internet use, *Computers in Human Behavior*, 23, 880–891

Andersen, K., & Witfelt, C. (2005). Educational design: Bridging the gap between computer-based learning and experimental learning environments. *International Journal of Continuing Engineering Education and Life-long Learning*, 15(1/2), 5-18.

Barrett, L. F., & Barrett, D. J. (2001). An introduction to computerized experience sampling in psychology. *Social Science Computer Review*, 19(2), 175-185. Retrieved May 11, 2007, from http://www.bc.edu/sites/asi/publications/lfb/01CompExperSampling.pdf

Beck, J.C., & Wade, M. (2004). *Got Game*. Boston: Harvard Business School Press.

Brosnan, M., & Goodison, P. (date non-specified). Anxiety, flow and boredom: Optimizing computer-based learning in the classroom. Retrieved December 22, 2008 from http://people.bath.ac.uk/pssmjb/blog/index_main.php?page=cyber (select Week 5).

Chan, T.S., & Ahem, T.C. (1999). Targeting motivation – adapting flow theory to instructional design. *Journal of Educational Computing Research*, 21(2), 151-163.

Chang, H.H., & Wang, I.C. (2008). An investigation of user communication behavior in computer-mediated environments. *Computers in Human Behavior*, 24(5), 2336–2356.

Chen, H. (2006). Flow on the net – detecting web users' positive affects and their flow states. *Computers in Human Behavior*, 22, 221-233.

Chen, H., Wigand, R. T., & Nilan, M. S. (1999). Optimal experience of web activities. *Computers in Human Behavior*, 15(5), 585-608.

Chen, J. (2007). Flow in games (and everything else). *Communications of the ACM*, 50(4), 31-34.

Chen, J. V., & Park, Y. (2005). The difference of addiction causes between massive multiplayer online game and multi user domain. *International Review of Information Ethics*, 4(12), 53-60.

Chiou, W-B., & Wan, C.-S. (2006). A further investigation of the motives of online games addiction. *Paper presented at the National Educational Computing Conference* (San Diego, July 5–7, 2006). Retrieved August 23, 2006, from http://center. uoregon.edu/ISTE/uploads/NECC2006/KEY_12738686/Chiou_NECC06ChiouWenBin_ RP.pdf

Choi, D., & Kim, J. (2004). Why people continue to play online games: In search of critical design factors to increase customer loyalty to online contents. *CyberPsychology & Behavior*, 7(1), 11-24.

Choi, D.H., Kim, J., & Kim, S.H. (2007). ERP training with a web-based electronic learning system: The flow theory perspective. *International Journal of Human-Computer Studies*, 65, 223–243.

Chou, T.-J., & Ting, Ch.-Ch. (2003). The role of flow experience in cyber-game addiction. *CyberPsychology & Behavior*, 6(6), 663-675.

Conner Christensen, T., Feldman Barrett, L., Bliss-Moreau, E., Lebo, K., & Kaschub, C. (2003). A practical guide to experience-sampling procedures. *Journal of Happiness Studies*, 4, 53-78.

Csikszentmihalyi, M. (1990). *Flow: The psychology of optimal experience*. New York: Harper and Row.

Csikszentmihalyi, M. (2000, first published in 1975). *Beyond boredom and anxiety: Experiencing flow in work and play*. San-Francisco: Jossey-Bass.

Csikszentmihalyi, M., & Larson, R. (1987). Validity and reliability of the Experience Sampling Method. *Journal of Nervous and Mental Disease*, 175, 526-536.

Davis, R., & Wong, D. (2007). Conceptualizing and Measuring the Optimal Experience of the eLearning Environment. Decision Sciences. *Journal of Innovative Education*, 5(1), 97-126.

Deci, E., & Ryan, R. (1985). *Intrinsic motivation and self-determination in human behavior*. New York: Plenum Press.

Dong, Y. & Lee, K. P. (2008). A cross-cultural comparative study of users' perceptions of a webpage: With a focus on the cognitive styles of Chinese, Koreans and Americans. *International Journal of Design*, 2(2), 19-30.

Dubnov, S. & Assayag, G. (2005). Improvisation Planning and Jam Session Design using concepts of Sequence Variation and Flow Experience. In *Proceeding of Sound and Music Computing* (SMC'05), Salerno, Italy. Retrieved October 3, 2006 from http://mediatheque.ircam.fr/articles/textes/Assayag05a/

Faiola A., & Smyslova, O. (2009). Flow Experience in Second Life: The Impact of Telepresence on Human-Computer Interaction. In: A. Ant Ozok and Panayiotis Zaphiris (Eds.). Online Communities and Social Computing. Third International Conference, OCSC 2009, Held as Part of HCI International 2009, San Diego, CA, USA, July 19-24, (pp. 574-583). Proceedings, *Lecture Notes in Computer Science*, Issue 5621.

Faiola, A., & Voiskounsky, A.E. (2007). Experience of MUD players: Investigating multi-user dimension gamers from the USA. In G. Salvendy and J. Jacko (Ed.), *Human-Computer Interaction - Ergonomics and User Interfaces, Theory and Practice, Proceedings of the 12th International Conference on Human-Computer Interaction (pp. 324-333)*. Beijing, China. (Mahwah, NJ: Lawrence Erlbaum Publishers).

Fernandez, A. (2007). Fun *Experience* with Digital Games: a Model Proposition. *Paper presented at the Interact 2007 Workshop* (September 10-11, 2007), Rio de Janeiro,

Brazil. Retrieved December 22, 2008 from http://www.fun-of-use.org/interact2007 /papers/FunExperienceWithDigitalGames.pdf

Finneran, C.M., & Zhang, P. (2005). Flow in computer-mediated environments: Promises and challenges. http://melody.syr.edu/pzhang/publications/CAIS_05_Finneran_Zhang_Flow.pdf

Fu, F.-L., Rong-Chang Su, R.-Ch., & Yu, Sh.-Ch. (2009). EGameFlow: A scale to measure learners' enjoyment of e-learning games. *Computers & Education*, 52, 101–112

Gackenbach, J. (2008). The Relationship Between Perceptions of Video Game Flow and Structure. Loading…, 1(3). Retrieved January 11, 2008 from http://journals.sfu.ca/ loading/index.php/loading/article/view/39/37

Gaggioli, A. (2005). Optimal experience in ambient intelligence. In G. Riva, F. Vatalaro, F. Davide, & M. Alcaniz (Eds.), *Ambient intelligence* (pp. 35-43). Amsterdam, The Netherlands: IOS Press. Retrieved July 16, 2006, from http://www. emergingcommunication.com/volume6.html

Gaggioli, A., Bassi, M., & Delle Fave, A. (2003). Quality of experience in virtual environments. In G. Riva, F. Davide, & W. A. IJsselsteijn (Eds.), *Being there: Concepts, effects and measurement of user presence in synthetic environments* (pp. 122-135). Amsterdam, The Netherlands: IOS Press. Retrieved July 16, 2006, from http://www.vepsy.com/communication/book4/4_08GAGGIOL.PDF

Ghani, J. A., & Deshpande, S.P. (1994). Task characteristics and the experience of optimal flow in human-computer interaction. *The Journal of Psychology*, 128(4), 381-391.

Heidman, L., & Sharafi, P. (2004). Early use of Internet-based educational resources: Effects on students' engagement modes and flow experience. *Behaviour & Information Technology*, 23(2), 137-146.

Hektner, J.M., Schmidt, J.A., & Csikszentmihalyi, M. (2007). *Experience sampling method: Measuring the quality of everyday life*. Thousand Oaks, CA: Sage Publications.

Hoffman, D. L., & Novak, T.P. (1996). Marketing in hypermedia computer-mediated environments: Conceptual foundations. *Journal of Marketing*, 60(3), 50-68.

Hoffman, D.L., & Novak, T.P. (2009). Flow Online: Lessons Learned and Future Prospects. *Journal of Interactive Marketing*, 23(1), 23-34.

Hsu, C., & Lu, H. (2004). Why do people play on-line game? An extended TAM with social influences and flow experience. *Information and Management*, 41 (7), 853-868.

Huang, M.-H. (2006). Flow, enduring, and situational involvement in the web environment: A tripartite second-order examination. *Psychology and Marketing*, 23(5), 383-411.

Ilsever, J., Cyr, D., & Parent, M. (2007). Extending Models of Flow and E-loyalty. *Journal of Information Science and Technology*, 4(2), 3-22.

Inal, Y. & Cagiltay, K. (2007). Flow experiences of children in an interactive social game environment. British *Journal of Educational Technology*, 38 (3), 455–464. Retrieved June 4, 2007, from http://www.simge.metu.edu.tr/journal/flowexperience.pdf

Jegers, K. (2006). Pervasive GameFlow: Understanding player enjoyment in pervasive gaming. In Th. Strang, V. Cahill, & A. Quigley (Eds.), *Pervasive 2006 Workshop Proc. Pervasive 2006*. Retrieved July 16, 2006, from http://www .ipsi.fraunhofer.de/ambiente/pergames2006/final/PG_Jegers_GameFlow.pdf

Jung, Y., Perez-Mira, B., & Wiley-Patton, S. (2009). Consumer adoption of mobile TV: Examining psychological flow and media content. *Computers in Human Behavior*, 25(1), 123–129.

Kearne, P.R., & Pivec, M. (2007). Immersed and How? That Is the Question. In Games In Action. Conference Proceedings. University of Gothenburg. Gothenburg, Sweden. Retrieved October 24, 2008 from http://www.learnit.org.gu.se/digitalAssets/862/862904_kearney_pivec.pdf

Keller, J., & Bless, H. (2008). Flow and Regulatory Compatibility: An Experimental Approach to the Flow Model of Intrinsic Motivation. *Personality and Social Psychology Bulletin*, 34(2), 196-209.

Kim, Y.-Y., Oh, S., & Lee, H. (2005). What makes people experience flow? Social characteristics of online games. *International Journal of Advanced Media and Communication*, 1(1), 76-92.

Konradt, U., Filip, R., & Hoffmann, S. (2003). Flow experience and positive affect during hypermedia learning. *British Journal of Educational Technology*, 34, 309-327.

Konradt, U., & Sulz, K. (2001). The experience of flow interacting with a hypermedia learning environment. *Journal of Educational Multimedia and Hypermedia*, 10(1), 69-84.

Korzaan, M. (2003). Going with the flow: Predicting online purchase intentions. *Journal of Computer Information Systems*, 43(4), 25-31.

Koufaris, M. (2002). Applying the technology acceptance model and flow theory to online consumer behavior. *Information Systems Research*, 13(2), 205-223.

Kubey, R., & Csikszentmihalyi, M. (2002). Television addiction is no mere metaphor. *Scientific American*, 286(2), 74-80.

Lee, I. & Kwon, H. (2005). Relations Among Flow, Information Processing Strategies, and Performance in a Computer-based Simulation Game. In P. Kommers & G. Richards (Eds*.), Proceedings of World Conference on Educational Multimedia, Hypermedia and Telecommunications 2005* (pp. 986-992). Chesapeake, VA: AACE.

Lemay, Ph. (2007). Developing a pattern language for flow experiences in video games. *Situated Play*, Proceedings of DiGRA (Digital Games Research Association) Conference. Tokyo, Japan, 449-455.

Li, B., & Browne, G.J. (2006). The Role of Need for Cognition and Mood in Online Flow Experience. *Journal of Computer Information Systems*, 46(3), 11-17.

Liao, L.-F. (2006). A flow theory perspective on learner motivation and behavior in distance education. *Distance Education*, 27(1), 45-62.

Lu, Y., Zhou, T., & Wang, B. (2009). Exploring Chinese users' acceptance of instant messaging using the theory of planned behavior, the technology acceptance model, and the flow theory. *Computers in Human Behavior*, 25(1), 29–39.

Luna, D., Peracchio, L.A., & de Juan, M.D. (2002). Cross-cultural and cognitive aspects of web site navigation. *Journal of the Academy of Marketing Science*, 30(4), 397-410.

Luna, D., Peracchio, L.A., & de Juan, M.D. (2003). Flow in Individual Web Sites: Model Estimation and Cross-Cultural Validation. In P.A. Keller, & D.W. Rook (Eds.), *Advances in Consumer Research*, Volume 30 (pp. 280-281), Valdosta, GA : Association for Consumer Research.

Malone, T., & Lepper, M. (1987). Making learning fun: A taxonomy of intrinsic motivation for learning. In R. E. Snow, & M. J. Farr (Eds.), *Aptitude learning and instruction*. Vol. 3. Conative and affective process analysis (pp. 111-140). Hillsdale, NJ: Lawrence Erlbaum.

Manssour, A. B. B. (2003). Flow in journalistic telework. *CyberPsychology & Behavior*, 6(1), 31-39.

Massimini, F., & Delle Fave, A. (2000). Individual development in a bio-cultural perspective. *American Psychologist*, 55(1), 24-33.

Mathwick, C., & Rigdon, E. (2004). Play, Flow, and the Online Search Experience. *Journal of Consumer Research*, 31(2), 324–332.

McKenna, K., & Lee, S. (1995). A love affair with MUDs: Flow and social interaction in Multi-User Dungeons. Retrieved October 2, 2002, from http://www.fragment.nl/mirror/various/McKenna_et_al.nd.A_love_affair_with_muds.html

Moller, A.C., Meier, B.P., & Wall, R.D. (2010). Developing an experimental induction of flow: Effortless action in the lab. In B. Bruya (Ed.), *Effortless Attention: A New perspective in the cognitive science of attention and action* (pp. 191-204). Cambridge, MA: MIT Press.

Moneta, J. B. (2004). The flow experience across cultures. *Journal of Happiness Studies*, 5(2), 115-121.

Montgomery, H., Sharafi, P., & Heidman, L.R. (2004). Engagement in activities involving information technology: Dimensions, modes, and flow. *Human Factors*, 46(2), 334-348.

Nacke, L., & Lindley, C.A. (2008). Boredom, Immersion, Flow – A Pilot Study Investigating Player Experience. In E. Thij (Ed.), *Proceedings of IADIS International Gaming Conference 2008: Design for engaging experience and social interaction* (pp. 103-107). Amsterdam, The Netherlands. Retrieved December 21, 2008 from http://gamescience.bth.se/download/16/.

Nakatsu, R., Rauterberg, M., & Vorderer, P. (2005). A new framework for entertainment computing: From passive to active experience. In F. Kishino, Y. Kitamura, H. Kato, & N. Nagata (Eds.), *Entertainment Computing - ICEC 2005. 4th International Conference on Entertainment Computing. Lecture Notes in Computer Science*, 3711, 1-12. Retrieved May 30, 2007, from http://www.idemployee.id.tue.nl/g.w.m.rauterberg/publications/ICEC2005(1)paper.pdf

Novak, T. P., & Hoffman, D. L. (1997). Measuring the flow experience among web users. Retrieved April 2, 2006, from http://sloan.ucr.edu/blog/uploads/papers/Measuring%20the%20Flow%20Experience%20Among%20Web%20Users%20%5BHoffman,%20Novak%20-%20July%201997%5D.pdf

Novak, T. P., Hoffman, D. L., & Duhachek, A. (2003). The influence of goal-directed and experiential activities on online flow experiences. *Journal of Consumer Psychology*, 13(1-2), 3-16.

Novak, T. P., Hoffman, D. L., & Yung, Y.-F. (2000). Measuring the customer experience in online environments: A structural modeling approach. *Marketing Science*, 19(1), 22-42. Retrieved February 4, 2006, from http://advertising.utexas.edu/vcbg/home/Novak99.pdf

O'Broin, D., & Clarke, S. (2006). INKA: Using flow to enhance the mobile learning experience. Retrieved August 24, 2006, from http://www.cs.tcd.ie/publications/tech-reports/reports.06/TCD-CS-2006-42.pdf

Oudeyer, P.-Y., & Kaplan, F. (2007). What is Intrinsic Motivation? A Typology of Computational Approaches. *Front Neurorobotics*, 1(6). Retrieved February 3, 2010 from http://www.ncbi.nlm.nih.gov/pmc/articles/PMC2533589/

Pace, S. (2004). A grounded theory of the flow experiences of web users. *International Journal of Human-Computer Studies*, 60(3), 327–363.

Pearce, J. M., Ainley, M., & Howard, S. (2005). The ebb and flow of online learning. *Computers in Human Behavior*, 21(5), 745-771.

Pearce, J. M., & Howard, S. (2004). Designing for flow in a complex activity. *Lecture Notes in Computer Science*, 3101, 349-358.

Pedrotti, J.T., Edwards, L.M., & Lopez, S.J. (2009). Positive Psychology Within a Cultural Context . In C.R. Snyder & S.J. Lopez (Eds.), *The Oxford Handbook of Positive Psychology* (pp. 49-57), Second Edition. N.Y. et al.: Oxford University Press.

Pilke, E.M. (2004). Flow experiences in information technology use. *International Journal of Human-Computer Studies*, 61(3), 347-357.

Polaine, A. **(2005).** The flow principle in interactivity. *Proceedings of the second Australian Conference on Interactive Entertainment. ACM International Conference Proceeding Series* (pp. 151–158)**, 123.** Sydney, Australia.

Rettie, R. (2001). An exploration of flow during Internet use. Internet *Research: Electronic Networking Applications and Policy*, 11(2), 103-113.

Roca, J.C., & Gagne, M. (2008). Understanding e-learning continuance intention in the workplace: A self-determination theory perspective. *Computers in Human Behavior,* 24(4), 1585-1604.

Rodriguez-Sanchez, A.M., Schaufelj, W.B., Salanova, A., & Cifre, E. (2008). Flow Experience Among Information and Communication Technology Users. *Psychological Reports*, 102(1), 29-39.

Rotto, L.I. (1994). Curiosity, Motivation and Flow in Computer-Based Instruction. *Paper presented at the 1994 National Convention of the Association for Educational Communications and Technology*, Nashville, TN. Retrieved January 6, 2009, from http://mailer.fsu.edu/~jkeller/EDP5217/Library/Curiosity%20&%20Attention/Attention/Rotto(1994)%20Computer-Based%20Instruction.pdf . Also available at: http://eric.ed.gov/ERICDocs/data/ericdocs2sql/content_storage_01/0000019b/80/13/4e/51.pdf

Ryan, R. M., & Deci, E. L. (2000). Self-determination theory and the facilitation of intrinsic motivation, social development, and well-being. *American Psychologist*, 55(1), 68-78.

Schultheiss, D. (2007). Long-term motivations to play MMOGs: A longitudinal study on motivations, experience and behavior. *Situated Play, Proceedings of DiGRA Conference.* Retrieved 11 December, 2008 from http://www.digra.org/dl/db/07311.00087.pdf

Seah, M., & Cairns, P. (2008). From immersion to addiction in videogames. In England, D. and Beale, R. (Eds.), Proc. of the 22nd British HCI Group Annual Conference (John Moores University, Liverpool, UK, 1 - 5 September 2008), vol 1, 55-63. Retrieved January 6, 2009 from http://www-users.cs.york.ac.uk/~pcairns/papers/Seah_Cairns_HCI2008.pdf

Sénécal, S., Gharbi, J-E., & Nantel, J. (2002). The Influence of Flow on Hedonic and Utilitarian Shopping Values. In S. Broniarczyk and K. Nakamoto (Eds.), *Advances in Consumer Research*, 29(1), 483-484.

Seligman, M.E.P., & Csikszentmihalyi, M. (2000). Positive psychology: An introduction. *American Psychologist*, 55(1), 5-14.

Sharafi, P., Heidman, L., & Montgomery, H. (2006). Using information technology: Engagement modes, flow experience, and personality orientations. *Computers in Human Behavior*, 22(5), 899-916.

Sherry, J. L. (2004). Flow and media enjoyment. *Communication Theory*, 14(4), 328-347.

Shin, N. (2006). Online learner's 'flow' experience: An empirical study. *British Journal of Educational Technology*, 37(5), 705-720.

Shoham, A. (2004). Flow experiences and image making: An on-line chat rooms ethnography. *Psychology and Marketing*, 21(10), 855–882.

Sicilia, M. & Ruiz, S. (2007). The Role of Flow in Web Site Effectiveness. *Journal of Interactive Advertizing*, 8(1). Retrieved January 6, 2009 from http://jiad.org/vol8/no1/ruiz/index.htm

Siekpe, J. S. (2005). An examination of multi-dimensionality of flow construct in a computer-mediated environment. *Journal of Electronic Commerce Research*, 6(1), 31-43.

Skadberg, Y.X., & Kimmel, R. (2004). Visitors' flow experience while browsing a web site: Its measurement, contributing factors and consequences. *Computers in Human Behavior*, 20(3), 403-422.

Smith, D. N., & Sivakumar, K. (2004). Flow and Internet shopping behavior: A conceptual model and research propositions. *Journal of Business Research*, 57(10), 1199-1208.

Smyslova O.V., Voiskounsky A.E. (2009). Usability studies: to meet or not to meet intrinsic motivation. *PsychNology Journal*, 7(3), 303 – 324.

Sweetser, P., & Wyeth, P. (2005). GameFlow: A model for evaluating player enjoyment in games. *ACM Computers in Entertainment* (CIE), 3 (3). Retrieved November 2, 2006, from http://www.itee.uq.edu.au/~penny/_papers/Sweetser-CIE.pdf

Takatalo, J., Nyman, G., & Laaksonen, L. (2008a). Components of human experience in virtual environments. *Computers in Human Behavior*, 24(1), 1–15.

Takatalo, J., Häkkinen, J., Lipsanen, J., Lehtonen, M., Kaistinen, J., & Nyman, G. (2008b). Pleasure and enjoyment in digital games. In T. Vanhala and J. Anttonen (Eds.), *Proceedings of EHTI'08: The First Finnish Symposium on Emotions and Human-Technology Interaction*. University of Tampere, Department of Computer Sciences, A-2008-3 (pp. 38-42). Retrieved January 4, 2009 from http://www.cs.uta.fi/reports/dsarja/D-2008-3.pdf

Thatcher, A., Wretschko, G., & Fridjhon, P. (2008). Online flow experiences, problematic Internet use and Internet procrastination. *Computers in Human Behavior*, 24(5), 2236-2254.

Trevino, L. K., & Webster, L. (1992). Flow in computer-mediated communication. *Communication Research*, 19(5), 539-573.

Tzanetakis, R., Vitouch, P. (2002). Flow-experience, the Internet and its relationship to situation and personality. *Abstract of a paper presented at the Internet Research 3.0: Net/Work/Theory* (Maastricht, The Netherlands). Retrieved January 24, 2004, from http://aoir.org/2002/program/tzanetakis.html

Voiskounsky, A. (2004). Current problems of moral research and education in the IT environment. In K. Morgan, C. A. Brebbia, J. Sanchez, & A. Voiskounsky (Eds.), *Human perspectives in the Internet society: Culture, psychology and gender* (pp. 33-41). Southampton and Boston: WIT Press.

Voiskounsky, A.E. (2007a). A Cross-Cultural Study of Flow Experience in the IT Environment: The Beginning. In G. Salvendy and J. Jacko (Ed.), *Human-Computer Interaction - Ergonomics and User Interfaces, Theory and Practice, Proceedings of the 12th International Conference on Human-Computer Interaction*. Beijing, China. (Mahwah, NJ: Lawrence Erlbaum Publishers). Lecture Notes in Computer Science, 4564, 202-211.

Voiskounsky, A.E. (2007b). Two Types of Repetitive Experiences on the Internet. *INTERFACE: The Journal of Education, Community and Values*, 7(6). Retrieved February 6, 2008 from http://bcis.pacificu.edu/journal/2007/06/voiskounsky.php

Voiskounsky A.E. (2008). Flow Experience in Cyberspace: Current Studies and Perspectives. In A. Barak (Ed.), *Psychological Aspects of Cyberspace: Theory, Research, Applications* (pp. 70-101). N.Y.: Cambridge University Press.

Voiskounsky, A.E. (2010). Internet Addiction in the Context of Positive Psychology. In: Yu.P. Zinchenko & V.F. Petrenko (eds.). *Psychology in Russia: State of the Art. Scientific Yearbook* (pp. 541-549), Moscow: Lomonosov Moscow State University; Russian Psychological Society Publ.

Voiskounsky, A.E., Mitina, O.V., & Avetisova, A.A. (2004). Playing online games: Flow experience. *PsychNology Journal*, 2(3), 259-281. Retrieved November 2, 2004, from http://www.psychnology.org/PSYCHNOLOGY_JOURNAL_2_3_VOISKOUNSKY.pdf

Voiskounsky, A.E., Mitina, O.V., & Avetisova, A.A. (2005). Communicative patterns and flow experience of MUD players. *International Journal of Advanced Media and Communication*, 1(1), 5-25.

Voiskounsky, A.E., Mitina, O.V., & Avetisova, A.A. (2006a). Flow experience and interaction: Investigation of Francophone online gamers. In F. Sudweeks, H. Hrachovec & Ch. Ess (Eds.), *Cultural attitudes towards technology and communication*. Proceedings, 5th International Conference (pp. 385-396). Murdoch, Australia: Publ. by School of Information Technology, Murdoch University.

Voiskounsky, A.E., Mitina, O.V., & Avetisova, A.A. (2006b). Cross-cultural investigation of online gaming: Models of flow experience and interaction in samples of Russian and French gamers. In *Reality and Game & Game and Reality*. Papers of the 37th Annual Conference of the International Simulation and Gaming Association (pp. 64-86). St. Petersburg, Russia: ENGECON Publ.

Voiskounsky, A.V., Mitina, O.V., & Avetisova, A.A. (2008). Flow experience and interaction in online gaming: Comparative study of Russian and Chinese MUD players. In F. Sudweeks, H. Hrachovec, & Ch. Ess (Eds.). *Sixth international conference on Cultural Attitudes Towards Technology and Communication* (pp. 410-421). Murdoch, Australia: Publ. by School of Information Technology, Murdoch University.

Voiskounsky, A.E., & Smyslova, O.V. (2003a). Flow-based model of computer hackers' motivation. *CyberPsychology & Behavior*, 6(3), 171-180.

Voiskounsky, A.E., & Smyslova, O.V. (2003b). Flow in computer hacking: A model. In C.-C. Chung, C.-K. Kim, W. Kim, T.-W. Ling, & K.-H. Song (Eds.), *Web and communication technologies and Internet-related social issues – HSI 2003. Proc., Second International Conference on Human.Society@Internet (Seoul, Korea, June 2003). Lecture Notes in Computer Science*, 2713, 176-186.

Vollmeyer, R., & Rheinberg, F. (2006). Motivational effects on self-regulated learning with different tasks. *Educational Psychology Review*, 18(3), 239-253.

Wan, C.-S., & Chiou, W-B. (2006). Psychological motives and online games addiction: A test of flow theory and humanistic needs theory for Taiwanese adolescents. *CyberPsychology & Behavior*, 9(3), 317-324.

Wan, C.-S., & Chiou, W-B. (2007). The motivations of adolescents who are addicted to online games: A cognitive perspective. *Adolescence*, 42(165), 179-198.

Wan, F., Nan, N., & Smith, M. (2008). Consumers' Optimal Experience on Commercial WEB Sites: A Congruency Effect of WEB Atmospheric Design and Consumers' Surfing Goal. In S. Bandyopadhyay (Ed.), *Contemporary Research in E-Branding* (pp. 78-94), *Hershey*, *PA*: Information Science Reference, IGI Global. Retrieved January 11, 2009 from http://www.ebrc.info/kuvat/2135_04.pdf

Wang, C.K.J., Khoo, A., Liu, W.C., & Divaharan, S. (2008). Passion and Intrinsic Motivation in Digital Gaming. *Cyberpsychology & Behavior*, 11(1), 39-45.

Webster, J., Trevino, L. K., & L. Ryan (1993). The dimensionality and correlates of flow in human-computer interaction. *Computers in Human Behavior*, 9(4), 411-426.

Weibel, D., Wissmath, B., Habegger, S., Steiner, Y., & Groner, R. (2008). Playing online games against computer- vs. human-controlled opponents: Effects on presence, flow, and enjoyment. *Computers in Human Behavior*, 24 (5), 2274-2291.

Wu, J.-J., & Chang Y.-S. (2005). Towards understanding members' interactivity, trust, and flow in online travel community. *Industrial Management & Data Systems*, 105(7), 937–954.

Zwick, D., & Dholakia, N. (2007). Observing Flow: A qualitative investigation of compelling web experiences and absorbing web environments. In *William A. Orme Working Paper Series, College of Business Administration, University of Rhode Island*. No. 2. Retrieved January 4, 2009 from http://www.cba.uri.edu/offices/research/workingpapers/documents/2007/ObservingFlowAqualitativeinvestigationofcompellingwebexperiencesandabsorbingwebenvironments.pdf

ABOUT THE AUTHORS

Manuel Viegas Abreu, Ph.D.

Emeritus Professor, University of Coimbra; abreu@fpce.uc.pt; Rua do Colégio Novo, 3001-802, Coimbra, Portugal. Phone: +351239851450, Fax: +351239851462

Valery I. Chirkov, Ph.D.

Associate professor, Department of Psychology, University of Saskatchewan, Saskatoon, SK S7N 5A5, Canada. Email: v.chirkov@usask.ca

Stefan Engeser, Ph.D.

Universität Trier, Fachbereich I – Psychologie, Abteilung Differentielle Psychologie, Persönlichkeitspsychologie u. Diagnostik. D-54286 Trier. Email: engeser@uni-trier.de; Tel.: ++49(0)651 201-2905; Fax: ++49(0)651 201-3979

Ulrich Geppert. Ph.D.

Senior research scientist, Max Planck Institute for Human Cognitive and Brain Sciences, Department of Psychology, Munich, Germany. Postal address: Forstanger 7a, D-86911 Diessen am Ammersee. E-mail: geppertdiessen@t-online.de

Frank Halisch, Ph.D.

Senior research scientist, Max Planck Institute for Human Cognitive and Brain Sciences, Department of Psychology, Munich, Germany. Postal address: Mallersthofener Str. 16d, D-85716 Unterschleissheim. E-mail: frank.halisch@t-online.de

Alfried Längle, M.D., Ph.D.

President, International Society for Logotherapy and Existential Analysis, Vienna. Ed. Suess-Gasse 10, A-1150 Vienna, Austria. email: alfried.laengle@existenzanalyse.org

Willy Lens, Ph.D.

Emeritus Professor, University of Leuven, Belgium. Willy.Lens@psy.kuleuven.be Dept. Psychology, Tiensestraat 102

B-3000 LEUVEN (Belgium). Phone: +32-(0)16.32.59.71; Fax: +32-(0) 16.32.60.99

Dmitry Leontiev, Ph.D.

Professor, Psychology Department, Lomonosov Moscow State University. Mokhovaya str. 11-5, Moscow 125009, Russia. Email: dleon@smysl.ru

Salvatore R. Maddi, Ph.D.

Professor, Department of Psychology and Social Behavior, University of California, Irvine. 4201 SBS Gateway, Irvine, CA 92697, USA
srmaddi@uci.edu

Maria Paula Paixão, Ph.D.

Associate Professor, University of Coimbra. mppaixao@fpce.uc.pt
Rua do Colégio Novo, 3001-802, Coimbra, Portugal. Phone: +351239851450; Fax: +351239851462

Catherine Patyayeva,

Ph.D., senior lecturer, Psychology Department, Lomonosov Moscow State University. Mokhovaya str. 11-5, Moscow 125009, Russia
Email: patyayeva@yandex.ru

Falko Rheinberg, Prof. Dr. (Emeritus)

Universität Potsdam. Karl-Liebknecht-Str. 24/25, 14476 Golm. Email: rheinberg-gladbeck@t-online.de

Eugene Subbotsky, PhD,

Reader in Developmental Psychology, Psychology department, Lancaster University, Lancaster, LA1 4YF, United Kingdom. E-mail: e.subbotsky@lancaster.ac.uk

Alexander E. Voiskounsky, Ph.D.

Senior research scientist, Psychology Department, Lomonosov Moscow State University, Mokhovaya str. 11-5, Moscow 125009, Russia. Email: vaemsu@gmail.com

INDEX

E

F

S

Y